Persuasive Peers

Persuasive Peers

SOCIAL COMMUNICATION AND
VOTING IN LATIN AMERICA

Andy Baker, Barry Ames, & Lúcio Rennó

PRINCETON UNIVERSITY PRESS
PRINCETON AND OXFORD

Published by Princeton University Press
41 William Street, Princeton, New Jersey 08540
6 Oxford Street, Woodstock, Oxfordshire OX20 1TR

press.princeton.edu

Library of Congress Cataloging-in-Publication Data

Names: Baker, Andy, 1972– author. | Ames, Barry, author. | Rennó, Lucio R., author.
Title: Persuasive peers : social communication and voting in Latin America /
Andy Baker, Barry Ames, and Lucio Renno.
Description: Princeton : Princeton University Press, [2020] |
Series: Princeton studies in global and comparative sociology |
Includes bibliographical references and index.
Identifiers: LCCN 2019056822 (print) | LCCN 2019056823 (ebook) |
ISBN 9780691205786 (hardback) | ISBN 9780691205779 (paperback) |
ISBN 9780691205793 (ebook)
Subjects: LCSH: Voting—Latin America. | Communication—Political aspects—
Latin America. | Social networks—Political aspects—Latin America. | Social
influence—Political aspects—Latin America. | Political participation—
Latin America. | Latin America—Politics and government.
Classification: LCC JL968 .B24 2020 (print) | LCC JL968 (ebook) |
DDC 324.98—dc23
LC record available at https://lccn.loc.gov/2019056822
LC ebook record available at https://lccn.loc.gov/2019056823

British Library Cataloging-in-Publication Data is available

Editorial: Meagan Levinson and Jacqueline Delaney
Production Editorial: Lauren Lepow
Text Design: Lorraine Doneker
Cover Design: Karl Spurzem
Production: Brigid Ackerman
Publicity: Kate Hensley and Kathryn Stevens

This book has been composed in Minion Pro with Myriad Pro
Printed on acid-free paper. ∞

Printed in the United States of America

1 3 5 7 9 10 8 6 4 2

Para nossos filhos, Della, Olivia, Elisa, Tomás e Celina

CONTENTS

ILLUSTRATIONS

TABLES

PREFACE

Casual conversations occur with great frequency in every human society, but few countries label them as colorfully as Brazil: *bate papo*. Literally translated, *bate papo* means to smack a bird's neck pouch back and forth. Brazilians invoke the term with an anticipatory and almost celebratory undertone; a *bate papo* with friends and family feeds the Brazilian soul. As the great thinker Sérgio Buarque de Holanda noted, "a horror of social distance seems to be . . . the most specific trait of the Brazilian spirit."[1]

When it comes to politics, a *bate papo* is a common way for Brazilians to process and learn about their complex (and, to most, disappointing) political system and the actors who compose that system. A 2018 survey showed that conversation with family, friends, and colleagues was the most important political information source for Brazilians when they decided how to vote.[2] More anecdotally, one is struck, while walking and eavesdropping on the streets of major Brazilian cities during election campaigns, by the sheer number of conversations about politics.

When it comes to scholarship on Brazilian voting behavior, however, *bate papo* is almost entirely missing. Political scientists studying Brazil, and the rest of Latin America as well, prefer to study the impact of formal, hierarchical structures: parties, civil society organizations, networks of clientelistic exchange, and, on occasion, mass media conglomerates. Implicit in this scholarship is the claim that Latin Americans are largely asocial and simply don't *bater o papo*.

This book seeks to come to grips with informal conversations and peer influences in Latin American voting behavior. We need hardly articulate why scholars overlook this form of communication. Informal conversations are difficult to quantify and measure, and peer influences rarely fit the dominant paradigm around rational, transactional behavior. Neither fact means that conversations and peer influences are unimportant. Little is more fundamentally human than being social: forming friendships, seeking intimacy, starting a family, caring for relatives. It is time for research on Latin American politics to incorporate what is truly social.

ACKNOWLEDGMENTS

By some measures, this research monograph has been brewing for a very long time. Back in the late 1960s, when Barry was a graduate student at Stanford, everyone read *The American Voter*, the classic from the Michigan school of voting behavior research.[1] Most students also read *The People's Choice*, the more sociologically minded contribution from the Columbia school.[2] It was clear that the Michigan school, as part of the triumph of methodological individualism, was winning the battle in political science, but it was hard not to feel that something was lost in its atomistic view of voters—especially its failure to incorporate social interactions. Still, Barry was a Latin Americanist and an institutions scholar, and Latin America was entering a dark period of military rule where voting was mostly irrelevant. So he just stored this controversy in his mind and went on with other interests.

In 1973 Barry moved to Washington University, St. Louis. Although that department was rapidly becoming a bastion of rational-choice scholarship, John Sprague and his students, especially Bob Huckfeldt, held out. Their work on the 1984 presidential election campaign in South Bend, Indiana, signaled to Barry that the insights of the Columbia school were alive and well, even if the 1984 election was a particularly uninteresting contest.[3] Besides, Barry could not escape the hunch that Brazilians, compared to Americans, were more prone to engage in meaningful political conversations, especially now that Brazil was democratizing. Political talk took place among family members at home; with friends at the bar, the *futebol* field, and the crèche; and with coworkers on the job. Brazilian voters, moreover, seemed much more likely than Americans to change their minds during campaigns.

By 2001 Barry had moved to the University of Pittsburgh. He was finishing *The Deadlock of Democracy*,[4] his monograph on the Brazilian electoral system and legislative politics, and he was looking for a new project. He hatched the idea of running a Huckfeldt-and-Sprague-inspired study of social networks and voting behavior in Brazil during the 2002 campaign and elections, complete with a three-wave panel design, interviews with discussion partners, and two cities selected for their stark political differences. Barry had a one-year-old child and was unable to spend a year alone in the field. So he partnered on a grant proposal with Andy, a newly minted PhD whom he had met at the ICPSR summer program in 1996, and Lúcio, a promising Brazilian graduate student at Pitt who added a neighborhood spin to Barry's nascent research design. That fall, we received a National Science Foundation (NSF) grant of reasonable size to conduct the study. Lúcio also received dissertation grants from the NSF and the Social Science Research Council.

The following year, Lúcio moved to Juiz de Fora and Andy to Caxias do Sul. Juiz de Fora was a natural choice: political science research had already been undertaken in the city, it was only two and a half hours from Rio de Janeiro, its size was manageable, it hosted a good university, and restaurants abounded. In addition, its politics revolved, as in much of the rest of Brazil, around personalities and pork-barrel projects. Caxias do Sul also turned out to suit us well: its population size and economy were similar to those of Juiz de Fora, but it was much more partisan and polarized. To be sure, it was a tough site. Caxias gets cold and Brazilian apartments lack central heating, but Andy is a hardy midwesterner.

We are aware (and somewhat embarrassed) that 2002 was a long time ago. Fortunately, new infusions of data have occurred since then, and we hope they keep the findings in this book fresh. With money from his endowed chair (the Andrew Mellon Professorship of Comparative Politics), Barry funded a fourth panel wave in the two cities in 2004 and then fifth and sixth waves in 2006. Andy was able to squeeze a discussant name generator onto the Mexico 2006 Panel Study. Barry and Lúcio (with Amy Erica Smith) placed one on the 2014 Brazilian Electoral Panel Study. Andy and two Pitt graduate students carried out in-depth interviews in Brazil and Mexico during their 2018 presidential races.

Still, it has certainly taken a long time to put together this monograph, although we have produced, jointly and separately, many articles along the way. There were distractions. Barry was department chair at Pitt and then mounted a multi-collaborator project on policy implementation in Brazilian states, Andy was waylaid into writing two other books, and Lúcio headed a government department in Brasília. We have even added four more children to our collective tally since 2002. But around 2014, a table of contents finally materialized—into Andy's head—and off we went. In this monograph Andy is deservedly first author, because he took the lead in both the analysis and the writing.

Given the length of time it took to develop and finalize this project, the amount of gratitude we owe is staggering. But let us attempt at least a partial listing of those who helped us. The data collection for the first three waves of the Two-City Panel was funded by the National Science Foundation (SES #0137088) and the Social Science Research Council. Data collection for the fourth through sixth waves was funded by the Andrew Mellon Professorship of Comparative Politics at the University of Pittsburgh. The National Science Foundation (SES #0517971) and *Reforma* newspaper provided funding for the Mexico 2006 Panel. *Reforma*'s Polling and Research Team, under the direction of Alejandro Moreno, conducted fieldwork. The Inter-American Development Bank funded the Brazilian Electoral Panel Study of 2014. We thank the Latin American Public Opinion Project (LAPOP) and its major supporters (the

United States Agency for International Development, the Inter-American Development Bank, and Vanderbilt University) for making the data available. Funding for research assistance, travel, and other occasional costs came from the University of Colorado Boulder, the University of Houston, Northeastern University, and the University of Pittsburgh. All of the code used to produce the analyses in this book is available for download at Andy's dataverse: https:// dataverse.harvard.edu/dataverse/andybaker. All six waves of the Two-City Panel are also available there. The two online appendixes (Translation Appendix and Sensitivity Analysis Appendix) are also at this dataverse. All other datasets are publicly available and have their own devoted websites.

This manuscript was a very different and far inferior product before we held a book conference in April 2018. Paul Beck, Carew Boulding, Jennifer Fitzgerald, Anand Sokhey, Jennifer Wolak, and Elizabeth Zechmeister gave trenchant and invaluable constructive criticisms that led to a serious rewrite. Even beyond the book conference, Sokhey and Wolak gave Andy ongoing intellectual (as well as occasional musical and confectionary) support. Anand was Andy's in-house mentor on social networks, and Jenny gave timely comments on everything Andy sent her way. We also received valuable feedback from the following friends and colleagues who read specific chapters: Ernesto Calvo, Eddie Camp, Benjamin Campbell, Theresa Coletti, Jorge Domínguez, Ken Greene, Dick Jessor, Chappell Lawson, Alejandro Moreno, Vicky Murillo, Simeon Nichter, Ezequiel González Ocantos, Brian Richter, Doug Schuler, Matt Singer, Rebecca Weitz-Shapiro, and the Institutions group of the University of Colorado Boulder Institute of Behavioral Science (Lee Alston, Jennifer Bair, Carew Boulding, Edward Greenberg, Joseph Jupille, Nelson Montenegro, Isaac Reed, and James Scarritt). Four friends also dropped everything to give quick feedback on the prospectus: David Bearce, Ken Greene, Nita Rudra, and Ethan Scheiner. Thanks also to Fred Hansen for assisting so much with the index. Finally, we could not be happier to be publishing this book with Princeton University Press. We are extremely grateful to Andreas Wimmer and Meagan Levinson for making that happen and to Lauren Lepow for providing wonderful copyediting.

The number of research assistants and field coordinators on whom we relied is also large, and we apologize to those we are forgetting. The list includes Ciara Coughlan, Dalton Dorr, Paulo Roberto Figueira Leal, Miguel García-Sánchez, Juan Carlos Rodríguez-Raga, and Sierra González Speegle. Marianne Batista and João Victor Guedes conducted some of the 2018 in-depth interviews. Marianne and José Incio Coronado generated the maps in chapters 5 and 6. Daniel Cabral and Giovanna Rodríguez-García arranged Andy's 2018 in-depth interviews in Brazil and Mexico. In the two cities, João Inácio Pires Lucas, Manoel Palácios, and Rubem Barbosa Filho secured institutional support from the Universidade de Caxias do Sul and the Universidade Federal de Juiz de Fora, and we received help from a host of field coordinators and supervisors: Alexandre Bernardo, Cássio Cunha Soares, Débora Resende, Diogo

Tourino de Sousa, Júlio César de Paula e Silva, Juliana Silva, Priscila Azevedo, Rodrigo Giacomet, and Soraia Marcelino.

This is not our first statement on the topic or with some of these data, but everything except chapter 7 is new analysis and content. Although it has been rewritten to fit the overall narrative, much of chapter 7 appeared as Joby Schaffer and Andy Baker (2015). "Clientelism as Persuasion-Buying: Evidence from Latin America," *Comparative Political Studies* 48, no. 9: 1093–126. This article won the 2017 Mitchell Seligson Prize for best scholarship that used LAPOP's AmericasBarometer data in the two preceding years, and we heartily acknowledge and appreciate Joby's contribution to this chapter. A few sentences from three other publications appear in the book: (1) Andy Baker (2009), "Regionalized Voting Behavior and Political Discussion in Mexico," in *Consolidating Mexico's Democracy: The 2006 Presidential Campaign in Comparative Perspective*, ed. Jorge I. Domínguez, Chappell Lawson, and Alejandro Moreno (Baltimore: Johns Hopkins University Press), 71–88; (2) Andy Baker, Barry Ames, and Lúcio R. Rennó (2006), "Social Context and Campaign Volatility in New Democracies: Networks and Neighborhoods in Brazil's 2002 Elections," *American Journal of Political Science* 50, no. 2: 382–99; and (3) Andy Baker, Barry Ames, Anand E. Sokhey, and Lúcio R. Rennó (2016), "The Dynamics of Partisan Identification When Party Brands Change: The Case of the Workers Party in Brazil," *Journal of Politics* 78, no. 1: 197–213.

Our respective families deserve the most gratitude. To live in Caxias, Andy left his wife, Lila, alone with the flying Houston cockroaches for five months. He is eternally grateful for this and for her other sacrifices and support over nearly 20 years of marriage. Barry owes everything to his parents, Irving and Mina Ames. Finally, we are especially grateful to our five children, Della, Olivia, Elisa, Tomás, and Celina, to whom we dedicate this book. Over the long course of its composition, they have been our most influential peers—entertaining us, making us proud, and turning us into better people.

ABBREVIATIONS

AMLO	Andrés Manuel López Obrador
APES	Argentine Panel Elections Study
ARG	Argentina
BEPS	Brazilian Electoral Panel Study
BGR	Bulgaria
BRA	Brazil
CHL	Chile
CHN	China
CNEP	Comparative National Elections Project
CNT	National Transport Confederation
COL	Colombia
CS	Caxias do Sul
CUT	Unified Workers Central
DOM	Dominican Republic
DV	Dependent Variable
ESP	Spain
GRC	Greece
HEG	Free Electoral Hour
HDI	Human Development Index
HH	Heloísa Helena Lima
HKG	Hong Kong
HUN	Hungary
IBOPE	Brazilian Institute of Public Opinion
ICPSR	Inter-University Consortium for Political and Social Research
IDN	Indonesia
ISO	International Organization for Standardization
ITA	Italy
IV	Independent Variable
JF	Juiz de Fora
KEN	Kenya
LAPOP	Latin American Public Opinion Project
LOWESS	Locally weighted scatterplot smoothing
MDB	Brazilian Democratic Movement
MENA	Middle East and North Africa

MEX	Mexico
MNL	Multinomial logit
MORENA	National Regeneration Movement
MOZ	Mozambique
MST	Landless Workers' Movement
NAFTA	North American Free Trade Association
NSF	National Science Foundation
OLS	Ordinary least squares
PAN	National Action Party
PCdoB	Communist Party of Brazil
PER	Peru
PFL	Liberal Front Party
PL	Liberal Party
PMDB	Brazilian Democratic Movement Party
PPB	Brazilian Progressive Party
PPS	Popular Socialist Party
PRD	Party of the Democratic Revolution
PRI	Institutional Revolutionary Party
PRN	National Renovation Party
PSB	Brazilian Socialist Party
PSDB	Brazilian Social Democratic Party
PSL	Social Liberal Party
PSOL	Socialism and Liberty Party
PT	Workers' Party
PTB	Brazilian Labor Party
SES	Socioeconomic status
SLV	El Salvador
TA	Translation Appendix
TWN	Taiwan
UK	United Kingdom
URY	Uruguay
VEN	Venezuela
WVS	World Values Survey
ZAF	South Africa

PART I

Introduction and Descriptive Background

1

Social Communication and Voting Behavior

The gift of speech . . . proves that man is a more social animal
than the bees.

—Aristotle[1]

THE PUZZLE OF VOTE CHOICE IN BRAZIL

Even by Brazil's lofty standards, the October 2014 presidential campaign was
exciting. Though surges by outsider candidates and other kinds of momentum
swings have been frequent in the country's recent presidential contests, the 2014
contest contained all the drama of a *telenovela* and a closely fought soccer
match. Early in the year, President Dilma Rousseff of the left-of-center Workers' Party (PT) held a commanding lead in the polls, a lead so safe that she was
seemingly on course to win in the first round of Brazil's majority runoff system (see figure 1.1). In a distant second place was Aécio Neves of the center-
right Brazilian Social Democratic Party (PSDB). As in Brazil's previous five
elections, it thus seemed that the top two finishers would come, despite the
country's 30-plus political parties, from these two parties.

Once campaigning had officially begun in July, however, Eduardo Campos
of the Brazilian Socialist Party (PSB) began to surge in the polls. After nearly
a month of steady gains, Campos was nipping at Aécio's heels for second place,
contending for a spot in the now increasingly likely second round. Tragically,
Campos died in a plane crash on August 13, but his running mate, Marina Silva,
immediately grabbed the party's baton and continued its ascent. Marina was
the ideal replacement.* She was a known quantity who four years earlier had
earned 19 percent of the first-round vote atop her own presidential ticket (for
a different party). Capitalizing on a surge of sympathy for the deceased
Campos, she zoomed past Aécio in the polls. By early September, with just a

---

*Throughout this book, we refer to politicians, after the first mention, with Brazilian short-
hand conventions; these sometimes eschew the formality of English by using first names or
nicknames.

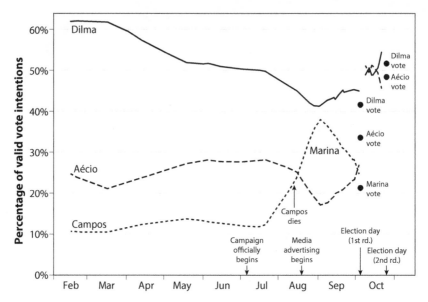

FIGURE 1.1 The Evolution of Vote Intentions for Major Presidential Candidates in Brazil 2014

Notes: Each line (LOWESS-smoothed with a bandwidth of .25) summarizes results from nationally representative polls and represents a candidate's estimated percentage of valid vote intentions (dropping undecided respondents). Actual election-day results are indicated with circle markers. Only the top three finishers are depicted.
Sources: Datafolha, IBOPE, Vox Populi.

month remaining, Marina had a 20-point lead on Aécio, even reaching a statistical tie with the front-runner Dilma in a few polls.

Then Marina's fortunes began to unravel. No single gaffe or mistake triggered her slide. In fact, Marina ran a disciplined campaign. Over the final 30 days, however, her support cratered almost as quickly as it had risen. By the eve of election day, she had fallen into a tie with Aécio in the contest for a second-round spot, and voters went to the polls on October 5 genuinely uncertain which of the two would earn the right to face the incumbent Dilma in the second-round election (also "runoff"). Was Brazil on the verge of producing the world's first female-only presidential runoff? Or would the country see its fourth consecutive PT-PSDB runoff?

In the end, the result was another PT-PSDB runoff, and it was not even close. Aécio defied the final polls by a wide margin, beating Marina by 12 points and finishing closer to Dilma than to Marina. After peaking near 40 percent of vote intentions in early September, Marina fell to just 21 percent on election day, only a minor improvement over her performance four years earlier. The second round began in a tie, but Dilma opened a small lead toward the end of the three-week campaign period and, in Brazil's closest-ever presidential contest, squeaked out a three-point victory.

This horse-race intrigue poses a major puzzle about the nature of Brazilian voting behavior and election outcomes. On the one hand, the election featured a huge and fascinating amount of change in voter preferences. It is clear from figure 1.1 that many voters were changing their minds as the contest unfolded. By our own panel-data estimates, at least 40 percent of the electorate shifted their vote intentions across party lines at some point during the campaign. This represents a high degree of volatility by international standards. On the other hand, this volatility ended in a predictable outcome. Aggregate vote intentions before the campaign's start were similar to the eventual first-round vote totals. Moreover, because pre-campaign vote intentions favored the two traditional parties, the campaign restored *os mesmos de sempre*, the same ones as always, to their usual places in the second round. What explains this aggregate predictability despite the high rates of individual-level voter volatility?

Some Incorrect Answers

To scholars of US campaigns and voting behavior, this puzzle of short-term change amidst medium-term stability has a familiar ring to it: enlightened preferences.[2] During political campaigns, many US voters vacillate between indecision and a particular candidate, thus making aggregate vote intentions somewhat volatile. Election outcomes, however, are highly predictable based on the political and economic fundamentals (e.g., macroeconomic health and the distribution of partisanship) in place before a campaign's start. Moreover, virtually all US voters end up choosing the candidate in line with the partisan predispositions and group affiliations they held before the campaign began.[3] Thus in the US a campaign serves to bring voters home to the partisan choice that has lurked beneath the surface all along—the one based on their most informed, and thus enlightened, preferences.

Although a powerful predictor in the US context, this explanation does not fit the Brazilian case. Because Brazil is a new democracy with an extremely high number of parties, Brazilians' partisan predispositions are weak.[4] In any given cross-sectional survey in 2014, just 15 to 20 percent of the electorate identified with the PT, less than half of Dilma's first-round total.[5] Panel data show that only half of Dilma voters declared themselves to be PT sympathizers at some point during the campaign, and the PT is the party that had Brazil's *largest* base of citizens. Aécio's PSDB and Marina's PSB had virtually no mass bases. Just 13 percent of his voters and 7 percent of hers declared themselves to be PSDB or PSB sympathizers, respectively, at least once during the campaign. Clearly, most voters were not returning to an underlying partisan leaning over the course of the campaign. Moreover, the sorting of voters into pro- and anti-incumbent camps based on stable economic perceptions cannot explain the volatility: most of the switching occurred between the nonincumbent candidates, Aécio and Marina. Finally, unlike US voters, Brazilian voters do mull different party choices, as evidenced by the 40 percent who crossed party lines. They do not simply end up where they began. The group of individuals lined up to vote for Aécio at the campaign's start was very different from the group that ultimately voted for Aécio on election day. In summary, the enlightened preferences argument does not export well to Brazil.

Strategic voting poses another possible answer to the puzzle. Perhaps the high degree of volatility arose as voters, and particularly strongly anti-Dilma voters, sought to coordinate around the most viable opponent to her candidacy, an instinct that would maintain Brazil's stubborn two-party duopoly in presidential elections.[6] Yet this hypothesis contains a logical failure: Brazil's president is chosen by majority, not plurality, rule. Two-round systems with strategic voting should reduce to three-party, not two-party, competition. In other words, there was no strategic reason for sincere Marina supporters to abandon her for Aécio, especially when she had a 20-point lead on him. At that point, the contest had reduced to a battle between the two for a second-round slot. Moreover, polling results for simulated second-round scenarios showed Marina to be the better competitor against Dilma. Strategically minded Dilma-haters should have voted for Marina.

Perhaps Aécio rode a wave of vote buying into the second round. After all, he had the backing of most of Brazil's conservative, and largely clientelistic, establishment parties, while Marina had virtually no machine infrastructure supporting her. Yet no empirical evidence or even speculation exists that a vote-buying operation of this scope occurred on Aécio's behalf. It would be a hard operation to keep secret, as Marina lost an estimated 20 million votes, nearly one-fifth of the electorate, in five weeks. In fact, research on Brazil shows that targeted vote-buying attempts have limited relevance for presidential politics because of the country's federalized and fragmented party system. Almost all vote-buying and party-contacting efforts are made on behalf of municipal and legislative candidates,[7] and these lower-level candidates avoid making upward endorsements of presidential contenders who are lagging in the polls.[8] Evidence from the broader literature on Latin American clientelism shows that vote-buying attempts are ineffective at producing this amount of preference change because parties do not even target swing voters.[9]

Perhaps the solution to the puzzle lies in the mass media and the relative balance of partisan information broadcast during the campaign. On this front, Marina's campaign did face a major disadvantage. In Brazil campaign commercials in the traditional electronic media (television and radio) are strictly regulated. The Federal Electoral Tribunal prohibits commercials before the final seven weeks of the campaign (figure 1.1), and airtime is allocated to candidates in proportion to the size of the legislative coalitions backing them. Hailing from a smaller party, Marina received half the airtime that Aécio did, and just one-sixth that of Dilma. Media consumption thus exposed citizens to relatively little pro-Marina content, potentially spelling her eventual demise. Two facts, however, undermine this hypothesis. First, figure 1.1 shows that Marina's surge continued several weeks after electronic media campaigning began, a fact leading some observers to conclude at the time that the amount of media exposure was unrelated to success.[10] Second, among voters who had expressed a mid-campaign intention to vote for Marina, those *least* exposed to campaign commercials were *more* likely to abandon her, according to our panel survey data. In other words, attention to electronic media correlated negatively, not positively, with changing one's mind. Direct exposure to the partisan balance in campaign commercials does not explain vote switching.

Socially Informed Preferences

Our solution to the puzzle lies in an arena of political life that scholars of Latin American politics have largely ignored: the arena of horizontal social ties and informal political discussion. During election campaigns, nearly every Brazilian voter converses about the candidates and parties. Some do it just once, some do it many times every day, and most do it at a frequency falling between these two extremes. Nearly all these conversations occur between peers— between spouses, siblings, work colleagues, neighbors, soccer teammates, lifelong friends, and so on. Such conversations thus occur between individuals with *horizontal* social ties, meaning no political elite is involved. Occasionally they occur between individuals connected by vertical ties—between a common voter and a politician or a party broker—but these instances are relatively rare. The vast majority of voters' political conversations occur not with a politician or a party worker. Instead, they occur spontaneously among otherwise socially connected individuals.

In Brazil's roller-coaster campaign of 2014, the voters most likely to change preferences across party lines were not those returning to an under-the-surface partisan leaning, nor those bought off by a party, nor those settling for second best to defeat their least-liked candidate, nor those who watched the most campaign commercials. According to our survey data, the voters most likely to switch preferences across party lines were those who had discussed politics with peers who disagreed with their mid-campaign vote intentions. These peers often persuaded them to change. Just as important, the voters least likely to switch were those who discussed politics only with peers who agreed with them—peers who reinforced their mid-campaign vote intentions. Between these two types of voters, the difference in the probability of switching preferences across party lines was more than 35 percentage points. Conversations with social ties produced both preference change and preference stability.

A model of horizontal social influence addresses the puzzle of short-term volatility amidst medium-term aggregate stability. We show that in Brazil the most important means of social influence during campaigns is deference to role-model peers. Many voters who are relatively uninformed and overwhelmed by politics seek advice on how to vote from discussion partners who have more political expertise than themselves. Thus the vote choices of the less informed are influenced by political experts in their social milieu. Over the course of the campaign, voters eventually settle on what we call their socially informed preferences, meaning the candidate preferences they acquire upon being influenced by their social ties. This process of social influence creates the high rates of vote switching in Brazil, as many voters update their preferences based on cues they receive from the political opinion leaders in their everyday lives.

Paradoxically, social influence also produces medium-term aggregate stability, meaning the main candidate contenders at the campaign's onset are the top finishers on election day, even if candidates who were initially also-rans experience compelling mid-campaign momentum surges. The deference to more knowledgeable peers produces this result because political experts tend to have more stable preferences. Acquiring socially informed preferences from opinion leaders brings less informed voters in line with more stable and predictable voting patterns. To be clear, the campaign exerts major influence in this formulation and determines the winner. In 2014 at least 40 percent of voters switched preferences across party lines, and relatively few of these simply circled back to pre-campaign predispositions. But polling surges by initially weak candidates are hard to sustain, as most voters end up choosing a candidate who was running well at the campaign's onset. Social influence induces a modicum of aggregate preference stability in Brazil's otherwise weak and volatile party system.

Brazil is not alone in these campaign patterns and voting behaviors. Latin American presidential campaigns often feature bandwagon effects and momentum swings that are large by international standards (e.g., Argentina 2015, Chile 2005, Ecuador 2006, Guatemala 2015, Mexico 2006, Peru 1990 and 2006).[11] Sometimes these are momentous enough to eradicate the traditional parties and players, but more typically they maintain the candidates who were strong at the campaign's start.[12] The process of horizontal political communication and voter gravitation toward socially informed preferences explains, we suspect, these aggregate campaign patterns in Latin America's other new democracies as well.

SCHOLARLY CONCEPTIONS OF THE
LATIN AMERICAN VOTER

This book illuminates the influence of horizontal social networks and political discussion on a central political act, voting behavior, in Latin America. It is thus a study of political communication and political intermediation. Political communication is the process whereby political information flows to and through a mass public. In modern societies, citizens learn and form opinions about politicians, policies, and politics through different information intermediaries, such as newspapers, Facebook, or party brokers.

The systematic study of political communication and political intermediaries in Latin America emerged rather recently, and it has focused almost exclusively on intermediaries of a top-down, vertical nature—namely, local elites and mass media. The largest body of research focuses on one of the *least* common forms of intermediation: direct vertical ties to politicians, parties, and politicized organizations, and especially the clientelistic form of these ties.[13] For example, research on clientelism, which predates the region's present democratic era, is now a booming area whose volume heavily outweighs research on all other intermediary types.[14] The focus on these top-down sources of persuasive political information reveals an assumption among scholars that formal organizational structures (parties, labor unions, social movements, churches, participatory budgeting forums) are the primary source of political information for voters.

Direct vertical ties to elites, however, are relatively rare and unrepresentative sources of political information. Vote-buying payoffs are delivered, by the most generous election-year estimates, to just a quarter of the citizenry, and large majorities of citizens expect to receive no private handouts during campaigns.[15] Steeped in hierarchy and transactional norms, clientelistic ties also lack the sincerity and intimacy of horizontal social ties with family and friends. As this research area has grown, moreover, its cumulative findings question the ability of clientelism to explain the changes in campaign preferences and momentum swings that are so common in Latin America.[16] Evidence that party machines prefer to pay off swing and potentially volatile voters is surprisingly thin. If anything, machines seem more likely to target individuals who are already their loyalists—to reinforce, reward, and mobilize.[17] In other words, changing the recipient's vote preference is often not the goal of the party machine or broker.

Latin American parties also engage in non-clientelistic forms of citizen contact. During campaigns, parties canvass, distribute leaflets, and hold rallies. These activities occur so infrequently, however, that they are but a minor source of political information for voters. For that reason, they are rarely objects of research.[18] Similarly, the vast majority of Latin American citizens are not party members and belong to no politicized organizations. In fact, most belong to no secondary association at all.[19] In sum, the top-down flows of persuasive political information that occur through direct vertical ties to politicized structures represent just a small share of political communications in Latin American societies.

A much smaller body of literature looks at what is nonetheless a far more frequent form of vertical political intermediation, mass media. Parties proselytize through print, broadcasting technologies, and the internet in the form of campaign advertisements, televised speech making, party websites, and other messaging techniques. Media professionals—newspaper journalists, TV news anchors, and leaders of media conglomerates—also contribute original content to the arena of political communication, with many injecting their own partisan biases.[20] Latin Americans are far more likely to get political information from mass media than from direct contact with parties and politicians, as a large majority consume some political news content at least once per week.[21] Because of the near ubiquity of mass media in Latin American societies and the fact that citizens have, at most, only occasional direct contact with politicians and parties, the vast majority of information about politics that circulates through a mass public originates from a media source. As a result, the relative distribution of scholarly attention to direct party contacts and mass media is inversely related to each one's actual importance for the acquisition of political information.

Still, the literature on mass media and citizen political behavior in Latin America has its own flaws. Although this literature focuses more on the heart of the matter, it is grounded in an incomplete model of influence. Models of media effects presume that attitudinal change is correlated positively with the degree of a citizen's exposure to specific media content. In other words, media influence occurs only among those directly exposed to it.[22] The problem with this assumption is that citizens talk about media content. Media stories and campaign commercials quickly become fodder for horizontal, peer-to-peer communications about politics and politicians. Consider these remarks from some of our Brazilian interviewees:

> At work, we read the newspaper and then comment on one thing or the other. [TA1.1]*

> [In my family] we didn't watch political news together. We left the TV on, and when someone saw something of interest, they commented on it.[TA1.2]

> [My friends and I] talk about the [political] videos that we see . . . Sometimes, one of us shares a video with our WhatsApp group. Then we always talk about it . . . We talk a lot about the videos that we share.[TA1.3]

The truism that people talk about the news means that "*empirical studies of media impact that fail to consider media's interaction with social networks risk bias.*"[23] For instance, the diffusion of a persuasive media message through social networks weakens the estimated relationship between media exposure and the probability of opinion change, even though social networks are actually disseminating that mediated information to those who were not directly exposed to it.[24] In fact, studies of campaign effects in Latin America often find that those

---

*The superscripted letters and numbers behind each quotation give the location of the original Portuguese in the Translation Appendix, which can be found online at https://dataverse.harvard.edu/dataverse/andybaker.

who are the least exposed to political news are *more* likely than the highly exposed to change vote intentions.[25]

Furthermore, the literature's overall emphasis on vertical intermediaries—
both direct and mediated information from politicians—assumes a level of
trust toward elites that is often lacking in Latin America. Many Latin American voters confront self-serving information from elites with a deep skepticism,
as politicians are typically not a credible breed.[26] For this reason, an exclusive
focus on vertical intermediaries struggles to understand the following Brazilian voters interviewed by our research team:

> INTERVIEWER: How do you decide how to vote?
> VOTER 1: I speak with people. . . . I don't believe what [politicians] say . . . If
> one comes to talk to me, I don't listen.
> INTERVIEWER: What about the free electoral hour [i.e., the televised bloc of
> campaign commercials]?
> VOTER 2: Nobody watches that! People only watch it when there's a clown
> show, when Tiririca [a famous clown elected as federal deputy] or
> someone like him is on. . . . It's a waste of time, just lies. We see who
> gets things done by talking with one another . . . Aside from that, it's
> all lies.[TA1.4]

Clearly, both voters distrust vertical intermediaries but trust their family and
friends.

Armed only with vertical understandings of political intermediation, research on Latin American voters "conceives the citizen as an independently
self-contained decision-maker," ignoring voters' embeddedness in peer networks.[27] For this reason, even when referring to groups and so-called social
factors, research on Latin American voting behavior is dominated by economistic and psychological approaches that see voters as social isolates. The economistic perspective envisions the causes of vote choice as some combination
of policy interests, clientelistic payoffs, and incumbent performance evaluations.[28] A social-structuralist approach to voting coalitions and behavior resides
within this economistic camp, treating groups with shared demographic traits as
collections of people with similar economic and policy interests.[29] The more psychological view of Latin American voters stresses their affinity for a party, their
tendency to succumb to persuasive appeals by candidates, and their emotional
orientations toward politics and political events.[30] This tradition depicts the
important group identity of partisanship as a product of vertical intermediation—
that is, of party activism, elite cues, and evaluations of politicians.[31]

In neither case are the so-called group or social factors actually about interpersonal communication. But what is a group if not a "collection of individuals who are interacting with one another"?[32] Viewing group affiliations and
demographic traits strictly as indicators of policy interests or psychological
identities is reductionist, since such affiliations and traits are also measures of

social context and thus the kinds of people by whom one is likely to be influenced.[33] The phenomenon of shared political attitudes among members of a group is a product of more than just common interests and identities.[34] In other words, a group is more than the sum of its individual parts: "the group formed by associated individuals has a reality of a different sort from each individual considered singly."[35]

Economistic and psychological conceptions of groups do have high explanatory value, but we wish to explore the *truly social* side of the Latin American voter. To gain a more complete understanding of political intermediation, voting behavior, and elections, scholars of the region must come to grips with the horizontal social ties and informal political discussion reported by voters in the quotes above. Beneath all the elite-level strategizing, messaging, and maneuvering that plays out through vertical intermediaries lies a world of social communication and peer effects that scholars of Latin American politics have roundly ignored.[36]

HORIZONTAL SOCIAL TIES, POLITICAL DISCUSSION, AND THE VOTE

Around 90 percent of Latin Americans report engaging in some form of politically relevant conversation. Nearly all these conversations emerge organically and spontaneously; humans are social animals. (Recall this chapter's epigraph.) Some conversations take place over social media, but even today most are face-to-face.[37] They require no motivation from office-minded elites, and they exist largely outside the realm of organized civil society. The vast majority of political conversations are thus informal, occurring within horizontal social networks of friends, family, and acquaintances. Social communication carries a uniqueness that distinguishes it in both character and consequence from other forms of political communication. In this section, we define this uniqueness, and then we describe the precise mechanism by which social influence shapes vote choices in Latin American electorates.

The Uniqueness of Political Talk

Social communication is an important and unique form of political intermediation in several ways.* In contrast to vertical forms of intermediation, discussion among peers is active and can even be authoritative for the common citizen. Political discussion is a two-way street, so it is often considered

---

*Throughout the book, we use the following important terms synonymously: "social communication," "discussion," "conversation," "horizontal intermediation," and "peer-to-peer intermediation."

a form of political participation that cultivates "leader-like" qualities.[38] Studies of citizens in established democracies show that a minute of political discussion has greater impact—on knowledge acquisition, on community standing, on civic skills, on tolerance for opposing views—than a minute of media consumption.[39]

Political discussion is also biased. Political information is usually communicated with partisan bias, but some sources are more biased than others. Even when media sources have a political leaning (a common state of affairs in Latin America), some journalistic norms and regulations around fact-finding and reporting do exist.[40] Adherence to these norms lends an air of impartiality to most major media outlets. Common citizens, in comparison, are not subject to these norms and regulations, and discussion partners inherently carry political biases. Moreover, social ties with politically disagreeing individuals tend to be harder to sever than attention to a media source: contrast the ease of navigating to a different newspaper website with the difficulty and even emotional pain of avoiding family conflict over politics at a holiday table. Overall, political discussion exposes individuals to more imbalance and bias than media consumption.[41]

Further, political discussion is intimate. Consumption of political news via print or a screen is an impersonal process, but social communication occurs with other thinking and emoting individuals who are part of one's life routines. Political discussion across disagreeing lines carries a gravity—a potential for social discomfort and interpersonal sanctioning—that media consumption lacks.[42] Even clientelistic relationships in which party brokers apply social pressure to induce voting-booth compliance carry lower stakes, as brokers are typically connected only to voters' extended, less intimate social contacts.[43] Moreover, the intimacy of political discussion means that it conveys information to voters in colloquial terms and in their own parlance. Consider the following remark from yet another Brazilian voter who does not consume mass media in isolation:

> I read *Valor Econômico* [a financial newspaper] every day on the web. I also read *Folha de São Paulo* and *Estadão* [two major newspapers]. But I don't understand everything. I ask my friends at work what they think. There are people there who understand a lot. I ask them to explain things to me when I don't understand something.[TA1.5]

Friends and family package political information in more comprehensible terms than the mass media.[44]

Finally, political discussion belongs to the masses. It exists largely beyond the purview, manipulation, and monitoring of politicians, party brokers, and civil society. Democratization in Latin America has opened new public spaces, such as participatory budgeting and neighborhood associations, for mass deliberation and debate, but even these are formal and organized in comparison to the "messy and radically decentralized" realm of informal conversation.[45] Elites in Latin America do have a vague awareness of this conversational domain, but they have limited abilities to manipulate it. Consider the following campaign statements by candidates in Brazil's 2002 presidential election:

> José Serra, in a final campaign commercial: "Until Sunday [election day], I want you to have one goal: Get one more vote. With your vote, plus one more, victory!" [This was accompanied by images of a child trying to convince his grandparents to vote for Serra.][TA1.6]

> Anthony Garotinho, at a rally: "Multiply your vote! Spread the number 40 among your undecided friends and relatives!" ["40" was the number voters needed to enter in electronic vote machines to vote for Garotinho.][TA1.7][46]

Serra and Garotinho were clearly aware of social communication's power, but they were unable to harness it. Both lost.

Importantly, horizontal intermediation is not a theoretical competitor to, nor is it mutually exclusive from, vertical intermediation. Much to the contrary, different intermediary types *interact*. In modern societies, the raw material—the content—of political discussion usually originates in the mass media, and in contexts where clientelism is commonplace, individuals talk about the favors they received from a party. In both cases, far from muting or competing with alternative intermediaries, social communication can *magnify* the effects of the information conveyed through them, creating a ripple or cascade effect.[47] Our approach thus firmly eschews social determinism.

Overall, its unique combination of traits makes political discussion a particularly effective intermediary in shaping vote choice. Our primary purpose is to demonstrate how horizontal social influences work during election campaigns in Latin America.

Mechanisms of Social Influence

The most common form of peer influence on vote choice in Latin America combines two mechanisms: role modeling and the deliberative exchange of information.* Voters engage in deliberation, meaning the exchange of information and opinions among discussion partners, but they do so with carefully chosen partners, particularly partners they consider to be trustworthy and knowledgeable role models on political topics.[48] To illustrate, consider the following comment from a Brazilian interviewee, to whom we give the pseudonym Eva:

---

*We use "peer influence" and "social influence" as synonyms.

EVA: I have an uncle. He is PT because he is a factory worker. He knows more. I ask
him whom I should vote for. My uncle is more involved in that stuff. He's
really linked to the PT.[TA1.8]

Eva's remarks illustrate in several ways how social influence took place in this
scenario and, we find, in many others in Latin America. It shows clear evidence
of the role-modeling mechanism—that is, one individual imitates the attitude
or behavior of a trusted peer.[49] What has occurred, however, is not role modeling in its purest form, since Eva has done more than just passively observe
and model the behavior of her uncle. Instead, she seeks out her uncle to converse with him. The discussion that took place in this appeal to the uncle's perceived expertise alludes to the other mechanism of social influence: the exchange of persuasive information through conversation. The content of the
message mattered, not just the messenger.[50]

The model of social influence that we posit is a hybrid of these two mechanisms. Voters discuss and defer. They seek to gather information through discussion, but they prefer to do so from role models: "some people have far more
influence than others, simply because the decisions of those people convey more
information. [People] are especially likely to follow those who are confident,
who have special expertise."[51] Learning about politics is an overwhelming
informational chore for voters in any country. This is especially so in our
primary case of Brazil, where the proliferation of parties and the weakness of
party cues make information shortcuts scarce. Faced with this situation,
many voters, and particularly less politically knowledgeable ones, take cues
from more knowledgeable peers.[52] Because knowledgeable peers carry a
credibility and confidence that reassure uncertain voters, they serve as
opinion leaders in informal social networks; they are persuasive peers. By
appealing and listening to their best-informed social contacts, many Latin
American voters acquire socially informed preferences over the course of a
campaign.

Another aspect of Eva's comment merits our attention. The role-modeling
uncle is a partisan and thus likely to be a stable voter, maintaining his candidate preference over the course of the campaign. In seeking and imitating
his opinion, Eva ends up with a preference on election day that is in line with
that of a more partisan and stable voter. She gravitates toward a dominant
preference in her social environment, creating aggregate stability even as
she herself vacillates during the campaign. The following observation about
persuasive peers from the literature on US politics, worth quoting at length,
describes what has taken place:

> Opinion leaders are much less likely to dramatically modify their own opinions
> due to changing opinion distributions in the aggregate. Their staying power, in
> turn, serves as an anchor on changes in public opinion. Rather than moving
> toward new opinions, they tend to pull the movement of public opinion back

toward their own beliefs. . . . The influence of opinion leaders lies in their own unwillingness to change their beliefs.[53]

Two simple sociograms (i.e., network diagrams) depict the scenario implied in Eva's remarks and visually summarize these main points. Frame A of figure 1.2 includes three actors, each depicted as a circle (also "node"): Eva, her uncle, and (for the sake of illustration) her father.* Eva does not mention her father in the quotation, but that is exactly the point: she mentions her uncle, not her father, as a primary source of mid-campaign political information and advice because her uncle is the more knowledgeable one. Eva has a relationship (or "tie") with both, as indicated by the diagonal "social" lines, but she chooses to have a "political" tie—meaning informal political discussions—only with her uncle. Her only tie to her father is social, so he is an apolitical contact. (A political tie can exist only when a social tie is present.) Eva's only political conversation partner, or "political discussant," is her uncle. Her uncle's greater political knowledge is captured by the thick ring (with vertically hatched lines) around his node; it is thicker than the rings of Eva and her father. The political tie is directional, with the arrowheads indicating the direction of flow of political information. Eva's incoming arrowhead is larger than her outgoing one, meaning she receives more political information and advice from her uncle than she gives to him. In sum, these graphical elements convey Eva's selection decision—that is, her choice to discuss politics with her knowledgeable uncle rather than her poorly informed father.

The figure also conveys our argument about partisan politics and vote choice. Both frames A and B of figure 1.2 color each node according to the actor's candidate preference. Frame A depicts a mid-campaign scenario, and frame B depicts the votes cast on election day. Eva's uncle is an unwavering *petista* (PT partisan), so his node is black at both times, meaning his preference is Dilma. (For the sake of illustration, we continue with the 2014 election example.) In contrast, Eva's node in frame A is tricolored, indicating that she is still undecided among Dilma, Aécio (white), and Marina (gray). We will assume her father is also undecided because, empirically, politically unknowledgeable individuals are less likely to be committed partisans with stable preferences. Across all three actors, as in the real world, political knowledge and stability of candidate preference are positively correlated. On election day (frame B), Eva casts a vote for Dilma, turning her node black, because of her uncle's influence. (Absent any assumed channel of social influence, we cannot be certain how her father votes.) Eva's tendency to deliberate and defer to a trusted role model pulls her toward the preference held by a strong partisan in her social milieu.

---

*Note that the spatial placement of the nodes is arbitrary and irrelevant. Because no elites are present, ties depicted in sociograms throughout this book are horizontal. The only exception to this statement is in chapter 7 (figure 7.1).

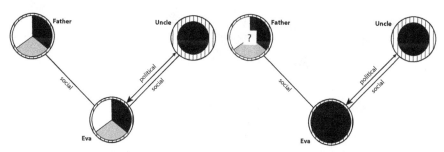

Frame A: Middle of Campaign

Frame B: Election Day

FIGURE 1.2 Eva's Network through Time

Notes: Node color indicates vote choice for Dilma (black), Aécio (white), or Marina (gray). A tricolored node means the actor is undecided. The thickness of the rings with vertically hatched lines indicates the amount of the actor's political knowledge. Arrowheads indicate amount (with arrowhead size) and direction of political information being exchanged.

Implications for Political Geography, Clientelism, and Democratic Citizenship

With a creative look at figure 1.2, one can imagine further theoretical implications of Eva's scenario. We derive three such implications and explore them in this book. First, persuasive peers can induce citizens to cast a vote that differs from the one they would have cast if they lived in a different social and political context. If some exogenous factor dictated that Eva's trusted political discussant were a stable Aécio voter rather than a stable Dilma voter, then the persuasive information emanating from this discussant would influence her toward an Aécio vote rather than a Dilma vote. This exogenous factor would thus be of utmost importance, and political geography is one such factor.

Frame A of figure 1.3 illustrates the role of geography, redrawing Eva's mid-campaign network while adding a simplified representation of the (hypothetical) political geography in which she and her two contacts are embedded. Imagine that Eva, her uncle, and her father live in a social environment—a neighborhood, a city, or even a state—in which stable Dilma voters are plentiful while stable Aécio voters are rare. These *potential* face-to-face discussants are portrayed by the smaller nodes now peppering Eva's sociogram in frame A. She talks to an infinitesimally small fraction of them, but they still matter because they constitute the pool from which she probabilistically chooses her knowledgeable contact. The pool leans pro-Dilma, making it likely that she ends up with a pro-Dilma tie who, as illustrated in figure 1.2, later leads her toward a Dilma vote by election day. In contrast, frame B shows a counterfactual scenario where Eva is embedded in a heavily pro-Aécio geographical environment. With

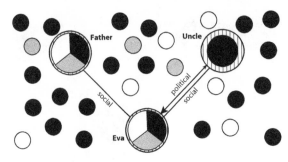

Scenario A: Eva in a Dilma-Leaning Context

FIGURE 1.3 The Effect of Political Geography on Eva's Mid-campaign Network *Notes:* See figure 1.2 for meaning of colors and symbols.

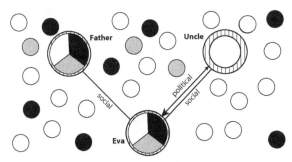

Scenario B: Eva in an Aécio-Leaning Context

this different partisan mix in her pool of potential political discussants, she ends up with an Aécio-voting discussant who (again by assumption derived from figure 1.2) later convinces her to vote for Aécio. The externally imposed factor of political geography shapes the distribution of partisan leanings among Eva's potential and actual social contacts and, because one of the contacts is a persuasive peer, influences her voting decision.

Second, clientelistic party machines should try to pay off voters who have large political discussion networks. Reconsider Eva's original (figure 1.2, frame A) mid-campaign network from the perspective of a strategically minded politician or broker armed with clientelistic payoffs. Traditional formal models of clientelistic targeting treat voters as horizontally isolated. These models would conclude that brokers should target Eva and her father because these two are more persuadable than Eva's uncle.[54] But the recognition of voters' horizontal social ties changes the calculus and better fits the balance of empirical evidence, which shows that clientelistic parties in Latin America tend to reward their loyalists.[55]

We illustrate by expanding Eva's original mid-campaign network using the following simple and realistic assumption: there are other voters like Eva. In

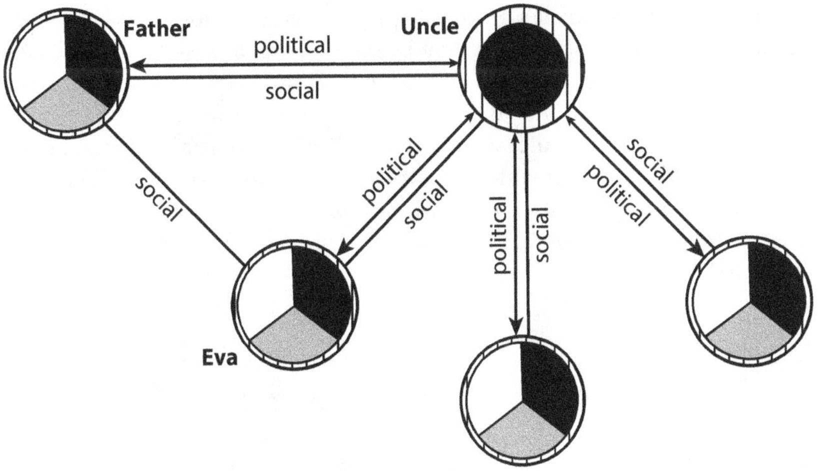

FIGURE 1.4 Eva's Mid-campaign Network Expanded
Notes: See figure 1.2 for meaning of colors and symbols.

other words, many other voters seek informed political advice from a knowledgeable peer. Figure 1.4 represents this expanded network. Because of his expertise, Eva's uncle attracts political ties and functions as an epicenter of political discussion and social influence. He is, in other words, a "hub" within
these informal social networks. (In this scenario, even Eva's father gets in on
the act by discussing politics with Eva's uncle.) From this perspective, a clientelistic party with limited resources should pay off the uncle, since the favor
could further energize him to proselytize the party's message to his many contacts. In other words, when the uncle is paid off, his impressive network magnifies the payoff's partisan message. If the party paid off Eva, its possible return from the favor would end with her.

Third, peer influence raises important normative questions about the quality and equity of political voice and democratic citizenship—questions that require empirical answers. Does social influence lead voters toward the candidate most aligned with their political values and issue positions? In figure 1.2
Eva's uncle led her to a particular candidate choice, but it is not clear whether
this is the *best* candidate for Eva's interests. Because of his own partisan de-
sires, Eva's uncle is surely not motivated to nudge Eva toward the candidate
maximizing *her* utility. This utility maximization could occur incidentally *if*
Eva's values and interests are similar to those of her uncle, perhaps because
the two have a shared city of residence or religious affiliation. But this is a big
if, one that can only be answered empirically. This scenario also points to a
second important question. Does informal political talk weaken or deepen
status-related differences in political knowledge and in the quality of citizens'

political voices? The uncle's greater degree of political knowledge and larger number of political discussants might be indicative of and even partly caused by his masculine identity, or by a higher social and economic status. After all, the acquisition of political knowledge requires resources, such as time, cognitive skills, and finances. Although radically decentralized and largely uncontrolled by elites, the informal airwaves of political discussion and social influence might still carry a "strong upper-class accent."[56] We address these questions and implications with our empirical analyses of network data in Latin America.

LATIN AMERICA AS A CASE

With these theoretical arguments and our empirical examinations, we seek to introduce scholars of Latin American politics to a world of social communication that has thus far evaded their view. There is some scholarship on peer influence in mass politics outside the US, but the vast majority of research on this subject is conducted on US citizens.[57] To those who misinterpret as bald imperialism our effort to export ideas from scholarship on the US to a Latin American context, we hasten to point out that this book also stresses the reverse flow of findings and ideas. Latin America offers a venue that is distinct in important ways from that of the US, and for multiple reasons scholars of mass political psychology in any country have much to learn about peer effects by paying attention to their workings in Latin America.

Most important, the laboratory of Latin American politics proffers many more instances of short-term changes in voter preferences, our primary dependent variable, than the US laboratory. The minimal effects paradigm of campaign influence is a stubborn one in the US, where citizens switch their vote intentions across party lines during presidential election campaigns far less frequently than Latin Americans. Panel surveys show that only about 5 to 8 percent, in sharp contrast to the aforementioned 40 percent in Brazil, switch during a US campaign.[58] Larry Bartels finds the average net impact of campaign persuasion over six elections to be just 1.8 percent in the US, and Robert Erikson and Christopher Wlezien claim that "only a small percentage of the vote is at play during the autumn in a typical election year."[59]

To get around this lack of variance, empirical work on peer-to-peer intermediation and candidate choice in the US uses dependent variables that are related to but distinct from changes in candidate preference—variables such as ambivalence about candidates or lateness in deciding.[60] Even in these studies, however, the appearance of indecisiveness and uncertainty is somewhat illusory. Recall the enlightened preferences tendency: virtually all US voters have partisan instincts to which, even if they have dabbled with indecision during the campaign, they return by its end. Similarly, the first modern studies of campaign effects, carried out by the Columbia school scholars, concluded that social influences activate and reinforce voters' preferences but rarely change them across party lines. In other words, if social influence exists at all during US campaigns, it produces preference stability and thus invariance.[61]

In Latin America, by contrast, the raw materials for social persuasion during campaigns are in place. Because most parties and party systems in the region are young, mass attachments to parties are poorly sedimented.[62] Many citizens possess relatively weak affinities for a candidate or a party at a campaign's onset, so they are open to social persuasion during the campaign. Unlike the US electoral system, moreover, those in Latin America feature proportional representation with, in most presidential elections, majority runoffs. Multiparty competition, therefore, is the norm, and more choices mean more opportunities for disagreement with, and then persuasion by, peers.[63] (Chapter 2 presents this evidence.) For these reasons, between one-third and one-half of all Latin American voters change their vote intentions *across party lines* (as in Brazil 2014) in the months before a presidential election. (Chapter 3 presents this evidence, showing high rates of change in Argentina and Mexico as well.) To summarize, Latin American campaigns and elections provide a rich arena for studying peer effects on changes in voter preferences because the region's elections feature substantial and important variation in this dependent variable.

Latin America is also distinct because neighborhoods are arenas of social influence. Scholars of the US generally agree that its neighborhoods are no longer forums for rich social interaction.[64] This does not accurately describe Latin America, where urban neighborhoods tend to have greater cohesion and organization, more residential stability, and better-defined borders.[65] Latin Americans discuss politics with their neighbors more than is typical in the US and in Europe (chapter 2). As a result, the region provides a unique opportunity to demonstrate when and how political discussion is a channel of neighborhood influence during campaigns.

The Latin American context can also inform theories of peer influence because clientelistic party machines are a thing of the past in the US, whereas the distribution by parties of jobs, gifts, and services in exchange for votes remains common in the region.[66] The contemporaneity of vote-buying efforts allows us to answer questions no longer relevant in the US. These questions incorporate the idea that clientelistic parties recognize the horizontal embeddedness of potential payoff recipients.

Finally, Latin America's fragile new democracies raise a unique set of normative questions about democratic citizenship in a horizontally networked world—questions that are unanswerable in the US context. Pundits and scholars of the US have made much of how social homogeneity and small-group echo chambers reinforce values and partisan polarization, with some groups allegedly drawn by these influences toward vote choices that are counter to their material interests.[67] The average social network in Latin America, by contrast, is more politically diverse and more likely to induce short-term preference change during a campaign. As a result, Latin American cases allow one to observe whether these factors produce some of the benefits, such as moving voters toward choices that align better with their interests, that advocates of deliberative democracy claim can arise from discussion and disagreement.[68]

METHODS OF ANALYSIS AND DATA

Horizontal social networks and the political discussions that take place within them can be difficult to measure and observe, a major reason why scholars of Latin America tend to ignore both. Measuring networks of social ties is time-consuming and expensive, and the direct observation of political conversations requires an ethnographic approach that can limit generalizability. It is easier to treat survey respondents as atomized social isolates and thus to reduce their attitudes, preferences, and information to individually held traits.

This book moves beyond this methodological individualism by measuring and analyzing voters' social contexts in several ways. Our primary method of inquiry is analysis of network (also "relational") data collected as part of nationally or municipally representative panel surveys. Some of these surveys also contain rarely measured neighborhood traits, enabling us to situate voters in a social environment that is broader in geographic scope than their immediate horizontal networks. In a few cases, we incorporate information from state-level social environments. Finally, we supplement these findings with data from open-ended, in-depth interviews about respondents' political ties and conversations as well as more traditional survey questions about the frequency of political discussion.

Egocentric Network Analysis

Our primary method of inquiry is longitudinal egocentric network analysis, conducted in the context of sample and panel surveys. Egocentric networks (also "egonets") center on a focal individual, as we did with Eva, who is called the "ego" or (in surveys) "main respondent." Egonets describe the number and nature of ties, if any, that this focal individual has with "alters" or (for conversational ties) "discussants." (We will use "ego" and "main respondent" synonymously and "alter" and "discussant" synonymously.) To provide an example, figure 1.5 shows the sociogram of two simple egocentric networks for egos E1 and E2. The lines indicate the presence of a tie between ego and alter (labeled as "A#"), and each ego ↔ alter pair is called a "dyad." In the figure, each of the two egos has three alters.[69]

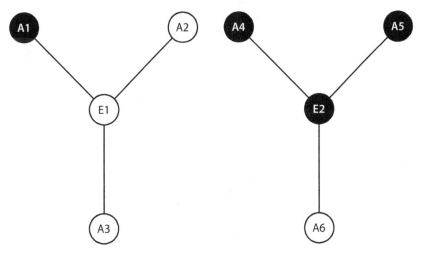

FIGURE 1.5 Sociograms of Two Egocentric Networks
Notes: Node color indicates vote choice for a hypothetical White or Black Party.
Lines indicate political ties.

Beyond these general elements of terminology and diagramming, our specific application of egocentric network analysis has several important features.
In our public opinion surveys, the egos are the standard interviewees chosen
by probabilistic sampling procedures. Each ego's unique set of alters is derived
via a question battery known as a network name generator: respondents are
asked to list the two or three people with whom they most discuss political
matters.[70] In other words, the ties we identify are *political*, meaning the ego
and alter discuss politics with one another. Eva's egocentric network in figure 1.2 shows two kinds of ties: social ties and their political subset. We occasionally refer to apolitical social ties (like Eva's father) or to potential ties in
the social environment (like the small nodes in figure 1.3) for conceptual reasons, but we do not directly observe apolitical ties, save one exception that we
exploit in chapter 2.[71] Stated differently, in our data the selection of *political*
discussants that is partly modeled and described in figures 1.2 and 1.3 *has already taken place.* Despite this, we can learn a great deal about the motivations and processes underlying citizens' selection of political discussants by
comparing the observed traits of alters to those of their egos and to the entire
sample.

The name generators are accompanied by name-interpreter questions that
ask egos to describe different traits of each alter, including a "proxy report" of
alters' intended or already-cast votes in the presidential election. With the name
interpreters (along with direct questions about ego's vote preferences), we can
identify the candidate preference of every node in each respondent's egonet.

This information allows us to, in essence, color-code each node in figure 1.5 for that actor's current political preference.

We have datasets with repeated measures of egocentric networks for four different presidential election campaigns in recent Latin American history. This book represents, in fact, the culmination of nearly two decades of collecting such data. The four elections are Brazil 2002, Brazil 2006, Brazil 2014, and Mexico 2006. The data on the first two were collected as part of the Brazil 2002–2006 Two-City Panel Study,[72] data for Brazil 2014 were collected as part of the Brazil 2014 Elections Panel Study (BEPS 2014),[73] and data for Mexico were collected as part of the Mexico 2006 Panel Study.[74] The Two-City Panel polled representative samples of respondents in the midsized Brazilian cities of Caxias do Sul and Juiz de Fora, and the other two panels are based on nationally representative samples. The Two-City Panel project conducted six waves of interviews: three in 2002, one in 2004, and two more in 2006. The Mexico 2006 Panel contains three waves, and BEPS 2014 contains seven. All four elections featured major momentum swings and high rates of individual-level preference change that we measure with these wave timings.

The precise protocols used to measure egocentric network traits vary somewhat across the different surveys, and we highlight these when relevant. Two merit brief mention here. First, the Two-City Panel includes interviews with many of the named discussants, itself a rarity in egocentric network measures in any country context.[75] These discussant interviews allow us to directly validate alters' preferences and to assess the accuracy of egos' reports of these preferences. Second, in BEPS 2014 main respondents were asked to list up to two discussants, whereas for the other three election studies they could list up to three.

The longitudinal nature of the egocentric network measures is crucial to our analyses and arguments about peer influences. For a study based on observational data that nonetheless wishes to estimate causal effects, longitudinal (panel) data are essential. Scholars of social influence consider longitudinal data to be "ideal" and a "Holy Grail," because "it is perilous to infer influence from relationships in cross-sectional surveys."[76] Figure 1.5 illustrates this. It might be tempting to conclude from a cross-sectional comparison of E1 and E2 that E1 is a White Party voter and E2 is a Black Party voter because both were influenced by the balance of opinion among their alters. After all, the majority opinion in the two networks correlates perfectly with the two egos' vote choices. But it is equally plausible that the majority of E1's network are White Party voters because, far from being influenced by them, White-partisan E1 *prefers* conversation partners with that stable trait. Black-partisan E2 also prefers to fraternize with fellow Black partisans and chose political ties with this in mind. This is the familiar, and seemingly universal, effect of homophily: humans prefer to have relationships with others who are like them and who share their views.[77] In politics, homophily is the tendency of citizens to avoid politically discordant relationships because disagreement can be uncomfortable.[78]

Panel data can address this selection effect. Our panel studies allow us to hold egos' and alters' constant across two observed time periods, and this enables us to assess whether changes in alters' preferences during the campaign are correlated with changes in egos' preferences. In this setup the choice of discussion partners is not a methodological confound because the alter or set of alters is constant through time. For instance, the Two-City Panel achieves this by holding the alters constant in two panel waves during the 2002 election campaign. Respondents listed their alters and their alters' vote intentions in an early panel wave conducted during the campaign, and respondents then reported the actual vote choices of these same alters in a panel wave conducted just after election day. In other words, if a main respondent listed João, Maria, and José as discussants in the earlier wave, that respondent was asked about the vote preferences of João, Maria, and José in that wave and then again in the post-election wave. Holding discussant identities constant in this way is preferred—yet rarely executed in political science studies—because it allows us to control for lagged alter preferences and thus the confound of alter selection.[79] In essence, our methodology adheres to the following prescription: "a proper study of social influence requires a dynamic, interactive framework that simultaneously focuses both on the source and the target of influence."[80]

Confounding from homophily is the greatest, but not the only, threat to achieving unbiased causal estimates of social influence. Latent homophily, environmental confounding, reverse causation, and measurement error also pose challenges, but we define these technicalities and our solutions to them as they arise in the chapters below. Experiments could address some of these shortcomings, and their recent proliferation in studies of horizontal intermediation and politics is welcome.[81] But experimental treatments that manipulate social communication are, by definition, artificial and lack the depth, intimacy, and realism of the social ties of everyday life.[82] Our primary research goal is to maximize external validity. Our measures of egocentric networks in panel surveys enable conclusions about social influences on actual voting behavior across electorates in Latin American elections.[83]

Other Methods of Analysis

Our longitudinal analyses of egonets with surveys generate conclusions about social influence that are generalizable to the real world and across a wide geographic scope while at the same time addressing, to the best extent possible with observational data, threats to making unbiased causal inferences. Still, this approach reveals rather little about the nature of the political conversations that took place between our egos and alters, save whether they were largely agreeing or disagreeing in nature. Participant observation and online text analyses have enabled scholars to observe discussion and interpersonal influence in action, but these methods require a deep commitment of time to a small number of physical or virtual sites.[84]

We balance these challenges by reporting quotations, as we did in a few instances above, gleaned from open-ended interviews that we and our research assistants conducted with individuals (many of them our survey main respondents) in Brazil and Mexico. In 2002, 2004, and 2018, our team conducted a total of about 80 such interviews with common citizens and another 60 with neighborhood leaders. The interviews probed the reasons respondents voted the way they did and the nature of the conversations they held in their horizontal social networks. These qualitative data offer clear examples of peer influences and elucidate the mechanisms through which those influences occurred. They also provide crucial information about voters' motivations for discussing or, as is sometimes the case, *not* discussing politics. When it is necessary to use a name in these quotations, we always use pseudonyms (like Eva) that nonetheless convey the gender of the referent. For each quotation, the original Portuguese or Spanish appears in an online Translation Appendix (TA). The quotation's precise location in the appendix is indicated by a superscripted identification number (e.g., TA3.1) that appears at the end of each quotation.

Despite our heavy reliance on the egocentric network data from the four Brazilian and Mexican elections, we also make use of many traditional, non-relational measures available in these and other surveys. Most innovative, the Two-City Panel sampled a critical mass of respondents (100 or more) in 22 different neighborhoods in each city. These data allow us to analyze rarely measured political aspects of respondents' neighborhood-level environments and to assess the degree to which neighborhood influences on vote choice are truly social in nature. The surveys for these four elections also include standard indicators of concepts such as the frequency of political talk and exposure to other political intermediaries (e.g., media, party contacting, and clientelism).

Finally, to present findings on a broader set of countries and elections, we report analyses of three cross-national survey datasets. The Comparative National Elections Project (CNEP) and the World Values Survey (WVS) convey important descriptive information about political intermediation in Latin America and provide points of comparison to countries in other world regions. In particular, the CNEP contains rich cross-sectional measures of exposure to all political intermediary types, including measures of egonets. The Latin American Public Opinion Project (LAPOP) includes cross-national information on the relationship between political talk and clientelism.

FOCUS AND PLAN OF THE BOOK

Our focus in this book is peer influence on *presidential* voting in Latin America. Presidential elections are the headlining contests for each country's most powerful post in a region where presidents are especially strong actors. Still, it is important to bear in mind that presidential races are least likely cases for our argument. The presidential election is the most visible election in any given country, and mass-mediated information is readily available for the citizen who wishes to decide without consulting social contacts. In contrast, elections to lower offices in our country cases are often low-information affairs. This is especially true of elections to legislative posts in Brazil, where an overwhelming number of candidates (literally hundreds) and parties (several dozen) run in every district. For voters, vertically mediated information about their legislative options is harder to come by, so they are probably *more* likely to ask peers to help them winnow down their choices for legislative elections than they are for presidential elections. In short, evidence of peer influence in presidential campaigns suggests that it is likely to exist during campaigns for other offices.

The plan of the book is as follows. The next chapter ("Latin American Political Discussion in Comparative Perspective") rounds out the background material of part I ("Introduction and Descriptive Background"). Chapter 2 fills a major gap in the literature on Latin American politics by providing sorely needed descriptive information about the region's political discussion networks, our principal explanatory variable. Using our panels, the CNEP, and the WVS, we report the absolute and relative prevalence of political discussion—compared to other countries and to other intermediaries—in Brazil, Mexico, and eight other Latin American countries. Latin American citizens discuss politics at a frequency that is typical or even above that prevailing in other countries, and their propensity to speak with residential neighbors is well above the global average. Chapter 2 then portrays the amount of political disagreement and the disparity in political expertise between discussion partners. Rates of disagreement over vote choices in Latin America are high relative to those in the US, and this is largely because the region's multiparty systems afford more opportunities for disagreement. Moreover, Latin Americans seek out discussion partners with relatively high political expertise, an important part of the socially informed preferences argument.

Chapters 3 through 6 constitute part II: "Social Influence and the Vote." They carry the core empirical material in support of the argument on social influence. Part II provides crucial descriptive findings about rates of preference change by voters during Brazilian and Mexican presidential campaigns. We then show that the volatility of voters' preferences is caused by political discussion and persuasive peers. In doing so, we also demonstrate in part II how social influences deepen the geographical clustering of the vote across neighborhoods and even across states.

Chapter 3, "Voter Volatility and Stability in Presidential Campaigns," reports novel descriptive facts on part II's primary dependent variable, the dynamics of vote choice during presidential election campaigns. Using all available panel data from Brazil and Mexico (plus one from Argentina), we estimate the amount of preference change that occurred in 10 election campaigns. Between any two panel waves, 17 to 45 percent of voters switched across party lines. We then depict campaign volatility at the national level, using nation-wide poll results to show how the horse race unfolded in our four main election cases (Brazil 2002, Brazil 2006, Brazil 2014, and Mexico 2006). These polling trends provide a brief historical background to our election cases and allow us to refute claims that the observed switching is based strictly on individual (and potentially socially isolated) calculations to avoid a wasted vote.

Chapter 4 ("Discussion Networks, Campaign Effects, and Vote Choice") is the book's core empirical chapter. It demonstrates that the dynamics of vote choice described in chapter 3 are caused by the discussion and social ties described in chapter 2. During campaigns, discussion with disagreeing partners tends to induce preference change in voters, while discussion only with agreeing partners reinforces vote intentions, causing preference stability. We demonstrate this relationship at multiple levels of analysis, estimating relationships in the Brazilian and Mexican panel surveys in ways that address threats to causal inference. Quotations from our qualitative data also illustrate social influence in action, showing vividly that many voters defer to their more politically knowledgeable social ties. In short, the votes cast on election day in Brazil and Mexico are socially informed. Chapter 4 also shows that the social influences that occur during campaigns determine who wins elections. Candidates whose mid-campaign supporters encounter high rates of disagreement from social ties struggle to hold on to these voters through election day. These voters' preferences are less reinforced in conversation, so many switch to different candidates. The candidate they previously supported collapses in the polls.

Chapter 5, "Neighborhoods and Cities as Arenas of Social Influence," is the first of two chapters linking political discussion to the geography of the vote (as illustrated in figure 1.3). Social influences induce many citizens to cast votes that differ from the ones they would have cast if they lived elsewhere. This chapter considers neighborhood effects on vote choice in two Brazilian cities. Nearly two-thirds of discussion partners in the two cities are residents of the same neighborhood. Neighborhoods with a stable and relatively homogeneous partisan leaning assimilate, over the course of a campaign, initially disagreeing residents toward that leaning. We show that this effect occurs through discussion between neighborhood coresidents in the politically polarized city of Caxias do Sul. In other words, the clustering of political preferences by neighborhood in Caxias is partly due to social influences and not, as in the case of the US, mere self-sorting. By contrast, the same level of political discussion in Juiz de Fora, a less polarized city where the partisan leanings of neighborhoods are amorphous, yields no assimilation effect.

Chapter 6 ("Discussion and the Regionalization of Voter Preferences") completes part II by scaling up the focus to larger subnational units. It illustrates how political discussion explains the geography of the vote across states and entire subnational regions. Political discussion during the Brazil 2014 and

Mexico 2006 campaigns drew many voters toward the political leanings of their states, deepening North versus South and other regional divides. Scholars tend to see the regional clustering of political preferences in Brazil and Mexico as the sum of individual-level interests, identities, and demographics (e.g., the Mexican North is conservative because its residents are relatively wealthy). We show that social influences make the regionalization of preferences much greater than the sum of these individual parts.

With the empirical evidence of peer influences on vote choice in hand, part III considers the implications of a horizontally networked world for other aspects of political behavior. Chapter 7, entitled "Clientelism as the Purchase of Social Influence," turns to elite behavior, demonstrating that clientelistic party machines try to pay off hubs—that is, voters with large political discussion networks who frequently engage in persuasion. In seeking to buy votes, the best strategy a party can pursue, as we argued using figure 1.4, is to target citizens who are well-connected opinion leaders in informal networks. These voters represent the machine's highest potential yield because they can magnify the effect of the payoff by diffusing positive information about the machine through their large social networks. We use LAPOP and the Mexico 2006 Panel Study to show that party machines do target well-connected voters throughout Latin America. We also show that a finding central to previous theories—namely, that loyal partisans are the most likely targets of clientelism—is driven by omitted-variable and endogeneity bias. In other words, scholarly expectations of party activity change when we recognize that parties operate in a world of horizontally networked voters.

Our final set of empirical exercises, chapter 8 ("Discussion, Societal Exclusion, and Political Voice"), explores the implications of horizontal intermediation for the normative issues of the quality and equity of political voice. Because its monetary costs are virtually nil, the realm of horizontal intermediation could be a haven for under-resourced and marginalized groups. Our analyses of data from the panel studies and the CNEP, however, show that political discussion in seven Latin American countries suffers from an exclusion problem. Individuals of high socioeconomic status (SES) are much more likely to discuss politics than individuals of lower status, and men discuss politics more than women. This has concrete consequences, as high-SES individuals and men have more political knowledge than low-SES individuals and women, respectively. Chapter 8 then considers whether these inequalities distort the political voice of marginalized groups. In Brazil and Mexico, the degree of engagement in horizontal intermediation is positively correlated with voters' abilities to choose the candidates who best represent their issue attitudes (i.e., their "correct" candidates). Because of this correlation, the poor are sometimes less likely than the rich to choose candidates who support their expressed values and beliefs about politics and policies. Moreover, the emergence of socially informed preferences during a campaign does not move voters toward their correct candidates.

Seen collectively, our findings paint a somewhat complicated picture of democratic citizenship in Latin America. Chapter 9 wrestles with these findings and strikes a balanced conclusion. On the one hand, the high rates of vote switching during campaigns, often as a result of informal discussion, reflect an open-mindedness and a responsiveness to counterargumentation that is absent in the more polarized and partisan US. In thinking about their vote decisions, moreover, Latin American voters seek informed advice, identifying knowledgeable peers from whom to learn. On the other hand, this social process during the campaign does not necessarily yield better decisions, at least according to the correct-voting criterion. Furthermore, this process is dominated by the upper class in a region that already suffers deep socioeconomic inequalities.

2

Latin American Political Discussion in Comparative Perspective

Sometimes someone else's opinion helps, you know?[TA2.1]

—*Brazilian voter (2004)*

In any democratic society, interest and engagement in politics vary enormously across citizens. One end of the spectrum features individuals who almost never discuss politics. A remark from one of our Brazilian respondents exemplifies this voter type:

> Politics makes me nauseous. . . . I avoid talking about it.[TA2.2]

On the other end of the spectrum, some individuals eat and breathe politics:

> My family is all about politics. We go to a party, and it's politics. We go to a funeral, and it's politics.[TA2.3]

> Yes, [I talk about politics] almost every day. Politics is in all of our lives, isn't it?[TA2.4]

In Latin America, most voters fall somewhere in between these extremes, but beyond this truism scholars of the region know rather little about the nature of informal political discussion. How frequently do Latin Americans discuss politics, and with whom do they discuss it? These are seemingly straightforward descriptive questions, but to date they have received only cursory answers. Fortunately, several surveys of the region's citizens have included questions about horizontal intermediation. This chapter analyzes data from the Brazil and Mexico panel studies and, to provide some comparisons to the rest of Latin America and the world, two major cross-national survey ventures: the World Values Survey (WVS) and the Comparative National Elections Project (CNEP). The chapter paints a descriptive picture of our main independent variable, informal political talk.

The first half of the chapter assesses how much informal political talk occurs in Latin America. It compares the amount of political talk to the amount of mass media consumption in the region and to the amount of political talk in other world regions. Political discussion in Latin America, we find, is about as prevalent as worldwide averages, although results vary by survey instrument and by country. The frequency of political discussion varies by types of conversation partners, as Latin Americans discuss politics with friends, family, and neighbors in descending order of frequency. This relative pattern is almost ubiquitous internationally, but Latin Americans stand out for discussing politics more with *neighbors* than do individuals in most other countries. Latin American citizens do discuss politics less often than they consume political news, but discussion, as an active and engaged form of intermediation, has a much greater impact on knowledge acquisition (per minute spent) than media consumption. These findings underpin and reinforce one of our central claims: informal political discussion is important in Latin America, and ignoring it means that scholars of Latin American mass politics miss a crucial part of the processes underlying the region's elections and voting behavior.

The second half of the chapter looks more closely at the political character of conversational exchanges. Crucially, Latin Americans prefer political discussants who are more politically knowledgeable than themselves. Citizens in the region, moreover, discuss politics with individuals who agree politically with themselves more frequently than chance would dictate. Still, political disagreement is not entirely purged or uncommon in interpersonal relationships, and this disagreement creates opportunities for social persuasion. Overall, the descriptive findings in this chapter lay the groundwork for the analyses of social influence presented in later chapters.

THE PREVALENCE OF POLITICAL DISCUSSION

How often do Latin American citizens discuss politics with family, friends, and neighbors? Politics is complicated for even the most engaged and knowledgeable citizens, so many shut it out. Millions of Latin American citizens, moreover, lack the socioeconomic resources that are highly correlated with political knowledge and engagement around the world.[1] For instance, many voters in Brazil told us in interviews that they lacked the "*estudo*" (studies or schooling) to understand and respond knowledgeably to our political questions. Political discussion requires at least some information, and it carries costs, including embarrassment and loss of self-esteem, if one reveals a lack of knowledge. Furthermore, political polarization is common in the region, and individuals often prefer to avoid conflictual political conversations.[2] Consider this remark from a Brazilian voter: "I don't talk about politics. It ends up in a lot of fighting."[TA2.5] Finally, some scholarly impressions of Latin America suggest that a culture of familism predominates, meaning individuals are hesitant to forge trusting ties and converse with nonrelatives.[3] Facing so many challenges, most Latin American voters may be reluctant to discuss politics in their peer networks, especially with peers who are not immediate family members.

These impressions are wrong. Politics is indeed complicated, but in Latin America (as elsewhere) it is rife with content—personalities, morality, group conflicts, distributive consequences, competition, violence—that citizens can easily grasp and that is highly communicable to their social contacts. This section shows that Latin American citizens engage in informal political discussion at a rate that is typical by international standards. The precise amount varies by country, by interlocutor type, and by measure, but the unequivocal overall conclusion is that horizontal political talk exists at frequencies that are important. Indeed, Latin Americans, according to some measures, are more likely to discuss politics with neighbors than are citizens elsewhere. To situate our measures of discussion frequency in the region, we provide various anchors of comparison. These anchors include rates of political discussion in other world regions, the frequency of mass media consumption within the region, and the frequency of discussion in the region at other points in time. Gauging political discussion frequency is challenging, so the endnotes provide some technical detail defending the measurement validity of the survey items.

International Comparisons

The WVS and the CNEP allow us to compare the amount of informal political discussion in Latin America with amounts in other world regions. From 1982 to 2001 the WVS asked, "How often do you discuss political matters with friends?" in 121 country years (e.g., Mexico 1990). Most country years are in the 1990s. We label this variable *Frequency of political discussion with friends*. (Note that all variable names are italicized in the main text.) The response options are "never," "occasionally," and "frequently." (Wordings and numerical codes for all survey questions used in this book are in appendix B, which lists variables in alphabetical order.) Frame A of figure 2.1 reports means by world region.[4] Latin American countries are below the global mean, but not by much—just 0.12 of a standard deviation and just a tiny portion of the overall range. Europe, which is generously sampled, pulls up the global mean, and the means across all other regions are nearly equivalent to those in Latin America.[5] Overall, Latin America in the 1990s was essentially equal to all non-European regions in its frequency of political discussion with friends, and Latin America's shortfall with Europe was minor.

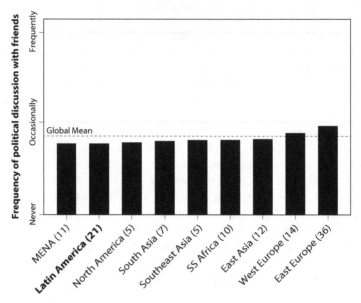

Frame A: By World Regions
Notes: Each bar is the grand mean of the relevant country-year means.
Numbers in parentheses are counts of country-year observations.
"MENA" = Middle East and North Africa. "SS Africa" = sub-Saharan
Africa.

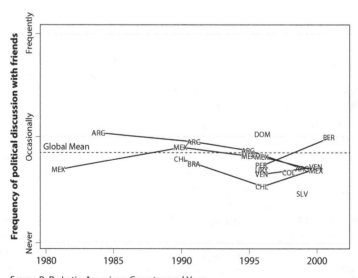

Frame B: By Latin American Country and Year
Notes: The placement of each point represents the mean for a country
year, and the points themselves are three-letter country ISO codes.

FIGURE 2.1 The Frequency of Political Discussion in 121 Country Years
Source: World Values Survey.

Frame B of figure 2.1 portrays the variation in means across Latin American countries and across time. This frame plots, using three-letter country ISO codes, the 21 observed country-year means for Latin America. Black lines connect repeated measures within a country. Respondents in some countries report more discussion, on average, than others (e.g., the Dominican Republic reports more than El Salvador), and the vast majority of observations cluster just below the global mean. No consistent temporal pattern exists: increases through time seemingly occurred in Mexico, Peru, and Venezuela, but declines occurred in Argentina and Chile.

Findings from the CNEP paint a different picture, suggesting that Latin Americans discuss politics as frequently as or even more frequently than voters in other world regions. Although the CNEP has fewer country years than the WVS, it differs in other ways that make it more useful for our purposes. CNEP interviews occur during election years and in reference to a recent or upcoming election, and they provide broader and more recent temporal coverage (1993 to 2018). The CNEP questionnaires also contain a rich set of questions about exposure to virtually all types of political intermediaries, including (with just a few exceptions) a three-question battery asking respondents how frequently they talked about "the most recent election campaign" with three peer types: family, friends, and neighbors. Response categories are "often," "sometimes," "rarely," and "never." Brazil has not been part of the CNEP, but we report comparable results from the 2002, 2006, and 2014 elections since our panel studies contain questions with wordings that are equivalent or nearly equivalent to these from the CNEP.[6]

Figure 2.2 presents results about horizontal political discussion from 33 elections across 20 countries and territories. Election cases are labeled with three-letter country ISO codes followed by a two-digit year, and the Latin American countries are in boldface. Frame A of figure 2.2 presents four pieces of information for each election. The placement of the lettered labels are the election (also country-year) means on each of the three queries: "fam" is the average for the *Frequency of political discussion with family* query, "frd" is the average for the *Frequency of political discussion with friends* query, and "nei" is the average for the *Frequency of political discussion with neighbors* query. The height of the gray bar is the grand mean of these three averages. The elections are sorted in descending order from left to right according to their value on this grand mean.[7] The y-axis spans the entire possible range of discussion frequency, from never to frequently. Frame B of figure 2.2 presents the percentage of respondents who discuss politics at any time during the election. More precisely, this is the percentage who did not respond with "never" to all three discussion queries. Admittedly, this is a low bar: answering "rarely" to just one of the three queries classifies the respondent as having discussed politics. Still, it is useful to know the share who claim to have discussed politics at all.

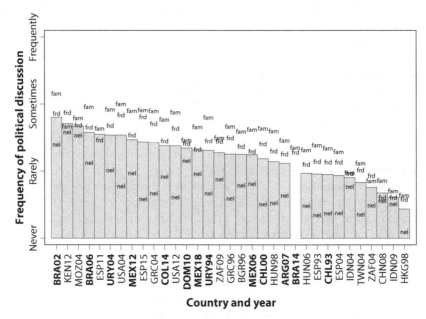

Frame A: Frequency by Type of Conversation Partner and Frequency Overall
Notes: "fam" = *Frequency of political discussion with family,* "frd" = *Frequency of political discussion with friends,* "nei" = *Frequency of political discussion with neighbors.* Each bar is the grand mean of these three means.

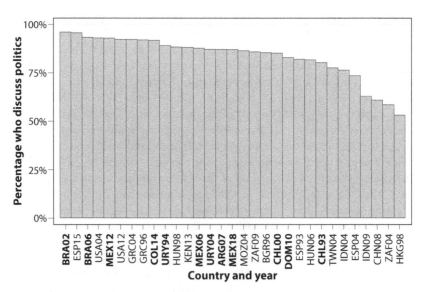

Frame B: Share of the Population that Discusses Politics
Notes: Each bar is the percentage of respondents who did not answer "never" to all three discussion queries from frame A.

FIGURE 2.2 The Frequency of Political Discussion in 33 Election Campaigns
Sources: CNEP, Two-City Panel, BEPS 2014.

The two frames contain three important findings. First, the amount of political discussion in Latin America is at or perhaps even above the international central tendency. Admittedly, this is not a systematic sampling of elections, so the true international central tendency remains unknown. In addition, recall that the Brazil 2002 and 2006 results are from just two cities that, based on the comparison with the nationally representative 2014 survey, appear to have rates of discussion that exceed Brazil's national average. Still, only 3 of the 13 Latin American observations are below the median for non–Latin American countries (which is between Bulgaria 1996 and Hungary 1998), and only one (Chile 2000) is decidedly below this median. If we consider the percentage who discuss politics at all, all but 1 (Chile 1993) of the 13 Latin American cases are above the non–Latin American median (Spain 1993).

The second finding is that Latin Americans talk politics most often with family members. Friends are a close second, and neighbors are third. In all the Latin American country years, the mean response on discussion frequency with family members is between the "sometimes" and "rarely" categories, with the mean closer to "sometimes" than "rarely" in 9 of the 13 cases. Rates of discussion with friends also fall in between these two categories, but in most Latin American cases they are closer to "rarely" than to "sometimes." Rates of discussion with neighbors cluster closest to the "rarely" category (except in Chile 1993, where they are closest to "never"). On the surface, this relative ranking might support the claim that a culture of familism prevails in the region, but even a casual second glance reveals that family contacts predominate in *almost all* the sampled countries.

These low relative rates of discussion with neighbors notwithstanding, our third central finding is that Latin Americans discuss politics with their neighbors—contra the alleged culture of familism—more than do citizens of most other countries. Of the 11 elections with the highest means on this variable, 8 are Latin American, and only Chile's 2 elections are below the non–Latin American median. Neighborhood discussion is especially common, compared to other countries, in the two Brazilian cities and in Colombia, the Dominican Republic, Mexico, and Uruguay. In summary, although the region was slightly below the global mean in the 1990s, informal political discussion has since become at least as common and widespread in Latin America as elsewhere. Moreover, discussion with neighbors is more common in Latin America than in most other world regions.

We also conduct an international comparison of *Egocentric network size* (also "degree"). This is the number of political discussants each respondent lists in response to a name-generator query.* Recall from chapter 1 that the name-generator wordings in the Two-City Panel and the Mexico 2006 Panel ask for strictly *political* ties and discussants. Typical name generators implemented

---

*Our measures of egocentric network size never include the one ego in the count.

in the US and elsewhere ask for a list of social alters, meaning individuals with whom the main respondent discusses "important matters." As a result, our queries about *political* discussants limit the opportunity for cross-national comparisons.[8] The safest comparison is with a name generator conducted on a 1996 survey of US citizens by the Spencer Foundation.[9] Like our panel surveys, it sought strictly political discussants and capped the list at three alters.

Because we calculate network size for multiple panel waves in Mexico 2006, a quick note on wave nomenclature is in order. So that readers do not have to remember the different panel-wave numberings for each study, we apply a common terminology across them throughout this book. For each of the four election years (Brazil 2002, 2006, 2014, and Mexico 2006), we have a "campaign" wave (also "*c* wave" or *c*) of interviews and an "election" wave ("*e* wave" or *e*). Campaign waves occurred during the legally defined campaign period, and election waves occurred soon after election day. For Brazil 2002, Brazil 2014, and Mexico 2006, we also have a "pre-campaign" wave ("*pc* wave" or *pc*) that occurred after major-party candidates were known but before the campaign's legal start. To reiterate, the temporal ordering is $pc \rightarrow c \rightarrow e$. With seven waves, the Brazil 2014 Panel Study is more complex, with multiple campaign waves and multiple election waves, but we save further details about this and the precise wave timings in all panels for chapter 3.

Figure 2.3 is a bar graph that reports the mean number of political discussants in Brazil, Mexico, and the US. For the Mexico 2006 Panel, the survey administered fresh name generators in both the campaign wave and the election wave, and the figure reports both sets of results. The horizontal length of each bar denotes the mean number of discussants that main respondents reported, and the means themselves are shown in black numbers. Figure 2.3 also categorizes discussants into two groups—relatives or friends—based on *Relationship to discussant* queries. The black portion of the bar (and leftmost white number) represents the mean number of relatives, and the dark-gray portion (and rightmost white number) is the mean number of friends. The light-gray portion captures the mean number of discussants that main respondents did not categorize into either group (e.g., "other" or "don't know").

The mean in almost every instance rounds to two political discussants. In the two Brazilian cities, the average is 2.10 in both election years,[10] and it is 1.80 in the US. In Mexico, the mean was lower (1.47) in the campaign wave, but it jumped to the US level (1.77) in the election wave. These means are close to those seen in response to important-matters name generators elsewhere. For example, in surveys conducted in six European countries and the US, James Gibson finds the country averages to have a similar central tendency (median of 2.08) with a narrow range (1.80 to 2.33).[11]

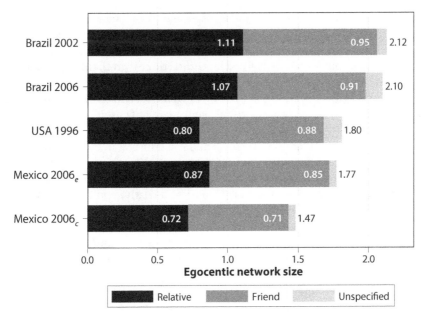

FIGURE 2.3 The Number of Political Discussants in Brazil, Mexico, and the US
Notes: Entries for the two Brazil elections are based on campaign-wave questions.
$N = 3,561$ (Brazil 2002); $N = 2,042$ (Brazil 2006); $N = 715$ (USA 1996); $N = 1,776$ (Mexico 2006c, campaign wave); $N = 1,594$ (Mexico 2006e, election wave).
Sources: Two-City Panel, USA Spencer Foundation 1996, Mexico 2006 Panel.

Two sources of measurement error mean that our estimates of the average number of political discussants are probably low.[12] First, these results *overestimate* the share of citizens with zero discussants. Some respondents cut corners at the beginning of a name generator, failing to report any discussants because they see it as an invasion of privacy or because they want to move the interview along.[13] In the campaign wave of the Mexico 2006 Panel, for example, a relatively high 38 percent of respondents reported themselves to be singletons or isolates, meaning they listed no discussants. Nonetheless, a large majority (68 percent) of these respondents said elsewhere in the questionnaire that they discuss politics at least rarely. In the election wave of this panel study two-fifths of the (now-lower) 28 percent of respondents who reported as singletons responded inconsistently in this way. In the end, only about 12–16 percent of the Mexican electorate, by our estimates, are true politically mute individuals— that is, individuals who respond consistently as non-talkers to both the name-generator and frequency-of-discussion questions. This is reassuring because it is closer to the estimate reported in frame B of figure 2.2.

Second, although the discussant name generators are capped at three, many Brazilians and Mexicans have more than three alters.[14] In Mexico 2006, for example, 40 percent of respondents listed three discussants, and many of these respondents would have surely listed more than three if given the opportunity to do so.

Figure 2.3 shows nearly a 50:50 family-to-friend ratio in the discussant lists for Brazil and Mexico. This is virtually equivalent to Gibson's cross-national median and to the ratio reported for the US, which further dismisses any claim that Latin Americans are abnormally familial and insular in their social ties.[15] The nationally representative BEPS 2014 shows a similar finding despite using a different political-discussant name generator wording. BEPS respondents heard a more guided query, first being asked to name a relative and then a nonrelative. Respondents were equally likely to offer names in response to both.[16]

Overall, citizens in Latin America discuss politics with a frequency that is typical by international standards. Moreover, they select family members and friends as political discussants with nearly equal frequency, although they speak a bit more often to the former than to the latter. Both patterns are the norm outside the region as well, but Latin Americans do deviate from one international norm by talking to neighbors at a higher rate than do citizens of other regions. Finally, the frequency of political discussion in Latin America relative to the rest of the world may have increased through time.

Comparison to Mass Media Consumption

How does the frequency of informal political discussion compare to rates of mass media consumption in Latin America? To answer this question, we face an important measurement challenge. Most survey questions on discussion frequency and network size cannot tell us precisely how much political discussion occurs. Of the four response options to the discussion frequency queries from the CNEP, only one ("never") provides a concrete rate, meaning a frequency that is anchored in time. This also complicates comparisons to the frequency of mass media consumption because the CNEP questions on media exposure use different response options—ones that *do* anchor responses in concrete timing intervals (number of days per week).

To resolve this problem, we turn to the Mexico 2006 Panel, which contains measures of discussion frequency that reference well-specified time intervals. The media-usage questions feature response options with nearly equivalent time intervals, allowing us to compare across these two intermediaries. In all three waves of the Mexico 2006 Panel, respondents were asked about their *Frequency of political discussion*: "How often do you talk about politics with other people? (30) Daily. (15) A few days a week. (4) A few days a month. (1) Rarely. (0) Never."[17] We score these categories at the interval level in units of days-per-month.[18] This creates comparability to media usage, which is measured with *Frequency of TV news consumption*: "Do you normally watch any news program on TV? [If "yes"] Which ones? How often do you watch them? (30) Daily. (15) A few times per week. (4) Once a week. (1) Sometimes. (0) [If "no"] Never."[19] Again, the unit of measurement is the number of days per month.

Figure 2.4 shows two sets of histograms. Frame A portrays three marginal distributions, one per panel wave, of political discussion frequency. Frame B portrays three marginal distributions of news consumption frequency. The figures also report (in the legend) the means at each panel wave.

In the months surrounding the 2006 election, Mexicans talked politics an average of 7 days per month. Despite the unfolding campaign and the election itself, this central tendency varied little through time. In contrast, Mexicans watched TV news an average of 15 to 19 days per month, roughly two to three times as often as they discussed politics. For reasons that are unclear, this central tendency declines through time, but even at its nadir just after the election it exceeds the *Frequency of political discussion* mean by 9 days.

News viewership is considerably more common than political discussion. Perhaps, for this reason, our focus should be on media consumption. Are we barking up the wrong tree by studying social communication? We think not, for two major reasons.

Most important, a mindless focus on the frequency or quantity of intermediary exposure overlooks the per-unit quality and impact of that exposure. Media consumption is a passive activity. Exposure to media does not necessarily mean that its content is understood and absorbed. Many households run their televisions all day and evening while their residents pay only sporadic attention. For these and other reasons, political-behavior scholars have long insisted on the distinction between media *usage* and media *reception*.[20] Political discussion, in comparison, is an active practice, an act of participation itself that requires mental engagement. On a per-minute basis, political discussion should have greater impact on attitudes and behaviors than media consumption.[21]

To test this hypothesis, we consider differences in the impacts of the intermediaries on campaign knowledge levels. Political discussion is a known cause of political knowledge, but, if our argument is correct, individuals should learn more from political discussion than from media consumption. Using the Mexico 2006 Panel, we measure *Campaign knowledge* with indexes (standardized to *z*-scores) compiled from objective quiz questions that measure whether respondents know each major-party candidate's campaign slogan. These questions were asked in the pre-campaign (four items) and campaign (three items) waves, and the overall indexes are calculated using item response theory models.[22] To answer the empirical question, campaign-specific knowledge is more appropriate than overall political knowledge. It captures information that is plausibly endogenous to the intermediary usage reported at the time of the

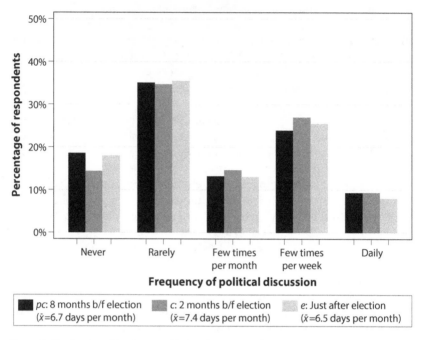

Frame A: Distribution of Frequency of Political Discussion by Timing

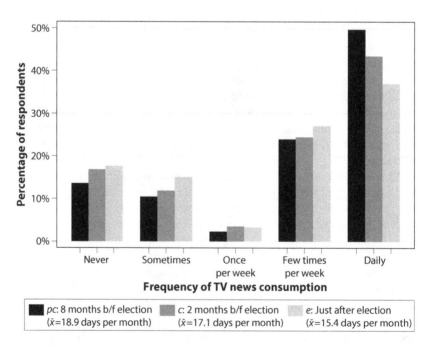

Frame B: Distribution of Frequency of TV News Consumption by Timing

survey wave—these slogans could not have been known prior to the start of the 2006 campaign.

Figure 2.5 depicts (as a rope-ladder plot) coefficients and 95 percent confidence intervals from three ordinary least squares (OLS) regression models. The dependent variable is *Campaign knowledge*. The figure provides value labels for the main coefficients of interest. (Appendix A reports full numerical results of all the statistical models whose main results we depict graphically.) The first regression (circle markers) uses pre-campaign data and contains, as independent variables, *Frequency of political discussion* and *Frequency of TV news consumption*. Because these two variables are in the same unit of measurement (days-per-month), their coefficients can be directly compared to weigh their relative contributions to campaign knowledge. The second regression (squares) uses campaign-wave data and contains both these independent variables plus, to provide a point of comparison, two measures of direct vertical intermediation from political parties (*Contacted by a party* and *Paid off by a party*). The third regression (triangles) also uses campaign-wave data but replaces *Frequency of political discussion* with *Egocentric network size*.

According to model 1, the effect of an extra day (per month) of political discussion on pre-campaign knowledge (0.025) is three times as large as the effect of an extra day of TV viewing (0.008).[23] Model 2 shows that the gap is smaller in the campaign wave, but the effect of discussion is still nearly twice as large. Model 3 reveals that egocentric network size also has a large effect, although this comparison is not as straightforward given the different units of measurement. The effect of an additional political discussant on campaign knowledge is equivalent to watching TV news daily for an extra two weeks each month! Thus two additional discussants yield the equivalent in knowledge of the difference between a person who never watches news and one who watches daily. The campaign-wave models also show that the effects of direct intermediation from political parties are minimal and statistically insignificant. In short, political discussion yields a larger effect on knowledge acquisition than the consumption of television news.

The second reason to avoid a simple focus on quantity for adjudicating the relative importance of intermediaries is that our central theoretical claims are not about the *amount* of political discussion. They are, rather, about *with whom one discusses*. In other words, what matters in creating social influence on vote choice is the "who," not the "how much." Most important, vote choice and vote switching vary with the preferences of political discussants, not

---

FIGURE 2.4 The Amount of Political Discussion and TV News Consumption in Mexico 2006
Notes: $N = 2,372$ (*pc*, pre-campaign wave); $N = 1,750$ (*c*, campaign wave); $N = 1,574$ (*e*, election wave).
Source: Mexico 2006 Panel.

Dependent variable: campaign knowledge

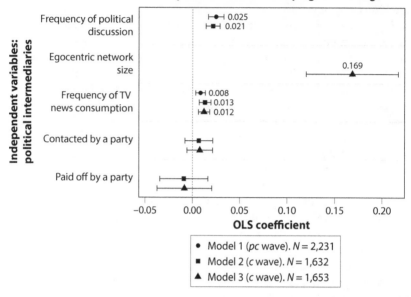

FIGURE 2.5 Campaign Knowledge by Exposure to Political Intermediaries in Mexico 2006: Coefficients from Three OLS Models
Notes: Each marker is an OLS coefficient with 95 percent confidence interval.
pc = pre-campaign, *c* = campaign. Table A.1 reports the complete set of coefficient estimates in numerical form.
Source: Mexico 2006 Panel.

with how frequently one discusses politics. To be sure, egocentric network size and the volume of political talk are relevant to some of our arguments, namely, those about clientelistic targeting (chapter 7) and correct voting (chapter 8). But the changing preferences and voting decisions that we document and explain in part II depend on the traits of one's political discussants, not on how often one discusses. The second half of this chapter describes the "who" in more detail, but our efforts to describe quantities of discussion in this first half are important in building the case that large amounts of influential political discussion occur in Latin America.

Online Political Discussion

Our comparison of political discussion to the consumption of television news seemingly calls for a similar comparison between peer-to-peer political intermediation and internet-based political intermediation. This is, however, a false dichotomy. The horizontal exchange of political information and opinions via social media is now commonplace. In other words, online discussion is a *subset* of the horizontal political discussion that constitutes our focus, just as vertical intermediation from journalists to voters and from parties to voters can also occur online. None of the discussion-frequency or name-generator queries used above orient respondents toward strictly face-to-face discussion, so respondents are free to consider online political talk when they answer them.

For two reasons, we do not belabor the distinction between face-to-face (offline) and online political discussion. First, doing so would turn this project into a technical study on the effects of different modalities. This would divert attention from our primary focus, which is a set of arguments and findings about the nature of social influence on vote choice in Latin America. Furthermore, recent findings show these modality effects to be small. "The structure of online social networks mirrors those in the offline world,"[24] and discussions in both forums are equally effective in boosting political knowledge, efficacy, and participation.[25]

Second, in Latin America face-to-face discussion remains far more prevalent than online discussion. According to the CNEP, the percentage of respondents who reported gathering or discussing campaign information over the internet was less than 5 percent in Uruguay (2004) and Mexico (2006) and just 14 percent in Argentina (2007). These contrast with a figure of 40 percent in the US around the same time (2004).[26] Analyses of more recent data show that the finding still holds. For instance, after being queried about discussion with family and friends, respondents to the BEPS 2014 were asked about their *Frequency of political discussion on social network websites* like Facebook, Twitter, Orkut, and so on. The mean responses on the "never/rarely/sometimes/frequently" scale were 2.5 times higher for the family and friends queries reported in figure 2.2 than for this query about online discussion. Almost three-fourths of respondents said they never discuss politics over social media, in contrast to just 25 percent and 30 percent, respectively, answering "never" to the family and friends queries. Using a nationally representative survey of Mexicans implemented in November of 2011, Moreno and Mendizábal find that just 4 percent followed information about campaigns on social networks like Facebook and Twitter.[27] In a poll conducted just after the 2012 election, the figure increased, but only to 15 percent.[28]

We conclude, then, that the boom in social media usage has produced no fundamental change in the nature of political discussion in Latin America. The study of online social networks in the region is an exciting new avenue of research on political intermediation,[29] but we lose little by ignoring the distinction between online and offline discussion. Anticipating continued growth in this topic of research, our concluding chapter returns to and further illustrates this point with a brief discussion of social media and texting app usage during the Brazil 2018 election—an election in which WhatsApp purportedly played a major role.

THE POLITICAL TRAITS OF DISCUSSANTS

We have now established that the *amount* of political discussion in Latin America is meaningful. When it comes to social influence on vote choice, however, the *traits* of discussion partners are more important than overall discussion quantity. In other words, source surpasses volume in importance, as certain discussant traits heavily shape the content and persuasiveness of discussion. In this second half of the chapter, we consider and describe two such attributes. The first is the absence or presence of gaps in political expertise between discussion partners. Whether individuals select political experts carries important implications for mechanisms of social influence. The second is the absence or presence of political disagreement within a relationship. Whether political disagreement exists shapes the kind of social influence that can occur between two conversation partners. Our survey data reveal the degree of relative expertise and of agreement in the conversational exchanges of respondents during the campaigns. They also allow a rich description of the kinds of political discussants that Latin American citizens select.

Political Expertise

Do Latin American citizens seek out discussion with politically knowledgeable individuals? We find that they do.[30] A key element of our argument about mechanisms of social influence is that some voters are willing to learn from and even defer to individuals whom they trust and find credible on political matters. Anthony Downs argues that voters can save time and effort by relying on peers to acquire political knowledge, effectively using these contacts as information shortcuts.[31] Voters might therefore privilege conversation with people they know to be well-informed about politics.[32] In practice, however, this may not always be easy. Voters' incentives to seek out accurate information and knowledge are often weak, and individuals who possess political expertise may not be available in their social milieu or be willing to talk. Three different data sources provide descriptive evidence on this topic: the ego and alter interviews in the Two-City Panel, the CNEP name-generator and name-interpreter questions, and the open-ended interviews.

The first is the Two-City Panel, which is particularly valuable because it contains interviews with main respondents and many of their discussants. The discussant interviews occurred soon after the 2002 election wave. We administered a political knowledge quiz to discussants and main respondents. The latter group received the battery twice, in both the pre-campaign wave and the election wave. The resulting *Political knowledge* variable is standardized so that zero is the mean value achieved among pre-campaign main respondents. (The standard deviation is one.) We limit the battery to three

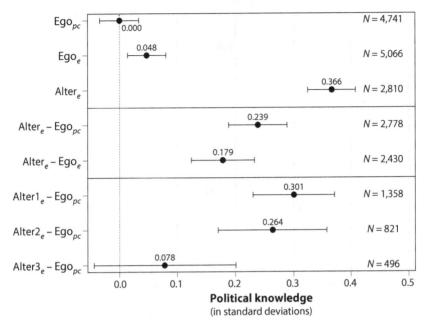

FIGURE 2.6 Political Knowledge among Egos and Alters in Brazil 2002
Notes: Each marker is a mean or a difference of means with 95 percent confidence interval. pc = pre-campaign wave, e = election wave.
Source: Two-City Panel.

knowledge items asked of both egos and alters, so comparison between the two is straightforward.

Figure 2.6 shows eight means and differences of means that are useful for discerning whether main respondents in these two Brazilian cities select discussants with more political expertise than themselves. The first set of means offers a naive test. These are three simple means: two for samples of egos and one for the sample of alters. The figure reports two different ego means, one from the pre-campaign wave (our preferred benchmark) and the other from the election panel wave.[33] The figure clearly shows discussants to be more knowledgeable about politics than the representative sample of egos. The difference, more than a third of a standard deviation, is substantively important. In short, the discussants whom main respondents choose are, on average, more politically knowledgeable than the average citizen.[34]

Still, this finding is naive. It does not demonstrate that main respondents *intentionally* seek out discussants with greater knowledge. Discussants are a nonrandom sample of individuals because, by definition, they discuss politics. In reporting the mean among discussants, we have removed all the individuals who do not discuss politics, so it is no surprise that mean political knowledge is higher among alters than among egos.[35]

Matched-pairs tests provide a more direct approach. We report two such results in the next set of two means in figure 2.6. Each alter is matched to her or his interviewed ego, and the means of the resulting differences in knowledge are shown in the figure. These results directly capture the amount of *relative* expertise in egos' discussant choices. The knowledge gap remains, whether we use the pre-campaign-wave measure of ego knowledge or the campaign-wave measure. Discussants are between 0.18 and 0.24 of a standard deviation more knowledgeable than the main respondents who named them.

The final set of means takes a different approach. Because socially provided political expertise is a finite resource, individuals may prioritize it when choosing how to allocate attention and conversation time within their existing networks. The Two-City Panel does not contain direct measures of conversation time per alter, but we can test whether the most knowledgeable discussants are the first ones who come to mind as main respondents answer the name generator. The bottom three means in figure 2.6 shows this to be the case. It repeats the matched-pairs test by each alter type: first-named (*Alter1*), second-named (*Alter2*), and third-named (*Alter3*). First-named alters are more knowledgeable than their egos by 0.30 standard deviations, a substantively important difference, and second-named alters are 0.26 more knowledgeable than their egos. A big drop-off occurs when we move to third-named alters, who are just (a statistically insignificant) 0.08 standard deviations more knowledgeable than their egos. Many Brazilians are clearly able to find two more knowledgeable discussants, and knowledgeable discussants are the first to come to their minds.

Using a second data source, the CNEP, we can directly model egos' decisions to create political ties with their existing social contacts. Recall from figure 1.2 that Eva chooses to speak to her uncle about politics because of his expertise, but she forgoes political discussion with her father because he lacks political knowledge. The CNEP allows us to explore whether a relationship exists between an alter's political knowledge and ego's decision to forge a *political* tie to that alter—given that the two are already socially tied. That is because the CNEP name generator produces *social* ties, many of which might be apolitical. In other words, it offers variation on whether social contacts are political discussants. The CNEP also contains nationally representative samples, moving us well beyond the two Brazilian cities.

CNEP respondents received a guided network battery in which they were first asked about their spouses' or partners' political traits. Then they were asked to list two important-matters discussants ("Alter 2" and "Alter 3"). Name-interpreter questions about the political traits of these social alters followed.[36] Among the subsequent name-interpreter questions was a query about the frequency of political discussion with each alter: "How often did you talk to this person about the recent election? (0) Never. (1) Rarely. (1) Sometimes. (1) Often." We create the following variables: *Spouse selected as a political alter, Alter 2 selected as a political alter,* and *Alter 3 selected as a political alter.* Each measures whether there is a political tie along with the existing social tie. These are our dependent variables in three statistical models, one for each alter type (spouse, alter 2, and alter 3). The main independent variable in each model, also asked separately for each alter, is *Perceived political knowledge of spouse/alter 2/alter 3:* "Generally speaking, how well informed would you say this person is when it comes to politics? (0) Not at all informed. (1) Not well informed. (2) Somewhat informed. (3) Very well informed." We expect that main respondents are more likely to discuss politics with social alters whom they view as politically knowledgeable than with alters they view as unknowledgeable.

Unfortunately, a reverse causation problem lurks: discussants may be knowledgeable because they learn through frequent conversations with the main respondents (figure 2.5), instead of being knowledgeable because main respondents *choose* them for their preexisting knowledge. Although it is an imperfect solution, the three models control for main respondents' *Campaign interest, Political knowledge,* and overall *Frequency of political discussion.*

Figure 2.7 summarizes the main results. The depicted quantities are the model-predicted shifts in the probability of selection as a political alter when the alter's perceived political knowledge is changed from not at all informed to very well informed. (The other independent variables are held constant at their means.) The shifts in predicted probabilities are statistically significant and substantively large, especially for spouses: politically knowledgeable spouses tend also to be political discussants, while spouses who are uninformed are likely to remain apolitical social alters. In results not shown, we also find that the *frequency* of political discussion with each social alter is highly correlated with the alter's (perceived) political knowledge. For these analyses, we maintain the original ordinal coding of the dependent variable* and estimate ordered logit models with the same independent variables. Main respondents are 60 to 70 percentage points more likely to discuss politics sometimes or often with a very well-informed alter than they are with an alter who is not at all informed. In sum, Latin American citizens prefer to discuss politics with their politically informed social contacts.

The third data source is our set of open-ended interviews. In these interviews, respondents' preferences for politically expert discussants—whom they see as role models—are striking. Perhaps the best general statement of the phenomenon is captured in this chapter's epigraph, which is one respondent's reflection on her own political conversations: "Sometimes someone else's opinion

---

*(0) Never. (1) Rarely. (2) Sometimes. (3) Often.

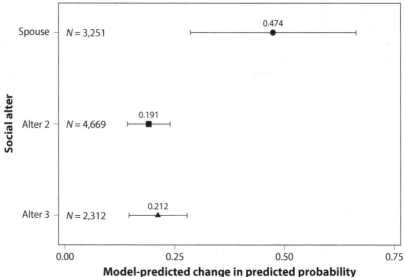

Dependent variables:
spouse/alter 2/alter 3 selected as a political alter

FIGURE 2.7 Selection of a Social Alter to Be a Political Alter by the Perceived Political Knowledge of That Alter in Four Latin American Countries: Predicted Changes in Probability from Three Binary Logit Models
Notes: Each marker is the model-predicted change in the probability (with 95 percent confidence interval) of a main respondent discussing politics with the social alter upon shifting *Perceived political knowledge* of that alter from "not all informed" to "very well-informed." Country election years are Argentina 2007, Chile 1993, Mexico 2006, Mexico 2012, and (for alter 2 only) Uruguay 1994. Table A.2 reports the complete set of coefficient estimates in numerical form.
Source: CNEP.

helps, you know?" This theme of receiving "help" for a political decision through social communication is common in the interviews:

> Here at home we discuss politics a lot. We help each other.[TA2.6]

> I read the *Folha de São Paulo* on the internet, and I talk with my friends, family. . . . We avoid touchier topics, heavier discussion, you know? But when things are still peaceful, we converse. Yes. It helps a lot.[TA2.7]

When seeking assistance in navigating a complex political world, individuals find the views of knowledgeable contacts to be the most credible and useful. In many instances, these experts are readily available in an individual's immediate and most intimate social circles. One Brazilian woman said she was "privileged" to have a husband who is knowledgeable about politics. Another said the following of her spouse:

> I watch a lot of television. I watch the news programs with my husband. He explains everything to me. I even converse with my friends and receive some things in my friends' groups on WhatsApp. But I don't understand them that much. It's my husband who explains things to me. I either ask him, or he's already explaining when we receive something together. He provides details about things. He follows a lot more than I do . . . He is a businessman, so he knows much more about how the country and state are doing.[TA2.8]

Other open-ended interview data clearly demonstrate that many voters pursue political discussion with individuals not because they are intimate and readily available social contacts, but because of their political expertise. Consider the following remarks from four different voters:

> The majority of people, I suppose, that I talk to about the topic [of politics]—that I am going to converse with—understand a lot. I speak with my geography professor, who works on political geography, about these things.[TA2.9]

> INTERVIEWER: [In a past interview] you told us that you speak about politics with Fernanda . . . Do you continue conversing with Fernanda?
> RESPONDENT: Yes, sometimes. When there's an opportunity, you know?
> INTERVIEWER: Is she your friend? Neighbor?
> RESPONDENT: No. She's actually a lawyer . . . She manages some houses around here . . .
> INTERVIEWER: Do you discuss politics with neighbors? Or with work colleagues? In other words, besides Fernanda, are there other people that you discuss politics with, or is it just her?
> RESPONDENT: It's mostly just with her. . . . In truth, I like to hear her ideas. . . . She knows a lot . . . I trust her opinion . . . She always knows what's going on.[TA2.10]

> I have some neighbors, and I have one neighbor who is a judge. So we've chatted [about politics].[TA2.11]

> INTERVIEWER: Is [your discussant] a relative or a friend?
> RESPONDENT: No. She's my boss. . . .
> INTERVIEWER: And does she know a lot about politics?
> RESPONDENT: A lot. . . . She has a beauty salon. And she worked many years, ten years, in a bank, Bradesco. She has a lot of knowledge.[TA2.12]

For each of these four voters, their alters' occupations were a mark of expertise and a credential worth mentioning. Other respondents saw expertise worth pursuing in a much broader social category defined by age:

I like talking to people who can do an analysis that is critical and intelligent about things. These people are usually older than me.[TA2.13]

I ask people with more experience, people who are older than me. They know more than me. I ask them "Which [candidate] is best? Who will be better?"[TA2.14]

A final type of voter sees expertise in individuals who are close to politicians or who work for politicians. In the following anecdote, the voter pays close attention to a politician and his family members when they discuss politics. Notice that the exchange of information and influence (if any) occurs through horizontal intermediation. The voter is adamant in saying that no vertical intermediation occurred: she was not canvassed or otherwise targeted for persuasion by the politician or his family. Instead, it is the information itself that she finds helpful.

> RESPONDENT: Francisco Spiandorello [a local politician] is my
>   neighbor. . . .
> INTERVIEWER: So, during election time, you know a lot of people who are
>   involved in the election, right?
> RESPONDENT: Yes, but I don't know much about politics. I know [some
>   things] because I work with the sister of Francisco Spiandorello. They
>   are very political. So I know things more through them.
> INTERVIEWER: During election time, do those people try to convince you
>   to vote a certain way?
> RESPONDENT: No. I just listen to their commentary. They comment a lot
>   about politics, you know? What gets done and what doesn't. But try
>   to convince me, no.
> INTERVIEWER: Does this help you when it comes time to vote?
> RESPONDENT: It helps me, you know? Because you see them discussing.
>   This helps you choose. But try to convince me? No.[TA2.15]

Overall, it is clear that individuals in Latin America seek out politically knowledgeable discussants. Downs was partially correct in saying that individuals use social contacts as an information source, but our qualitative data suggest that not all settle for what is available in easy-to-find contacts. Instead, many seek out political expertise beyond their most intimate ties.

Political Disagreement

Political disagreement is a central concept in the literature on informal political discussion.[37] The amount of contact and conversation that occurs across lines of political difference—so-called dangerous discussion—is an inherently important trait of any society and political system, and the absence or presence of disagreement dictates the nature of social influence that can occur within a relationship.[38] If the homophily instinct is so overwhelming that individuals never engage in dangerous discussion, then social influence is largely about the reinforcement of political preferences. In politically agreeing relationships, social influence serves to reassure individuals that their preferences need no reexamining.[39] Societies whose discussion partners are almost always in political agreement feature a "homogeneity problem," with individuals walled off into like-minded groups, unexposed to the arguments and values of other sides.[40] Social influence in this setting occurs by *forestalling* attitude change, a process we label "social reinforcement." Conversely, the presence of political disagreement in an ongoing relationship indicates a tolerance and empathy for competing views and for differently minded people.[41] Dangerous discussion, moreover, provides the opportunity for political talk to induce genuine shifts in preferences. If, after initially disagreeing, one person convinces the other to change her or his opinion, then social influence has occurred as "social persuasion."

This subsection quantifies the amount of political disagreement in Latin America's discussion networks and dyads, but we must settle two important measurement issues before proceeding. First, this book defines agreement and disagreement in an ego $\leftrightarrow$ alter dyad using the *vote* intentions (the preferences held during campaigns) or *vote* choices (the candidates selected on election day) of both ego and alter, and our analyses of social influence in part II consider the effect of alters' vote preferences on those of their egos.* Some of the surveys contain a measure of alters' partisanship, but partisanship, whether measured by self-report or by proxy report, is suboptimal as a measure of political preferences. Vote choice is a discrete, concrete, and observable behavior, whereas partisanship is a continuous latent attitude. Measures of vote choice are thus more accurate. Even in places where partisan identities are stable and deeply held, as in the US, they are measured with substantial error.[42] The comparative absence and instability of mass partisanship in Latin America only increase the amount of measurement error. In Brazil, for example, the vast majority of voters for non-PT presidential candidates lack a positive partisan identity entirely.[43] Given these considerations, this book uses vote intention and vote choice in its empirical evaluations of disagreement and agreement within political ties.

With this first measurement decision in place, a second important decision is how to categorize dyads in which one person is nonopinionated, meaning an undecided voter or a nonvoter. (We describe citizens with a candidate preference as "opinionated" and those without a candidate preference as "nonopinionated.") Scholars of political networks hold varying perspectives on the definition and measurement of disagreement in a discussion dyad.[44] According

---

*The relevant variables names are *Ego vote intention/choice* and *Alter vote intention/choice*.

to the most restrictive definition, disagreement is the presence of party discordance; to be classified as disagreeing, the two partners must both be opinionated and support different candidates.[45] According to the more inclusive definition of disagreement, the absence of party concordance is a sufficient condition for disagreement; any pair of individuals not supporting the same candidate, including pairs in which one individual is not supporting *any* candidate, is in disagreement.[46] Consider, for instance, a mid-campaign dyad with an ego intending to vote for Dilma and an alter intent on abstaining. According to the restrictive definition, this dyad does not feature disagreement. According to the inclusive definition, it does.

Which conception of disagreement is more valid? Sound logics underlie both. From the standpoint of the restrictive definition, ego's vote decision in the example is not subject to social persuasion because alter is not advocating for a candidate and not persuading ego to make a directional change. (This assumes that ego will not abstain.) This restrictive definition presumes that social persuasion requires open and direct persuasion to a different side. From the standpoint of the inclusive definition, ego's preference is more subject to change than if alter preferred Dilma because ego's preference is not reinforced by the alter. Even though the abstaining alter is not attempting to persuade ego to switch to a different candidate, the alter is also failing to provide social reinforcement of ego's vote intention.[47] In the end, we choose throughout this book to conduct analyses using both definitions. The main text, however, presents results using the restrictive definition, while results based on the inclusive definition are reported only in appendix A. Substantive conclusions rarely differ across the two.

With these technicalities in place, we report the prevalence of political disagreement between peers during Brazilian and Mexican presidential campaigns. Open-ended interviews reveal that voters take various approaches toward political disagreement. On the one hand, many express discomfort with disagreement and conflict, so the homophily instinct is strong:

> I keep to myself. I don't like to fight over politics, asking for votes. . . . Forget that!
> I see what the people do around here. Wow, God help me! What's it all for? It's
> just not worth it. It wears on me. It creates ill will. That's why I prefer to keep to
> myself.[TA2.16]

> It is difficult talking about politics nowadays—not only with neighbors, but also
> with friends, because each one has different ideas.[TA2.17]

> Each [of my friends and family] thinks differently from one another now. When
> we begin [to converse] and see that so-and-so is there, or so-and-so is there, then
> we prefer to change the subject and talk about our work.[TA2.18]

On the other hand, some citizens clearly embrace disagreement and thrive on give and take:

Look. Sometimes there are clashes. "I don't believe this. I don't agree with that." But these exchanges of experiences, of information, they're enriching! The greater the diversity, the more I learn.[TA2.19]

INTERVIEWER: Have you argued with anyone?
RESPONDENT [WHO IS A STREET VENDOR]: [Here] in the street? Yes. Yes. "I'm going to vote for so-and-so," "so-and-so is this, so-and-so is that," "no, no, don't say that," "you're going to do what?!" So, little arguments, but then one goes to one side, the other goes to the other side and afterwards everything is peaceful.[TA2.20]

Others fall in between, tolerating disagreement and not letting it deter their discussions:

[My friend] is a factory worker also, but he understands things. He's got more schooling than me, you know? I like to talk to him sometimes. He's got different opinions. Sometimes I don't agree with them. . . . But he's a person who is cool to converse with. He's a person that, if I say something, he doesn't get offended. He doesn't fight just for that reason.[TA2.21]

INTERVIEWER: Do you discuss politics much with your family?
RESPONDENT: Always. There are always fights. . . .
INTERVIEWER: And your friends. Are they diverse also or more united?
RESPONDENT: No. They all talk politics, and they always have different ideas from one another.[TA2.22]

I'll vote for Haddad for president, and my husband for Bolsonaro. Sometimes we'll have a spat. I want to punch him and vice versa. But we understand that, above all, respect and love have to prevail.[TA2.23]48

What is the net result of these competing instincts on rates of political agreement and disagreement in the social networks of Latin Americans? Egocentric network data from our panel studies and the CNEP permit estimation of these quantities at the national level for available election years. Figure 2.8 shows results from the panel studies. It uses data from campaign waves, rather than election waves, since we are presently interested more in the nature of discussant selection than in social influence. Election-wave rates of disagreement are more subject to a genuine process of social influence, as we document in chapter 4. We classify the egocentric networks of main respondents into four categories based on egos' vote intentions and those of the alters they reported. "Agreement only" networks are those in which all opinionated alters share the same vote intention as the ego. An ego who reports no discussants or only nonopinionated discussants* is tallied as a "Singleton."49 Networks with "Agreement

---

*Named discussants whose vote intention/choice was not known by their main respondent are also tallied (along with undecided and abstaining discussants) as nonopinionated.

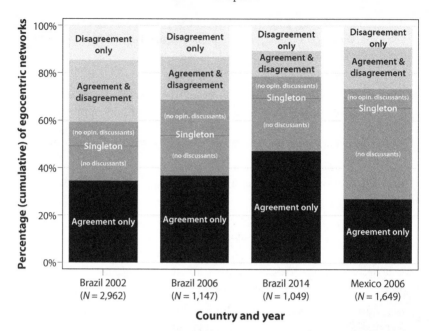

FIGURE 2.8 The Distribution of Political Agreement and Disagreement with Ego in Egocentric Networks in Brazil and Mexico
Notes: Results are from campaign waves. Samples are limited to opinionated egos only.
Sources: Two-City Panel, BEPS 2014, Mexico 2006 Panel.

& disagreement" are those with at least one alter agreeing with ego and at least one alter disagreeing with ego. Finally, networks containing only alters who disagree with ego are "Disagreement only" networks.

To characterize the findings from figure 2.8 very broadly, the electorates in these four cases are roughly divided into thirds. One-third of citizens are in wholly homogeneous networks, facing no disagreement. Another third are singletons. The final third are in heterogeneous networks, facing some disagreement. Dividing into thirds oversimplifies, but the exceptions have clear explanations. The BEPS 2014 surely overestimates the share of agreement-only networks because it capped the name generator at two discussants, and the marginal rate of disagreement grows with every discussant named.[50] Recall also that the Mexico 2006 Panel—along with probably all the surveys—overestimates the number of singletons.

With these caveats in mind, we tentatively conclude that a majority of voters in Brazil and Mexico are not exposed to political disagreement through peer networks. Whether the observed rates are seen to be abnormally high and indicative of severe polarization and a homogeneity problem depends on the points of comparison. For example, rates of exposure to disagreement are even lower in the US. Less than a quarter of respondents to the American National Election Studies in 2000 reported at least one disagreeing discussant, and this result was in response to a name-generator battery capped at four, not three.[51]

The CNEP also contains estimates of cross-national rates of political disagreement, thereby introducing more context and comparison for this question.[52] In three different scatterplots, figure 2.9 reports on the y-axis the cross-national rate of disagreement for the three types of social alters: spousal dyads, ego ↔ alter2 dyads, and ego ↔ alter3 dyads. The *Percentage of dyads that agree* is measured using *Ego vote choice* and *Alter vote choice* (as reported by the main respondent). Disagreement is defined with the restrictive definition. Disagreement exists when the two nodes preferred *different* parties or candidates. Agreement exists when the two nodes preferred the *same* party or candidate. If either node in the dyad had no candidate preference, the dyad is dropped from the analysis.

When we compare rates of dyadic disagreement cross-nationally, an important confound is the number of party options. All else equal, more parties means more opportunities for disagreement.[53] We account for this by plotting rates of disagreement as a function of that election's *Effective number of parties/ candidates* (x-axis).[54] The effective number of parties is a fitting benchmark since it is the reciprocal of the probability that two randomly chosen individuals voted for the same party.[55] Using this concept, each figure also includes a dashed line that depicts this benchmark—that is, what disagreement would be if discussion partners were paired at random *and* if no intra-dyadic influence were to occur.

For the observed data, scatterplot points appear as three-letter country ISO codes followed by two-digit year. Black points are Latin American countries and gray points are countries from other regions. The best-fit line from a quadratic regression is drawn as a solid black line.

According to figure 2.9, the rate of agreement in a country is indeed a negative function of the number of parties, as traced out by the solid lines. The bivariate correlations range from −0.57 to −0.69, and Latin American countries (with the exception of Chile 1993) tend to fall close to the best-fit line. The figure clarifies the distinction between the US and Latin America. Dyads in the US feature more agreement than all comparable dyad types in Latin America when the US acts like its normal two-party self—that is, in 2004 and 2012 but not in 1992.[56] Latin America's multiparty systems create more opportunity for political disagreement, and this in turn is reflected in voters' social networks. In fact, the figure clearly shows that the US, where most of the research on social influence in politics has taken place, is the exception. The other set of exceptions are Mozambique and South Africa (a pair of dominant-party systems) and two-party Taiwan. Rates of agreement in Latin American countries are much more representative of the international norm than rates of agreement in the US.

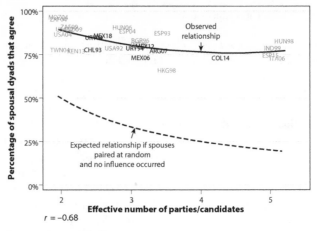

Frame A: Spousal dyads

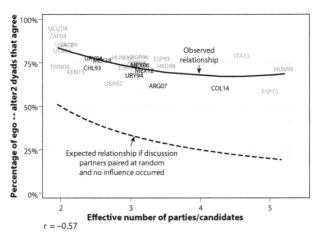

Frame B: Ego ↔ Alter2 dyads

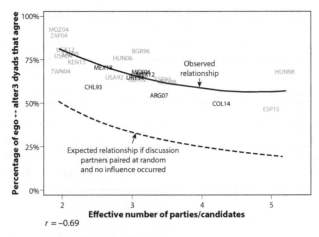

Frame C: Ego ↔ Alter3 dyads

Although rates of dyadic agreement are lower in Latin America than in dominant- and two-party systems, they are still well above the dashed line. This denotes the presence of homophily and/or peer influence. Indeed, this fact obtains for *every* country: the observed relationships between rates of disagreement and the effective number of parties are not as negatively sloped as chance alone would dictate. Dyads, especially spousal dyads, are more like-minded than the number of parties alone would dictate.[57] With just these cross-sectional data—some of which are pre-election measures and others of which are post-election measures—it is impossible to decipher the relative contributions of homophily and influence, but in later chapters we model both with our panel data.

We close this discussion of political disagreement by comparing across intermediary types, considering whether individuals agree politically with their mass media sources to the same extent that they agree with their social contacts. On the one hand, individuals may agree more with their television news sources or newspapers because they can so easily select among them: "it is much easier to change channels than to change discussion topics."[58] On the other hand, scholars have long documented a hostile media effect, wherein citizens are convinced that professional media sources are biased against their political views.[59] A middle position holds that individuals have less desire to be politically selective when choosing a media source and that journalistic norms sometimes encourage the sharing of multiple viewpoints.[60]

The CNEP data reveal that none of these hunches are true. Instead, most citizens, in Latin America and elsewhere, decline to attribute any political bias to their media sources.[61] Individuals are either oblivious to the biases of their news sources or wish to think their sources are unbiased. This contrasts starkly with the overwhelming propensity to report (or at least guess at) their discussion partners' political preferences. Figure 2.10 portrays this comparison with a bar chart. We measure *Respondent reports political bias of [intermediary]* for each of six political intermediaries: spouse, alter 2, alter 3, television news, newspaper, and radio. Respondents were asked to report the political biases of sources that that they themselves cited, meaning their named discussants and their favorite television news show, newspaper, and radio program. Respondents either (1) report the intermediary's political bias or say (0) "no party" or

---

FIGURE 2.9 Rates of Political Agreement within Discussion Dyads in 29 Election Years in 18 Countries
Notes: Each scatterplot point denotes the relevant country year with the three-letter country ISO code followed by the two-digit election year. The solid black lines are from quadratic regressions. Black points are Latin American cases, and gray points are countries from other regions.
Source: CNEP.

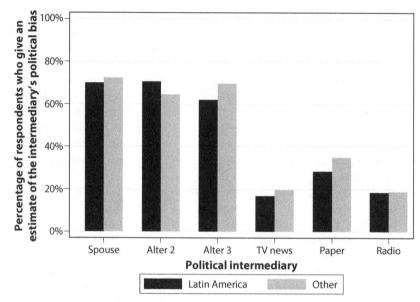

FIGURE 2.10 The Propensity of Respondents to See Political Bias in Their Political Intermediaries in 34 Election Years in 20 Countries
Notes: Survey administrators did not ask all six items of *Respondent reports political bias of [intermediary]* in every country year, so the set of available country years varies slightly for each intermediary.
Source: CNEP.

"don't know." The bar heights capture the percentage of respondents who report a political preference for each intermediary. Respondents naming no source in response to a question are dropped in the calculation of that intermediary's percentage.

Large majorities of respondents report their perceptions of the vote choices of their social contacts, but only a minority report that their mass media sources support a particular political party. The percentages perceiving a political bias in the content of their favorite television and radio news shows are particularly low, less than 20 percent in Latin America and beyond. In fact, the gap between the set of horizontal intermediaries and the set of vertical intermediaries is surely *understated* because CNEP did not request explicitly political discussants. In the Mexico 2006 Panel, for example, main respondents declined to report a vote preference for just 12 percent of their named political discussants, and in the Two-City Panel the figure is 19 percent. In short, Latin Americans recognize political bias in their conversation partners, but they are far less likely to see bias in their mass media sources.

To recap, Latin Americans discuss politics with agreeing discussants—much like their counterparts in other countries—more frequently than chance alone would dictate. They are not, however, completely unexposed to political disagreement through their peer networks, and in fact their networks are less politically homogeneous than those prevailing in the US. Finally, the political biases of social contacts are better communicated to individuals than the biases of traditional mass media outlets.

Accuracy

Before proceeding with the remainder of the book, we must briefly address a final important point on measurement. The preceding subsection and many of the analyses in part II typically use main respondents' *perceptions* (also "proxy reports") of their discussants' vote choices as the measure of discussants' *actual* vote choices. This is largely for practical reasons, as the expense of obtaining discussant-validated preferences through direct alter interviews is high. Nonetheless, it is important to consider how much measurement error these proxy reports contain.

In the US perceptions are largely accurate. Respondents to a nationally representative sample in 1992 were correct 81 percent of the time when they reported the presidential choice of a voting discussant and 78 percent of the time when including abstaining discussants.[62] Still, when individuals in the US were wrong, they tended to project their own preferences onto their discussants. This is but one example of the false consensus effect, whereby individuals overestimate similarity and agreement between themselves and others.[63] The false consensus effect, when present, artificially inflates estimates of social influence on vote choice.[64] Network scholars in the political-behavior field have tried to get around this uncomfortable fact by arguing that it is the *perception* of discussants, and not the reality, that matters.[65] This argument, however, stretches the concept of peer influence too far: apparent agreement in a dyad could just be the result of a main respondent's projection of this agreement rather than the discussant's genuine influence on the main respondent. Measures of alters' preferences need to be reasonably accurate.

Our Two-City Panel is the only survey dataset (to our knowledge) that contains interviews with both sides of political-discussion dyads in Latin America. It thus provides the means to observe the accuracy of main respondents' perceptions of their peers' political preferences. The dataset contains interviews, conducted in 2002 soon after the second round of the presidential election, with 2,808 of our main respondents' discussants. This questionnaire measured the discussant's self-reported, first-round vote choice. The election wave of main-respondent interviews, conducted two to three weeks earlier and just after the first round, contains egos' perceptions of the presidential vote choices of these discussants.

In the two cities, main respondents are accurate 82.3 percent of the time when the interviewed discussant actually voted for a candidate. This compares to a baseline of 30 percent if egos randomly guessed alters' preferences in proportion to the candidates' national vote totals. Main respondents are accurate in 78.8 percent of their answers if the sample of discussants is expanded to include nonvoters. In other words, accuracy in these two Brazilian cities is remarkably similar to accuracy in the 1992 US study.[66] Finally, there is no evidence of widespread projection. When main respondents did misperceive a discussant's vote choice, they projected their own candidate preference just 48.2 percent of the time. In other words, although the proxy reports of main respondents are not errorless, we can use these reports of their discussants' preferences with confidence. It is particularly reassuring that the use of these perceptions will not inflate estimates of social influence via false-consensus effects.

CONCLUSION

Latin Americans discuss politics with their peers. The frequency of these discussions cannot be considered high in any absolute sense, but Latin Americans do discuss politics at rates typical of global norms. They discuss politics with (in descending order of frequency) family members, friends, and neighbors—a pattern that is seemingly universal—although Latin Americans are a bit chattier with their neighbors than is common elsewhere. They discuss political topics less frequently than they consume them on television, but political talk has a greater impact on knowledge acquisition. This collection of findings on discussion frequency suggests that, in overlooking horizontal political intermediation, scholarship on mass political behavior in Latin America misses a major part of voters' political experiences.

Typical Latin American citizens also discuss politics with individuals who are more knowledgeable than themselves. This disparity is often the result of intentional choice. Voters seek the guidance of relatively expert contacts as they try to gather information about candidates and politics. This evidence is crucial to our understanding of how and why persuasive peers exert social influence during election campaigns in the region.

Finally, Latin Americans discuss politics with agreeing individuals more frequently than random selection of discussion partners would dictate. Political disagreement, nonetheless, is by no means absent from political talk. It is more prevalent, in fact, in Latin America's multiparty systems than in the commonly studied two-party US. The observed rates of political disagreement in our cross-sectional reports suggest the potential for peer influence: *social reinforcement*, because of the high rates of agreement, and *social persuasion*, because disagreement is still present. Alternatively, the fact that dyadic agreement is more prevalent than chance alone dictates may just indicate the presence of homophily (selection into like-minded networks), while disagreement may indicate the failure of an attempt at social persuasion. To resolve this methodological problem, part II utilizes our panel data to distinguish discussant selection from social influence.

PART II

Social Influence and the Vote

3

Voter Volatility and Stability in Presidential Campaigns

In my head I'm thinking "Ah, I'm going to vote for this guy, I'm going to vote for that guy." Things like that. And then you're about to vote, but at the last minute you're not certain who the right choice is. I say one thing, and then at the last minute you go with someone else.[TA3.1]

—*Brazilian voter (2018)*

Rapid changes in voter preferences, like those reported in the epigraph, are common in Latin America, so common that the region's voters have been called "unmoored."[1] Three of Latin America's more transformative and authoritarian presidents rose to power from minuscule beginnings on the strength of highly effective campaigning. Alberto Fujimori of Peru achieved a landslide second-round victory in 1990 after beginning the campaign with a new party and less than 2 percent of vote intentions. Hugo Chávez came from nowhere to win Venezuela's 1998 presidential election by 16 points, beating out (among others) Irene Sáez, who fell from 70 to 3 points over the course of the campaign. Rafael Correa's 10-year stint as the Ecuadorian president began in 2007 with a long-shot candidacy that started the campaign at just 6 percentage points.

Still, most Latin American campaigns do not match these headliner cases for volatility. Many countries, including our two main cases, Brazil and Mexico, have more institutionalized party systems than those that produced these presidencies. Committed partisans who are immune to campaign influences and who vote for the same party in repeated elections exist in every Latin American country. And some of the region's elections, such as the landslide win in Mexico in 2018 by Andrés Manuel López Obrador, are predictable affairs lacking any horse-race intrigue. In the end, how volatile are the preferences of Latin American voters during presidential election campaigns?

This chapter provides descriptive evidence about preference volatility from recent presidential elections in Brazil, Mexico, and Argentina. Preference stability and volatility during campaigns constitute the dependent variable in our core empirical chapters (4 through 6), so the description here is important for setting the stage. In describing the nature of this dependent variable, the current chapter also establishes the historical and political background that readers need to understand our main presidential election cases (Brazil 2002, Brazil 2006, Brazil 2014, and Mexico 2006) and the datasets used to study them.

We begin, in the next two sections, by drawing from research on electoral volatility as well as research on Brazilian and Mexican politics to provide some straightforward theoretical reasons for high (by international standards) campaign volatility. Latin America's party systems are highly fragmented, and they have relatively weak societal roots. At the same time, voters' preferences are not completely whimsical: many voters do hold stable partisan and candidate preferences during campaigns. In fact, Mexico's party system has been among Latin America's most societally rooted, while Brazil's party system has shown some regularities and (until 2018) increasing institutionalization, especially in the offerings in presidential elections. Election outcomes clearly reflect both preference continuity and preference change during campaigns.

How much continuity? How much change? To answer these questions, we turn to two forms of survey data. We first estimate—using panel data from our four election cases plus six others—the amount of individual-level preference change that occurred during campaigns. The number of voters who switch preferences across party lines, as a share of all voters, is relatively high by international standards, and these rates of switching are higher in less partisan Brazil than in more partisan Mexico and Argentina. Clearly, however, many stable voters are also found in these settings.

The second half of the chapter turns to candidate-level preference change by looking at time series of aggregated vote intentions and vote choices from before, during, and just after the campaigns in our four election cases. These aggregate trends show volatility, but this volatility exists within finite bounds. While plotting and describing aggregate campaign dynamics, we also detail the timing of our survey panel waves.

In focusing on the main dependent variable, this chapter makes a brief detour from the book's focus on social networks and influence. Nevertheless, the chapter contributes to the overall argument in an important way by showing that preference change during campaigns is genuine and sincere. Most preference change during campaigns occurs across party lines, and we dismiss, in the final empirical section of this chapter, the important counterargument that preference change occurs strictly as a result of strategic voting calculations. The strategic voting counterargument holds that individuals switch their vote intentions across party lines during a campaign not because of genuine persuasion and sincere preference change but, instead, to cast a more effective vote against a least-preferred candidate. The evidence shows that strategic switching accounts for a relatively small share of voter volatility in our election cases.

THE ROOTS OF VOTER VOLATILITY
IN LATIN AMERICA

Latin American voters have more volatile partisan preferences than their counterparts in older democracies. To date, the evidence for this volatility has come from changes in party vote shares *between* contiguous elections: inter-election volatility or, more commonly, electoral volatility. On average, Latin American voters are more likely to cross party lines between consecutive elections than their counterparts in older democracies.[2] This is easily observed through a comparison of average scores across regions on the Pedersen index, the leading measure of electoral volatility. The Pedersen score for a particular election is the net change from the previous election in all parties' vote percentages.* Higher scores mean higher electoral volatility. The average Pedersen score in Latin America's legislative elections between 1980 and 2010 was 23.0 percent. In comparison, it was just 4.2 percent in the US over the same stretch of time. Similarly, for presidential elections electoral volatility averaged 25.9 percent in Latin America and just 8.8 percent in the US over these 30 years. To be sure, the US is not a typical point of comparison: it is an extreme case, exhibiting the lowest average electoral volatility in the world. Still, Western Europe, even after experiencing a steady increase in electoral volatility in recent decades, exhibited legislative volatility averages that were less than half (10.4 percent versus 23.0 percent) as high as Latin America's over the same period.[3]

The remainder of this section describes two main causes of Latin America's high inter-election volatility: weak partisanship and party fragmentation. We then argue that these underlying causes should also create relatively high *campaign* volatility, that is, preference change *during* campaigns.

Reasons for High Electoral Volatility

Although high by the standards of the world's oldest democracies, Latin America's rates of electoral volatility are typical of those observed in other third-wave democracies.[4] The young democracies of Africa and Asia have also experienced volatility in legislative elections at rates in the mid- to high-20s, and averages in post-Communist Eastern Europe are even higher.[5]

These similarities across the developing world and their contrasts with the developed world point to causes of electoral volatility that are common across

---

*More specifically, it is half the sum of the absolute values of the changes between two consecutive elections in every party's vote share (Pedersen 1979).

new democracies. Perhaps the most important cause is the age of the party system. Because Latin American parties tend to be younger, they have weaker roots in their electorates than parties in older democracies. Survey evidence confirms that it can take many years to build stable mass partisanship.[6] In turn, votes cast by individuals with strong attachments to long-standing parties are more immune to the economic, political, and social events that unfold between elections. In short, the relative absence of mass partisanship leaves many Latin American citizens psychologically unconnected to the party system and willing to change their vote across party lines in response to the kinds of events that occur between elections.

Moreover, some evidence on the cross-national correlates of electoral volatility suggests the existence of a cohort effect. Regimes founded in the age of mass media have new party systems that are not entrenched in long-standing class and organizational structures. These regimes seem to have permanently higher levels of electoral volatility, and their electorates have permanently weaker partisan roots.[7] Latin America's levels of electoral volatility, for example, have failed to decrease over time. Quite to the contrary, mean volatility in presidential elections moved from 33.4 percent in the 1980s to 36.6 percent in the 2010s.[8] In addition, the number of partisans in Latin America has not noticeably increased since democratization began.[9]

Latin America's multiparty competition also contributes to its high rates of electoral volatility, although this cannot necessarily explain its volatility gap when compared to Western Europe. Proportional representation in legislative elections plus, in many instances, two-round presidential elections proliferate parties and candidates. Theoretical justifications linking party-system fragmentation to greater volatility are numerous. In spatial models, the propensity to substitute party competitors is easier when their numbers are high.[10] Simulations show that societies with more partisan options have more volatile preferences in the aggregate.[11] Empirically, there is a positive relationship between the effective number of parties and electoral volatility.[12] Overall, Latin America has rates of electoral volatility exceeding those in older democracies because of the region's weaker partisan roots and fragmented party systems.

Campaign Volatility

The same factors that cause high rates of electoral volatility in Latin America should also contribute to high rates of preference change by voters *during* campaigns, yet here research is sparse. If strong partisanship immunizes an individual's vote choice from the influence of ongoing events, then weak partisanship should leave one open to campaign influences. And if party-system fragmentation increases electoral volatility by easing substitution among options, then it should also increase preference change during campaigns. In short, weak mass partisanship and multiparty competition contribute to high *intra*-election volatility, or more simply "campaign volatility." Campaign volatility, in turn, contributes to high *inter*-election volatility. Campaign volatility, in other words, is a constitutive element of electoral volatility. Despite this, scholars of Latin America and other new democracies have largely ignored the portion of total inter-election volatility that occurs during campaigns. Instead, they attribute high volatility to other, slow-moving factors: institutions (electoral rules and party-system fragmentation), sociodemographics (rates of unionization and ethnic fragmentation), or macroeconomic factors (growth and inflation).[13]

Electoral volatility and its slow-moving causes also receive greater attention because they are easy to measure. Calculating electoral volatility requires only parties' vote shares, and country-level measures of political institutions, demography, and macroeconomic variables are also widely available. An analysis of aggregated *campaign* volatility, by contrast, requires surveys of vote intentions at various points throughout a campaign period. Such data are often available but harder to compile and more error-ridden than election returns.[14] More difficult yet is the precise quantification of the number of volatile voters, which requires the rare and expensive panel study. The fast-moving factors that explain persuasion and volatility during campaigns—namely, the information communicated through political intermediaries—are also difficult and costly to measure. These challenges notwithstanding, failing to gauge campaign volatility leaves our understanding of electoral volatility incomplete.

PARTY SYSTEMS IN BRAZIL AND MEXICO

Brazil and Mexico, our two primary country cases, differ from one another in the depth of their electorates' partisan roots and in the number of parties. Since Brazil and Mexico democratized in 1985 and 2000 (respectively), they have maintained very different party systems. Brazil's is highly fragmented with weak roots in the electorate, while Mexico's, until 2018, was a relatively stable three-party system with less ephemeral partisan constituencies. Before 2018, both party systems were more institutionalized and stable than the Latin American average, but their post-democratization trajectories reveal them to be less institutionalized and stable than the systems prevailing in older democracies.[15]

Brazil

Brazil's parties have weak roots in the electorate. By most measures, the overall prevalence of partisanship is below the international average and certainly below averages in older democracies.[16] Using the most restrictive survey measure of partisanship, partisans constitute about 25 percent of the Brazilian electorate, compared to 60 percent in the US. Using the most permissive measure puts the prevalence of partisanship between 30 and 45 percent in Brazil, compared to about 85 percent in the US.[17] Among the non-leftist parties that have collectively dominated legislative and gubernatorial representation, only the Brazilian Democratic Movement Party (PMDB) could boast of a critical mass of partisans in the few decades after democratization. Even this has shriveled in recent years to almost nothing.

Moreover, party labels provide limited information about candidate ideology or policy stances. Politicians switch parties with regularity and for strictly opportunistic reasons.[18] Many parties have changed names at least once, and electoral and legislative coalitions of strange bedfellows are common. All three practices water down the stability and meaningfulness of party brands, so much so that party labels are often unknown. For example, in a 1999 poll administered more than four years after his first inauguration, only 36 percent of respondents correctly identified the party affiliation of President Fernando Henrique Cardoso.[19]

Brazil also has extreme numbers of parties in its federal and state legislatures, numbers that surely contribute to voters' confusion and low rates of mass partisanship.[20] Elites have created a fragmented party system driven by high district magnitude and an open-list proportional representation electoral system that complicates the diffusion of clear partisan cues. In 2014, for example, the lower house had 14.1 effective electoral parties, and 33 parties held seats in the Chamber of Deputies in 2019. In federal and state lower-house elections, voters choose from among literally dozens of parties and hundreds of candidates. Most voters forget for whom they voted within a few months of a legislative election.[21]

Overall, then, Brazil has weak partisan roots and extreme party-system fragmentation, conditions that make it an excellent case for studying electoral and campaign volatility. We temper this point, however, with two additional observations. First, the PT has been a notable exception to the standard story of weak partisan roots. In general, half of all partisans in Brazil have been *petistas*, even though the party has never received more than 20 percent of the vote in federal lower house elections.[22] During the first 20 years after its founding in 1980, the PT upheld a consistent leftist program and constructed deep organizational roots in civil society.[23] In doing so, it crafted a stable party brand and an ever-growing pool of mass adherents who, like many voters in developed countries, maintained an enduring political identity with the party and its policy goals.[24] Policy moderation and scandal diluted the PT's brand while it held the presidency from 2003 to 2016, but even through this the PT retained a larger mass base than any competitor.[25]

Second, the extreme number of parties in Brazil's legislature has *not* been duplicated in its presidential elections, which are the focus of our research. Instead, every presidential election, except the first after redemocratization in 1989 and the most recent in 2018, has largely been a two-candidate race between the PT and PSDB nominees. Their summed first-round vote totals averaged 80 percent in all six elections between 1994 and 2014.[26] Elites from Brazil's enormous and fragmented non-leftist camp have largely coalesced around a single candidate from the PSDB, despite the fact that the party has only occasionally been the largest non-leftist party. For its part, the PT nominated either Luiz Inácio Lula da Silva or his protégé, Dilma, in every election prior to 2018. The presidential field has featured viable third- and even fourth-place candidacies— politicians enticed by the hope of squeaking into a second-round matchup in Brazil's majority runoff system. In fact, these candidacies have provided the most interesting campaign dynamics and volatility, something we document below. In the end, however, no such candidate exceeded 22 percent of the vote between 1994 and 2014; every winner and second-round qualifier was either a PT or a PSDB affiliate.[27] Importantly, although eventual-winner Jair Bolsonaro (Social Liberal Party, PSL) in 2018 was the first candidate since 1989 from neither of these two parties to make the second round, he began that year's campaign as one of the two front-runners.

Mexico

Mexico's party system contrasts with the party system of Brazil on both the strength of mass partisanship and the extent of fragmentation. Its first three elections under a truly competitive, democratic regime occurred in 2000, 2006, and 2012. In these races, partisan roots in the electorate were comparatively strong. Rates of partisanship were around 45 percent according to the most restrictive survey metric and 55 to 75 percent according to the most permissive one.[28] Both sets of percentages are nearly twice as high as those prevailing in Brazil.

A party system whose longevity was exceptional by developing-country standards, along with a comparatively programmatic orientation, aided the formation of enduring partisan identities in the electorate. Two of Mexico's major parties, the centrist Institutional Revolutionary Party (PRI) and the right-leaning National Action Party (PAN), were over 60 years old in 2000, a rarity in a world region with high degrees of regime and party-system instability.[29] The PRI had built up a pool of adherents, mostly in rural areas, based on decades of pork barreling, while its two main opponents appealed to voters on more programmatic grounds. The PAN had steadily constructed a reputation by appealing to middle-class and observant Catholic voters, especially in the North, on the basis of a market-friendly, socially conservative platform. The Party of the Democratic Revolution (PRD) was much younger (founded in 1989), but it had cultivated roots with civil society groups in Mexico City and the South based on a consistent leftist critique of the economic and political status quo.[30] In other words, in contrast to most of Brazil's major parties, Mexico's parties had "tight links to core electoral constituencies."[31]

Furthermore, elite competition among these three major-party alternatives was stable from 2000 to 2012, keeping electoral volatility and party fragmentation relatively low. In these first three presidential elections, the three major parties collectively attracted nearly 95 percent of the vote, and in lower-house elections they garnered 85 percent. Despite Mexico's plurality rule, the effective number of electoral parties in presidential elections has been similar to the number prevailing in Brazil's two-party dominant affairs. Mexico averaged 3.01 effective parties from 2000 to 2012, while Brazil's (first-round) contests averaged 2.76 parties from 1994 to 2014. For all of these reasons, scholars have argued that Mexico's political party system is "remarkably institutionalized compared to other new democracies in Latin America and around the world."[32]

Again, we must temper these observations. Mexico may appear to have a party system akin to those prevailing in more established democracies, leaving relatively little space for campaign volatility. Such a conclusion, however, is unwarranted. Partisan identities at the individual level are less stable in Mexico than in established democracies.[33] One study found that just 55 percent of *priístas* (PRI partisans) maintained their self-declared *priísta* identity over a nine-month period, and about 70 percent of *panistas* (PAN partisans) and *perredistas* (PRD partisans) did so. In comparison, in the US and UK more than 85 percent of partisans repeated the same partisan affiliation after one year, and in the UK 75 percent did so after four years.[34]

In addition, rates of mass partisanship in Mexico have declined steadily, from a peak of almost 80 percent in 1997 to a low of 45 percent in 2017.[35] In 2018, 53 percent of voters cast a ballot for the victorious Andrés Manuel López Obrador (AMLO), who had split from the PRD to form an entirely new party (National Regeneration Movement, MORENA) just four years prior. In 2018, moreover, Mexicans elected their most fragmented congress ever, and the three traditional parties received just 39 percent of the lower-house vote. That so many voters in 2018 were willing to abandon traditional parties attests to the fact that mass partisan identifications in the period we study were weaker than partisan identifications observed in older democracies.

In summary, the parties and party systems of Brazil and Mexico are less rooted in their electorates than those of older democracies. Party systems in both countries are also more fragmented than party systems in the most commonly studied established democracies—namely, the UK and the US. We expect to observe substantial amounts of preference volatility during presidential election campaigns in our two country cases. In addition, given Mexico's deeper partisan roots during this period, we expect to see less campaign volatility in Mexico than in Brazil.

CAMPAIGN VOLATILITY AT THE INDIVIDUAL LEVEL IN BRAZIL AND MEXICO

We first estimate rates of individual-level campaign volatility—that is, shares of voters who change vote preferences during a campaign. Our examination of individual-level change provides valuable descriptive insights that move well beyond those provided by the Pedersen index. Not only does the Pedersen index measure only the volatility occurring between elections, it is also limited to aggregated and net volatility. The Pedersen index is thus a highly imperfect proxy for the number of individuals who change vote preferences, especially the number who change *during* campaigns. Of course, the downside of estimating genuine individual-level instability is its cost; it requires election panel studies. Across the universe of Latin American countries and all Latin American presidential elections, we are able to estimate rates of vote switching in only ten presidential elections, and all but one of these elections occurred in Brazil or Mexico.[36]

For any two points in time, we define the degree of individual-level volatility as the percentage of twice-opinionated respondents who *Changed vote preference*. The formula for any given pair of time points—and in practice panel waves—is as follows:

$$\frac{\#\ of\ twice\text{-}opinionated\ respondents\ who\ switched\ between\ t\ and\ t+x}{\#\ of\ twice\text{-}opinionated\ respondents\ in\ t\ and\ t+x} \times 100\%,$$

where t indexes panel waves, and x is an integer between one and one minus the total number of panel waves for the given study. To set terminology, individuals in the numerator are "switchers," and all others are "non-switchers." "Opinionated voters" in a given wave are those who report a preference for a candidate, so individuals with candidate preferences in both waves t and $t+x$ are "twice-opinionated voters." Limiting the sample (for now) to twice-opinionated voters defines switching as preference change that occurs *across party lines*. In other words, individuals who switch between indecision and a candidate preference, or between a candidate preference and abstention, are *not* treated as switchers. They are not tallied in the numerator or the denominator and are dropped from this calculation.

This formula creates a high bar for classifying a change in attitudes as genuine preference volatility, but it is the bar we want. Research on US elections shows that most individual-level changes during campaigns are between indecision (or other forms of nonopinionation) and support for a single candidate. The "holy grail of campaign effects," meaning genuine persuasion across party lines, is largely absent: "One of the best established findings in voting research is that [US] voters rarely hold a preference for a candidate and then change it to the opponent."[37] In contrast, we expect to observe higher rates of switching across party lines in Brazil and Mexico, a sign that genuine persuasion and preference change are taking place. Excluding nonopinionated voters carries the additional advantage of eliminating a confound from our estimated percentages. The different survey projects invited nonopinionation with differing numbers and types of categories (e.g., "don't know," "no response," "would/did not vote"). The rate of nonopinionation across the waves varies from

5 to 25 percent partly for this artificial reason.* For the interested reader, we do subsequently report results that contain nonopinionated voters in the numerator and denominator.

We use the following nomenclature throughout the book to avoid ambiguity about campaign dynamics. Individuals intending to vote for a candidate *during the campaign* are that candidate's "supporters" (e.g., Dilma supporters), and their candidate preferences at any given time during the campaign are their vote "intentions." Referring to these as the candidate's "voters" would be a misnomer, since not all of them ultimately voted for that candidate on election day. A candidate's "voters" are those who do *cast a vote* for the candidate in the election; this is their vote or candidate "choice." When referring to the collective set of a voter's campaign vote intentions and election-day vote choice, we use candidate or vote "preferences." Vote switchers, for instance, are those who changed preferences during the campaign.

Our estimates of individual-level volatility come from a set of nine panel studies conducted on ten total elections. The set includes the workhorse panel studies of this book: the Two-City Panel, the BEPS 2014, and the Mexico 2006 Panel. It also includes the Brazilian Electoral Panel Study of 2010[38] (BEPS 2010), the Brazilian Electoral Panel Study of 2018[39] (BEPS 2018), the Mexico 2000 Panel Study,[40] the Mexico 2012 Panel Study,[41] and the Mexico 2018 Panel Study.[42] To complete the set of available Latin American cases, we also calculate and report estimates from the Argentine Panel Elections Study 2015 (APES 2015).[43] Because these latter six datasets do not contain longitudinal social network data, this will be their only appearance in this book. The reader should bear in mind that all estimates are based on national samples except those for Brazil 2002 and 2006, which are based on the Two-City Panel.

Figure 3.1 is a simple scatterplot of rates of vote switching by time. The unit of analysis in the figure is the wave pairing or wave dyad, and we use every possible panel-wave dyad from all 10 elections. For instance, a four-wave panel offers not just the consecutive $1 \rightarrow 2$, $2 \rightarrow 3$, and $3 \rightarrow 4$ dyads but also the $1 \rightarrow 3$, $2 \rightarrow 4$, and $1 \rightarrow 4$ dyads.[44] The *y*-axis is the percentage of twice-opinionated respondents who *Changed vote preference* between the paired waves, and the *x*-axis is the amount of time (in months) between the paired waves. The points in the figure are shown as two-digit numbers to indicate the year and thus the panel study. Points for Brazil are in black and those for Mexico are in gray. The one point for Argentina is also in black and identifiable as the only "15." The rightmost point for each panel is in bold and corresponds to the amount of switching between the earliest (pre-campaign) wave and the final (election)

---

*We drop voters who, in an early wave, intended to vote for a candidate (e.g., Roseana Sarney in Brazil 2002, Eduardo Campos in Brazil 2014) who subsequently exited the race. These voters were forced to switch, so we do not wish to inflate the degree of volatility by tallying them as switchers.

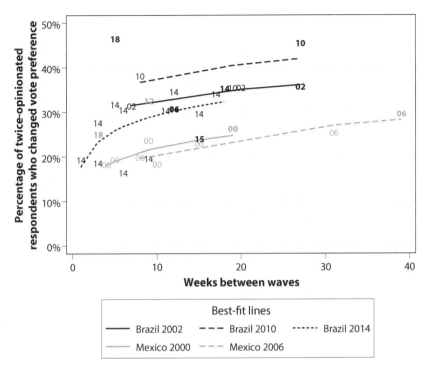

FIGURE 3.1 Rates of Voter Preference Change among Twice-Opinionated Respondents during Brazilian, Mexican, and Argentine Presidential Campaigns
Notes: The *y*-axis variable is *Changed vote preference.* The placement of each point captures values for a pairing of two panel waves, and the point markers themselves are the numbers of the relevant election year. Best-fit lines are from quadratic regressions. Black denotes Brazilian cases and the one Argentine ("15") case. Gray denotes Mexican cases.
Sources: APES 2015, Two-City Panel, BEPS 2010, BEPS 2014, BEPS 2018, Mexico 2000 Panel, Mexico 2006 Panel, Mexico 2012 Panel, and Mexico 2018 Panel.

wave. Finally, the figure also shows five quadratic regression lines, one for each of the five elections with three or more panel waves (Brazil 2002, 2010, 2014; Mexico 2000, 2006). These are the best-fit lines that summarize the bivariate relationship between *Changed vote preference* and time for each of these five elections. We have only two panel waves each for the other five elections, so these five appear as single points in the scatterplot (Argentina 2015; Brazil 2006, 2018; Mexico 2012, 2018).

Plotting the results at the wave-dyad level and as a function of time facilitates direct comparability across the election cases. Raw comparisons of the amount of switching over an entire panel study would be confounded by the number of total waves and by how early polling began. Also, comparisons between two waves that fail to account for the time gap between the waves would be confounded by the length of this gap.

Figure 3.1 contains several important findings. First, rates of preference change in Latin America are, by international standards, above average. Most of the percentages in Brazil, Mexico, and Argentina are relatively high, ranging between 20 percent and 50 percent. In comparison, the share of twice-opinionated US voters who switch across party lines during campaigns is between 5 percent and 8 percent, and in the UK it is only slightly higher at 8 to 13 percent.[45] Evidence from other democracies is sparser, but rates of switching may be slightly higher in countries like the Netherlands (18 percent to 27 percent), Canada (19 percent), and especially New Zealand (31 percent).[46] Regardless, twice-opinionated citizens in Latin America are more likely to change candidate preferences during campaigns than voters in more established democracies. At the same time, a majority of respondents in any panel-wave dyad have stable preferences.

As predicted, voters are more volatile in Brazil than in Mexico. The 21 Brazilian dyads cluster in the 25 to 38 percent range (a mean of 31 percent), although 4 are below 20 percent and 2 are incredibly high, exceeding 45 percent. In contrast, the Mexican dyads ($N=11$) cluster between 18 and 30 percent (a mean of 24 percent), with the sole exception of the Mexico 2012 dyad (33 percent). (Argentina is at this mean of 24 percent.) If the 2012 and 2018 dyads are any indication, Mexico's declining rate of partisanship has been steadily producing higher rates of switching since 2000, and Brazil's rates of switching also show no sign of diminishing.[47]

The passage of time between waves does increase rates of switching, but not by much. The four quadratic regression lines are positively sloped, but not steeply so. For explaining rates of volatility, election- and country-specific effects that do not vary through time are just as important as time, if not more so. The panel with the largest number of waves (Brazil 2014) shows that the relationship with time is one of diminishing returns. The effects of time are steep at very small values (of one to two months), but they tail off after three months, with the line seemingly approaching an election-specific asymptote. This finding counters the possibility that the observed switching is merely voters vacillating during the campaign before they return on election day to a very predictable home—a home that fits their pre-campaign predispositions. In figure 3.1 the rightmost points in bold are not vertically lower than the other points to their left from the same election, so there is no return to a pre-campaign preference, as is common in the US. Rather, the rate of vote switching increases slightly as time passes.

Figure 3.2 contains results that incorporate nonopinionated respondents. "Once-opinionated" respondents are those who ended the dyad with a candidate preference but began it without one. ("Never-opinionated" respondents who lacked an opinion in both waves are dropped from the analysis, since we

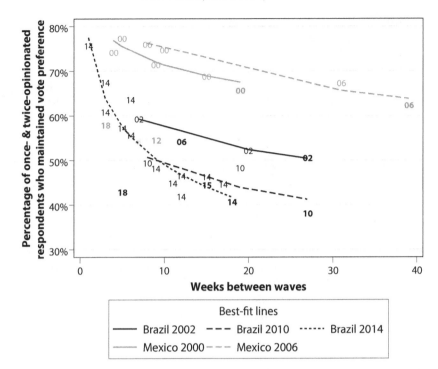

FIGURE 3.2 Rates of Voter Preference Stability among Once- and Twice-Opinionated Respondents during Brazilian, Mexican, and Argentine Presidential Campaigns
Notes: The *y*-axis variable is *Maintained vote preference*. The placement of each point captures values for a pairing of two panel waves, and the point markers themselves are the numbers of the relevant election year. Best-fit lines are from quadratic regressions. Black denotes Brazilian cases and the one Argentine ("15") case. Gray denotes Mexican cases.
Sources: APES 2015, Two-City Panel, BEPS 2010, BEPS 2014, BEPS 2018, Mexico 2000 Panel, Mexico 2006 Panel, Mexico 2012 Panel, and Mexico 2018 Panel.

are interested in understanding those who ultimately cast a vote.) In contrast to figure 3.1, figure 3.2 plots, as a function of time, the percentage who *Maintained vote preference*:

$$\frac{\# \textit{of once- and twice-opinionated non-switchers between } t \textit{ and } t + x}{\# \textit{of once- and twice-opinionated respondents in } t \textit{ and } t + x} \times 100\%$$

Under this new definition, the share of stable voters varies more dramatically across time and countries. It can be as high as 75 percent over a short span, but it can also be as low as 40 percent over a longer one. Time has starker consequences in this analysis, since the number of undecided voters falls as the campaign progresses. The figure depicts even sharper country-level differences: Mexico has more stability than Brazil. (The observation from Argentina is again closer to Mexico's than to Brazil's.) On balance, majorities have stable candidate preferences, but in Brazil these majorities are often slim when they exist at all. Either way, in both settings many voters are open to persuasion during election campaigns. In subsequent chapters we show how peer influences help explain this volatility of preferences.

AGGREGATE CAMPAIGN VOLATILITY
IN BRAZIL AND MEXICO

How did these individual-level maneuverings add up to and, ultimately, affect candidate fortunes in our presidential election cases? In this section we answer this question for the four election cases that will be the focus of our analyses of egocentric network data in the remaining chapters of part II. The discussion provides readers with the necessary background for understanding the contexts and competitors in these elections, and it places the timing of our panel waves in relation to election-related events.

Brazil 2002

The October 2002 presidential election in Brazil will be remembered most for the convincing victory of Lula, a non-elite, left-leaning candidate of the PT. Despite Lula's impressive 22-point margin of victory (in the second round) and the interpretation that his victory implied a leftist mandate, his success was not always a foregone conclusion during the lengthy pre-campaign and campaign season. Two different candidates, neither of whom survived to the second round, were technically tied with Lula at different junctures of the campaign.

Figure 3.3 illustrates this volatility by plotting vote intentions for the five main candidates during the 10 months preceding the first-round election of October 6. The lines are smoothed results from trial heats ("Whom would you vote for if the election were today?") in repeated, nationally representative cross-sectional surveys. To avoid clutter, this and the subsequent three figures show only the smoothed lines, suppressing results from each of dozens of polls used to estimate the lines.[48] The figure gives some context for these numbers by providing a time line of important events, including the campaign's legal start and the initiation of the Free Electoral Hour (HEG, *horário eleitoral gratuito*), which is the seven-week period in which all television and radio stations must devote two hours per day to campaign commercials. Before the HEG, candidates are not allowed to advertise in these electronic media forums.

Lula's competitors, in order of finish, were José Serra (PSDB), the incumbent party's candidate and Lula's second-round opponent; Anthony Garotinho

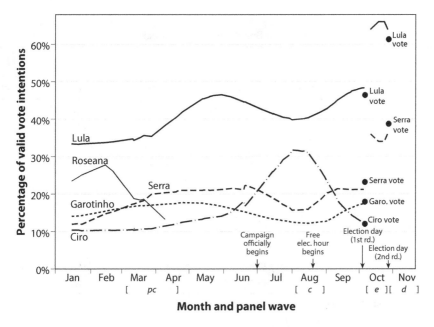

Month and panel wave

FIGURE 3.3 The Evolution of Vote Intentions for Major Presidential Candidates in Brazil 2002
Notes: Each line (LOWESS-smoothed with a bandwidth of .25) summarizes results from nationally representative polls and represents a candidate's estimated percentage of valid vote intentions (dropping undecided respondents). Actual election-day results are indicated with circle markers. Only the top four finishers and Roseana Sarney are depicted. *pc* = pre-campaign wave, *c* = campaign wave. *e* = election wave, *d* = discussants wave.
Sources: Datafolha, IBOPE, Vox Populi, CNT.

(PSB), a populist evangelical and former governor of Rio de Janeiro state; and Ciro Gomes (Popular Socialist Party, PPS), a former governor and finance minister running for the second time. Vote intentions are also displayed for Roseana Sarney (Liberal Front Party, PFL), a strong early candidate from Brazil's clientelistic right who departed the race in April amidst a corruption scandal. Table 3.1 serves as a quick reference for important information about the candidates, including their vote totals, parties, ideological leanings, and incumbency status.[49] The table also reports the naming conventions for each candidate used throughout the book. We use whatever convention prevails in the respective country. In Brazil this sometimes entails using a nickname or first name, primarily when the politician has a very common surname. In Mexico the convention is often just the paternal surname.

Although Lula's vote intentions followed a wavy path, he was always the front-runner. More interesting are the seismographic patterns and fierce jockeying

TABLE 3.1.
Results and Candidate Information for Brazil's 2002 Presidential Election

	First-round result	Second-round result	Political party	Ideology	Notes	Naming convention
Luiz Inácio Lula da Silva	46.44%	61.27%	Workers' Party (PT)	Center-left	4th time running	Lula
José Serra	23.19%	38.72%	Brazilian Social Democratic Party (PSDB)	Center-right	Incumbent party. 1st time running	Serra
Anthony Garotinho	17.86%		Brazilian Socialist Party (PSB)	Center-left	1st time running	Garotinho or Garo.
Ciro Gomes	11.97%		Popular Socialist Party (PPS)	Center	2nd time running	Ciro

Notes: First-round results do not total to 100% because of the omission of minor candidates.

for position among Lula's challengers, movements made all the more important by Brazil's runoff system. Roseana in February, Serra in April, and Ciro in August all held seemingly solid second-place positions. At their peaks, Roseana and Ciro were technically tied with Lula in some polls. Ciro rode the most erratic roller coaster, zooming from fourth to second and then, in the final two months, falling to a disgraced fourth by election day. At his peak in August, Ciro was widely expected to be Lula's second-round opponent, but between that peak and election day Ciro's candidacy imploded. Even third-place finisher Garotinho added some suspense at the end of the campaign by making a run at Serra's second-round spot.

Erikson and Wlezien define two kinds of momentum swings in campaigns, both exemplified in figure 3.3.[50] A "bump" is a permanent surge in vote intentions, a surge that begins during the campaign and lasts through election day. Lula benefited from a 12-point net bump (which the press dubbed the "Lula wave") between March and the early October election. In contrast, a "bounce" or (in the language of network theory) a "fad" is an ephemeral shift, a shock whose effects decay to zero or near zero before election day. Ciro's August high was an archetypal bounce, as he surged from 10 points to over 30 and then back to low double digits when votes were cast. In short, the 2002 election featured substantial aggregate volatility, and this volatility affected the race—especially for second place—in important ways. Similarly, recall from figure 3.1 the high rates of individual-level volatility; 30 to 35 percent of twice-opinionated respondents switched between each pair of panel waves.

Nonetheless, one cannot escape the observation that the volatility seems far from random. In fact, the election results did not differ much from the trial heats reported between April and June, after the field was winnowed down to its eventual four but before the formal campaign began. Lula had a large lead, and Serra had a precarious hold on second. After the Ciro bounce faded, the race returned to its pre-campaign standing and, indeed, to the standing of previous races: a two-party race between the PT and the PSDB.[51]

Stated differently, most of the electoral volatility that occurred *between* the 1998 presidential election, when the PSDB candidate Cardoso defeated Lula by 27 points, and this 2002 election occurred *before* the 2002 campaign. The Pedersen score of electoral volatility between these two elections, 1998 and 2002, is 33.8 percent. By converting the vote intentions at the *start* of the 2002 campaign to vote shares, we can calculate a Pedersen score of volatility between 1998 and this time point. It equals 34.2 percent. Between the campaign's start and election day 2002, however, the Pedersen score is just 10.0 percent. In other words, most of the electoral volatility occurred in the three-plus years before the campaign, as the 2002 campaign returned final vote totals to their pre-campaign levels. This illustrates our central puzzle: more than a third of voters switched, but the campaign's end was predictable from its beginning.

Figure 3.3 also carries important information about the timing of the Two-City Panel. On the *x*-axis, the figure denotes the timing of the first three panel waves. Recall that these have the following labels: the pre-campaign wave (*pc*, wave 1 of this study), the campaign wave (*c*, wave 2), and the election wave (*e*, wave 3). The figure also identifies when the wave of interviews with discussants (*d*) occurred, immediately after the second-round election. This is the only one of the four elections for which we have such a wave. Overall, these panel waves were well-timed to capture voter volatility, as the study contains observations from well before, during, and after the Ciro fad.

Brazil 2006

Four years later, Lula won re-election in a slightly more predictable contest. At the campaign's onset, Lula had the wind at his back because the economy had been growing strongly since 2004. His greatest challenge was answering accusations that he knew about, or was even involved in, a massive legislative vote-buying scheme that came to light in 2005, the infamous *mensalão* scandal. Orchestrated by top party officials and even some of Lula's aides, the *mensalão* deeply tarnished the PT's name.[52] Despite his opponents' attempts to capitalize on the corruption scandal, Lula's involvement in the scheme remained murky. He maintained a healthy lead throughout most of the campaign, consistently polling above the 50 percent mark needed to obviate a second round. (See figure 3.4.)

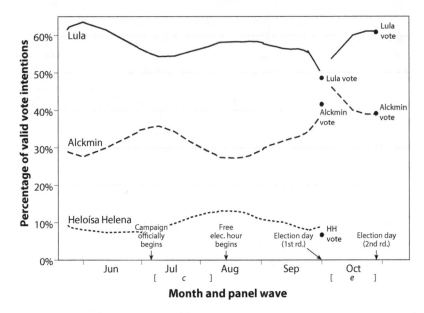

FIGURE 3.4 The Evolution of Vote Intentions for Major Presidential Candidates in Brazil 2006
Notes: Each line (LOWESS-smoothed with a bandwidth of .25) summarizes results from nationally representative polls and represents a candidate's estimated percentage of valid vote intentions (dropping undecided respondents). Actual election-day results are indicated with circle markers. Only the top three finishers are depicted. *c* = campaign wave, *e* = election wave, HH = Heloísa Helena.
Sources: Datafolha, IBOPE, Vox Populi, CNT.

The volatility of his opponents' support, nevertheless, provided some intrigue. (See table 3.2 for more on the candidates.) The runner-up, Geraldo Alckmin of Serra's PSDB, consistently ran about 20 points behind Lula during the campaign, only to experience a bump of more than 10 points in the month before election day. The polling in figure 3.4 suggests that Alckmin clearly stole some supporters from Lula during this late surge. To the surprise of many observers, Alckmin closed to within seven points of Lula in official first-round tallies, forcing a second round. Alckmin, however, failed miserably to capitalize on this second-round breath of life. He began the four-week campaign period nipping at Lula's heels in polls, but he quickly faded and lost by the 20-point margin that stood through much of the campaign.

Although her bounce was not nearly as pronounced, third-place finisher Heloísa Helena Lima was the Ciro of 2006. She ran to Lula's left under the banner of PSOL (Socialism and Liberty Party), a new party formed from a split with the PT over Lula's policy moderation. As a relative unknown, Heloísa Helena

TABLE 3.2.
Results and Candidate Information for Brazil's 2006 Presidential Election

	First-round result	Second-round result	Political party	Ideology	Notes	Naming convention
Luiz Inácio Lula da Silva	48.61%	60.83%	Workers' Party (PT)	Center-left	Incumbent. 5th time running	Lula
Geraldo Alckmin	41.64%	39.17%	Brazilian Social Democratic Party (PSDB)	Center-right	1st time running	Alckmin
Heloísa Helena Lima	6.85%		Socialism and Liberty Party (PSOL)	Left	1st time running	Heloísa Helena or HH

Notes: First-round results do not total to 100% because of the omission of minor candidates.

began the campaign in single digits, but she surged to nearly 15 percent at the campaign's height. She faded, clearly to Alckmin's benefit, to a mere 7 percent on election day.

Notwithstanding these shifts as well as the 30 percent rate (at least) of individual-level switching, it is worth noting again the points of stability during the campaign. The candidates never switched places, and the race was always a contest between the same two parties as in 2002. The Pedersen score from campaign start to election day was just 7.9 percent. Something predictable in the aggregate arose out of something volatile at the individual level.

As for the timing of data collection, the Two-City Panel conducted two waves of interviews during this election year. These are the fifth and sixth waves of the overall study (a fourth wave occurred in 2004), and for the 2006 campaign they are, respectively, the campaign wave and the election wave. The campaign wave was again well-timed—near Alckmin's trough and Heloísa Helena's peak.

Brazil 2014

The opening to this book described aspects of Brazil's 2014 election campaign, so this subsection repeats the exercise more briefly just to convey the timing of panel waves and provide more information about the candidates. Recall that Dilma Rousseff (PT) began the year with a commanding lead in her bid to be re-elected. (See figure 3.5.) As the size of her lead declined over the subsequent months, Aécio Neves, of Serra's and Alckmin's PSDB, and Eduardo Campos of Garotinho's PSB competed for the other runoff slot. (See table 3.3.) Soon after closing in on Aécio for second place in the polls, Campos died in a plane

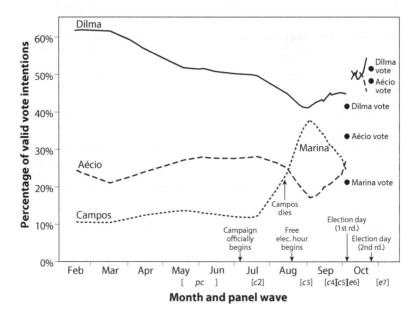

FIGURE 3.5 The Evolution of Vote Intentions for Major Presidential Candidates in Brazil 2014
Notes: Each line (LOWESS-smoothed with a bandwidth of .25) summarizes results from nationally representative polls and represents a candidate's estimated percentage of valid vote intentions (dropping undecided respondents). Actual election-day results are indicated with circle markers. Only the top three finishers are depicted.
pc = pre-campaign wave, *c* = campaign wave. *e* = election wave.
Sources: Datafolha, IBOPE, Vox Populi.

accident. Marina Silva, his running mate, quickly replaced him. Marina continued the party's upward trajectory in the polls, but it was merely an ephemeral bounce.[53] On election day, Aécio surpassed Marina by 12 points, finishing closer to Dilma than to Marina. Despite his late surge in the first round, Aécio lost to Dilma in the second round by three points.

By this point, it goes almost without saying that despite the horse-race intrigue provided by Campos's death and the Marina fad, election-day vote shares are more similar to those prevailing before than during the campaign. In fact, a common pattern prevailed in all three Brazilian races: a third-party candidate rose and then fell, leaving the traditional PT versus PSDB battle intact and the election-day results similar to the distribution of pre-campaign intentions. It is this stability amidst volatility that we explain with our argument about social influence.

Figure 3.5 shows the campaign dynamics depicted in chapter 1 but adds the timing of the seven panel waves from BEPS 2014. To clarify, no respondents

TABLE 3.3.
Results and Candidate Information for Brazil's 2014 Presidential Election

	First-round result	Second-round result	Political party	Ideology	Notes	Naming convention
Dilma Rousseff	41.59%	51.64%	Workers' Party (PT)	Center-left	Incumbent. 2nd time running	Dilma
Aécio Neves	33.55%	48.36%	Brazilian Social Democratic Party (PSDB)	Center-right	1st time running	Aécio
Marina Silva	21.32%		Brazilian Socialist Party (PSB)	Center-left	2nd time running	Marina

Notes: First-round results do not total to 100% because of the omission of minor candidates.

were eligible to respond to all seven waves. Survey administrators contacted a random half of the *pc* wave (wave 1) respondents for reinterview in the next wave (*c2*), and they contacted the other half in the following (*c3*) wave. Administrators again split the sample between the next two waves, *c4* and *c5*. They then attempted reinterviews with all *pc*-wave respondents in the first-round election wave (*e6*) and the runoff-election wave (*e7*). To distinguish among the four campaign waves and the two election waves, the labels contain the overall wave number behind *c* and *e*.

Mexico 2006

The controversial 2006 Mexican presidential election saw multiple fluctuations in candidate fortunes as the race unfolded. Figure 3.6 depicts the evolution of vote intentions in the nine months before election day. The contenders from the three major parties were, in order of finish, Felipe Calderón of the incumbent and right-leaning PAN, López Obrador of the leftist PRD, and Roberto Madrazo of the centrist PRI. (See table 3.4.) Calderón began the pre-campaign period in October—once the field of major-party candidates was defined—8 to 10 points behind the front-runner López Obrador and in a technical tie with Madrazo. At this time, Calderón began a gradual bounce that put him in the lead just two months before election day. Madrazo faded into a firm third place, while López Obrador struggled to regain his lost lead. To heighten the intrigue, Calderón did fall back in the campaign's waning days. Estimates based on the final set of polls, conducted and released before the eight-day polling blackout period, suggest that López Obrador had retaken a slim lead.

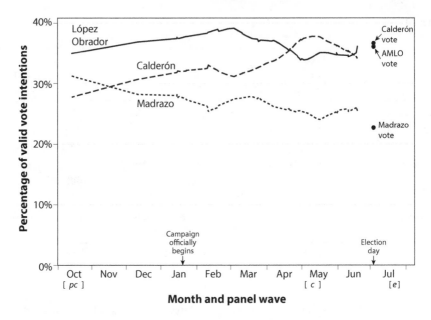

FIGURE 3.6 The Evolution of Vote Intentions for Major Presidential Candidates in Mexico 2006
Notes: Each line (LOWESS-smoothed with a bandwidth of .25) summarizes results from nationally representative polls and represents a candidate's estimated percentage of valid vote intentions (dropping undecided respondents). Actual election-day results are indicated with circle markers. Only the top three finishers are depicted. *pc* = pre-campaign wave, *c* = campaign wave. *e* = election wave.
Sources: ARCOP, Alduncin y Asociados, Beltran & Asociados, CEO, Consulta Mitofsky, Covarrubias, Data Opinion Publica y Mercado, Demotecnia, El Imparcial, El Universal, GCE, GEA-ISA, Indemerc, Ipsos, Lavin & Associates, MEBA, Marketing Politico, Parametria, Reforma, Rvox, Saba Consultores, Tactica Marketing & Comunicacion, Mexico 2006 Panel.

Mexico's 2006 election is most remembered for what happened next, as the closeness of the contest became a visible and genuine test of the nation's nascent democratic institutions. Returns from the 75 percent of polling stations that reported first showed López Obrador with a seemingly insurmountable two-point lead, but Calderón made up the gap among the late-reporting stations. Once all votes were tallied, he had nipped López Obrador by half a percentage point. Over the subsequent weeks, López Obrador vigorously contested the outcome as fraudulent, mounting multiple legal challenges, occupying Mexico City's central square for weeks with his supporters, and even declaring himself the country's legitimate president in an alternative ceremony held before the official inauguration day. While our goal is not to explain these post-election events, the volatility of vote intentions before election day and, espe-

TABLE 3.4.
Results and Candidate Information for Mexico's 2006 Presidential Election

	Result	Political party	Ideology	Notes	Naming convention
Felipe Calderón	35.89%	National Action Party (PAN)	Right	Incumbent party. 1st time running	Calderón
Andrés Manuel López Obrador	35.31%	Party of the Democratic Revolution (PRD)	Left	1st time running (2018 winner)	López Obrador or AMLO
Roberto Madrazo	22.26%	Institutional Revolutionary Party (PRI)	Center	1st time running	Madrazo

Notes: Results do not total to 100% because of the omission of minor candidates.

cially, López Obrador's blown lead surely exacerbated the post-election crisis by heightening his and his supporters' sense of anger and loss.

In sum, Mexican voters' shifting preferences made for a nail-biting affair. All three major candidates held second place at least once, and the lead changed hands three times in the second half of the campaign. Again, however, volatility had its limits, as each candidate fluctuated within a band of 10 percentage points.

Figure 3.6 notes the timing of the three waves of the Mexico 2006 Panel. The pre-campaign wave is valuable because it occurred just after the major-party candidate field had been defined yet long before election day—before Calderón's bounce and during López Obrador's initial lead. In turn, the campaign wave caught vote intentions when Calderón was at his peak.

STRATEGIC SWITCHING?

Are most of these changes in voters' preferences the result of strategic voting calculations? If widespread, volatility due to strategic switching could pose a challenge to our argument about social persuasion. Voters may switch preferences across party lines not because of sincere preference changes resulting from the peer-to-peer intermediation that is central to our argument. Rather, voters may be switching as they make strategic calculations in reaction to candidates' changing fortunes. In both Brazil and Mexico, these fortunes are well known. Polls, many of which we used in the preceding section, are numerous and well-publicized during presidential campaigns. Voters may be immune from campaign and social influences but still shift across party lines in response to these polls, casting a ballot for a second choice in the hope of keeping a least-preferred one out of office. Preference volatility may just be voters acting alone on strategic urges.[54]

We doubt that strategic switching explains much of the individual-level campaign volatility in these two countries. Some evidence suggests that strategic voting in new democracies is rare, since expectations and information about future behavior by parties and voters are uncertain and unstable.[55] For example, the extreme number of legislative parties in Brazil far outruns the nation's already-permissive electoral system. Still, we must take the possibility seriously, as these are two of Latin America's more institutionalized party systems, and informational constraints are not always severe. In fact, candidates for executive posts in Brazil and Mexico have been known to ask supporters of poorly polling candidates for their *voto útil* (useful vote, the opposite of the English-language wasted vote). This brazen (and always contested) request can guide individuals toward strategic votes. We briefly consider whether strategic-voting maneuvers can plausibly explain most of the switching in Brazil and Mexico.

The Absence of Strategic Switching in Brazil

Strategic voting in Brazil's presidential elections is complicated by its majority runoff system. Brazilians have the following saying: "In the first round you vote with your heart. In the second round you vote with your head." Maurice Duverger himself expected little strategic voting under runoff rules on the premise that voters would vote sincerely in the first round.[56] Subsequent scholars have developed more specific expectations—expectations that vary dramatically by assumption and context—while still admitting that "under runoff rules ... strategic voting is often more complicated [than under plurality rule]."[57] The most common theoretical assertion is that the strategic voting equilibrium is $M+1$ candidates. M (district magnitude) in the first round under majority-runoff rules is two, so the electorate should concentrate all votes in just three candidates. Even a brief look at the aggregated polls and results from the three Brazilian election cases allows us to dismiss the notion that strategic switching was widespread.

Consider the 2002 campaign, which featured Ciro's fad. Again, according to the $M+1$ rule, fourth-place (and below) candidates should receive no votes in the first round. Their sincere supporters should end up casting a strategic vote for one of the top three candidates.[58] Despite this, Ciro, the fourth-place finisher, received 12 percent of the vote. Even more damning to the claim of strategic switching is the timing of Ciro's rise and decline. At his peak, Ciro was in a firm second place and seemingly a shoo-in for the second round. That his supporters abandoned him to vote for a more viable candidate, one who needed help to qualify for the second round, is nonsensical. Ciro *was* the most viable anti-Lula candidate at that time. Moreover, his negative ratings boomed as his polling numbers declined, largely because he committed a series of gaffes (described in chapter 4). The switching away from Ciro was clearly sincere.

An alternative strategic-voting scenario holds that Lula's sincere supporters strategically defected from him in the first round to influence who would be his second-round opponent. Perhaps many switched late to Garotinho in the hope of creating an all-leftist second round or in the belief that Garotinho would be a weaker opponent than Serra. The aggregated trends strongly counter this argument. Recall from figure 3.3 that Lula's support grew, rather than fell, in the final weeks of the campaign. More important, Lula had a genuine shot at winning a majority in the first round, which would have foreclosed the need for a runoff. In fact, this was the only real source of intrigue in the campaign's final weeks, and it provided strong incentive for Lula's supporters to hold fast.

This alludes to yet a third possibility. Perhaps anti-Serra voters switched from Ciro to Lula to advance Lula's goal of winning a majority in the first round. At this point, the strategic-voting hypothesis claims so many possible maneuvers that it borders on the nonfalsifiable, which perfectly illustrates the point that strategic voting is extremely difficult in Brazil's majority runoff context, especially given the obstacles to voter coordination around a single strategy. Regardless, recall that sincere Ciro supporters should not have abandoned him mid-campaign, when he was in second place, just to prevent Serra or Garotinho from forcing a second round. Again, Ciro's demise could only have occurred because of sincere switching away from him.

In the 2006 campaign, strategic voting considerations could not have played a role in causing preference volatility. No notable fourth-place candidate, from whom strategic voters might defect, ever existed. Moreover, Heloísa Helena's losses due to switching cannot be explained from a strategic standpoint. Recall from figure 3.4 that neither of the top two candidates, Lula and Alckmin, needed help from her supporters to get into the second round. Heloísa Helena's late decline belies a case that she benefited from strategic defections by Lula supporters to help create an all-leftist second round. Finally, it is not possible that her sincere supporters strategically defected to Lula to help him win in the first round. In fact, it was Alckmin who surged toward the end of the first round, and our panel data show that he received more of Heloísa Helena's campaign-wave supporters (36 percent) than Lula received (24 percent).

Finally, recall the 2014 campaign, which featured the dramatic rise and fall of Marina and the corresponding fall and rise of Aécio. Again, with just three major candidates, no strategic switching from weaker candidates can explain the observed swings in fortunes between Aécio and Marina. Aécio's late surge makes sense only as the result of sincere shifts, mostly from Marina to him. Our panel data show 24 percent of Marina's campaign-wave supporters switching to Aécio and just 15 percent switching to Dilma. Shifts between the second- and third-place candidates had no bearing on Dilma's desire to avoid a second round. Perhaps most damning to the strategic-voting hypothesis, polls publicized at the time showed that Marina had a *better* shot than Aécio at defeating Dilma in the second round, so Marina clearly attracted no last-minute strategic support for this reason.[59]

Strategic Switching in Mexico

In contrast to Brazil, Mexico's presidency is determined by the plurality rule, which provides, to those wishing to cast a strategic vote, much clearer information and easier voter coordination. Supporters of a third-place candidate may abandon that candidate near election day to cast a *voto útil* (also *voto cruzado*) for one of the top two. This straightforward form of strategic voting may drive some campaign volatility in Mexico, but it cannot account for most of it. To start, in the strategic $M+1$ voting equilibrium, just two candidates would receive votes. Despite this, between 20 and 30 percent of Mexican voters chose third-party or minor candidates in the elections from 2000 to 2012. Furthermore, recall from figure 3.1 that Brazilians switch more frequently than Mexicans during campaigns, even though the information and incentives for strategic voting are much more straightforward in Mexico.

Admittedly, this argument does not entirely foreclose the possibility of strategic switching. In the 2006 election, some *priístas* and other sincere Madrazo supporters who feared a López Obrador or Calderón presidency may have switched to one of these two front-runners in the hope of averting what they saw to be a worst-case scenario. In fact, PAN campaign advertisements attempted to stoke fear of López Obrador as a dangerous leftist and as a callow unknown whose party had never governed. These ads were aimed just as much at Madrazo supporters as they were at López Obrador supporters, and PAN leaders made open appeals for the *voto útil*—appeals against which Madrazo and the PRI vehemently protested. Moreover, recall from figure 3.6 that Madrazo's support declined steadily throughout the campaign, perhaps because it grew increasingly clear that his bid was doomed. He even underperformed his final polling tally by a few percentage points.

Fortunately, panel data allow us to estimate an upper bound on the share of voters who may have switched for strategic reasons. The Mexico 2006 Panel Study contains an estimate of the number of pre-campaign and campaign-wave Madrazo (and minor-party) supporters who ultimately voted for López Obrador or Calderón. Their share of all switchers serves as an upper-bound estimate on the amount of switching that was due to strategic voting. We repeat this exercise for two other elections with panel data (2000 and 2012), as possibilities for strategic voting were equally present then. Prior to his victory in the 2000 campaign, for example, Vicente Fox asked for the *voto útil* of Cuauhtémoc Cárdenas supporters in order to oust the long-governing PRI.[60]

Table 3.5 reports these upper-bound calculations. The table specifies two types of candidates: "top-two candidates" (e.g., López Obrador and Calderón in 2006) and all "other" (third-place or worse) candidates (e.g., Madrazo and minor-party candidates in 2006). These are based on order of finish in the election results, and they also describe the candidates' placement in the polls throughout the campaign. The specification of these candidate types defines four (2×2) types of vote switching. The possible strategic voting type is a switch from an other candidate to a top-two candidate: row 1 in the table, which is shaded for emphasis. For example, in 2006 this category contains individuals who switched from Madrazo or a minor-party candidate to López Obrador plus those who switched from Madrazo or a minor-party candidate to Calderón. The three other categories are switches that, by definition, cannot be motivated by strategic voting, such as a switch (row 2) between top-two candidates (e.g., between López Obrador and Calderón) or a switch (row 3) from a top-two candidate to a third-place one (e.g., from López Obrador or Calderón to Madrazo). We use only panel-wave dyads that terminate with an election wave, and entries are percentages of all twice-opinionated switchers; hence the percentages in each column sum to 100.

The figure confirms that a majority of switchers could not have switched for strategic reasons. Collectively, sincere switches—switches that could not possibly be strategic—outnumbered potentially strategic switches in all three elections. These indisputably sincere switches are the three unshaded rows: switches between top-two candidates, switches between other candidates, and switches toward other candidates. For the 2000 and 2012 elections the upper bounds on the number of strategic switches are quite low, less than 35 percent of all switching.

Admittedly, in the 2006 election on which we focus, a plurality of switchers in each of the two panel-wave dyads did so from Madrazo or a minor-party candidate to one of the top-two finishers, a potentially strategic move. Recall, however, that these relatively high figures of 46 to 48 percent are an upper bound. Switches for truly strategic reasons are just a subset of this. The relatively high percentages seen in 2006 did not obtain in the 2000 or 2012 election, a sign that the practice of switching in this ostensibly strategic direction is not a habit for the Mexican voter. It is clear from the rates of switching in the other three categories that sincere changes of preference are common and thus may plausibly characterize many of these apparent strategic ones. Finally, we close this discussion by stressing that strategic switching and social influence are *not* incompatible. Supporters of a weak candidate may be persuaded by supporters of a stronger candidate to switch, precisely for strategic reasons, to avoid a wasted vote.[61] In other words, part of the informational content exchanged within networks of political discussion can be strategic, since strategic concerns can be a useful tool of argumentation (e.g., "C'mon, friend. Don't waste your vote on Madrazo!").

TABLE 3.5.
Different Types of Vote Switching during Three Mexican Presidential Election Campaigns

Switching Type	Mexico 2000			Mexico 2006		Mexico 2012
	wave 1 → wave 4	wave 2 → wave 4	wave 3 → wave 4	$pc \rightarrow e$	$c \rightarrow e$	wave 1 → wave 2
(1) Other candidate → Top-two candidate (*possibly strategic*)	20.8%	28.9%	29.7%	48.3%	46.8%	34.4%
(2) Top-two candidate → Top-two candidate	53.9%	45.5%	51.5%	35.5%	31.7%	34.9%
(3) Top-two candidate → Other candidate	22.0%	20.6%	15.8%	15.0%	16.5%	28.6%
(4) Other candidate → Other candidate	3.3%	5.0%	3.0%	1.2%	5.1%	2.1%
Total	100%	100%	100%	100%	100%	100%
N	241	121	101	291	198	189

Notes: Entries are column percentages. Calculations are based on repeated measures of *Ego vote intention/choice*. "Other candidates" are those who did not finish as one of the top two contenders. p = pre-campaign wave, c = campaign wave, e = election wave.
Sources: Mexico 2000 Panel, Mexico 2006 Panel, and Mexico 2012 Panel.

CONCLUSION

Latin America's presidential campaigns and elections exhibit both change and continuity. On the one hand, preference volatility is common and consequential. Candidates' fortunes undergo bumps and bounces, especially in Brazil, of magnitudes rarely seen in established democracies. During campaigns, the shares of voters who change preferences are high by international standards. Virtually all this volatility is sincere preference change, as evidenced in two ways. Switches across party lines, and not just waffling between indecision and one party, are common, and switches of a strategic nature do not dominate.

On the other hand, stability and continuity also exist, even in a region where electoral volatility between elections is high. A majority of voters do not switch across party lines during campaigns. In addition, at the aggregate level, campaigns have a certain predictability, belying any claim that voters are switching with each new campaign event and each new piece of information. Election-day returns are never that distant from aggregated pre-campaign vote intentions. Although outsiders occasionally ride campaign bumps to victory in Latin America, such events are generally rare, and they certainly did not occur in any of our four election cases. In none of the four did the campaign reshuffle the main contenders. In fact, in Brazil the main two contenders, even amidst extreme party-system fragmentation and after various campaign twists and turns, always reduced to the PSDB and the PT.

The findings of this chapter reinforce the puzzle raised in chapter 1. During the campaign, individual-level volatility is high, but net changes in aggregate vote shares from before the campaign to election day are modest. The explanation for this trend from scholars of US elections would point to a very individualized and atomized process: voters are returning to their own enlightened preferences—preferences that were under the surface all along. Figure 3.1, along with the findings presented in subsequent chapters, shows this not to be the case. Instead, voters arrive at their final decisions via a social process of discussion with peers. The next three chapters provide evidence.

4

Discussion Networks, Campaign Effects, and Vote Choice

My family doesn't have a lot of education. My mom, my stepfather, and my brothers, when they are going to vote, ask "write here who you're going to vote for." I write it on a small piece of paper. They take it, and they vote.[TA4.1]

—*Brazilian voter (2018)*

The political hit job was incredibly effective. In early-August polls during Brazil's 2002 presidential campaign, José Serra of the incumbent PSDB unexpectedly found himself trailing Ciro Gomes. Running under the label of a minor party, Ciro had skyrocketed from just 10 percent to nearly 35 percent of predicted vote intentions, surpassing Serra in the process and seemingly cinching a second-round spot with front-runner Lula. (Revisit figure 3.3.) Ciro boasted that he could smell victory, and many leaders in Brazil's conservative elite endorsed him as his polling numbers swelled. Mid-August, however, saw the start of Brazil's unique Free Electoral Hour (HEG), a period when candidates could televise campaign commercials. Serra went on the offensive. His team broadcast footage of Ciro in a series of gaffes. As a guest on a radio show, Ciro called a phone-in listener "stupid." He angrily pushed and swore at a cameraman on the campaign trail. He joked that his celebrity wife's primary role in his campaign was to sleep with him. The media backed the emerging narrative about Ciro,[1] reporting other campaign gaffes. At one public forum, Ciro lashed out at an Afro-Brazilian university student, alleging that the student was claiming ungranted speaking privileges because he was a "good-looking black guy." Ciro also famously said he did not "give a damn" about international investors and markets. The attacks and the negative reportage were consequential. Ciro began a free fall in the polls, losing about three million voters *per week* on his way to a disgraced fourth-place finish at 12 percent. Serra, meanwhile, vaulted to a second-round spot.

With the media conveying so much negative information about Ciro, one might expect the degree of exposure to mass media to be a strong predictor of who abandoned him, but this was not the case. In fact, according to the Two-City Panel, the August supporters of Ciro who stuck with him through election day were *more* likely to have viewed his gaffes, the debates, and the attacks than those who abandoned him. A better predictor of stability in support for Ciro lies in the social networks of his early-August supporters. Ciro supporters who were embedded in networks of other Ciro supporters when he was peaking in August were 25 percent less likely to abandon him by election day than those Ciro supporters who did *not* have their leanings reinforced by pro-Ciro discussants. What mattered was not direct observation of the attacks and negative reportage, but whether the attacks were reinforced in conversation with social contacts. The process of arriving at their socially informed preference led many voters away from Ciro.

This chapter provides the primary empirical foundations for our argument about socially informed preferences. Information exchanged by voters in their networks of political conversation causes change and stability in preferences during election campaigns. The chapter opens by laying out some general hypotheses about social influence. It then demonstrates peer influence at the individual level of analysis, showing that voters embedded in networks that entirely agree with them are less likely to change preferences during the campaign than voters embedded in networks that at least partly disagree with them. The chapter then moves to the lowest level of analysis, the dyad, to show the large effect of alters' opinions on the vote choices of their egos, and we address several methodological challenges at this stage. We then scale up to the candidate level of analysis to demonstrate, as in the opening anecdote, that social influence has important effects on election outcomes. Candidates whose supporters face relatively high rates of disagreement in their networks during the campaign are less likely to maintain these supporters through election day than candidates whose supporters face low rates of disagreement. Using our quantitative and qualitative data, we also elaborate on the informational mechanism of peer effects on vote choice, and we show how these peer effects explain the aggregate stability that prevails from before the campaign to election day, even though instability at the individual level is high.

NETWORK TRAITS AND PREFERENCE CHANGE

Political discussion and horizontal influences do not inherently induce preference change. Rather, *some* kinds of discussions and network structures encourage volatility, while others encourage stability. This section presents some predictor variables and their associated hypotheses. Because the hypotheses

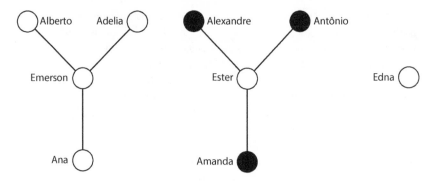

FIGURE 4.1 Political Agreement and Disagreement in Three Egocentric Networks
Notes: Node color indicates vote intention for a hypothetical White or Black Party.

are devoid of the names of candidates and the precise partisan direction of influence, we are able to generate expectations across country cases and at multiple levels of analysis.

The most important influence on individuals' propensities to change their attitudes is the extent to which their social ties agree with them. An ego embedded in a social context of complete agreement has a minimal probability of experiencing attitudinal change. In this scenario political discussion with alters creates social reinforcement of ego's opinions. Conversely, when social interaction occurs across lines of political difference (dangerous discussion), it holds the potential to induce attitudinal change. An ego embedded in a network with at least one discussion partner with whom ego disagrees has a higher probability of experiencing preference change. In this scenario the alter who disagrees with ego can induce social persuasion.

Our primary test of social influence at the individual level is the disagreement hypothesis: an ego's propensity to switch vote intentions during a campaign is a positive function of *Network disagreement*, which is the share of alters who disagree with ego. To illustrate, consider the two leftmost egocentric networks in figure 4.1. Each node has a fictional proper name. Egos' names start with "E" (like Eva in chapter 1), while alters' names start with "A." All ties between egos and alters are political. Emerson supports the White Party and so do all his alters. Network disagreement is 0/3 = 0 for Emerson. Ester also supports the White Party, but all three of her alters support the Black Party. For Ester, network disagreement is 3/3 = 1. The disagreement hypothesis predicts that Ester has a greater probability of subsequently switching than Emerson. (Network disagreement can also take on values between 0 and 1.)

The disagreement hypothesis aggregates to two higher levels of analysis, the candidate and the country levels. At the candidate (or party) level, the hypothesis is as follows: candidates whose mid-campaign supporters are embedded in networks with relatively high rates of disagreement will lose a greater share

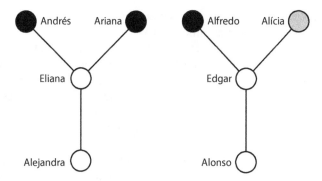

FIGURE 4.2 Political Heterogeneity in Two Egocentric Networks
Notes: Node color indicates vote intention for a hypothetical White, Black, or Gray
Party.

of those voters by election day than candidates whose mid-campaign supporters are embedded in networks with low rates of disagreement. A candidate's
bubble will burst, turning a bounce into a fad, if that candidate's mid-campaign
supporters tend to be embedded in networks that challenge rather than reinforce their preferences. At the country level, the amount of preference volatility is higher in countries with relatively high rates of network disagreement
and lower in countries with lower rates of network disagreement.

Now consider a second measure and hypothesis. In the rightmost network
of figure 4.1, Edna is a *Singleton*, meaning she has no discussants. Network disagreement for Edna is undefined (0/0), but her social context contrasts with
those of Emerson and Ester. Emerson hears only voices that affirm his preference; these are efforts at social reinforcement. Ester encounters only voices
committed to changing her mind; these are efforts at social persuasion. Edna
faces neither extreme. Her predispositions are neither reinforced nor opposed,
so her probability of switching should be in between those of Emerson and
Ester. We thus introduce the singleton hypothesis: the probability that a singleton switches preferences will fall between those of an ego facing no disagreement and one facing only disagreement.

The third and final individual-level measure accounts for diversity (also
called heterogeneity) within the network. Consider the two networks in figure 4.2. At 0.66, Eliana and Edgar have the same rate of network disagreement.
The disagreement in Eliana's network is united because Andrés and Ariana are
both Black Party supporters. The disagreement in Edgar's network is diverse,
however, because Alfredo and Alícia support opposing parties. Diversity among
the disagreeing alters is clearly a dimension that can vary independently of the
amount of disagreement itself. In other words, the concept of heterogeneity is
distinct from network disagreement, although network scholars sometimes use
the two terms synonymously. In our usage, disagreement refers to attitudinal

differences between an ego and that ego's alters, while heterogeneity refers to attitudinal differences strictly among alters.[2]

The simple example in figure 4.2 illustrates an analytical advantage of the multiparty competition present in the Latin American context: it allows us to tease out the different consequences of these two concepts. Though network disagreement and network heterogeneity are central independent variables in studies of social influence, research on the US often conflates them.[3] For instance, scholars from the Columbia school famously argued that cross pressures exerted from a network made individuals more likely to change preferences during campaigns, but they were ambivalent about the concept's precise meaning. In some scenarios, citizens embedded in networks that leaned against their current predispositions were defined as cross-pressured. "The stability of a preference . . . varies with the chances of social support for it," so this definition stressed disagreement as the cause of preference change.[4] Elsewhere the Columbia school focused more on heterogeneity or diversity, defining cross-pressures as "the conflicts and inconsistencies among the factors which influence vote decision."[5] This conflation stems from the near collinearity between the two concepts in the US two-party system. In figure 4.2 the only reason heterogeneity among the disagreeing alters can exist is the presence of a Gray Party. Without this third party, disagreement alone would capture the dimension of interest.

The relevant new variable is *Disagreeing alters' diversity*, which captures the heterogeneity among the alters who disagree with ego. (To clarify, the variable name treats "disagreeing alters" as alters who disagree with their egos.) Conceptually, this variable captures whether disagreement is communicated to an ego from a united front or a divided front. It is nonzero only when ego has at least two alters who disagree with ego *and* these alters are not in full agreement with one another. When at least two alters disagree with ego and do not agree with one another, the variable is the probability that two of them chosen at random (with replacement) hold opposing preferences. *Disagreeing alters' diversity* moves independently of network disagreement.[6] For Eliana it is zero and for Edgar it is 0.5.[7]

Because heterogeneity is often conflated with disagreement, scholars tend to see diverse networks as a cause of attitudinal instability.[8] Once we redefine the concept as heterogeneity among alters who disagree with ego, however, the position that diversity promotes attitude change becomes theoretically dubious. An alter has more influence on an ego when that alter's views are shared by other alters in the egocentric network. The persuasive argument of a disagreeing discussant is less likely to produce change in ego's attitude if the argument is undermined by competing arguments made by other alters,[9] whereas redundancy within a network contributes to social persuasion. This is the concept of autoregressive influence.[10] Thus our heterogeneity hypothesis holds that, all else equal, *Disagreeing alters' diversity* should lower, rather than raise, the probability of vote switching.

SOURCES OF CHANGE AND STABILITY
AT THE INDIVIDUAL LEVEL

The Brazil and Mexico panel studies contain the necessary data to explore the effects of political discussion on the volatility of voters' preferences. The necessary data are repeated measures of main respondents' preferences, of discussants' preferences, and (thus) of network preferences. We apply a general vocabulary and framework of analysis to uncover the roots of preference change and continuity across the four election cases. This section tests our general hypotheses at the individual level, and the subsequent sections move to different levels of analysis.

Dependent and Independent Variables

For the individual-level analyses, the dependent variable is *Changed vote preference*, the same binary indicator that was aggregated to calculate the percentages reported in figure 3.1. Change (1) and stability (0) are defined across the period between the campaign and the election wave and only for twice-opinionated main respondents, so changes are those that occur across party lines.[11]

Our primary independent variables are the three network measures introduced above: network disagreement, singleton, and disagreeing alters' diversity. For the three Brazilian elections, the identities of all named alters in each egonet are held constant across the two waves. In other words, egos generated their list of alters and proxy-reported these alters' candidate preferences in the campaign wave, and then egos again proxy-reported the preferences of these same alters in the election wave.[12] (In the case of the Brazil 2002 election wave, we use discussant self-reports of election-wave vote choice when they are available.) Recall from chapter 1 that this approach provides an important methodological advantage over the alternative of conducting name generators afresh in both waves because it addresses the homophily confound. Shifts in alters' preferences between the campaign and election day waves are due to (perceived) preference change by alters, not to shifts in which alters are named.[13] The two Mexico 2006 name generators, however, were conducted independently from one another.[14] With this setup, addressing the homophily confound requires the extra methodological maneuver of limiting observations to repeated alter ↔ ego pairings. We implement this analysis later in the chapter when we report dyad-level results. The current section reports the individual-level results for Mexico 2006, recognizing that they may be biased by homophily.

Scholars of emerging, and especially Latin American, democracies have attempted to explain the volatility of voter preferences during campaigns not with *horizontal* influences but with *vertical* political intermediaries, namely, clientelism and mass media. The vertical intermediary that has received the most attention is direct party-to-citizen contact, mainly in its clientelistic form. Models for Mexico 2006 include a variable measuring whether respondents were *Paid off by a disagreeing party*, which should be positively correlated with vote switching. Disagreement is based on the main respondent's vote intention during the campaign wave. These models also include *Not paid off by a party*, so the implied baseline category is those who received a benefit from an agreeing party. Unfortunately, no measure of clientelism exists for the other three election cases, but for the Brazil 2002 and 2006 elections we have measures of party contacting. This is itself a form of intermediation—of which clientelistic contacts are a subset. Respondents reported whether and by whom they were contacted, and the survey wordings allowed for reports of multiple contacts by different parties.[15] *Contacted by a disagreeing party*, which should be positively correlated with vote switching, is the percentage of this list of party contacts that disagreed with the main respondent. The models also include *Not contacted by a party*, so the implied baseline is those contacted only by agreeing parties.

As for the influence of the mass media, recall our claim that the mass media are ultimately the source of most political information held in the public mind. Nonetheless, we depart from standard studies of media effects on Latin American voting behavior by arguing that attitudinal change is not a function of direct exposure to mass-mediated information. Various measures of main respondents' exposure to political news and to campaign advertising, included in our models, test this media-exposure hypothesis. The exact set of measures varies by election case. First, *Exposure to disagreeing media* is a continuous variable. It is available for Brazil 2002 and Mexico 2006 (called *Exposure to disagreeing TV news* in the latter case). This variable is based on media content coding and survey questions that allow us to construct the media diets of main respondents.[16] High values reflect respondents who consumed media content critical of their campaign-wave candidate, and low values correspond to respondents consuming media content supportive of their campaign-wave candidate. This variable should be positively correlated with vote switching. Second, *HEG exposure* is available for the Brazil 2002 models. This is particularly useful because Ciro took a beating in this forum. The standard hypothesis of media effects is that campaign-wave Ciro supporters who watched a lot of the HEG programming were more likely to switch than Ciro supporters who did not. Finally, no media content coding exists for the Brazil 2006 and 2014 election cases, but these two surveys do contain measures of overall *Media exposure*. Interacting this measure with campaign-wave vote intentions (e.g., *Marina vote intention × Media exposure*) provides a generic test of whether overall attention to political news caused switches away from a particular candidate.[17] More precise details on the measurement of all these variables are reserved for appendix B.

Results

In this subsection we report two sets of analyses. The first set consists of very trim models that reveal how campaign-wave network traits correlate with subsequent preference change and stability. The second set addresses some methodological challenges by considering whether *changes* in network traits correlate with *changes* in preferences. This second set of analyses includes the measures of exposure to other intermediaries.

Figure 4.3 depicts simple results on the relationship between campaign-wave network traits and the propensity to switch.* These are the predicted probabilities of switching derived from four binary logit models (one per election). For independent variables, each contains only the three network traits laid out above.[18] With these three, we create five ego types. The first ego type faces only disagreement from alters, and the alters are politically united ("Disagreement only (homog.)" in figure 4.3). This type is exemplified by Ester in figure 4.1 and should have the highest probability of switching of all five types. The second ego type ("Disagreement only (heterog.)") also faces only disagreement from alters, but the alters are not united among themselves (e.g., ᛉ). Given the autoregressive influence hypothesis, we expect this type of ego to have a lower probability of switching than the first. The third type of ego encounters a mix of "Disagreement & agreement," as exemplified by Eliana in figure 4.2,† and the fourth type is a "Singleton" (Edna in figure 4.1). These two should have probabilities of switching that fall in between the disagreement-only types and the fifth type, which is the "Agreement only" ego type exemplified by Emerson in figure 4.1.

Understanding figure 4.3 and similar figures in this book involves making statistical comparisons between two different point estimates, so let us clarify how to do this properly in rope-ladder plots. Recall that a confidence interval can be understood as all the null hypotheses that cannot be rejected. Thus when one tests the null hypothesis of equivalence between two different point estimates, the correct visual test is not whether their confidence intervals *overlap*. Instead, the correct test is whether either point estimate falls *inside* the confidence interval of the other. If at least one does, then the null hypothesis of equivalence cannot be rejected. If neither does, then the null of equivalence is rejected. For instance, even though the confidence intervals for "Disagreement only (heterog.)" and "Disagreement & agreement" overlap in the case of Brazil 2002, we reject the null hypothesis that these two voter types have equivalent probabilities of switching because neither of the two confidence intervals encompasses the point estimate of the other.

In all four elections, egos facing only disagreement are much more likely to switch than those facing only agreement. The differences in probability

---

*The coefficients and more model details are reported in appendix A.

†As in the example of Eliana, we set the disagreement to be homogeneous.

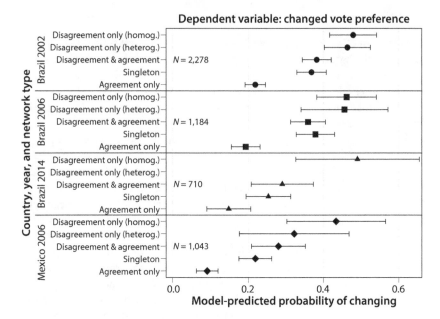

Dependent variable: changed vote preference

FIGURE 4.3 The Likelihood of Changing Vote Preference between Campaign and Election Waves by Campaign-Wave Network Traits: Predicted Probabilities from Four Binary Logit Models

Notes: Each marker is the model-predicted probability (with 95 percent confidence interval) of a main respondent changing vote preference across party lines between the campaign and election wave. Dependent variable for each model is *Changed vote preference*. All four samples are limited to twice-opinionated main respondents. All network traits are measured at the campaign wave. Table A.3 reports the complete sets of coefficient estimates in numerical form.

Source: Two-City Panel, BEPS 2014, Mexico 2006 Panel.

between the two vary between 0.25 and 0.35—differences that represent huge increases of between 100 and 400 percent over the baseline probabilities. Moreover, the probabilities that singletons switch always fall in between these two extremes, as do those of egos who face a mixture of agreement and disagreement. Taken collectively, these patterns suggest that alters can induce switching through persuasion when disagreement is present, and they can prevent switching through reinforcement when agreement is present. Either way, social influence occurs.[19] The one falsified expectation in figure 4.3 is the hypothesis about disagreeing alters' diversity. Egos with alters who disagree with them from a homogeneous front are not more likely to switch than egos with alters who disagree with them from a hetereogeneous front.[20]

These results are suggestive, but they fail to address the confound of network selection. Consider the following scenario. Emerson intentionally chooses only alters who agree with him precisely because he is a fervent partisan. He maintains the same preference throughout the campaign because, as a strong partisan, he resists new countervailing information from the media, not because his discussants reinforce his vote intention.[21] Conversely, Ester is independently minded and thus does not choose discussants based on their candidate leanings. She ends up with three discussants who disagree with her, yet she subsequently switches not because of their influence but because she is open to hearing new persuasive information from the media. In this scenario, the correlation between switching and network disagreement is spurious.

To address the selection effect, we estimate another set of logit models that incorporate network dynamics. These include as independent variables not just lagged network measures, subscripted by c and measured in the campaign wave, but also contemporaneous network measures, subscripted by e and measured in the election wave. $Network.disagreement_c$, for instance, is the share of alters at the campaign wave who disagree with ego in the campaign wave, and $Network.disagreement_e$ is the share of alters at the election-wave stage who disagree with ego's campaign-wave vote intention. (To avoid confusion, multiple-word variable names with a subscript contain a period between words.) Measuring and including both variables assesses whether the balance of preference *change* among alters is correlated with ego's propensity to switch. To reiterate, in Brazil the identities of these alters are constant, while in Mexico they can change. For the three network traits, the primary hypothesis tests are captured by the coefficients on the election-wave variables. These are the effects of *changing* network traits on whether the main respondent changed vote preference. The logit models also contain controls for exposure to vertical intermediaries.[22] Figure 4.4 conveys the main results, showing the coefficients for the network traits under the "horizontal" heading. (Table A.4 reports the full numerical results, and table A.5 shows results when the inclusive definition of agreement is used.)

Across all four elections, the coefficient on election-wave network disagreement is positive and statistically significant. The change in the proportion of alters who disagree with ego's campaign-wave vote intention correlates positively with the probability that ego switches by election day. The substantive effects (not shown) are equal in size to those when dynamics are not incorporated (in figure 4.3). Individuals with only agreeing alters in both waves have very low probabilities of switching—single digits in all four cases. This provides strong evidence of social reinforcement. These probabilities increase dramatically, by 30 to 45 percentage points, if election-wave discussants instead become all disagreeing ones—that is, providers of social persuasion. A third alternative is a change to singleton status, which yields, as expected, changes in probability that are about one-third to one-half these sizes.

The coefficients on lagged network disagreement are much smaller than those on contemporaneous disagreement. In Brazil 2006 the lagged coefficient is even negative and statistically distinguishable from zero, although this

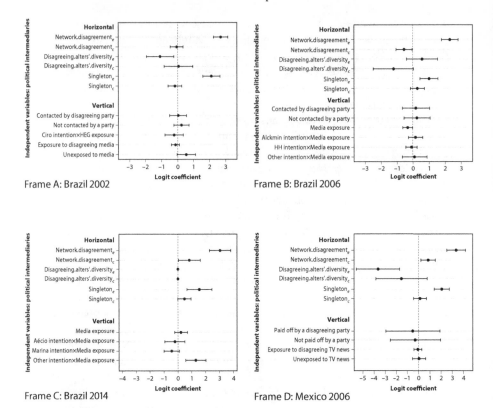

FIGURE 4.4 Changed Vote Preference by Network Traits in Brazil and Mexico: Coefficients from Four Binary Logit Models
Notes: Each marker is a logit coefficient with 95 percent confidence interval. Dependent variable for each model is *Changed vote preference*. All four samples are limited to twice-opinionated main respondents. Sample sizes are reported in figure 4.3. c = campaign wave, e = election wave. Measures of vote intention are from campaign waves, while measures of vertical intermediation are from election waves. Table A.4 reports the complete sets of coefficient estimates in numerical form. *Source:* Two-City Panel, BEPS 2014, Mexico 2006 Panel.

effect is swamped in size by the election-wave coefficient. The small size of the lagged coefficients makes clear that citizens are highly sensitive to the *ongoing discussion* that occurs in the weeks before election day.

In these dynamic models diversity now shows signs of life. A change during the campaign from a network like Eliana's, where disagreeing alters have zero diversity, to one like Edgar's, where disagreeing alters disagree with one another (in figure 4.2), lowers the probability of switching in Brazil 2002 by 10 percentage points. In Mexico 2006 it lowers the probability of switching by a sizable 18 points. In comparison, diversity among disagreeing alters has no statistically discernible effect in Brazil 2006. The difference lies in the fact that Brazil 2002 and Mexico 2006 featured much stronger third- and fourth-party options, and thus more opportunities for diversity among disagreeing alters, than Brazil 2006. Regardless, network diversity, when properly understood and measured in a multiparty context, does not increase (as is commonly thought) the probability of voter volatility. Rather, it tends to decrease it. This clarifies some conceptual ambiguities in the social network literature on US politics. Network diversity and disagreement are distinct phenomena. All else equal, disagreement induces attitudinal change while diversity reinforces existing attitudes.

The coefficients on measures of other intermediaries are virtually all statistically zero. Across the four election cases, direct exposure to different media sources is unrelated to the probability of vote switching. In Brazil 2002 and 2006, the partial correlation between party contacting and vote switching is negligible, and in Mexico 2006 receiving a clientelistic enticement also fails to move the needle. To clarify, we cannot and do not argue, based on these null results, that mass media and party contacting are wholly irrelevant to preference formation and change during campaigns. The results merely suggest that voters directly exposed to these forms of vertical intermediation are no more likely to switch than voters who are not directly exposed. These intermediaries may still have indirect effects on preferences once their content is repackaged and channeled through horizontal networks.

Still, we doubt that contacts and clientelism produce major effects on presidential vote choice, at least in Brazil. In the Two-City Panel more than 85 percent of party contacts promoted a candidate for a legislative post (federal or state deputy), while less than 5 percent promoted a presidential candidate. Previous research on Brazil and other Latin American countries also confirms that contacting and clientelism for high offices occur relatively rarely, simply because these practices cannot move enough votes.[23]

DYADIC SOCIAL INFLUENCE

The individual-level analyses above treat each egocentric network as a single observation, but an egocentric network with, for instance, three alters (like those in figure 4.2) can also be treated as three separate cases, one for each dyad. In dyadic analysis, each observation is an ego ↔ alter (main respondent ↔ discussant) pairing; this can also be thought of as an alter-level analysis.[24]

Dynamic specifications on dyadic data are one of the best ways to assess causality with observational network data.[25] Besides the obvious boost in statistical power, this approach brings several advantages. It can assess the precise political direction of social influence. Scoring alter and ego preferences in their natural nominal categories can confirm (or disconfirm) whether alters influence their egos in the direction of their preferences.[26] Also, the dyadic approach can more easily control for egos' prior political predispositions and then discern whether social influence exists while holding predispositions constant. Moreover, the dyadic approach can seamlessly maintain nonopinionated alters and egos in the sample, since we score nonopinionation as one among the various nominal vote intention/choice categories. In other words, we integrate opinionated and nonopinionated actors into a single model of vote choice and do not need to choose between restrictive and inclusive definitions of disagreement. Finally, dynamic dyadic analyses provide a clear framework for addressing the methodological challenge of reverse causation, because they can employ the past preferences of stable alters as an exogenous variable. We also consider the challenges of latent homophily and environment confounding (defined below) within this dyadic framework. In a final subsection we exploit the methodological advantages of Brazil's runoff elections.

Modeling Overview

The dependent variables for the dyadic analyses are nominal measures of *Ego vote choice*. Recall that this is an election-wave measure, as vote *choice* refers to the actual vote cast. To designate the different possible choices, we assign a different integer to each of the J presidential candidates and implement multinomial logit (MNL) models. We estimate one model for each of our four election cases. Each model estimates $J-1$ sets of coefficients: one set for each candidate except the omitted baseline candidate. The candidate of the incumbent party, notated with j^b, is the omitted baseline category.[27] Candidate j's coefficients are thus the estimated effects on the probability of voting for j (e.g., Lula in 2002) versus j^b (Serra). The set of coefficients for this pairwise comparison is labeled "$\Pr(Y_e=j)/\Pr(Y_e=j^b)$", where Y_e is the *Ego vote choice* dependent variable.

Our primary independent variables are two measures of alter's preferences: *Alter vote choice* and *Alter vote intention*. The first is a contemporaneous measure: alter's vote choice on election day. The second is a lagged measure: alter's vote intention during the campaign wave. These independent variables are broken into a series of dummy variables. For example, the full set of vote-choice dummy variables for the 2002 models are as follows: *Alter vote choice = Lula*, *Alter vote choice = Garo.*, *Alter vote choice = Ciro*, and *Alter vote choice = none*. *Alter vote choice = Serra* is the omitted baseline category.[28] The hypothesis that peer influences occur over an unfolding campaign is tested with these contemporaneous coefficients. The direction of change in an alter's preference between the campaign and election waves should correlate with the ego's change in preference over this same period. This specification works only in the presence of repeated observations of each alter's vote preference, which is rare in egonet research on voting behavior.[29]

In specifying these dyadic models, we reject social determinism. It is a truism that individuals bring their own background information and political biases to any campaign and to the social interactions they have over the course of that campaign. Despite our focus on horizontal intermediation, individuals' vote choices are not simply the sum of peer influences during a campaign, even in new democracies where volatility is high. Rather, a citizen's ultimate vote choice is the result of a self-other balance, meaning a combination of pre-existing attitudes and ongoing social influences.[30] According to the minimal-effects paradigm of campaign influence, the self weighs heavily in US presidential elections: most voters return to their pre-campaign dispositions on election day. To support our argument about peer effects during campaigns, we *must* show that alters can draw individuals away from their pre-campaign dispositions.

Our models thus include a robust set of controls for ego's political leanings and political predispositions. Most important are two lagged measures of the dependent variable: *Ego.vote.intention*$_{pc}$ and *Ego.vote.intention*$_c$. These are the main respondent's vote preferences (included as a full set of dummy variables) in the pre-campaign wave (second lag) and in the campaign wave (first lag), respectively. The inclusion of the first lag means that all other independent variables are explaining preference change between the campaign wave and election day.[31] The models also include measures of the main respondents' economic evaluations, incumbent evaluations, partisanship, and positional issue stances. These are all measured at the pre-campaign wave.[32]

Results

Figure 4.5 plots the most important results from each of the four models. These MNL models produce many coefficients, both because they estimate J-1 sets of coefficients and because egos' lagged preferences and alters' contemporaneous and lagged preferences are broken into full sets of dummy variables. To maintain focus on the main hypotheses, figure 4.5 plots only the coefficients for each *Alter vote choice* dummy variable. The full lists of estimated coefficients are reserved for appendix A.

The plots show coefficients for each of the J-1 pairwise comparisons. For instance, underneath the "Pr(Y_e = Lula)/Pr(Y_e = Serra)" heading in the Brazil 2002 frame are the estimated effects of alter's vote choice on the probability of ego's voting for Lula relative to the probability of voting for Serra. The most important coefficient in this set has a boldface label; this coefficient should be large and statistically distinguishable from zero. For instance, the large and statistically nonzero point estimate on *Alter vote choice* =Lula means that an ego whose alter switched preferences to Lula between the campaign and election waves was herself far more likely to switch to a Lula vote choice than an ego whose alter held a stable Serra preference across both waves. The coefficient

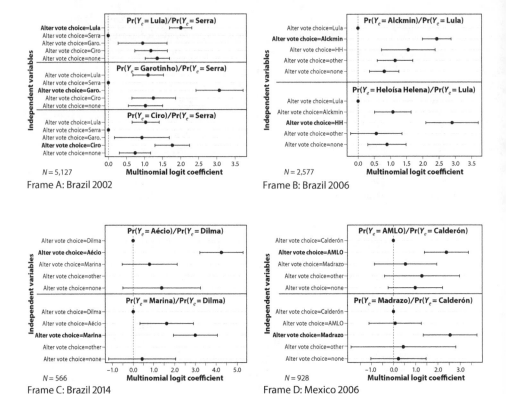

FIGURE 4.5 Ego's Vote Choice (Y_e) by Alter's Vote Choice at the Dyadic Level in Brazil and Mexico: Coefficients from Four Multinomial Logit Models

Notes: Each marker is a multinomial logit coefficient with 95 percent confidence interval. Dependent variable for each model is *Ego vote choice*. *Alter vote choice* is measured at the election wave. Models also contain lags of *Alter vote intention*, two lags of the dependent variable, and other independent variables. Tables A.6 through A.9 report the complete sets of coefficient estimates in numerical form. Coefficients on *Alter vote choice = other* for Brazil 2014 were estimated but are not shown because they have very wide confidence intervals that would affect the display.

Source: Two-City Panel, BEPS 2014, Mexico 2006 Panel.

(constrained-to-zero) on the omitted baseline category (e.g., *Alter vote choice = Serra*) is shown to provide the proper point of comparison.

No other coefficients in this set should fall outside these two extremes. We call these, with some exaggeration, the coefficients for irrelevant options. For example, in the top part of frame A the coefficient on *Alter vote choice = Garo.* falls in between those for *Alter vote choice = Lula* and *Alter vote choice = Serra*. This means that the effect of having a Garotinho-voting alter on the probability an ego votes for Lula (instead of Serra) is neutral, falling between the more positive effect of having a Lula-voting alter and the more negative effect of having a Serra-voting alter. It would undermine our argument to find that, even as (say) Lula-voting alters induced a Lula vote, Garotinho-voting alters were *more* likely to do so.

These technicalities aside, the results provide strong empirical support for the impact of persuasive peers in the final weeks of these election campaigns. In every instance, the primary coefficient of interest, with the boldface label, is large and statistically nonzero. A good example is the first coefficient entry under Brazil 2002. To understand its substantive effects, consider the following hypothetical egos: one has an alter with a stable Serra preference in both waves, and the other has an alter who switches from Serra to join the Lula bandwagon just before election day. The latter ego has a higher predicted probability—about 25 percentage points higher—of voting for Lula than the former ego. This latter ego also has a lower probability, by about 20 percentage points, of voting for Serra. Among alters, of course, a more common shift in 2002 was the Ciro-to-Serra switch as Ciro fizzled out. This switch by an alter was associated with a decline of 8 points (50 percent below the baseline) in ego's propensity to vote for Ciro and an increase of 19 points in ego's propensity to vote for Serra.

The other major fad among our election cases also followed a social logic. In Brazil 2014, when a Marina-supporting alter switched to Aécio or to Dilma, the ego's probability of sticking with Marina fell by over 30 points. Effects for other candidates and elections are also substantively important, and the results confirm the hypotheses for irrelevant options as well. None of the coefficients on alter vote choice for irrelevant options fall below zero or above the corresponding coefficients on the boldface variables. Indeed, most follow the tidiest possible result: their confidence intervals include neither zero nor the point estimate of the coefficient on the variable in boldface.[33]

These effects exist while main respondents' political predispositions are held constant. Factors not shown in the figure, such as previous vote intentions and pre-campaign partisanship, do matter, albeit to varying degrees across the elections and candidates. (See appendix A.) Overall, these dyadic results confirm a key finding from the individual-level estimates: changes in discussant preferences correlate with changes in main respondents' candidate preferences.

Robustness Checks

The dyadic results reveal strong correlations between changing alter and changing ego preferences late in election campaigns. Still, some methodological challenges remain, namely, reverse causation, latent homophily, and environmental confounding.

We first explore the reverse causation (or reflection) problem.[34] When an ego and an alter change candidate preferences in unison, the corresponding coefficient (labeled in boldface) in figure 4.5 increases in magnitude, but from this we cannot discern who has influenced whom. From one perspective, this is not overly concerning. Bidirectional social influence is still social influence, so the central argument holds. Because our intent is to model peer effects on the main respondent, however, bidirectionality inflates estimates of this pathway.

Estimating models on a sample that, by definition, does not contain ego-to-alter persuasion over the observed time period can help to isolate the alter-to-ego effect. For a new set of analyses, we limit the dyadic samples to pairings in which the discussant does not change preference between the campaign and election waves. These are labeled the "stable alters" samples. The gravitation of egos toward their alters' stable preferences over the final weeks of the campaign indicates the alter's influence on ego, but not the reverse. The model setup and presentation largely mimic those in the preceding subsection. The one exception is that these stable-alters models include only *Alter vote intention*—that is, the alter's preference at the campaign wave—because the alters have identical preferences at the campaign and election waves. Figure 4.6 shows the rope-ladder plots.

Limiting the sample in this way does not affect the primary conclusions. (The coefficients testing the main hypotheses again have boldface labels.) These new coefficients are, on average, only slightly smaller, but they all remain statistically significant. The coefficients on some of the irrelevant alternatives do muddy the waters slightly. For example, a stable Heloísa Helena–supporting alter in Brazil 2006 was just as likely as a stable pro-Alckmin alter to induce an ego to switch to Alckmin. (See the top half of the Brazil 2006 frame.) At the same time, a stable Heloísa Helena–supporting alter was more likely to induce an ego to switch to her than was a stable pro-Alckmin alter. (See the bottom half of frame B.) Inconsistencies such as these play out in a few other cases (e.g., stable Garotinho versus stable Lula alters, and stable Aécio versus stable Marina alters), but they seem to be largely the result of the greater estimation uncertainty surrounding third-place candidates. In the end, the results in figure 4.6 show an important effect: many egos move toward the stable preferences of their alters.

Next, we consider the overlapping challenges of latent homophily and environmental confounding, both of which are forms of omitted-variable bias.[35] As we have stressed, there is rare but powerful methodological leverage in our ability to hold alters constant across two panel waves. Yet the human propensity toward homophily could still artificially inflate the coefficients. Egos may tend to select alters who share with them a certain trait for which we do not control. If so, *and* if the presence of this trait is correlated with individual-level *changes* in voter preferences between the campaign and election waves, then our main coefficients would be inflated by latent homophily.[36] By way of example, imagine that Elena names her husband Adão as a political-discussion partner, and imagine also that the two initially met through their shared careers

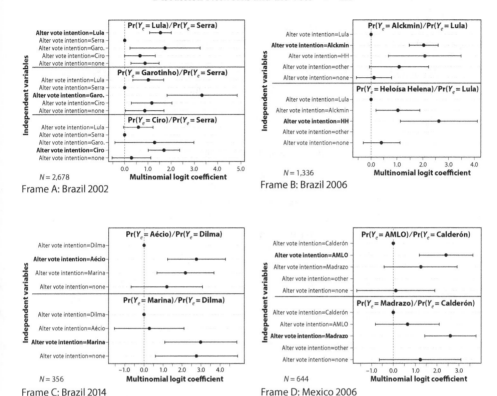

FIGURE 4.6 Ego's Vote Choice (Y_e) by Alter's Vote Intention at the Dyadic Level in Brazil and Mexico (Stable Alters Only): Coefficients from Four Multinomial Logit Models

Notes: Each marker is a multinomial logit coefficient with 95 percent confidence interval. Dependent variable for each model is *Ego vote choice. Alter vote intention* is measured at the campaign wave, although for this sample it is always equivalent to *Alter vote choice* (election wave). Models also contain two lags of the dependent variable and other independent variables. Tables A.6 through A.9 report the complete sets of coefficient estimates in numerical form.

Source: Two-City Panel, BEPS 2014, Mexico 2006 Panel.

in the business world, a variable we have not measured. Let us further assume that both were Ciro supporters in the middle of the campaign, but both later abandoned Ciro for Serra because of Ciro's gaffe about international investors—not because Elena and Adão influenced one another. Their parallel shifts increase the correlation between ego and alter preferences, but no peer effect has occurred.

Now consider the related problem of environmental confounding (also the "correlated" or "common shocks" problem). Because of homophily, egos tend to select alters (whether intentionally or not) who share with them a set of political intermediary sources, many of which we have not included in the models. If so, *and* if exposure to these different informational sources correlates with individual-level changes in voter preferences between the campaign and election waves, then our main coefficients are inflated by environmental confounding. Consider an alternative narrative for the dyad of Elena and Adão. If they both change from Ciro to Serra because they follow the endorsement of the same financial newspaper, then their parallel shift in preferences has increased the correlation between ego and alter preferences with no peer influence taking place.

We tackle these problems with multiple strategies. Most important, we conduct sensitivity analyses for each of the 18 coefficients with boldface labels in figures 4.5 and 4.6. Sensitivity analyses reveal how large the omitted-variable bias would need to be to shrink each of those coefficients, and thus our estimates of peer effects, to statistical insignificance.[37] Our results, reported in the online Sensitivity Analysis Appendix,* roundly confirm our argument that genuine social influence is taking place. For almost every one of these coefficients, it would take an omitted variable that has an almost impossibly high correlation with both the alter's vote-switching pattern *and* the ego's vote-switching pattern to reduce our estimate of genuine social influence to statistical zero.

As a second strategy, we estimate models on only dyads of friends, meaning we limit the sample to dyads in which the discussant is not related to the main respondent.[38] Two discussion partners living under the same roof are much more likely to have the same political information sources—a shared newspaper, magazine, or television—than two not living in the same home. In other words, the risks of environmental confounding are weaker for ego ↔ alter pairs who do not live together. The panel surveys do not directly measure whether egos and alters live together, but it is safe to assume that most non-related pairs do *not*. We report results of these friends-only models in the online Sensitivity Analysis Appendix. They too confirm the findings of the original models. Despite the smaller sample sizes, 16 of the 18 relevant coefficients remain statistically significant in these friends-only models.

We are not surprised that these last two sets of robustness checks confirm the results in figures 4.5 and 4.6 because there is great value in controlling for lagged vote preferences, as we do in these original models. In our setup, latent homophily is *not* the straightforward and common occurrence of an ego selecting, sometime before the campaign wave, a discussant who shares ego's vote intention. Rather, it refers to something that is much rarer since it is hard for actors to anticipate and intentionally choose: the selection of a discussant who later ends up with the same vote-*switching* pattern as ego owing to shared and

---

*The Sensitivity Analysis Appendix can be found online at https://dataverse.harvard.edu /dataverse/andybaker.

unmeasured individual-level traits. Also, environmental confounding only biases our estimates when a shared and unmeasured informational source invokes an identical vote-switching pattern in ego and alter. To the extent that information environments are the result of political predispositions such as vote intention and partisanship, the original models address these methodological challanges. Overall, our robustness checks confirm that these potential omitted-variable problems pose minimal threats to our inferences.

Social Influence in Runoff Elections

Our final exercise with dyadic data—one that also contains methodological advantages—asks whether vote choices in presidential runoffs are also socially informed. Since democratization in 1985, six of Brazil's eight presidential election winners have been determined in a second-round election contested by the top two vote winners in the first round. These runoff elections are thus expected and important parts of presidential selection in Brazil, although to date the first-round winner has won every second round. Runoffs provide methodological benefits that we exploit in this subsection, and we use them to show that second-round vote choices are also subject to peer influence.

The runoff scenario provides another means of measuring alters' preferences that are temporally prior to those of egos. The three weeks between the first and second rounds are, effectively, a battle between two candidates to attract voters whose first-round candidate did not survive to the runoff. In essence, these voters are forced to switch between the first and second round. We focus on this subset of voters in each election and consider whether they move toward the first-round vote choice of alters whose candidate *did* survive to the runoff. In Brazil 2002, for example, did first-round Ciro voters vote in the second round for the candidate (either Lula or Serra) who was better supported in their social networks?

We stay at the dyadic level. The dependent variable is *Ego runoff vote choice*, now measured (at the election wave) as a simple binary indicator. In keeping with our convention of treating incumbents as the baseline category, a second-round vote intention for the candidate of the incumbent party (Serra in 2002, Lula in 2006, Dilma in 2014) is scored a zero, and vote intention for the opposition (Lula in 2002, Alckmin in 2006, Aécio in 2014) is scored a one. The primary independent variables are $Alter.vote.intention_c$, meaning alter's vote intention at the campaign wave, and $Alter.vote.choice_e$, meaning alter's first-round vote choice.

We estimate three models, limiting the sample for each to main respondents who did *not* vote for either of the first-round's top two finishers. We are strictly interested in whether those voters who were forced to change candidates between rounds one and two (Ciro and Garotinho voters in 2002, Heloísa Helena voters in 2006, and Marina voters in 2014) moved toward the preferences of their discussants who were not forced to change. Again, the methodological advantages are vast compared to cross-sectional analyses of discussion effects.

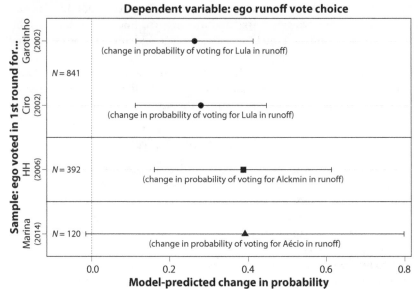

Dependent variable: ego runoff vote choice

FIGURE 4.7 Ego's Runoff Vote Choice by Alter's First-Round Vote Choice in Brazil: Predicted Changes in Probability from Three Models
Notes: Each marker is the model-predicted change in probability (with 95 percent confidence interval) of a main respondent voting for the opposition candidate in the runoff election. Dependent variable for each model is *Ego runoff vote choice*. Table A.10 reports the complete set of coefficient estimates in numerical form.
Source: Two-City Panel, BEPS 2014.

With this setup, selection of discussants for their political leanings is not a confound, since we are *by definition* estimating the effects of an initially disagreeing alter on an ego (e.g., the effect of an alter who voted for Lula or Serra in the first round on an ego who voted for Ciro in the first round). Similarly, alter preferences are, by definition, established prior to the ego preferences we are trying to explain. These models contain the same set of independent variables, including the campaign-wave measure of ego's first-round vote intention, as the models for figures 4.5 and 4.6.

Figure 4.7 summarizes the evidence from these three models by plotting predicted changes in the probability of vote choice in the runoffs. These changes in probabilities are generated under the assumption that alters had stable preferences in the campaign and election waves—that is, we change both *Alter .vote.intention$_c$* and *Alter.vote.choice$_e$* while holding other variables constant at their means. (To avoid cluttering the figure, we describe the results from changing only *Alter.vote.choice$_e$* in the text.)

In 2002 Garotinho-voting and Ciro-voting egos with an alter who had voted for Lula in the first round were about 30 points more likely to vote for Lula in the runoff than Garotinho-voting and Ciro-voting egos with an alter who had voted for Serra in the first round. In 2006 the gap was nearly 40 percentage points. First-round Heloísa Helena voters tended to vote in the runoff for the candidate preferred by their Lula- or Alckmin-voting discussant in the first round. (When alters are unstable, we still find a statistically significant effect of 20 percentage points.) Finally, we find for 2014 that the discussant effect on the runoff vote choices among first-round Marina voters is substantively large—nearly 40 percentage points—although the sample size is small and the estimated effect is not quite statistically significant at the 95 percent level. (When alters are unstable, we do find a statistically significant effect of 53 percentage points.)[39] To summarize, Brazilian runoff vote choices, like first-round vote choices, are socially informed.

SOCIALLY INFORMED PREFERENCES

These statistical results demonstrate that the election-day choices of Brazilian and Mexican voters are subject to a process of peer influence that occurs during the campaign. For this reason, we consider their ultimate vote choices to be socially informed preferences. For some voters, this process provides social reinforcement, entrenching them in their pre-campaign leanings. For others, it provides social persuasion, convincing them to change their minds. The next subsection offers complementary evidence of the social-influence process we have established, and the subsequent subsection illuminates the mechanism of social influence.

Complementary Evidence

Qualitative data provide vivid examples of the peer-influence process taking place in Brazil. Some individuals admit to being influenced by others:

> INTERVIEWER: And your neighbor. When you conversed with him about politics, did you agree or disagree?
> RESPONDENT: Look, in those elections for president, we agreed. Just like I said. My family and he and some friends influenced me. . . . He's a hardcore *petista*.[TA4.2]

> INTERVIEWER: Do you think your family influences you a lot when it comes time to vote?
> RESPONDENT: Look, in the last elections they did influence me.[TA4.3]

Others were aware that they themselves were persuasive peers—not as vertical intermediaries through processes of canvassing or brokerage, but through their informal social exchanges:

> INTERVIEWER: Did you have a friend who tried to convince you to vote a certain way? . . .
> RESPONDENT: It was I who tried to convince others.
> INTERVIEWER: Okay. You tried to convince others?
> RESPONDENT: I try and I succeed, you see. I succeed with many people.
> INTERVIEWER: Really? What do you say? How do you talk? What are your arguments?
> RESPONDENT: I'm not one to argue, you know? I go slowly.
> INTERVIEWER: You go ahead and get it, huh?
> RESPONDENT: Yep.
> INTERVIEWER: And you change a lot of minds.
> RESPONDENT: I do.[TA4.4]

> INTERVIEWER: And when you spoke with Pedro, did you have similar opinions? Did you agree or disagree?
> RESPONDENT: He changed. Before, he was very conflicted in his thinking. Today, he thinks the same as me.
> INTERVIEWER: Did you try to convince him?
> RESPONDENT: In a manner of speaking.[TA4.5]

Many respondents said that their family members voted jointly for the same candidate, but only after a process of deliberation throughout the campaign. Some families approach the election as a collective and seek to arrive at a *voto unido*, a united vote:

> My daughter influences me. In my family, we all vote for the same person. [*A família vota unida*].[TA4.6]

> We converse together at home and decide who we're going to vote for. . . . At home, we vote for the same person. [. . . *a gente vota junto*].[TA4.7]

> My wife and I talked. I voted for the person *we* thought was best. [emphasis added][TA4.8]

> INTERVIEWER: In the middle of the year, you intended to vote for Ciro? . . . But then you decided to vote for Lula. Why did you change your mind?
> RESPONDENT: Look, I think it was mostly because of interference from my family. They [were all saying] "I'm going to vote for Lula. I'm going to vote for Lula. Vote for Lula."[TA4.9]

Another voter recognized the social-influence process within his marriage, although he pointed out that the *voto unido* emerged slowly over many years.

INTERVIEWER: Do you and your wife generally vote for the same candidate?

RESPONDENT: Yes. . . . She agrees [with me], yes. We talk a lot about this [politics]. Generally, we vote for the same candidates. . . . Before, not so much. But it's a lot of years together, you know? Married for more than 30 years. We've ended up thinking in a very similar way, even though we used to disagree.[TA4.10]

Direct evidence of a very different flavor is found in survey data on who fills out voters' election-day crib sheets. To register their choices for the five or six offices in play, Brazilian voters must enter five to six different numbers, each of which has between two and five digits, into an electronic voting machine. Authorities thus encourage voters to take *colas eleitorais* to the voting booth. *Colas* are (perfectly legal) crib sheets containing candidates' numbers. In fact, an important part of campaigning and vertical intermediation in Brazil is for parties to distribute professionally printed *colas* with prefilled numbers. According to a 2002 nationwide survey, 74 percent of respondents used a *cola* and a quarter of these (16 percent of the electorate) said they used one filled out by someone else.[40] Because *colas* are distributed en masse by parties, is this evidence of vertical intermediation and top-down influence? Not necessarily. Two-thirds of those who used a *cola* filled out by someone else said that it had been filled out by a friend or family member, and a majority of these (55 percent) claimed that this person influenced their vote. (Recall this chapter's epigraph.)

The Informational Mechanisms of Social Influence

Network scholars categorize mechanisms of peer influence into two very broad types: normative and informational.[41] Normative influence occurs through a demonstrational or role-modeling effect, whereby individuals mimic the attitudes and behavior of others to achieve social approval. Discussion need not even occur, and the social pressure to conform is often implicit and self-imposed. Informational mechanisms of social influence, however, do involve an intentional exchange of relevant content through discussion. Informational mechanisms need not always be intentionally persuasive, but a prerequisite for informational social influence is that the content be biased and thus conducive to attitudinal and behavioral change or reinforcement.

The mechanism of peer influence in Brazil and Mexico is informational. Influence occurs through active and explicit discussions about politics, but influence is also informational in the sense that voters are seeking data and guidance from politically expert individuals. Reliance on social contacts, and especially more knowledgeable social contacts, to guide one toward a vote decision is a perfectly natural psychological response to the unease created by confusion and indecision: "whenever an individual is faced with uncertainty, he or she turns to others for information and validation. . . . it is the need to feel certainty or confidence in one's beliefs that drives social influence."[42] Uncertainty about politics runs high in any political system, but it runs especially high in new democracies and, as in Brazil, in highly fragmented party systems. Under this uncertainty, voters turn to trusted and relatively expert sources in their intimate social networks.

Our qualitative data show evidence that voters seek not just information from the political experts in their immediate social environments, as we showed in chapter 2, but also social influence. Consider the following quotes, which link the relative political expertise of a discussant directly to social influence:

My mom doesn't know anything about politics. I tell her how to vote. [TA4.11]

INTERVIEWER: Do you and your husband vote for the same person?
RESPONDENT: You could say so, yes. He helps me decide . . . And, as I said, I don't understand a lot. I'm not that engaged. He knows a lot . . . so he helps. And there's not much of an alternative, you know? Conversations with friends over politics are very superficial . . . At home it's different. When the news is on, we watch it together. Then I ask him, and he explains it. During these explanations, whoever is the good candidate and whoever is the bad candidate emerges. And that's how it's decided how I vote. We haven't decided yet [in this election] . . . But when we decide, we will certainly vote for the same candidate.[TA4.12]

INTERVIEWER: How do you learn about the candidates?
RESPONDENT: My friends usually talk about politics around election time. Before that, they don't say much of anything. In this period, they bring information, share things, converse in the gatherings we have each week. From there, I begin to have an idea about who is viable and who isn't. After sorting through it, I look for them on the internet. My family helps also.[TA4.13]

INTERVIEWER: In these conversations when you discuss politics with [your colleague], do you have identical opinions or were they different opinions?
RESPONDENT: No. Given our consensus, they are the same ideas. We discuss and arrive at a consensus.
INTERVIEWER: Is he a person who has a lot of knowledge about politics?
RESPONDENT: A lot. A lot.[TA4.14]

As further evidence, the 2002 nationwide survey shows that relying on social contacts to fill out one's *cola eleitoral* is a strategy of the less educated. The least educated were far more likely than the most educated (by 35 percentage points) to defer to someone else in this way.[43]

SOCIALLY INFORMED PREFERENCES
AND AGGREGATE OUTCOMES

Thus far, this chapter has compiled a set of micro-level findings on the formation of socially informed preferences during Brazilian and Mexican election campaigns. In this section we demonstrate how these findings explain important macro-political outcomes, namely, who wins elections and how countries differ in their degrees of campaign volatility. In other words, we first aggregate to the candidate level and then to the country level. In doing so, we elaborate further on the paradox of aggregate-level medium-term stability amidst individual-level change.

Findings at the Candidate Level

The results (in figures 4.3 and 4.6) on the effects of alters' campaign-wave intentions aggregate to the candidate level in the following way: a candidate whose campaign-wave supporters are embedded in networks with a relatively high rate of disagreement is less likely to retain those supporters through election day than a candidate whose supporters are embedded in networks with low rates of disagreement. To test this, we score the 13 major-party candidates (counting Lula twice for 2002 and 2006) across the four election cases on two variables. The dependent variable, *Lost supporters*, is the percentage of a candidate's campaign-wave supporters who did not vote for that candidate on election day—that is, the number of a candidate's campaign-wave supporters that he or she lost by election day as a share of her/his campaign-wave supporters.[44] The independent variable, *Mean disagreement in the networks of supporters*, is the aggregation (to the candidate level) of the campaign-wave measure of (individual-level) network disagreement, meaning the average level of disagreement that a candidate's supporters had in their networks at the time of the campaign wave.

This aggregated measure of disagreement varies dramatically by candidates and, in support of the hypothesis, is highly correlated with candidates' abilities to hold on to their campaign-wave supporters. Candidates whose mid-campaign supporters face a relatively high rate of disagreement are more likely to lose them before election day, while candidates whose mid-campaign supporters face high rates of agreement and reinforcement are more likely to retain them. The bivariate correlation between the two variables, shown in the figure 4.8 scatterplot, is exceedingly high at +0.79. Candidates whose campaign-wave supporters faced a relatively low rate of disagreement—those plotted on the left-hand side of the graph—were much more likely to hang on to these supporters over the duration of the campaign. This includes all four (first-round) winners: Lula 2002, Lula 2006, Dilma 2014, and Calderón 2006. In compari-

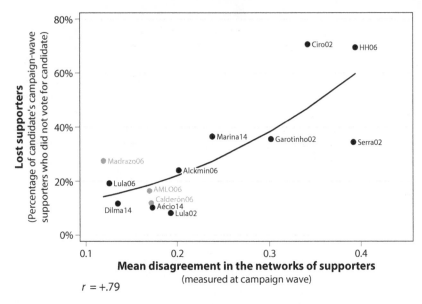

FIGURE 4.8 Rates of Preference Change by Network Disagreement at the Candidate Level in Brazil 2002, 2006, 2014, and Mexico 2006
Notes: Line is predicted values from a quadratic regression. Brazilian candidates are in black, and Mexican candidates are in gray.
Source: Two-City Panel, BEPS 2014, Mexico 2006 Panel.

son, several candidates faced a relatively high rate of disagreement in their networks—one-quarter appears to be a natural cutoff between low and high scorers on this variable. These candidates were far more likely to lose a high share of their supporters to another candidate by election day; the dependent variable increases as rates of disagreement grow. Candidates in Brazil who began *and* ended the campaign in third (Garotinho in 2002, Heloísa Helena in 2006, Marina 2014) or fourth place (Ciro in 2002) constitute all but one of these cases.

These cases include all three candidates who experienced polling collapses after surging to ephemeral peaks in the middle of campaigns (Ciro, Heloísa Helena, and Marina). A brief discussion of each case illustrates how social influence makes it difficult for outsiders—meaning candidates who begin the campaign in third place or worse—to sustain their polling surges. The discussion also illuminates the paradox of aggregate-level stability amidst individual-level change.

Recall first the case that opened the chapter, the Ciro fad of 2002. According to the Two-City Panel, only 29 percent of Ciro's campaign-wave supporters cast a ballot for him in October, whereas 92 percent of Lula's campaign-wave supporters did so. The rate of disagreement in the networks of Ciro supporters at his peak was nearly twice as high (0.34) as was disagreement in the networks of Lula supporters (0.19), so the social architecture around Ciro supporters made him vulnerable to a collapse. One obvious reason is that, owing to Lula's lead in the polls, there were fewer Ciro supporters than Lula supporters to be had as discussion partners. In other words, the pools of potential discussants in the social environments of Ciro supporters contained more disagreement than the pools in the social environments of Lula supporters. This speaks to the supply of preferences in a voter's social environment. Recall from figure 1.3 that the distribution of preferences in ego's surrounding environment shapes the distribution of opinions among the alters that ego ultimately has. (Chapters 5 and 6 illustrate this point empirically.) Similarly, the Serra outlier in figure 4.8 is driven by his deep unpopularity in one of the two cities. His supporters in Juiz de Fora were few and far between—that is, in low supply—and thus hard to find as discussion partners.

The polling gap between Ciro and Lula, however, was not *that* great at the time of Ciro's peak—just 10 percentage points. In other words, the network disagreement that Ciro's campaign-wave supporters faced was high by the standards of someone polling that well, and the raw math of the supply of preferences in one's social environment cannot entirely account for the 1.6 standard deviation difference in network disagreement between Ciro and Lula supporters. The same applies to Heloísa Helena and Marina. In the 2006 campaign wave, Heloísa Helena was only 10 points behind Alckmin in the two-city polling, yet we find a 20-point gap (more than two standard deviations) in the rate of disagreement in their supporters' respective networks. Similarly, Marina was polling *ahead* of Aécio and just behind Dilma at the time of the 2014 campaign waves, but Marina's supporters faced substantially *more* disagreement in their networks than did supporters of the other two candidates.* Ultimately, the partial correlation between the two variables in figure 4.8 falls by just 7 points (to +0.72) when accounting for the supply of disagreeing potential discussants in the electorate, which we measure as the complement of each candidate's campaign-wave share of vote intentions. Something more than the supply of preferences in the social environment is at play.

Instead, supporters of outsider candidates face more disagreement in their discussion networks because, in deferring to more politically knowledgeable conversation partners, they are also influenced by voters with more stable preferences—voters who are less likely to be lured by the hype of an outsider's rise and who stand by their pre-campaign vote intentions.[45] Formal theoretical results on networked communities illustrate the importance of fixed agents or inflexibles, meaning local opinion leaders who are themselves immune to

*Among undecided campaign-wave respondents, moreover, 75 percent of their opinionated discussants supported one of the two major-party candidates while just 25 percent supported Marina, even though Marina was polling close to 40 percent.

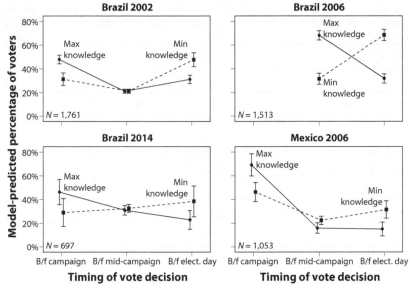

Frame A: Timing of Vote Decision: Predicted Percentages from Four Ordered Logit Models

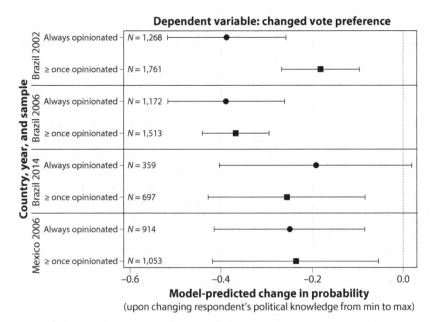

Frame B: Changed Vote Preference: Predicted Changes in Probability from Eight Binary Logit Models

peer effects but who have outsized influence on others.[46] This fits psychological evidence on the confidence heuristic; individuals who are the most committed to their views tend to wield the most persuasive influence on others.[47] Columbia school studies also found that voters who were undecided during much of the campaign (crystallizers) gravitated toward the preferences of individuals in their social group who expressed a stable opinion early in the campaign.[48]

Figure 4.9 shows that political knowledge increases preference stability. Frame A depicts *Timing of vote decision* as a function of political knowledge. We designate respondents who expressed the same vote intention/choice in the pre-campaign, campaign, and election panel waves (e.g., Lula, Lula, Lula) as having decided (1) "before the campaign." At the opposite extreme, respondents whose campaign-wave intentions do not match their election-wave vote choices (Lula, Ciro, Lula *or* Lula, don't know, Lula) are designated as deciding (3) "before election day." A middle category, (2) "before mid-campaign," picks up respondents whose final two expressed preferences (don't know, Lula, Lula *or* Garotinho, Lula, Lula) match one another but not the first. We regress this variable on respondent's *Political knowledge*, estimating one regression per election case. Frame A reports model-predicted values, specifically the predicted distributions of timing of decision for two groups: the highly knowledgeable ("Max knowledge") and the highly uninformed ("Min knowledge").

In all four election cases, knowledgeable voters decided well before uninformed ones. In Brazil 2002, for example, about 50 percent of highly knowledgeable voters had an unwavering commitment in place months before the campaign's onset, whereas only about 30 percent of uninformed voters had one ($p < .001$). The model predicts that half of uninformed voters decided in the campaign's final six weeks, while less than a third of highly knowledgeable ones did so. This pattern is repeated in the other three cases, as the coefficient on political knowledge is statistically significant for all four elections. (See table A.11.)

Frame B takes a closely related approach. The underlying models have *Changed vote preference* as a binary dependent variable, and each point estimate in the figure is the difference between the most knowledgeable and the least knowledgeable citizens in their probability of changing vote preference

---

FIGURE 4.9 Preference Stability by Degree of Political Knowledge in Brazil and Mexico: Model Predictions

Notes: Each marker in frame A is the model-predicted percentage (with 95 percent confidence interval) of making one's vote decision at the designated time. Each marker in frame B is a predicted change in the probability (with 95 percent confidence interval) of changing one's vote preference. "≥ once opinionated" denotes "at least once opinionated." Table A.11 reports the complete sets of coefficient estimates in numerical form.

Source: Two-City Panel, BEPS 2014, Mexico 2006 Panel.

during the campaign. In this instance, we treat any preference change over the three different panel waves (pre-campaign, campaign, and election wave) as a change.[49] In the interest of not equating changes from nonopinionation to opinionation with changes across party lines, the figure provides results (as in chapter 3) for two different definitions of switching. For both sets of results, the only voters scored as non-switchers are those who named the same candidate in all three waves. From there, whom we tally as switchers varies across the two sets of results. The "Always opinionated" results (circle markers) use only respondents who are opinionated in all three waves, so switchers are those who changed across party lines. The "≥ once opinionated" designation is short for voters[50] who are "at least once opinionated," so switchers for this set of results (squares) are those who either crossed party lines or were undecided at least once.[51]

Non-switchers are more politically knowledgeable than switchers in every case in frame B of figure 4.9. The relationship is not simply induced by the presence of more indecision among the politically uninformed, as the effect of knowledge is typically *larger* for the always-opinionated samples. Moreover, the relationships are strong ones. The changes in probability are, with one exception, between 20 and 40 percentage points. These are huge effects, especially when we recall that the overall rates of switching are between 20 and 40 percent. In other words, moving from no knowledge to high knowledge reduces the probability of switching by at least half.

This evidence, it is worth adding, is a final nail in the coffin of the media-exposure hypothesis. The most politically knowledgeable voters tend to be the most exposed to political news from the mass media, yet they are the *least* likely to switch. Media content matters, but whether it induces preference change depends not on direct exposure to the media source but rather on the way the content plays in voters' social networks.

Again, consider the Ciro collapse of 2002. When campaign commercials and news reporting turned decidedly against him at his mid-campaign peak, it was not the most media-exposed Ciro supporters who abandoned him. To some extent, it was quite the contrary, as illustrated in figure 4.10. The point estimates are average rates of media exposure among three groups: Ciro supporters early in the campaign wave (August 5 to 13), Ciro supporters late in the campaign wave (August 14 to 31), and the Ciro campaign-wave supporters who stuck with him through election day (Ciro voters). The figure reports each group's average level of exposure (in standard deviations) to three different types of media: television news (*TV news exposure*), HEG (*HEG exposure*), and all political news (*Media exposure*). The campaign-wave sample is split into early and late because, usefully, the Ciro implosion unfolded as the survey was in the field; his support was far lower late in this wave than early in the wave.[52]

If the most media-exposed individuals were the ones who abandoned Ciro, then the means should shift leftward through time. Clearly, this is not the case. If anything, the supporters that Ciro successfully held had a *higher* level of ex-

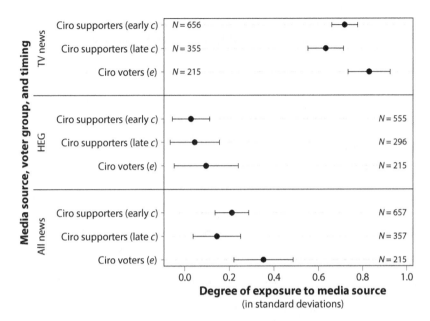

FIGURE 4.10 The Degree of Exposure to Media among Ciro Supporters and Ciro Voters by Source and Timing in Brazil 2002
Notes: Each marker is an observed mean with 95 percent confidence intervals. Variables used to define media source are (from top to bottom) *TV news exposure, HEG exposure,* and *Media exposure.* The sample of Ciro voters is limited to those who were Ciro supporters in the campaign wave. *c* = campaign, *e* = election. *Source:* Two-City Panel.

posure to TV and overall news than his full set of campaign-wave supporters. Much of the negativity about Ciro spread horizontally through social networks, reaching and persuading individuals who were not heavy consumers of media.

The following exchange from our in-depth interviews is illustrative. The respondent is a campaign-wave Ciro supporter who was ultimately influenced by stable Lula voters from her social milieu.

INTERVIEWER: What happened to make you lose faith in Ciro?
RESPONDENT: Mostly conversations with my family. We talked about how Lula had better proposals, stuff like that. . . .
INTERVIEWER: And your family also followed your trajectory? They also supported Roseana, and then Ciro, and then ended up voting for Lula?
RESPONDENT: No. They went straight with Lula.
INTERVIEWER: From the beginning?
RESPONDENT: From the beginning.
INTERVIEWER: Why weren't you with him in the beginning?

RESPONDENT: I don't know. It was the first year that I ever voted, you
  know? . . . I experimented with different things and saw that Lula was
  better . . . But [my family] didn't force me to vote for him. . . .
INTERVIEWER: Say a little about those conversations [with your family].
  When did they happen: meals, parties, gatherings?
RESPONDENT: They were more during the political hour [HEG] during the
  election campaign. We would watch news.
INTERVIEWER: You would get together to watch television and watch the
  [HEG]?
RESPONDENT: That's right.[TA4.15]

In short, the propensity to defect from Ciro was not a function of *direct* exposure to the negative media narrative. Rather, it was a function of exposure
to conversation partners who were supporting another candidate and who
thereby passed along this negativity. Ciro supporters were particularly susceptible to this type of influence because they faced relatively high rates of
political disagreement in their networks. The reason for this rests in this subsection's broader point. When outsider candidates are riding high in the polls,
they face an underlying vulnerability in the social architecture of their support: the most influential voters in horizontal social networks are unlikely to
support outsiders because these voters tend to have stable preferences. They
support the candidates who polled well in the pre-campaign period.[53] As a
result, voter movement toward socially informed preferences creates the paradox of short-term individual-level instability but medium-term aggregate
stability.

Findings at the Country Level

Our candidate-level findings also inform a brief conclusion about cross-national
differences in rates of switching and voter volatility. Recall from chapter 3 (figure 3.1) that Mexico has lower rates of cross-party switching during campaigns than Brazil. Figure 4.8 also shows that Mexican voters are embedded
in networks with less disagreement than Brazilian voters. Of the five candidates whose supporters faced the lowest rates of political disagreement, three
are the Mexican candidates from 2006. Overall, Mexican voters are slightly
more stable during campaigns because they are less likely to be embedded in
social contexts that countervail their opinions.

The fact that Mexico has higher rates of mass partisanship than Brazil contributes to this cross-national difference—partisans are less volatile during
campaigns. The difference remains, nevertheless, even after we account for rates
of mass partisanship.[54] The residual difference can be partially explained by
the fact that Mexicans tend to reside in more politically homogeneous micro-

environments. Mexico's party system and political preferences are rooted in stable constituencies and sociological divides, particularly along lines of class, religion, urbanicity, skin color, and region. In turn, "social homogeneity breeds political homogeneity."[55] Perhaps the exception that supports this rule is that the other two candidates whose supporters faced extremely low rates of disagreement were Lula in 2006 and Dilma in 2014, both *petista* presidential candidates in elections that took place *after* the emergence of a sharp regional cleavage between 2002 and 2006. (We document this political geography in greater detail in chapter 6.) In summary, social influence explains important cross-national differences in the amount of preference volatility among voters.

CONCLUSION

For our four election cases, the stability of political preferences during campaigns is a product of their social reinforcement. Socially reinforced preferences tend to be stable, while countervailed preferences tend to be volatile. This has implications at multiple levels of analysis. Voters who face political disagreement from at least one of their peers during a campaign are more likely to switch than voters who do not face disagreement. As a result, a candidate whose supporters confront lots of political disagreement in their mid-campaign networks is likely to experience a painful fall to earth, just as Ciro, Heloísa Helena, and Marina did in Brazil's roller-coaster contests.

In this atmosphere of thriving peer influences, many voters follow the lead of political experts in their social networks. This is not a silent process of imitating the behavior of a role model, nor is it a process in which the voter responds to quiet social pressure applied by intimate alters. Instead, voters seek out information and advice from those with greater political expertise. In so doing, many are persuaded by someone who decided *before* the campaign began, a fact that carries aggregate-level implications. By election day, the opinions of voters who supported pre-campaign leaders tend to hold sway in the electorate, and the distribution of votes actually cast bears close resemblance to the distribution of vote intentions in the pre-campaign period, even though a large share of voters switch across party lines during the campaign.

This process provides a modicum of aggregate stability between the campaign's start and its finish in the moderately entrenched party systems of Brazil and Mexico. Because direct media exposure itself does little to induce preference change, voters are not aimlessly shifting their choices with each mass-mediated campaign event. Successful candidates, as a result, are not those who had the best final debate or received the most favorable coverage in the campaign's closing weeks. Social influence does not result in a process whereby the best campaigner, regardless of party size, emerges victorious. To be sure, true party outsiders have won presidential elections in both countries, as evidenced by the victorious Fernando Collor do Mello (1989), Jair Bolsonaro (2018), and AMLO (2018) candidacies. None of these candidates, however, *began* their respective campaigns as also-rans. In fact, all began with polling leads.

This chapter's micro- and macro-level findings have implications for meso levels of analysis, meaning levels that fall in between. In particular, scholars of Latin American politics have studied the role of neighborhoods, cities, and even larger regional areas in shaping mass preferences and election outcomes. Peer influence is important for understanding why political preferences cluster within these geographic agglomerations. These meso levels exert their influence on the choices of voters by creating social environments within which voters exercise a constrained choice of discussants. The next two chapters consider the impact of neighborhood (chapter 5) and region (chapter 6) on voting decisions.

5

Neighborhoods and Cities as Arenas of Social Influence

Interviewer: "Where do you discuss politics the most? At work? At home? In the neighborhood?"
Brazilian respondent: "At the bar, here in the neighborhood. . . ."
Interviewer: "So when you chat [at the bar], this topic comes up?"
Respondent: "It almost always comes up."[TA5.1]

—*Brazilian voter (2004)*

Interviewer: "Do you converse [about politics] a little with neighbors?"
Brazilian respondent: "Yes. Yes."
Interviewer: "Is there one in particular?"
Respondent: "I've got a business, you know? We have a small grocery store."
Interviewer: "So when people come into the store, sometimes the topic comes up? Is that it?"
Respondent: "Yes. Sometimes." [TA5.2]

—*Brazilian voter (2004)*

Neighborhoods are an important part of life in Brazil's cities. Urban neighborhoods have a clear legal existence with circumscribed borders. They are well-labeled on standard municipal maps (not to mention many street signs), and they are even a required part of postal mailing addresses. Most urban neighborhoods in Brazil also have a tangible organizational presence embodied in the neighborhood association. Neighborhoods are a major source of friendships and acquaintances, and many neighborhoods feature gathering places, as illustrated in the epigraphs, that provide arenas for discussion of important matters.

Because neighborhoods are so important, scholars of Brazilian politics have produced rich portrayals of their roles in politics and elections.[1] These accounts focus on the clientelism that occurs at the neighborhood level in urban slums (*favelas*). Candidates for legislative and mayoral posts exchange promises of a neighborhood amenity or service in exchange for a neighborhood leader's delivery of residents' votes. Although these studies are compelling, most Brazilians do not live in *favelas*, and this kind of neighborhood-level clientelism is otherwise rare. Are neighborhoods thus irrelevant to voting behavior outside the poor urban neighborhoods where clientelism seemingly reigns?

This chapter demonstrates how neighborhoods can influence voters even in lieu of clientelistic linkage patterns. We argue that a neighborhood's political bias can exert a discernible effect on the voting decisions of its residents through the mechanism of informal discussion. Analyses of the Two-City Panel reveal that individuals speak frequently with neighborhood coresidents about politics, and these conversations assimilate residents into the neighborhood's partisan leaning during a campaign. For this type of effect to occur, however, the neighborhood must have a stable partisan leaning, and here the political character of the city matters. We document the presence of stable partisan leanings in the politically polarized city of Caxias do Sul (henceforth "Caxias") and the absence of stable leanings in the city of Juiz de Fora (JF). We then find neighborhood effects on vote choice in Caxias but not in JF. In Caxias, neighborhoods shape the supply of political leanings among potential discussants and, as a result, the actual distribution of candidate preferences in citizens' networks. In turn, these different network leanings nudge voters' preferences in different directions over the course of a campaign.

Beyond presenting findings on the mechanisms underlying the geography of vote choice in Latin America, this chapter fills an important gap in the broader research agenda on neighborhood effects. Within each city, the Two-City Panel randomly selected 22 neighborhoods and conducted about 100 first-wave interviews in each. This large N per neighborhood makes our inquiry unique in the realm of neighborhood-effects research, where the vast majority of studies in all disciplines have an N of 50 or fewer per neighborhood.[2] Moreover, our research design uniquely combines egocentric network measures with neighborhood-level measures. Many scholars of neighborhoods attribute neighborhood effects to interpersonal influences without ever measuring the nature of social contacts: "[a] limitation of neighborhood-effects research has been its lack of attention to measuring peer networks."[3]

We begin by depicting the legal, cultural, and social importance of the neighborhood unit in the day-to-day lives of Brazilians. Much, if not most, political discussion takes place among neighborhood coresidents. Then, after describing the nature of mass politics in the two cities, the chapter brings together these two units of analysis—city and neighborhood—to describe the political character of the neighborhoods in each municipality. Empirical analyses then demonstrate how social interactions channel neighborhood effects in Caxias do Sul but not in Juiz de Fora. In making this empirical case, we lay out a methodology to discern the degree to which the preferences in voters' spatial surroundings influence voters via horizontal intermediation, and we use this same methodology in the next chapter when we scale up our geographical focus from neighborhoods to states.

NEIGHBORHOODS AND VOTING IN BRAZIL

About 85 percent of Brazilians live in cities. In these urban areas, as in most Latin American cities, neighborhoods have clear legal boundaries and cultural orientations. In comparison, despite the large volume of sociological research on neighborhood effects in the US, scholars have long struggled to draw neighborhood boundaries, and critics have complained of a lack of "theoretically motivated definitions of neighborhood."[4] Some US researchers, for example, use zip codes as the relevant contexts, but zip codes average three to five square miles and are much larger—and surely more impersonal—than the typical Brazilian neighborhood.[5]

In addition, most urban neighborhoods in Brazil have a devoted neighborhood association, although the importance of these associations varies sharply across and within cities. At the very least, all neighborhood associations have a president who is expected to articulate neighborhood demands to bureaucrats and elected officials, but most associations far exceed this bare minimum. Many have a dedicated building, a sizable budget, and a staff that can exceed 20 people. In many instances, neighborhood associations provide crucial services, including the management of health clinics, public works projects, and preschool programs; the organization of community social events and self-help groups; and the representation of the neighborhood in participatory budgeting forums. More informally, neighborhood leaders are often expected to resolve disputes among residents and, where necessary, to maintain peace between police and drug gangs. Again, the contrast with the US is stark, where housing associations—where they do exist—serve mostly to establish and enforce deed restrictions.

Finally, Brazilian neighborhoods are meaningful because of residential stability and cohesion. Residential mobility is relatively low: "in Latin America, neighbors are not just anonymous faces. Families live in the same city and the same neighborhood for years, sometimes for generations. Thus, what happens in the local community, even in the largest cities, is part of the individual's immediate reality."[6] In the Two-City Panel, for example, 90 percent of residents had lived in the city for more than four years, and 77 percent had lived in their neighborhoods for four years or more. Because of residential stability, Brazilian neighborhoods have a relatively high degree of social capital and cohesion.[7]

Neighborhood Effects as Social Influence

Brazilian neighborhoods can also have a well-defined political relevance. Because of the weight they hold legally, organizationally, and culturally, neighborhoods can influence voting behavior. But how, precisely, might they do so? Merely showing a correlation between the political preferences of individuals and the aggregated preferences of their neighborhoods reveals little about the nature of neighborhood effects—or even that they truly exist. This simple approach would effectively leave the process of neighborhood influence up to an ill-defined "social telepathy."[8] For the Brazilian case, we argue that neighborhoods affect vote choice through peers: "neighborhood effects are forms of social interactions."[9] Neighborhoods, if they have a stable and clear partisan leaning, influence the distribution of candidate preferences held by conversation partners in voters' social networks, thereby shaping the persuasive content that voters encounter when they discuss politics. By influencing the political bias of information to which individuals are exposed via social communication, a neighborhood can assimilate voters toward the neighborhood's partisan leaning over the course of a campaign.[10]

In advancing this argument, we make an important conceptual distinction between two aspects of an individual's social context. "Social networks" are composed of the relatively small number of contacts that individuals themselves choose. Networks, the focus of the preceding chapter, are largely constructed at an individual's discretion, but this discretion occurs under environmentally imposed constraints. Neighborhoods are one of several broader "social environments" in which individuals and their networks are embedded.[11] An individual's social environments are the spatial agglomerations within which that individual engages in social interaction. Neighborhoods, along with cities, counties, states, regions, and even countries, are social environments that impose a structure, shaping the distribution of preferences among an individual's *potential* discussants. Our claim of neighborhood effects lies in the fact that neighborhoods influence the supply of different political preferences among potential contacts, and these differences in supply are reflected in egos' conversations and social networks.

Is it even plausible for social communication to be a mechanism of neighborhood influence? Scholars of US politics have found social influences among neighbors to be largely absent: "the causal effect of neighborhoods on individual voting and political opinions is quite small."[12] In Robert Huckfeldt and John Sprague's 1984 South Bend data, the average ego ↔ alter pair lived almost three miles apart, a far greater distance than that encompassed by standard neighborhood size.[13] More recently, Betsy Sinclair finds that the average US discussant lives more than *five hours* away from the main respondent.[14] Intimate ties among neighborhood residents are thus not the norm in the US, and they have not been the norm for decades.[15] Research in Great Britain has also found discussion among neighbors to be rare.[16]

Brazil is different. Most Brazilian neighborhoods feature a rich array of casual meeting places where conversations occur—open-air restaurants and bars, athletic fields, bus stops, community centers, health clinics, and the ubiquitous newsstands and taxi stands. As preliminary evidence, recall from chapter 2 (figure 2.2) that residents of our two Brazilian cities (and many other Latin American countries) discuss politics with neighbors more frequently than citizens of other world regions.

A deeper look at the Two-City Panel also shows that informal political discussion occurs with great frequency among neighborhood coresidents. Figure 5.1 provides estimates of the share of ego ↔ alter dyads that are characterized by neighborhood coresidency. During the discussant interviews, alters reported their neighborhood of residence, so we can observe how frequently they share a neighborhood with the egos who named them. To extrapolate coresidency figures from these interviewed discussants ($N = 2{,}729$) to *all* of the named discussants ($N = 11{,}351$), we use main respondents' reports of their *Relationship with discussant* (spouse, child, other relative, neighbor, work- or schoolmate, and other). For each relationship category, we impute the rate of coresidency gleaned from the interviewed discussants to all of the named discussants, whether they were interviewed or not.

In the pie chart, slices are shaded by relationship type. Within each type, solid slices represent our estimates of the proportion of named discussants who share a neighborhood with their main respondent, and slices with hatching are estimates of the proportion not sharing a neighborhood with their main respondent. Spouses and neighbors, by definition, live in the same neighborhood and are depicted as solid slices. The other categories (child, other relative, work- or schoolmate, and other) are bifurcated into their coresidency share and its complement (not coresidents). Children and other relatives are more likely than not to live in the same neighborhood (and surely often under the same roof), while a large minority of work- and schoolmates also share a neighborhood with the main respondent. In the end, we estimate that fully 64 percent[17] of dyads are composed of neighborhood coresidents.[18]

Family members are an important source of neighborhood coresidents, since many discussants live with their main respondents. Admittedly, neighborhood influences do not occur if individuals speak *only* to fellow household dwellers. For neighborhood political preferences to diffuse into a household, at least one household member must have a tie to a nonfamily member living nearby—otherwise the household is an isolated unit experiencing no outside influence. When this minimal condition is in place, family members can be a conduit of neighborhood influence.[19] To summarize, political discussion in these two Brazilian cities has a heavy spatial bias, as individuals who discuss politics with one another are likely to live in the same neighborhood.

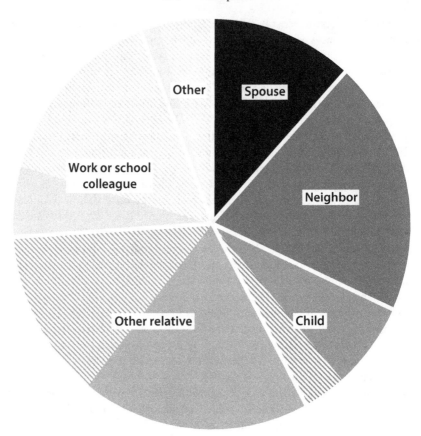

FIGURE 5.1 The Distribution of Discussants by Relationship Type and Neighborhood
Coresidency Status in Brazil 2002
Notes: Solid slices denote shares of discussants who are neighborhood coresidents
with their main respondents. Hatched slices denote shares of discussants who are not
neighborhood coresidents with their main respondents. Percentages for *Relationship
with discussant* are calculated from the $N=11,351$ discussants who were named by
main respondents. Percentages for coresident status are calculated from the $N=2,729$
discussants who were interviewed and asked for their neighborhood of residence.
Source: Two-City Panel, campaign wave.

Other Mechanisms of Neighborhood Influence

Horizontal interaction among coresidents is not the mechanism of neighborhood influence that has appeared most frequently in scholarship on Brazilian
elections. Instead, scholars have focused on the top-down influence of local
elites. This focus has particularly dominated thinking about neighborhood
politics in *favelas*. Robert Gay, for instance, called the relationship between

neighborhood association presidents and politicians in Rio de Janeiro's *favelas* "nakedly transactional."[20] Neighborhood presidents essentially auction off their political endorsements to the federal or state deputy candidate who makes the most generous commitment of club goods to the neighborhood. In exchange for a promise of state funds to pave a neighborhood road, for example, presidents will not only endorse legislative candidates, but they will also become their brokers or ward bosses (*cabos eleitorais*), campaigning on their behalf in the neighborhood. In other words, most scholarship related to neighborhood contexts in Brazil argues that neighborhoods influence voters' decisions through clientelistic exchange and, in turn, vertical communication from neighborhood leaders.

There are good reasons to think that in most Brazilian neighborhoods this is not how politics works. *Favela* politics is well researched in Brazil,[21] but the vast majority of Brazilians do *not* live in *favelas*. Furthermore, two-thirds of respondents to the Two-City Panel said they never discussed politics with neighborhood association leadership, and a trifling 4 percent said that a neighborhood leader tried to convince them to vote a certain way. When asked for whom their neighborhood president voted in the presidential contest, only 15 percent even hazarded a guess, and for lower-level elections (the elections stressed in earlier work), the tallies ranged from just 4 to 7 percent. In short, political influence is rarely exerted through neighborhood leaders in Caxias and JF.

Moreover, the vertical clientelistic influences documented in previous work are most relevant to elections for state and local candidates, not to the presidential elections on which we focus. Common citizens can rely on their neighborhood president's endorsement to navigate the hundreds of legislative candidates in Brazil's open-list electoral system. Some simply ask their neighborhood leader for whom they should vote, knowing that the leader has been negotiating.[22] This channel of influence exists in part because citizens have so little information from the media about state and local candidates. Information about presidential candidates, by contrast, is more widespread.

Our fieldwork in Caxias found that clientelism is rare. While many of the city's neighborhood leaders were indeed political activists, they were activists out of the relatively long-standing partisan commitments typical of the city and state.[23] In fact, in Caxias we occasionally observed active *anti*-clientelistic sentiment and behavior. One of us was interviewing a neighborhood-association vice president and partisan activist in the local headquarters of his party when a coresident walked in and asked for two bags of concrete mix to finish constructing his house. The gift, it was clearly implied, would secure his vote. Far from complying, the neighborhood leader admonished the requester, lectured him about the value of an unpurchased and "free" vote (*"o voto é livre"*), and told him to leave. With tail between legs, the resident did so. The most clientelistic behavior we heard about occurred when a neighborhood leader said a politician gave him a sewing machine—small potatoes in a relatively wealthy city—for the neighborhood mothers' group.[24]

Another potential mechanism of neighborhood influence, also top-down in orientation, lies in organizational agents of collective socialization.[25] This mechanism includes a diverse array of possibilities, such as party-contacting efforts, politically biased leadership in secondary associations, and candidate endorsements by religious clergy.[26] In the 2000 mayoral election in Caxias, for instance, the PT campaign worked to promote its candidate through evangelical churches in lower-class neighborhoods on the city's periphery.[27] In some Rio de Janeiro neighborhoods, even samba clubs endorse and campaign for candidates in their local areas.[28] In other words, parties' promotional efforts are almost never evenly distributed across neighborhoods.[29]

These vertical and institutional factors may contribute to cross-neighborhood differences in voting behavior in Brazil, and because of their more formal and structured natures, they have been a central focus of political intermediation research in Latin America.[30] Our empirical analyses measure and control for some of these factors, but such organizational influences have their limits, especially in a world teeming with horizontal social interactions. Participation in civil society organizations and party contacting pale in frequency and in intimacy when compared to informal conversations. The Two-City Panel asked respondents how frequently they participated in meetings of different *Secondary associations*, including sports clubs, labor unions, self-help groups, political parties, arts and cultural clubs, and new social movements. Only 31 percent of respondents attended at least one group meeting more than a few times per year, and only 15 percent of friends came from secondary associations.[31] As for political party activity, just 30 percent reported that a candidate or party contacted them in the weeks preceding the 2002 election.[32] In comparison, fully 58 percent said they got together to talk with friends at least once per week, and another 19 percent said they did so once or twice per month.[33] Horizontal intermediation thus occurs at a frequency and intimacy that are far greater than other possible channels of neighborhood influence.

MUNICIPAL CONTEXTS

In selecting the municipalities for the Two-City Panel, we sought midsized cities in order to make data collection and mastery of the cities manageable. The two cities also needed to possess similar socioeconomic traits. Caxias do Sul, in the southern state of Rio Grande do Sul, and Juiz de Fora, in Minas Gerais, made an ideal pair. The two cities were similar in population size in 2002, with 375,000 residents in Caxias and 470,000 in JF, and they had identical human development indexes (0.70). Both economies were heavily service-oriented, with formal employment in each dominated by shopping centers and a large university.[34] Each city had a lively industrial sector as well, led by a Mercedes-Benz factory in JF and a Marcopolo bus factory in Caxias. Distributions of income were virtually identical, with Gini coefficients around 0.40 in each.[35] In addition, their geographies of income disparity fit a familiar pattern in Brazil's midsized cities: a densely populated and wealthy neighborhood, called in both cases the Centro, was centrally located, and average incomes declined with distance from the center. The poorest neighborhoods, often called *bairros populares*, were on the peripheries.

While we did select cities that were matched socioeconomically, we wanted them to vary politically. Politics in Caxias was polarized and highly partisan, while politics in JF centered around personalism and pork-barrel exchanges. We discuss these different political characters in turn.

Politics and Voters in Caxias do Sul

Politics in the state of Rio Grande do Sul is known for its *bipartidismo*, or "two-partyism." The state polarizes between left and anti-left.[36] This contrasts with the personalism and extreme partisan fragmentation of much of the rest of the country.[37] As the state's second-largest city, Caxias is no exception to this polarization, although the label *bipartidismo* exaggerates the extent to which its competing political groups congregate in just two parties. In the 1990s and 2000s, a single party, the PT, did indeed dominate the city's left, heading electoral coalitions with smaller leftist parties like the PSB and the Communist Party of Brazil (PCdoB). Heir to a left militancy extending back to the 1945–64 democratic period, the PT in Caxias had at least three full-time employees at an active office, and the party won the mayorship in 1996 and 2000. The anti-left—a term more descriptive than "right" because opposition to the PT ranged from center to right—was more fragmented, with representation from the PMDB, PFL, PSDB, the Brazilian Progressive Party (PPB), the Brazilian Labor Party (PTB), and others. The center-right PMDB was far and away the largest party in this coalition. The PMDB leadership in Caxias (and in the wider state) was more programmatic than its pork-barreling national counterpart. It was also the only party other than the PT that could boast of a critical mass of partisan identifiers in the city's electorate, although by the late 1990s the PMDB was less embedded in the civil society of Caxias than the PT.[38]

Mass political identities and attitudes in Caxias around this time were a harbinger of the polarization that had emerged throughout Brazil by 2018. *Petistas* and adherents of the anti-left viewed each other with mutual antipathy, both politically and often personally. *Petistas* saw their opponents as shills for the domestic and international capitalist elite, an elite that sought to maintain and even reinforce the country's deep social inequalities. In return, the anti-left deemed *petistas*, many of whom were proud socialists, to be lacking in standards of achievement and hard work. An anecdote from one of our

TABLE 5.1.

Presidential Election Returns in Caxias do Sul in 2002

	First round	Second round
Lula	44.3%	51.2%
José Serra	39.7%	48.7%
Anthony Garotinho	9.6%	
Ciro Gomes	5.9%	

Source: Tribunal Superior Eleitoral.

interviews illustrates the depth of distaste: a right-leaning community leader hated the incumbent *petista* mayor so much that he described in vivid metaphoric detail how the mayor was enacting policies that were the moral equivalent of Nazi gassing operations.

In contrast to many polarized contexts (e.g., the present-day US), the opposing partisans in Caxias lived side by side in an urban area (although, as we document below, they were distributed unevenly by neighborhood). On election night in 2002, for example, hundreds of *petistas* celebrated Lula's victory in one corner of the city's central square, while in the opposite corner another crowd celebrated the gubernatorial triumph of Caxias's favorite son and PMDB candidate Germano Rigotto. The two camps were roughly equal in size in the city. In the decade before 2002, Caxias had seen a string of executive elections that were relatively balanced two-candidate contests between a *petista* and a candidate from the non-leftist camp. In 1998 Lula lost in the city to incumbent President Cardoso (PSDB but endorsed by the PMDB) by just 10 points, despite losing by 22 points nationwide.[39] In 2000 a bitter mayoral race between a PT and a PMDB candidate ended with the former winning by a mere 900 votes (0.4 percent).

Table 5.1 illustrates that this balance continued in the 2002 presidential election, our election case in this chapter. In the first round Serra ran behind Lula by a mere 4.6 points in Caxias despite finishing 23 points behind nationwide. In the second round Serra fell short by just 2.5 points despite losing again by 23 points nationwide. The city's two-partyism is also evident in how poorly the third- and fourth-place finishers performed relative to their first-round nationwide tallies. Both Garotinho and Ciro performed 50 percent worse in Caxias than they did nationwide. Finally, in our pre-campaign-wave polling for 2002, 23 percent of Caxias residents identified as *petistas* and 18 percent as *pemedebistas* (PMDB partisan).[40]

Low rates of ticket splitting (by Brazilian standards) are also evidence of meaningful partisanship and two-partyism in Caxias. According to our estimates, in 1998 just 22 percent of Caxias voters split their tickets across party lines between the presidential and gubernatorial elections.[41] Voters also tended to vote for the same party through time: 90 percent of Lula's 1998 voters cast their 2000 mayoral ballot for the PT's candidate (Pepe Vargas), while 66 percent of 1998 Cardoso voters did so for José Ivo Sartori of the PMDB.[42] Perhaps most telling is the fact that only 31 percent of Lula voters in 2002 caved to the allure of having a favorite son, Rigotto, in the gubernatorial mansion: the majority (65 percent) of Lula voters chose Rigotto's *petista* opponent (Tarso Genro).[43] Finally, in 2002 just 41 percent of Caxias voters split their tickets between the presidential and federal deputy levels,[44] a number far below Brazil's estimated rate of 68 percent.[45]

Politics and Voters in Juiz de Fora

Politics is much less partisan and more oriented around personalism in Juiz de Fora than in Caxias.[46] Parties, especially non-leftist parties, are mostly non-ideological shells and mere necessities of political ambition. At best they command passing loyalties from elites.

Consider the example of JF's favorite son, Itamar Franco. By 2002 politics in the city had revolved around the personage of its native-born Itamar for more than three decades. He had started in the city's local offices in the 1950s, eventually becoming mayor in the late 1960s, and from 1975 to 1990 he was a federal senator for Minas Gerais under the party banners of the Brazilian Democratic Movement (MDB) and then the Liberal Party (PL). Although Itamar long had center-left policy instincts, in 1989 he affiliated with the right-leaning National Renovation Party (PRN) to become its nominee for the vice presidency, a post he won on the ticket with Collor. A mere two years later he broke with the party to distance himself from its neoliberal economic policies and the soiled reputation of Collor, who resigned after impeachment late that year. Itamar assumed the presidency for just over two years (all of 1993 and 1994) but remained unaffiliated with any party during that time. In 1994 Itamar endorsed Cardoso (PSDB), his centrist former finance minister and the choice of the conservative establishment. Defeating Lula, Cardoso won the presidency handily, largely because of his role in ending, as finance minister, Brazil's perennial struggles with high inflation. In 1997, Itamar affiliated with the PMDB in a bid to seek that party's presidential nomination, but the party rebuffed him, choosing to endorse Cardoso for re-election. The PMDB instead nominated Itamar to run for governor of Minas Gerais, a post he won in 1998. By early 2002, he had been the state's governor for three years and made another bid to be the party's presidential nominee. Once again he was rebuffed, as the party endorsed Serra (PSDB). Itamar, who had publicly feuded with his former cabinet minister and erstwhile endorsee President Cardoso, heartily backed eventual winner

TABLE 5.2.
Presidential Election Returns in Juiz de Fora in 2002

	First round	Second round
Lula	63.9%	83.4%
José Serra	9.0%	16.6%
Anthony Garotinho	16.6%	
Ciro Gomes	9.6%	

Source: Tribunal Superior Eleitoral.

Lula. Itamar died as a federal senator in 2011 after yet again switching parties, this time to the PPS.

Itamar's journey through six different parties is just one example of how parties only weakly structure elite politics in JF. With such thin and ephemeral brands, parties fail to develop a base of stable mass partisans.[47] Evidence abounds that partisanship was less stable and meaningful in JF than in Caxias. After voting heavily for the PMDB in the 1998 gubernatorial election and in the 2000 mayoral election,[48] JF residents overwhelmingly ignored the PMDB's endorsement of Serra in 2002 and instead embraced Lula. Table 5.2 shows that Lula won the city in a landslide, outperforming his national tally by 18 points, while Serra finished fourth, 14 points behind his own national tally. These results contrast clearly with the left/anti-left polarization in Caxias.

Although table 5.2 seems to paint JF as a bastion of committed ideological leftism and *petismo*, this was not the case. Just eight years earlier, Lula underperformed his national tally in JF, partly because his victorious opponent, Cardoso, was the heir apparent and endorsee of Itamar himself, then the term-limited incumbent president. Compared to the PT in Caxias, the PT in JF was less militant and more conservative, as the party had no permanent structure and depended on its elected city councillors to organize party activities. The city's larger than average—although far from militant—industrial working class and university-affiliated population probably contributed to Lula's success, but, as we show below, voting preferences are about much more than these structural factors.

The PT's weakness despite Lula's strength and JF's personalism are further demonstrated by its high rates of ticket splitting. In the 1998 gubernatorial election, for example, just 12 percent of the city's voters chose the PT candidate (Patrus Ananias de Souza) despite Lula's 44 percent tally in the city that same year. In fact, the vast majority (78 percent) voted for Itamar himself in the 1998 gubernatorial race. In other words, in contrast to Caxias, most Lula voters (90 percent according to the Two-City Panel) split their tickets by voting for their favorite son instead of the *petista*. In total, 62 percent of JF residents split

TABLE 5.3.
The Distribution of Partisanship in Juiz de Fora and Caxias do Sul in 2002

	Juiz de Fora		Caxias do Sul	
	March 2002: *pc* wave	October 2002: *e* wave	March 2002: *pc* wave	October 2002: *e* wave
PMDB	15.5%	5.3%	18.0%	15.3%
PT	23.8%	40.3%	23.1%	24.3%
Other	9.1%	7.6%	8.5%	6.7%
Nonpartisan	51.6%	46.8%	50.4%	53.7%
Total	100%	100%	100%	100%
N	2,363	2,514	2,293	2,485

Notes: Entries are column percentages. Calculations are based on repeated measures of *Partisanship. pc* = pre-campaign. *e* = election. *e* wave samples are larger because fresh respondents were added in both the campaign and election waves.
Source: Two-City Panel.

their tickets between those two offices in that year, three times our estimate for Caxias. Similarly, in the election for JF's mayor just two years later, the PT candidate (Agostinho César Valente) received a mere 6 percent of the vote. Finally, rates of split-ticket voting between the presidential and federal deputy levels in JF in 2002 were, at 59 percent, closer to the national average of 68 percent and nearly 50 percent higher than in Caxias. In essence, the city's strong support for Lula in 2002 was about Lula, not Lula's PT.

Mass Partisanship in the Two Cities

Our own polling on *Partisanship* from 2002 confirms that political identities differed sharply between the two cities. A naive view of our pre-campaign results in March of 2002, reported in table 5.3, would suggest a striking degree of similarity between the two cities. Rates of both PMDB and PT partisanship were roughly the same across the two. After the campaign, however, the configurations diverged sharply. In JF the early adherents of Itamar's PMDB abandoned the party en masse, as its ranks fell by two-thirds over the course of just six months. Meanwhile, the number of *petistas* grew by two-thirds to a whopping 40 percent of the city, a clear bandwagon effect for Lula.[49] Rather than following the party's endorsement and voting for Serra, 65 percent of pre-campaign *pemedebistas* actually voted for Lula, and just 9 percent voted for Serra! *Pemedebismo* was merely a passing fad that did not serve as an unmoved mover structuring voting behavior in JF. By comparison, in Caxias percentages

TABLE 5.4.
Stability and Change in Partisanship in Juiz de Fora and Caxias do Sul in 2002

	pc wave / *e* wave	PMDB	PT	Other	Non-partisan
Juiz de Fora	PMDB	22.8%	0.7%	4.2%	1.9%
	PT	31.9%	82.8%	26.8%	26.7%
	Other	7.2%	3.3%	31.8%	6.0%
	Nonpartisan	38.1%	13.2%	37.1%	65.4%
	Total	100%	100%	100%	100%
Caxias do Sul	PMDB	59.4%	2.1%	16.1%	9.7%
	PT	6.6%	72.6%	7.4%	10.0%
	Other	4.8%	2.7%	37.7%	4.8%
	Nonpartisan	29.3%	22.7%	38.8%	75.7%
	Total	100%	100%	100%	100%

Notes: Entries are column percentages, meaning the percentage of the pre-campaign-wave category that falls into the election-wave category. Calculations are based on repeated measures of *Partisanship*. Shaded cells are those corresponding to no change in partisanship. *pc* = pre-campaign. *e* = election.
N = 1,704 in JF. *N* = 1,537 in Caxias.
Source: Two-City Panel, tables 1 and 2 in Baker et al. (2016).

remained stable, as the rate of *pemedebismo* never experienced the collapse it did in JF.

Table 5.4 confirms the hunches derived from these aggregates by comparing individual-level rates of partisan change between the pre-campaign and election waves. Entries are column percentages, so each column is the election-wave distribution of partisanship by pre-campaign-wave category. The cells on the shaded diagonals correspond to stable partisans or stable nonpartisans, and those on the off-diagonal cells correspond to switchers.

The most revealing entries are the top two in the first column in JF. Stated simply, by election day more pre-campaign *pemedebistas* were *petistas* (31.9 percent) than *pemedebistas* (22.8 percent)! Moreover, 26.8 percent of other party identifiers and 26.7 percent of those claiming no party identification in the pre-campaign wave rallied to the PT shortly after election day. In other words, there was a strong PT bandwagon effect in JF. By contrast, no similar pattern is evident in Caxias. *Pemedebismo* was much more stable (59.4 percent), with few *pemedebistas* jumping on the PT bandwagon. *Petismo* was ostensibly more stable in JF (82.8 percent compared to 72.6 percent), but this is merely a further reflection of the Lula bandwagon effect—Lula kept pre-campaign *petistas* in JF on his bandwagon.[50]

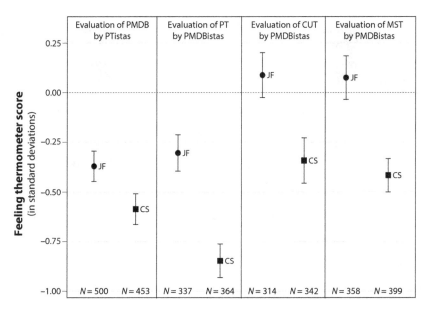

FIGURE 5.2 Feeling Thermometer Scores for the Opposing Party and for Two Leftist Movements by City in Brazil 2002

Notes: Each marker is an observed mean of an adjusted feeling thermometer score with 95 percent confidence interval. Respondent feeling thermometer scores are first adjusted for the response-set problem, meaning their original raw score is subtracted from the average score they gave to all parties/groups. The resulting variable is then standardized. "JF" denotes Juiz de Fora respondents. "CS" denotes Caxias do Sul respondents.

Source: Two-City Panel.

Finally, polling on interparty and intergroup sentiment shows that partisanship and political affiliations were less meaningful in JF. The left half of figure 5.2 shows the feeling thermometer scores[51] (expressed in standard deviations) that PT and PMDB adherents gave to the opposing party in the pre-campaign wave, months before the election kicked into high gear. The leftmost pair of estimates shows that *petistas* in Caxias do Sul (CS) disliked the PMDB more than did *petistas* in JF. An even larger difference emerges when we look at *pemedebistas'* attitudes toward the PT, as shown in the pair of estimates just to the right of the first two. Caxias's *pemedebistas* scored the PT more than a half standard deviation worse than did JF's *pemedebistas.*[52] Moreover, Caxias's *pemedebistas* were almost three times as likely as their counterparts in JF to say, in the campaign wave, they would never vote for Lula. (This result is not pictured.)

The two sets of estimates in the right half of the figure reinforce the claim that *pemedebistas* in Caxias viewed leftist forces with a much deeper skepticism than did *pemedebistas* in JF. The right half reports *pemedebistas'* scores for

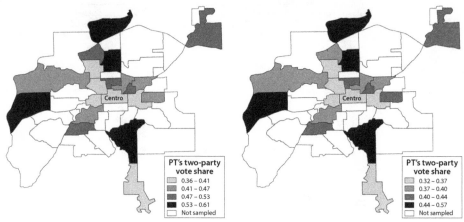

Frame A: Presidential Results in Caxias   Frame B: Gubernatorial Results in Caxias

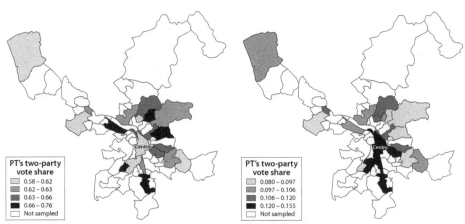

Frame C: Presidential Results in Juiz de Fora   Frame D: Gubernatorial Results in Juiz de Fora

FIGURE 5.3 The PT's Two-Party Vote Share in 1998 Executive Elections by Neighborhood in Caxias do Sul and Juiz de Fora

Notes: Thresholds between categories are drawn at quartiles. Unshaded neighborhoods were not sampled for the Two-City Panel. Juiz de Fora neighborhoods with little to no population are not shown.

Source: Tribunal Regional Eleitoral do Rio Grande do Sul, Tribunal Regional Eleitoral de Minas Gerais.

two controversial civil society groups that were closely allied with the PT: the Unified Workers Central (CUT)—a major leftist umbrella group for labor unions—and the Landless Workers' Movement (MST)—a Marxist social movement that carried out occupations of rural farmland. Caxias's *pemedebistas* scored these two groups nearly a half standard deviation worse than did *pemedebistas* in JF.

Overall, the stability, depth, and impact of mass partisanship differed dramatically between the two cities. Mass partisanship in JF consisted largely of ephemerally expressed orientations toward personalities. Partisanship in Caxias, by contrast, was more stable, providing a meaningful lens through which many voters viewed politics and candidates.

NEIGHBORHOOD POLITICAL LEANINGS IN JUIZ DE FORA AND CAXIAS DO SUL

Because of these political differences between the two cities, we expect to see that neighborhoods had relatively stable partisan leanings in Caxias but not in JF. Evidence of this exists on at least three counts.

First, because of JF's higher rates of split-ticket voting, its neighborhoods had much less consistent PT and PMDB voting patterns across concurrent elections than neighborhoods in Caxias. Consider the maps in figure 5.3. These shade the 22 randomly selected neighborhoods in each city—the 44 neighborhoods where the interviews of the Two-City Panel occurred[53]—by the *PT's two-party vote share* (using official returns) in the presidential (frames A and C) and gubernatorial (frames B and D) elections of 1998. The two Caxias maps are virtually indistinguishable from one another. Strong Lula neighborhoods were also strong neighborhoods for Olívio Dutra (PT candidate for governor), and strong Cardoso neighborhoods were also strong neighborhoods for Antônio Britto (PMDB candidate for governor). The neighborhood-level correlation in vote returns between the two elections is a massive +0.93. In comparison, the two JF maps appear to be plotting completely unrelated variables. The correlation is *negative* at −0.31, shocking for concurrent elections, and the PT performed an average of 50 points worse in the gubernatorial election than in the presidential election, as evidenced by the lower vote shares in the legend.

Second, the political leanings of Caxias neighborhoods are much more stable. The next set of maps in figure 5.4 plots returns for the mayoral race in 2000 as the PT's share of the two-party vote. Again, this new Caxias map is almost a carbon copy of the two in figure 5.3. The neighborhood-level correlation with the 1998 presidential results is +0.94, and the correlation with the 1998 gubernatorial results is +0.92. In JF, by contrast, the variable correlates at just +0.24 with the 1998 presidential results and just +0.11 with the 1998 gubernatorial results.[54]

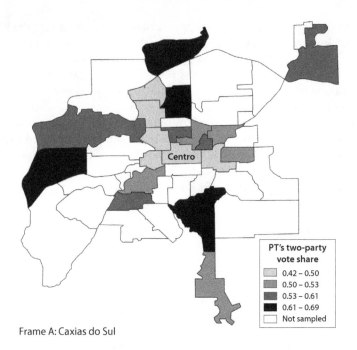

Frame A: Caxias do Sul

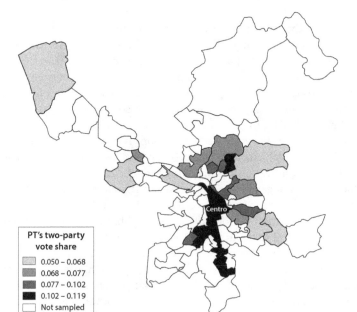

Frame B: Juiz de Fora

Finally, these stable neighborhood-level political preferences existed in Caxias in part because they were rooted in relatively slow-moving socioeconomic realities, a rootedness that was absent in the JF case. In Caxias the PT performed better in the periphery, where incomes are lower, than it did in and near the city's center. Figure 5.5 depicts this geographical distribution of income by mapping *Neighborhood income level*, defined as the neighborhood's median monthly household income from the pre-campaign wave interviews. As its political correlate, we define an index labeled *Neighborhood PT support*, which is the PT's average vote share in the three executive elections mapped in figures 5.3 and 5.4.[55] In Caxias the correlation between this variable and neighborhood income level is −0.66, but no such relationship exists in JF, where the correlation is just +0.07.

Together, these large differences in political character between our two cities present something of a puzzle. Caxias voters appear to be highly partisan and stable across concurrent and consecutive elections, whereas JF voters are more fickle with their partisanship. Yet recall from chapter 3 that rates of vote switching during the 2002 campaign were high in the Two-City Panel: 31 percent between the campaign and election waves. Incredibly, most of this switching occurred in Caxias. Fully 37 percent of Caxias voters switched, *more than the 27 percent figure of JF!*

Why are there such high rates of neighborhood-level stability through time in Caxias alongside relatively high rates of individual-level instability during campaigns? The answer lies in the way social influence creates neighborhood effects. In particular, voters in pro-PT neighborhoods who toyed with voting for Ciro, Garotinho, or Serra during the campaign were assimilated into the neighborhood line—a vote for Lula—by election day. For instance, Caxias respondents who intended to vote for Serra at the campaign wave were three times as likely to switch to Lula by election day if they lived in one of the most pro-PT neighborhoods (21 percent switched to Lula) than if they lived in one of the most anti-PT neighborhoods (7 percent).[56] Similarly, among respondents intending to vote for Ciro at the campaign wave, those living in pro-PT neighborhoods were almost twice as likely to ultimately vote for Lula (30 percent) as were those living in anti-PT neighborhoods (17 percent).[57]

Lacking a clear partisan message from their neighborhood, however, voters in JF did *not* gravitate toward a neighborhood leaning. If anything, they

FIGURE 5.4 The PT's Two-Party Vote Share in 2000 Mayoral Elections by Neighborhood in Caxias do Sul and Juiz de Fora
Notes: Thresholds between categories are drawn at quartiles. Unshaded neighborhoods were not sampled for the Two-City Panel. Juiz de Fora neighborhoods with little to no population are not shown.
Source: Tribunal Regional Eleitoral do Rio Grande do Sul, Tribunal Regional Eleitoral de Minas Gerais..

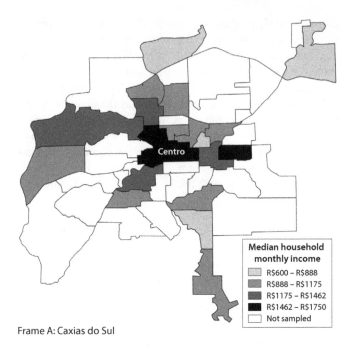

Frame A: Caxias do Sul

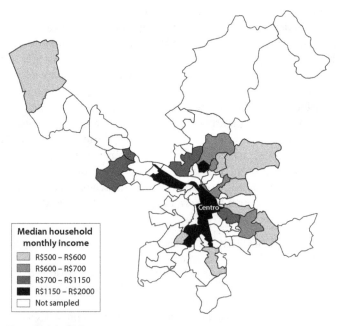

Frame B: Juiz de Fora

were brought into the city's pro-Lula line regardless of where they lived. According to the Two-City Panel, Lula's share of vote intentions in the city went from 48 percent in the pre-campaign wave to 53 percent in the campaign wave, and then 70 percent of election-wave respondents ultimately voted for him. In Caxias, neighborhoods were a conduit for inter-election stability but intra-election volatility. In JF, they did not matter. We demonstrate these patterns and the social mechanisms underlying them in the remainder of the chapter.

METHOD

We seek to show that these relationships in Caxias between neighborhood-level political preferences and individual vote choices are attributable, at least in part, to political discussion within social networks. For this to be the case, three empirical conditions must hold. First, the distribution of preferences in the neighborhood must shape the distribution of political preferences in residents' social networks. In other words, the neighborhood social environment, which imposes a supply of different political beliefs among an ego's *potential* discussants, has an imprint in ego's actual networks. (Recall figure 1.3.) Second, this balance of opinion in social networks must influence individuals' vote choices. This was demonstrated empirically in the previous chapter, but the current chapter does so again using a slightly different approach and measure. Third, these network effects must account at least somewhat for the correlation between neighborhood-level partisan leaning and individual-level vote choices. In other words, the correlation between ego's vote choice and the partisan bias of ego's neighborhood should fall toward zero when we control for network measures. If any one of these three conditions fails to hold, then horizontal intermediation is irrelevant to the variation across neighborhoods in aggregated vote returns.

We proceed in two main steps, estimating two sets of statistical models on ego-level data. The methodological logic follows that of a mediation analysis, with political preferences in ego's neighborhood as the first mover (X), the balance of political opinions in ego's campaign-wave social networks as the mediator (M), and ego's vote choice as the outcome (Y).[58]

FIGURE 5.5 Income Levels by Neighborhood in Caxias do Sul and Juiz de Fora in 2002
Notes: Neighborhood income levels are defined as the median monthly household income of the neighborhood. Thresholds between categories are drawn at quartiles. Unshaded neighborhoods were not sampled for the Two-City Panel. Juiz de Fora neighborhoods with little to no population are not shown.
Source: Two-City Panel, pre-campaign wave.

The first set of models estimates the parameters in the $X \rightarrow M$ relationship. These are models of social network construction or, more simply, discussant selection. They model the balance of alters' preferences in each ego's campaign-wave social networks as a function of the partisan leaning of ego's neighborhood as well as ego's individual traits, such as partisanship and pre-campaign vote intentions. If social interactions do account for neighborhood influence, then the political leanings of egos' neighborhoods should be correlated with the average political leanings among their alters, even after we account for the individual-level (ego) traits that shape whom egos select as discussants. This is the first empirical condition. In Caxias, for example, pro-Lula discussants should be more prevalent in the network of an ego whose neighborhood tends to support the PT than in the network of an otherwise similar ego whose neighborhood has supported the PMDB.

The second set of models estimates the parameters in the $X \rightarrow Y$ relationship while holding M constant. These are models of ego's vote choice. The models build iteratively from trim models with only neighborhood political preferences as independent variables to fuller models that add ego-level traits and then the network measures. In doing so, we observe whether the network measures exert an important effect on vote choice (the second condition). Just as importantly, their inclusion must shrink the coefficient on neighborhood preferences (the third condition). If so, then the network measures are partially accounting for the correlations between neighborhood leanings and individual-level vote choices. In Caxias, for instance, the estimated coefficients on the PT leanings of neighborhoods should fall when we introduce discussant preferences into a model of ego's vote choice. Because our expectations for the two cities differ, we execute this procedure separately for each city.

This method for assessing the extent to which social communication channels neighborhood effects is applicable to higher levels of geographical aggregation as well. As a result, we use it again in the next chapter to explore the *regional* clustering of candidate preferences in Brazil and Mexico.

NEIGHBORHOOD ENVIRONMENTS AND THE SELECTION OF DISCUSSANTS

We first report results from the models of discussant selection. In this step the dependent variables (**M**) are campaign-wave measures of social network composition at the ego level, namely, the proportion of named discussants that support each candidate: *Pro-Lula share among alters*, *Pro-Serra share among alters*, *Pro-Garotinho share among alters*, and *Pro-Ciro share among alters*. For example, if a main respondent named three discussants whom she perceived to be voting for Lula, Lula, and Serra, respectively, she would receive the following scores on the four variables: Pro-Lula share among alters = 0.67, Pro-Serra share among alters = 0.33, Pro-Garotinho share among alters = 0, and Pro-Ciro share among alters = 0.[59] Since these four variables must sum to one for each respondent, we model them jointly as compositional data.*

Our list of independent variables captures the fact that network construction may be a function of both supply and demand.[60] The distribution of preferences in a citizen's social environment—in this case the neighborhood—dictates the supply of each partisan viewpoint among potential discussants. Within this supply constraint, citizens exercise discretion when choosing discussants, demanding politically like-minded alters far more than chance would dictate. In theory, if this homophily instinct is strong enough, an individual could overcome the environmental constraint on supply and still craft a homogeneous and agreeing network. In other words, neighborhood influences on network construction are not inevitable.

Our primary independent variable gauges supply. A neighborhood's political leaning (X) is measured with the *Neighborhood PT support* index introduced above. Scholars of neighborhood effects have long argued against using aggregated results from the election or event at hand to "explain" individual behavior, since these results are themselves the sum total of individual- and neighborhood-level effects.[61] In our case, using 2002 presidential vote returns to explain behavior in 2002 would be tautological. Instead, we use this index of neighborhood voting returns, an index based on three *previous* elections to executive offices.

To measure demand, the models include measures of ego's political predispositions and demographics. Individuals may select into a neighborhood for reasons of homophily, because they prefer its residents' political biases or some other trait correlated with the neighborhood's partisan leaning. As a result, an observed correlation between neighborhood political orientations and individual political behaviors, such as the network-construction and vote-choice variables we seek to explain, could be spurious.[62] The models thus control for *Ego vote intention* and *Partisanship*, both measured in the pre-campaign wave. Although we do not wish to overload the models with demographic variables, they also include measures of *Socioeconomic status* and gender (*Woman*). They also contain *Evangelical church attendance*, which could be important given the candidacy of Garotinho, an evangelical Christian.

The model estimates confirm our expectations: neighborhood leanings are highly correlated with the distribution of political preferences in egos' networks in Caxias but not in JF. Interested readers can find the estimated coefficients

---

*The proper model for this case is a fractional multinomial logit (Papke and Wooldridge 1996). It is "fractional" because the dependent variable is a proportion and not nominal as in a standard multinomial logit, but it is still a "multinomial logit" in functional form and in the fact that the predicted probabilities for the four categories sum to one for each observation. As in a standard multinomial logit model, there must be an omitted baseline category for the dependent variable. Once again, the incumbent party candidate Serra is omitted.

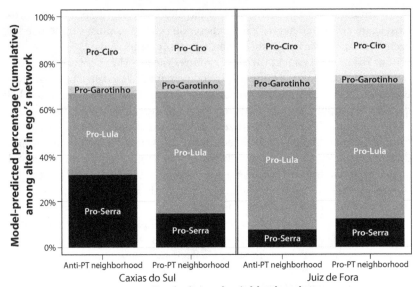

FIGURE 5.6 The Distribution of Vote Intentions among Alters by Neighborhood Type and City in Brazil 2002: Predicted Percentages from Two Fractional Multinomial Logit Models
Notes: Each bar portion is a model-predicted percentage. Dependent variables (*Pro-Lula share among alters, Pro-Serra share among alters, Pro-Garotinho share among alters,* and *Pro-Ciro share among alters*) are measured in the campaign wave. Table A.12 reports the complete sets of coefficient estimates in numerical form. $N = 1,307$ in JF. $N = 1,183$ in Caxias.
Source: Two-City Panel.

in table A.12, but to convey this relationship more intuitively, figure 5.6 depicts the model-predicted consequences of neighborhood leanings on political leanings in main respondents' networks. It shows the distribution of vote intentions among alters for four types of egos. Moving from left to right, they are (1) a resident of Caxias's most anti-PT neighborhood, (2) a resident of Caxias's most pro-PT neighborhood, (3) a resident of JF's most anti-PT neighborhood, and (4) a resident of JF's most pro-PT neighborhood. Note that the exercise varies only neighborhoods within each city. All other variables, including vote intention during the pre-campaign wave, are held at their means to generate these predicted values.

The Caxias half of the figure shows a large neighborhood effect on the balance of vote intentions in egonets. Upon moving from the weak PT to the strong PT neighborhood, the predicted share of pro-Serra discussants in the egocentric network falls by half, and the share of pro-Lula discussants increases by half. This shifts the ratio of Lula-to-Serra discussants from nearly one-to-one to nearly four-to-one. The ratios of pro-Serra discussants to pro-Garotinho and to pro-Ciro discussants also shift dramatically as we move from one neighborhood to the other in Caxias. This shift occurs despite the fact that the absolute proportions for these two other candidates change little between the two neighborhoods, a testament to the fact that neighborhoods in Caxias influenced only the selection of discussants who espoused a candidate from the two-party establishment. In sharp contrast, neighborhood political leanings in JF have no reverberations in political discussion networks. The absolute changes in the distributions between the two neighborhoods are small and even wrongly directed.

Our models have demonstrated that even in an urban setting like Caxias, with its relatively equal balance of left and anti-left partisans, individuals live in social environments that vary by partisan ethos. Neighborhood environments influence the supply of political preferences among potential discussants and, as a result, the central tendency of vote intentions in the social networks of Caxias residents. In an ever-shrinking world, distance and space still matter, as neighborhoods—most less than a few square kilometers in size—filter socially supplied political information, at least in cities where neighborhoods have stable partisan orientations.

DISCUSSION AND NEIGHBORHOOD
EFFECTS ON VOTE CHOICE

The previous section confirmed the first empirical condition for Caxias: the partisan leanings of neighborhoods shape the distribution of political opinions within discussion networks. Our next step is to ask whether these opinions within discussion networks account for neighborhood effects on vote choice.

The dependent variable in this second set of models is the nominal measure *Ego vote choice*. These models, like those above, control for vote intention in the pre-campaign wave (*Ego vote intention*). This amounts to a lagged dependent variable, so the coefficients on all other independent variables are capturing campaign effects—that is, the variables' influence on the *changes* in voter preferences that occurred over the course of the campaign. The inclusion of the lag helps address the homophily confound that arises from selection into neighborhoods.

For Caxias we run four multinomial logit models in succession. Each model adds independent variables to the preceding one. Model 1 includes only *Neighborhood PT support* (plus the lagged vote intention dummies present in all models). It captures the unconditional correlation between neighborhood leanings and change in vote preference. Model 2 contains the neighborhood variable *plus* individual-level factors (partisanship, issue positions, gender, and SES). These are individual-level factors that might account for the observed correlation between neighborhood leanings and the dependent variable. In some studies, alleged neighborhood "effects" are just spurious correlations, reflecting the fact that individual-level traits are unbalanced across neighborhoods. In this scenario neighborhood "effects" are not true causal effects, so we refer to them in quotation marks. Model 2 attempts to control for at least some of these individual-level traits. Next, model 3 contains the neighborhood variable and these individual-level factors *plus* measures of exposure to other political intermediaries (party contacting and evangelical church attendance). Differences across neighborhoods in party mobilization and clergy activities could be a channel for neighborhood influence. Finally, model 4 contains all three sets of aforementioned factors *plus* measures of alters' preferences, meaning the dependent variables (**M**) from the previous section on discussant selection.

To reiterate, early models are nested in later models. Building up to the most fully specified model allows us to observe the extent to which conditioning on additional factors *eliminates* lingering correlations between *Neighborhood PT support* and the dependent variable of *Ego vote choice*. Our goal is to understand the mechanisms underlying any observed correlation between neighborhood preferences and individuals' vote choices. When conditioning on factors that account for the influence of neighborhood on individual vote choice (e.g., discussants' preferences), the correlation between neighborhood leanings and the dependent variable should shrink toward zero.[63] Although our argument is that neighborhood context matters, we are in essence trying to get context to "not count"—to attenuate its coefficients to zero—by specifying precisely how neighborhood context exerts its influence on individuals during campaigns.[64]

Table 5.5 reports the most important numerical results for Caxias. Full results are in table A.13. Because the first empirical condition failed for JF, this section reports only the Caxias results. (Results for JF are in table A.14.) Vote for Serra is the omitted baseline for the nominal dependent variable. The table shows only the coefficients for Lula vote (relative to Serra vote) and for Garotinho vote (relative to Serra vote), and for each candidate it shows only those coefficients directly relevant to the argument.[65] We focus first and primarily on the Lula results in the left half of the table, where the model 1 column reports the coefficient on neighborhood leanings while controlling only for lagged vote intentions. Statistically, *Neighborhood PT support* is highly significant. Over the course of the campaign, voters with equivalent pre-campaign vote intentions were more likely to remain with or gravitate to Lula in pro-PT neighborhoods than in anti-PT ones. Similarly, voters with equivalent pre-campaign vote intentions were more likely to remain with or gravitate toward Serra in pro-PMDB neighborhoods than in anti-PMDB ones.

A variety of factors could explain the large coefficient on neighborhood leanings in model 1. Perhaps there is no contextual effect at all. Rather, certain individual traits, such as PT partisanship and attitudes of economic statism, could be more plentiful in pro-PT neighborhoods than in anti-PT ones, and by election day citizens end up voting in line with these predispositions. In other words, apparent neighborhood "effects" might be simply the result of the spatial clustering of similar individuals. Model 2 includes individual factors such as these. (To reduce clutter, the coefficients are not shown). Their inclusion does shrink the neighborhood coefficient by about 25 percent, but it is still sizable and statistically distinguishable from zero.

Next, model 3 adds measures of respondents' exposure to alternative political intermediaries—namely, party contacting and evangelical church attendance. (Again, the coefficient values are saved for appendix A.) Recall from the previous chapter that party contacting does not induce changes in vote choice, and here the ineffectiveness of party contacting is reaffirmed. In fact, the coefficient on neighborhood preference grows, counter to our goal of explaining it away. Cross-neighborhood differences in party-contacting activity (and in evangelical church attendance) do not account for these neighborhood effects on vote choice.

Finally, model 4 introduces the network measures, and here the table does report their coefficients. The statistical significance of two of the variables reaffirms, using slightly different measures, the findings from the previous chapter: political networks induce changes in main respondents' vote choices. More important, the inclusion of network factors further attenuates the neighborhood coefficient, this time to statistical insignificance. The coefficient declines by 26 percent (22 percent of the original coefficient). This is virtually equivalent in size to the drop that occurred between models 1 and 2 when individual traits were introduced. The social-interaction channel of neighborhood effects is clearly important in Caxias, as important as the part of neighborhood "effects" that is spurious because of the geographical clustering of individual-level factors.

The right half of the table repeats the exercise for Garotinho vote (relative to Serra vote). Garotinho received only 10 percent of the Caxias vote, so this is not fundamental to understanding how the election unfolded in the city. Still, it demonstrates the nature of other factors that correlate with neighborhood political leanings. The neighborhood coefficient in model 1 is just shy of statistical significance, and it shows that voters were more likely to stand by or gravitate toward Garotinho in pro-PT neighborhoods than they were in anti-PT ones. This is not surprising. Garotinho ran under a left party banner and appealed to evangelical voters, who tend to cluster in Caxias's poorer (and thus more pro-PT) neighborhoods. Indeed, the inclusion of individual-level traits in model 2, which includes economic issue stances, shrinks the neighborhood coefficient by almost half. In turn, the inclusion in model 3 of political intermediaries, and particularly a measure of evangelical church attendance, attenuates the coefficient to statistical zero.[66] This set of findings simply illustrates that neighborhood effects can be apparent for multiple reasons. Influences

TABLE 5.5.
Ego's Vote Choice by Neighborhood's Political Leaning and Possible Mediators in Caxias do Sul 2002: Results from Four Multinomial Logit Models

Dependent variable categories:	Lula vote Serra vote				Garotinho vote Serra vote			
	Model 1	Model 2	Model 3	Model 4	Model 1	Model 2	Model 3	Model 4
Mediators:	None	Individual traits	Individual traits & other intermediaries	Individual traits & other intermediaries & discussants	None	Individual traits	Individual traits & other intermediaries	Individual traits & other intermediaries & discussants
Neighborhood "Effects": Neighborhood's Political Leaning								
Neighborhood PT support	0.279* (0.089)	0.203* (0.089)	0.238* (0.094)	0.176 (0.099)	0.230* (0.108)	0.125 (0.107)	−0.042 (0.143)	−0.089 (0.143)
Discussants' Vote Intentions (c wave)								
Pro-Lula share among alters				1.875* (0.331)				1.417* (0.479)
Pro-Garotinho share among alters				−0.162 (0.677)				1.282 (0.679)
Pro-Ciro share among alters				−0.154 (0.357)				0.332 (0.483)
Singleton				0.672* (0.293)				0.563 (0.423)

			Omitted baseline			Omitted baseline
Pro-Serra share among alters	Included	Included	Included	Included	Included	Included
Other Variables						
Ego vote intention (pc wave) (4 vars.)	Included	Included	Included	Included	Included	Included
Individual traits (pc wave) (6 vars.)	Not included	Included	Included	Not included	Included	Included
Other political intermediaries (c wave) (5 vars.)	Not included	Not included	Included	Not included	Not included	Included

Notes: Entries are multinomial logit coefficients with robust standard errors (corrected for clustering by neighborhoods) in parentheses. Dependent variable for each model is *Ego vote choice*. pc = pre-campaign, c = campaign, e = election. Coefficients for $\frac{Ciro\ vote}{Serra\ vote}$ were estimated but are not shown. Table A.13 reports the complete set of coefficient estimates in numerical form.

$N = 1,143$. * = $p < .05$.

Source: Two-City Panel.

exerted through the social-interaction channel are not inevitable, as they clearly require a strong neighborhood partisan ethos.

The results from JF, reported in table A.14, also confirm this last point. The coefficients on neighborhood leanings are actually wrongly signed. Moreover, the addition of network measures does not affect their sizes, even though the network measures themselves are statistically significant. Discussion was influential in JF, but it was irrelevant to the *neighborhood* geography of the vote.

CONCLUSION

Neighborhoods in Brazil are well-defined and often vibrant arenas of social interaction. Indeed, most political discussion takes place between neighborhood coresidents. Neighborhoods, as a result, can play an important role in guiding voters toward their socially informed preferences during campaigns. For this to happen, however, the neighborhood social environment must hold a relatively clear and stable political leaning, something that is often a function of the political character of the municipality.

The preferences of voters in Caxias do Sul, a polarized city in which neighborhoods have stable political leanings, do move toward the political centers of gravity of their neighborhoods over the course of a campaign. By contrast, in Juiz de Fora, where politics is less partisan and less polarized, preferences do not move in this manner. In Caxias this movement toward a neighborhood leaning is not simply the product of voters activating their dormant individual traits—traits that tend to cluster by neighborhood. Nor does the movement result from vertical intermediation efforts, such as party canvassing and clientelism, that are distributed unevenly across neighborhoods. Instead, a primary cause of this movement is horizontal intermediation. Because the neighborhood social environment shapes the supply of potential discussants and therefore the distribution of opinions that voters in Caxias encounter in their social networks, political talk assimilates many voters toward their neighborhoods' partisan leanings during the campaign. The result in Caxias is individual-level instability during campaigns but neighborhood-level stability between them.

The extent to which these findings travel to other municipalities in Brazil remains an open question. Are most Brazilian neighborhoods like those in Caxias, with strong neighborhood effects, or like those in JF, where effects are minimal? Neighborhoods in Brazil certainly carry a high potential for exerting influence through peer effects, since they have levels of politically relevant social interaction that are high by international standards. What remains uncertain is whether the typical Brazilian neighborhood exhibits a strong and stable partisan leaning. We suspect that Caxias and Juiz de Fora are on opposite ends of a continuum.

Neighborhoods and cities are just one of many environments that can shape the socially supplied information to which voters are exposed and that, in turn, can influence vote choice. Another social environment, one unequivocally characterized by strong and stable political leanings in both Brazil and Mexico, is the state and even the broader regions of which states are a part. The next chapter scales up, using the method deployed in this chapter, to demonstrate how social networks channel *regional* preferences.

6

Discussion and the Regionalization
of Voter Preferences

Political discussion [is] the vehicle through which dominant
preferences within the larger community are transmitted to the
individuals who are members of that community.
—*Robert Huckfeldt and John Sprague*[1]

Marta is middle-aged, married, an observant Catholic, and a homemaker in a middle-class family in Celaya, a midsized city in north-central Mexico. She is neither partisan nor involved in politics, but she does hold reasonably well-formed conservative views on social issues and pro-market views on economic issues. Partly for these reasons, she voted in the 2000 and 2006 presidential elections for candidates of the right-leaning PAN. For her part, María is also middle-aged, married, a faithful Catholic, and a homemaker in a middle-class family.* Like Marta, María holds conservative social views and pro-market economic ones, and she is also nonpartisan and mostly inactive in politics. Unlike Marta, though, María lives a six-hour drive south, in the midsized city of Chilpancingo, and in those same two presidential elections she voted for the centrist PRI.

Why would two women with similar socioeconomic profiles and policy opinions vote differently in the same election? Most models of voting behavior base predictions strictly on the individual traits of voters, so they struggle to explain the divergent choices of Marta and María. The two face the same choice set, and Mexico's electoral system counts their presidential votes equally. Since they occupy the same point in the issue space, spatial models dictate that they would vote for the same candidate. Standard psychological models also fail, as neither woman has an expressed partisanship that would incline her

*Although their names are fictional, Marta and María are loosely based on real survey respondents to the Mexico 2006 Panel (folio numbers 282 and 1349).

toward one candidate. In short, their observed individual-level traits offer no answer.

The one descriptor that does differentiate these two women might offer a clue: they live in different parts of the country. Mexico does have a deep and persistent regional political cleavage. Marta lives in the state of Guanajuato in the north-central Bajío region, the PAN's heartland. María lives in the southern state of Guerrero in the Pacific Coast region, where the PAN is extremely weak and where the leftist PRD and centrist PRI compete for political supremacy. Like most voting models, standard accounts of Mexico's politics attribute its regional political cleavages to individual traits, such as northerners' greater wealth and Catholic religiosity. To reiterate, however, Marta and María are equivalent on these traits. Something else must explain why they each cast votes in line with the partisan leanings of their respective regions.

The crucial difference, we argue, is that María and Marta are embedded in distinct social environments—social environments that communicate very different partisan content. Marta's North is a social context in which she is much more likely to encounter *panista* voters in her day-to-day conversations, while María's southern surroundings have far more *priístas* than *panistas*. Marta tends to hear pro-PAN information in her social activities, while María hears frequent anti-PAN arguments. These peer interactions, in turn, influence their voting decisions. As in the epigraph, conversations can assimilate individuals toward the political leanings of their geographical surroundings.

This chapter brings together the two very different research literatures on political discussion and regional political cleavages. It scales up the argument from the preceding chapter to paint regions, like neighborhoods and cities, as relevant social environments. We demonstrate that casual conversations about candidates and politics expose voters to the political biases of their regional social environments. Region shapes the distribution of candidate preferences within voters' networks of political discussion. As a result, social interactions assimilate individuals toward their regions' political biases, strengthening geographical clustering and geographical divides within countries.[2] In playing this role, peer effects induce individuals to take on political preferences that differ from those dictated by their personal traits alone.

This is not an argument about the *emergence* of regional cleavages. Countries still have unique political histories and geographically clustered interests that spawn a variety of region-specific political affiliations and preferences. In other words, politics and policy very much matter. Our point, instead, is that a regional cluster of citizens who overwhelmingly vote for the same candidate is more than a mere agglomeration of voters with similar policy interests and partisan affiliations. In fact, many individuals in the cluster do not hold or share the interests and identities predominant in their region, but they nonetheless go with the flow of their political surroundings because of persuasive peers.

The chapter proceeds as follows. The next section describes the nature, the history, and the individual-level sources of the regional political cleavages in Brazil and Mexico. The subsequent section lays out the theoretical foundations for the ways in which social environments and political discussion deepen the regionalization of voter preferences. We then provide evidence for our argument by using the two egocentric network data sources that feature national representativeness: BEPS 2014 and the Mexico 2006 Panel. We execute an empirical exercise that is equivalent in process to that implemented in the preceding chapter. The results show that the supply of political preferences in respondents' social environments—this time defined as their state of residence— shapes the distribution of preferences in social networks. In turn, controlling for the political leanings of respondents' social networks weakens the partial correlations between regional political leanings and individual vote choices. Discussion, in other words, channels regional effects on vote choice.

REGIONAL POLITICAL CLEAVAGES IN
BRAZIL AND MEXICO

Voter preferences in Brazil and Mexico divide by region. Table 6.1 gives a sense of this regionalization by showing party- and country-level measures of party nationalization. (We treat "regionalization" and "nationalization" as antonyms.) The scores are based on the most widely used indicator of party nationalization.[3] At the party level, the indicator is one minus the Gini coefficient on party vote share across states.* A party receiving nearly equivalent shares of the vote in all states has a high nationalization score, while a party running very strongly in some states and very weakly in others receives a relatively low nationalization score. In turn, the national-level score is the weighted mean (weighted by each party's national vote share) of all party-level nationalization scores. Note that nationalization scores tend to run high in an absolute sense: closer to 1 than to 0, with scores below 0.60 empirically rare. Seemingly small absolute differences are thus meaningful. Nationalization scores can be calculated for any election type (presidential, lower house, upper house, gubernatorial). Given our focus, table 6.1 reports scores for presidential elections in Brazil and Mexico.

By international standards, the presidential elections of Brazil and Mexico have a low to intermediate degree of party nationalization, meaning regionalization in our two cases is high but not severe. Brazil and Mexico have roughly similar scores, ranging from 0.82 to 0.85 in Mexico and 0.78 to 0.86 in Brazil, though Brazil has become more regionalized through time. As a point of comparison, these scores are very similar to that obtained in elections for the US

---

*The Gini coefficient measure of inequity varies between 0 and 1, with higher scores indicating greater inequity across a set of units.

TABLE 6.1.

Party Nationalization Scores for Brazilian and Mexican Presidential Elections

	Brazil				Mexico			
	Nation	PT	PSDB		Nation	PRI	PAN	Left
1998	.86	.85	.90	1994	.85	.95	.80	.68
2002	.86	.94	.81	2000	.84	.90	.86	.69
2006	.82	.84	.81	**2006**	**.82**	**.86**	**.81**	**.79**
2010	.83	.86	.79	2012	.85	.92	.81	.81
2014	**.78**	**.82**	**.77**	2018	.84	.84	.77	.88

Notes: This chapter's two election cases are shown in bold. "Left" is based on PRD results from 1994 to 2012 and MORENA results in 2018.

Source: Authors' calculations.

House of Representatives in 2000 (0.84), the election year that added "red and blue America" to the lexicon. In short, there is plenty of regionalization to understand and explain in our two country cases.

These national numbers alone reveal little about the directionality and spatial distribution of regionalized preferences, and they also say little about the clear differences in the table across parties. The remainder of this section briefly describes previous scholarship on the nature and roots of regionalization in the two countries. These scholarly narratives are largely grounded in the fact that individuals with similar economic and, in Mexico, religious traits cluster together by region. Since parties appeal to individuals on the basis of economic interests and religious values, political preferences take on the clustering and uneven spatial distribution of these interests, values, and identities. In other words, these explanations see regional clustering as the mere aggregation of individual-level interests.

The Regionalization of Voter Preferences in Brazil

Regionalism has long been an intrinsic element of Brazilian politics. The government officially divides the country into five regions: North, Northeast, Southeast, South, and Center-West. (See figure 6.1.) The states in the North and Northeast are Brazil's poorest and most unequal. Figure 6.1 depicts this regional variation vividly by shading Brazil's counties (*municípios*) by their Human Development Index (HDI).[4] (A higher HDI means better human development.)

From the advent of Brazil's first democratic regime (1945–64) through the early years of its New Republic (1985–present), politics in the economically dominant Southeast and South had a more programmatic orientation. In the 1980s the southeastern state of São Paulo, the country's most populous state,

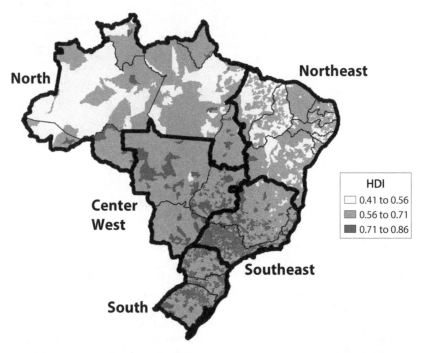

North

Northeast

Center
West

Southeast

South

HDI
☐ 0.41 to 0.56
◻ 0.56 to 0.71
■ 0.71 to 0.86

FIGURE 6.1 Brazilian Regions and Counties by Human Development Index in 2010
Source: Silva, Meireles, and Costa (2017).

spawned both the PT and the PSDB, the two programmatic, left-of-center parties that would eventually come to dominate presidential contests and the
presidency. By contrast, the poorer North and Northeast hosted a clientelistic,
pork-barreling form of politics in which conservative parties dominated
every level of government.[5] Because of the North and Northeast's relative
poverty, politics itself was a source of wealth, with key families dominating,
often intergenerationally, the most powerful political posts. In the 1991–94
legislature, for instance, 40 percent of all deputies from the Northeast state of
Bahia had a close relative in politics, compared to 5 percent in São Paulo.[6]
Turnover in legislative positions held by northeasterners was lower, and the
resulting seniority gave these deputies an advantage in the hunt for pork-barrel
projects.

How did these patterns play out in presidential elections? After 1985, when
the military regime ended and democracy returned, the top two contenders
in the first three presidential contests (1989, 1994, 1998) were Lula of the leftist
PT and a victorious candidate running to his right (Collor in 1989, and centrist Cardoso in 1994 and 1998). Lula's electoral base was in the urban middle
class and in the Southeast and South, and that base was moderately national-

ized. (Recall the PT's nationalization score of 0.85 in 1998.) In two of those contests (1994 and 1998), eventual winner Cardoso headed a PSDB that had moved to the center from its left-of-center beginnings but that polled more strongly in the poorer North and Northeast.

After these three failed attempts, in 2002 Lula finally won the presidency. Although he still drew disproportionately from the South and Southeast, he finished so strongly nationwide that he made important inroads into the North and Northeast, and he posted the PT's highest nationalization score to date (0.94). It was after Lula's successful re-election in 2006, however, that scholars began speaking of a new geographical political alignment and of his "new constituency."[7] The North and Northeast now polled more strongly for Lula than the South, Southeast, and Center-West, and his nationalization score fell by a dramatic 10 points (0.84). Poorer regions voted for the PT, while wealthier regions voted for the PSDB. Figure 6.2 brings this realignment into stark relief by juxtaposing Lula's 2002 and 2006 electoral maps.

The geographical realignment had two causes. First was the pro-poor policies of Lula's first term, particularly the increased real minimum wage along with the establishment of the targeted social program Bolsa Família.[8] The real minimum wage rose by 70 percent between the two elections, making a substantial difference to the roughly 35 percent of northeasterners and northerners who earned the minimum.[9] In addition, the conditional cash-transfer program Bolsa Família provided income support to roughly 11 million families (40 million people) in the inter-election period. The share of northeasterners receiving the benefit (17 percent) outnumbered the share in the Southeast (8 percent) by more than two-to-one.[10] In sum, poverty and inequality declined in the country's poorest regions between 2002 and 2006, and that decline dramatically boosted support for the incumbent.[11]

The realignment's second impetus was the losses Lula experienced among his erstwhile urban middle-class constituencies in the South and Southeast. These losses had two sources. One was the distaste of these constituencies for the new pro-poor policies.[12] The other was a massive corruption scandal that tarnished the PT's name, a scandal that disgusted many in the middle and upper classes.[13]

In the two elections that occurred after 2006, including the 2014 election on which we focus here, this new alignment sharpened. Following the realignment of 2006, the PT began to displace permanently the conservative, clientelistic politics of previous eras in the North and Northeast.[14] PT candidate Dilma won the presidency in 2010 and 2014 with geographical constituencies and vote totals that were similar to Lula's in 2006. (See figure 6.3.) Meanwhile, the PT's efforts to claw back the losses it had experienced in wealthier regions proved largely fruitless, with some exceptions in parts of Dilma's home states of Minas Gerais and Rio Grande do Sul. In 2014 Aécio of the PSDB polled much more strongly than Dilma in the South and Southeast. Brazil had its most

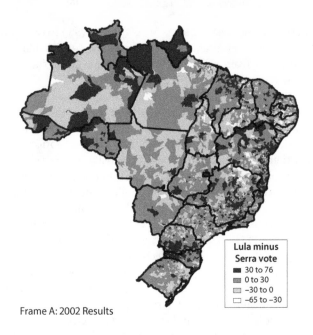

Frame A: 2002 Results

Lula minus
Serra vote
■ 30 to 76
▨ 0 to 30
▢ −30 to 0
☐ −65 to −30

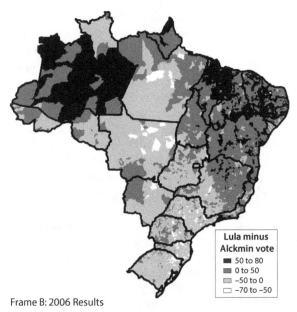

Frame B: 2006 Results

Lula minus
Alckmin vote
■ 50 to 80
▨ 0 to 50
▨ −50 to 0
☐ −70 to −50

FIGURE 6.2 Brazil's Political Realignment: PT Vote Share minus PSDB Vote Share by County in 2002 and 2006
Notes: First-round results.
Source: Silva, Meireles, and Costa (2017).

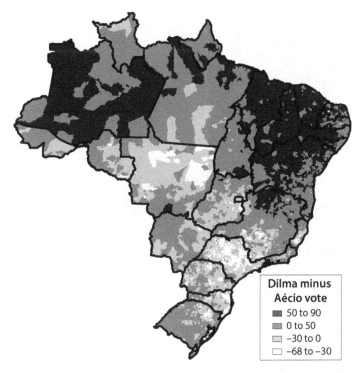

FIGURE 6.3 Brazil's Regional Political Cleavage: PT Vote Share minus PSDB Vote Share by County in 2014
Notes: First-round results.
Source: Silva, Meireles, and Costa (2017).

highly regionalized presidential election, with a left-leaning north and a right-leaning south.[15]

The Regionalization of Voter Preferences in Mexico

Unlike Brazil, Mexico does not divide its states cleanly into a few official regions, but region does have a high political relevance. Well-being varies across these regions in a mirror image of the Brazilian pattern: northern states are wealthier than southern ones, although Mexico City (before 2016 the Federal District) in the south-central area is the wealthiest unit. (See figure 6.4.) The regions also have cultural and religious differences. Northerners are whiter, and most of Mexico's indigenous population resides in the south. Northerners also tend to be more observant and conservative in their Catholicism; the Bajío region, located in the north-central area (including María's Guanajuato), is known as Mexico's Bible Belt, while Mexico City is more secular.[16]

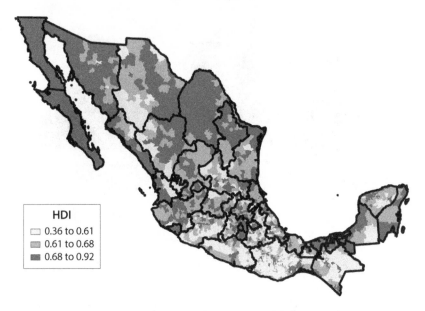

FIGURE 6.4 Mexican States and Counties by Human Development Index in 2010
Source: Programa de las Naciones Unidas para el Desarollo (2014).

Some studies of Mexican voting behavior stress region as a central, if not *the* central, "cause" of vote choice:[17] "Region, not class, remained the dominant cleavage in electoral politics [in 2006]. Our findings thus support the conventional wisdom that Mexico has increasingly become a nation of 'blue [*panista*] states' and 'yellow [*perredista*] states.'"[18] What are the contours of such a strong regionalization of voter preferences?

In 1988 the hegemony of the PRI, Mexico's long-standing ruling party, began to crack. Opposition parties filled the void, but they filled it in a highly uneven manner, at least geographically. Throughout the 1990s the PRI remained the only truly national party, with an exceedingly high nationalization score of 0.95 in its 1994 presidential election victory. The PAN was a capable challenger to the PRI in the North, while the PRD was its main competitor in the South. Neither of these two opposition parties had any meaningful presence in the other's stronghold. The PRD, for instance, had a very low nationalization score of 0.68 in 1994. Because of this arrangement, some analysts spoke of an electoral "bifurcation" or "two separate two-party systems," instead of a three-party system.[19] In many northern states only the PRI and the PAN were competitive, while southern states typically had a PRI/PRD divide.

The historic presidential election of 2000, won by the PAN's Vicente Fox, finally ended the PRI's perennial grip on the presidency. Fox had a sufficient national following to outpoll the *perredista* candidate, Cuauhtémoc Cárdenas,

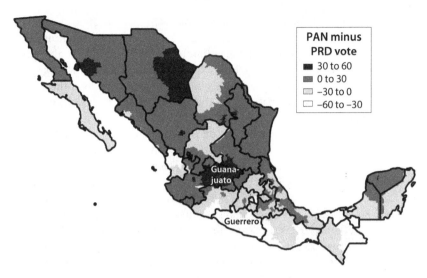

FIGURE 6.5 Mexico's Regional Political Cleavage: PAN Vote Share minus PRD Vote Share by Congressional District in 2006
Source: Instituto Nacional Electoral (2006).

in many southern states, and the PAN boosted its nationalization score from 0.80 to 0.86. Still, the PAN's increased nationalization reflected the weakness of Cárdenas rather than a fundamental change in Mexico's political geography. Fox's best tallies were in the North and Cárdenas's in the South. The PRI remained a nationalized, but now losing, party (0.90), drawing evenly from Mexico's various regions.

The 2006 election—our focus in this chapter—saw the PRI concede even more to the PRD and PAN in numerous states, but the regional divide persisted. The PAN's candidate, the victorious Calderón, performed much more strongly in the North than in the South, while *perredista* candidate López Obrador again outran Calderón in the South and in Mexico City. Figure 6.5, which maps vote returns at the district level, depicts a clear political fault line running horizontally near the country's geographical midpoint. (This line loosely corresponds to the northern borders of Michoacán and Hidalgo states.) Calderón won all but 3 of the 18 states lying to the north of this fault line, while López Obrador won all but 2 of the 14 states (plus Mexico City) lying to its south. This occurred despite a major boost in the PRD's nationalization score (from 0.69 to 0.79). (Note that we label Marta's very *panista* Guanajuato and María's very *perredista* Guerrero for reference.) Invoking parties' symbolic colors, by 2006 experts were speaking of the mostly "blue" northern states and the largely "yellow" southern states.

Although this chapter analyzes survey data only for the 2006 election in Mexico, it is worth mentioning that Mexico's regional patterns continue unchanged. In the 2012 presidential election, the victorious PRI remained the country's most nationalized party. The PRD maintained its trend toward greater nationalization but still won most of its votes in Mexico City and the South. Despite performing weakly nationwide, the PAN continued to draw its vote disproportionately from the North. Finally, the smashing 31-point victory by López Obrador in 2018—now running under the party banner of MORENA—should not disguise the ongoing regionalization of Mexico's vote. The country's nationalization score was largely unchanged. (Recall table 6.1.) López Obrador famously won a plurality in all but one state, but his victory resulted from an upward shift of about 30 points, compared to his 2006 and 2012 performances, that was roughly equal in size across the states.[20]

Scholars emphasize three reasons for Mexico's regionalized political cleavage: wealth, urbanization, and religiosity. The most frequently cited reason is the regional disparity in economic prosperity.[21] Because middle- and upper-class voters tend to be more supportive than poor voters of market-friendly policies, the wealthier North prefers the right-of-center PAN while the less-developed South favors the statist PRD.[22] Indeed, the advent of the export-oriented *maquila* sector and the North American Free Trade Agreement (NAFTA) were partially responsible for the North's greater prosperity. The second explanation is rooted in Mexico's urban/rural divide. Before the PRI's decline, its best polling was in rural areas, while the PAN did best in urban centers.[23] This remained the case after the PRI's defeat in 2000. During the 1990s and 2000s, the PRD did steal many opposition voters from the PAN in Mexico City, making the capital its stronghold.[24] But the overall urban/rural cleavage remained and helps explain why a largely urban North held political preferences distinct from those of a more rural South. Finally, the PAN is culturally conservative, with tight linkages to the Roman Catholic Church. The PAN opposes capital punishment, abortion rights, and same-sex marriage, and these stances resonate with the observant northerners of the Bible Belt. Meanwhile, the historically anticlerical PRI and the largely secular PRD attract voters with less traditional beliefs, and these more secular voters cluster in Mexico City and the South.

THE NATURE OF REGIONAL EFFECTS

Studies of Brazilian and Mexican voting behavior have demonstrated that the socioeconomic and issue-related factors discussed above help to explain regional cleavages, but they typically account for only a small part of the correlation between individuals' region of residence and their vote choices. Regression models of Mexican voting behavior, for instance, generally include measures of the three individual-level factors (wealth, urban/rural residence, and religiosity), but statistically significant regional coefficients, often measured with dummy variables, remain.[25] These lingering regional "effects" exist because respondents with similar individual traits—but distinct regional locations—have different propensities to vote for each candidate.* To illustrate once again with Marta and María, this finding simply means that a middle-class, economically liberal, culturally conservative, urban female homemaker residing in a northern state has a higher probability of voting for the PAN than a southern woman with the same traits.

Previous studies too often treat a set of statistically significant regional "effects" as a genuine finding rather than an invitation to more research. The presence of nonzero coefficients on regional dummy variables means that region of residence explains residual variance in vote choice that the individual-level factors cannot. Stated differently, region-of-residence measures are atheoretical fixed-effects variables—proper nouns—that, when statistically significant, identify *unexplained* differences in voting behavior.[26] The same principle holds even if the regional measures are continuous measures of the region's political preferences. Our scholarly goal should be to account for the remaining unexplained differences with specific mechanisms, not treat them as a theoretical end point for understanding voting behavior. While most scholarship on the geography of vote choice in Brazil and Mexico shows that regional clustering is much more than the mere aggregation of individual-level traits and interests, it fails to demonstrate precisely *why* these remaining cross-regional differences exist.

We argue that peer effects explain why many individuals with similar traits and attitudes vote differently by region. Social influence induces disparities between individual-level patterns and aggregate outcomes. Again by way of example, Marta the northerner occupies a social environment with far more *panista* voters than María the southerner. The supply of potential *panista* discussants who would pull Marta away from the non-*panista* options is high in her blue state of Guanajuato, so social influence during campaigns persuades or reinforces her toward the PAN. For her part, María encounters far fewer *panista* discussants in her yellow state of Guerrero, so peer influence moves her preference elsewhere.[27] In these scenarios, social influence is *not* the first mover in creating regional political cleavages, and country expertise is imperative if we are to understand the historical process that created a particular pattern of political geography.[28] Observers must also recognize, however, that the regional clustering of voter preferences is more than the simple sum of individual parts. It also stems from differences in the political preferences of influential peers.

---

*We again put "effects" in quotation marks when referring to regression coefficients on geographical variables because these coefficients reveal little about how and whether region *causes* voting behavior.

To test this explanation, we employ a sequence of methodological techniques akin to those of the preceding chapter. Recall that the sequence follows the logic of a mediation analysis. If discussion networks do deepen the regionalization of politics, three conditions must hold. First, the distribution of preferences in individuals' social environments must influence the distribution of preferences in their discussant networks. The preceding chapter treated neighborhood as the relevant social environment, while in this chapter the relevant social environment is the state. Second, social networks must influence individuals' vote choices. Chapter 4 showed this to be the case in Brazil 2014 and Mexico 2006, but this chapter does so again with a different measurement approach. Third, the balance of political opinions in the discussion networks must account, at least to some degree, for regional "effects" on vote choice. If any of these three conditions is empirically untrue, then social influence is not a reason for the regional clustering of vote choice.

REGIONAL ENVIRONMENTS AND THE SELECTION OF DISCUSSANTS

Let us consider first whether the environmentally determined supply of potential discussants influences the distribution of preferences in citizens' social networks. As in chapter 5, this first step estimates models of ego's discussant selection. Our dependent variables are measures of discussants' vote intentions, namely, the proportion of ego's alters who support each candidate. In Brazil the set of dependent variables is *Pro-Dilma share among alters*, *Pro-Aécio share among alters*, and *Pro-Marina share among alters*. In Mexico the set is *Pro-Calderón share among alters*, *Pro-AMLO share among alters*, and *Pro-Madrazo share among alters*. Again, we measure these dependent variables at the campaign wave and model them as compositional data.[29]

We operationalize the social environment using state political preferences. States are a high level of aggregation, but they are the most relevant social environment for this chapter's focus on regionalism.[30] The median state in both countries has more than two million people, so individuals clearly do not sample their discussants from across their entire states. This chapter's central point, however, is that social contacts and discussion are a channel through which the biases in very large regional communities are communicated to and absorbed by individuals. Vote shares of parties in the prior presidential election serve as our measure of the supply of vote intentions among potential discussants. In both Brazil 2014 and Mexico 2006, vote shares from the prior election are a highly accurate measure of the political bias experienced by respondents in their regional social environments. No realignments or other major shifts in political geography occurred between our observed election and the previous one, and the three main party contenders were the same in both.[31] In Brazil our primary independent variables are *State PT support* (the omitted base category), *State PSDB support*, and *State Marina support*. In Mexico the independent variables are *State PAN support* (omitted baseline category), *State PRD Support*, and *State PRI support*.[32]

The models also contain individual traits that measure the demand for certain preferences in one's network. If homophily is especially strong, then the aggregate distribution of political preferences in individuals' social environments may be irrelevant. For example, *priístas* in Mexico City, where they are a trifling minority, may still seek out *priísta* discussants, avoiding political conversations with citizens who represent their environment's majority opinion. To account for this tendency, the models include measures of *Ego vote intention* (a lagged dependent variable), *Partisanship*, and a few demographic traits.

Discussant Selection in Brazil

According to the model results, the state-level social environment exerts an important impact on the ratio of pro-Dilma to pro-Aécio discussants in egos' social networks. (The full set of coefficients appears in table A.15.)[33] Pro-Dilma discussants were more common in the North and Northeast, in states where she had performed strongly four years earlier. Pro-Aécio discussants were more common in the South and Southeast, in states where the PSDB had done well four years earlier. Figure 6.6 illustrates the substantive effects of the state social environment by plotting predicted values for three different states. Each bar shows the predicted distribution of candidate support in the network of a voter whose individual traits are at the national averages. As illustrated with the Marta and María examples, we take statistically identical citizens (at least on the individual-level variables we include in the model) and vary only their state of residence. The leftmost bar corresponds to Maranhão, a state typical of the Northeast in its enthusiasm for Dilma in 2010. In 2014 pro-Dilma alters in Maranhão outnumbered pro-Aécio ones by nearly six-to-one in its average egocentric social network. By comparison, in the wealthy southern state of Santa Catarina (the middle bar), where the PSDB performed well in 2010, pro-Aécio alters outnumbered pro-Dilma ones during the 2014 campaign. In addition, we show the effect across the entire range of the independent variable by looking at Roraima. Roraima is a very small northern state that was an exception to its regional pattern in the 2010 presidential election in being the country's most pro-PSDB state. In Roraima during the 2014 campaign, the ratio of pro-Aécio to pro-Dilma discussants was almost three-to-one, despite Aécio's 20-point deficit in national polls at the time. A typical resident of Roraima was more than five times as likely to have a pro-Aécio discussant as was an otherwise identical resident of Maranhão.[34]

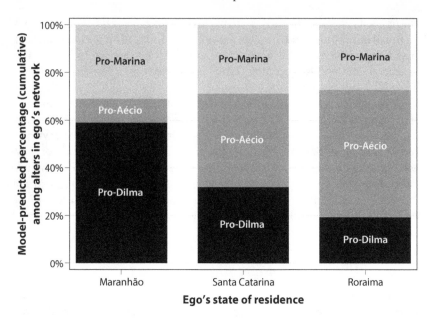

FIGURE 6.6 The Distribution of Vote Intentions among Alters by State in Brazil 2014: Predicted Percentages from a Fractional Multinomial Logit Model
Notes: Each bar portion is a model-predicted percentage. Dependent variables (*Pro-Dilma share among alters, Pro-Aécio share among alters, Pro-Marina share among alters,* and *Pro-other share among alters*) are measured in the campaign wave. Table A.15 reports the complete set of coefficient estimates in numerical form. $N = 749$. *Source:* BEPS 2014

State context had weaker, albeit statistically significant, effects on the share of pro-Marina discussants in Brazilians' discussion networks. The figure shows minimal differences in this share across the three states, but the relevant coefficients on *State Marina support* are statistically significant in the model. Comparing the model-predicted percentage of pro-Marina discussants from her strongest state (Brasília, the Federal District) to the percentage from her weakest state (Piauí) yields a difference of 16 points (45 percent to 29 percent). While this is a substantively important gap, it is more muted than the 30-point difference we observe when we compare the strongest and weakest states of the two major-party candidates. Marina's vote in 2010 was just as regionalized as that of her opponents,[35] but her support was not an entrenched and visible part of the political character of most states. Between 2010 and 2014, she switched between small parties and, as we noted earlier, entered the 2014 race only after the unexpected death of Campos. As a result, it is not surprising that her support within egocentric networks is only moderately linked with her previous

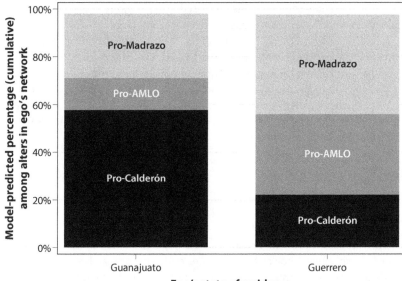

FIGURE 6.7 The Distribution of Vote Intentions among Alters by State in Mexico 2006: Predicted Percentages from a Fractional Multinomial Logit Model
Notes: Each bar portion is a model-predicted percentage. Dependent variables (*Pro-Calderón share among alters, Pro-AMLO share among alters, Pro-Madrazo share among alters,* and *Pro-other share among alters*) are measured in the campaign wave. Percentages do not sum to one hundred because of the exclusion of percentages for other candidates. Table A.16 reports the complete set of coefficient estimates in numerical form. $N = 948$.
Source: Mexico 2006 Panel.

vote in the state, whereas network support for Aécio and for Dilma *are* strongly linked to their previous performance in the state.

Discussant Selection in Mexico

Figure 6.7 shows similarly large model-predicted effects in Mexico. (The coefficients are reported in table A.16.) The figure shows predicted percentages for two hypothetical individuals who are average on all individual-level traits but differ by their state of residence. The first resides in Marta's Guanajuato in the north-central region. The predicted share of pro-Calderón discussants exceeds 50 percent, roughly four times the share of pro-AMLO alters and twice that of pro-Madrazo ones. In María's Guerrero, the predicted share of pro-Calderón discussants shrivels to 20 percent. The pro-AMLO share nearly triples in size and now outnumbers the pro-Calderón share by about 15 percentage points.

Also, the pro-Madrazo share has increased by half and is now twice the pro-Calderón share.[36] These substantive effects are very large.

In both countries, then, the regional social environment influences discussant choice above and beyond individual-level traits. Aggregate political leanings in a state dictate the supply of different political opinions among a voter's pool of potential discussants. This supply, in turn, influences the political biases to which the voter is exposed via informal conversation. We know from chapter 4 that these discussions exerted an influence on final vote choice in these two elections, but do they account for regional effects?

DISCUSSION AND REGIONAL EFFECTS ON VOTE CHOICE

We now repeat the preceding chapter's second exercise of estimating successively more fully specified models of *Ego vote choice*. This procedure discerns the extent to which individual-level factors, exposure to vertical political intermediaries, and then opinion in egocentric networks diminish the partial correlation between the political leaning of the regional environment and vote choice. Once again, all models control for vote intentions at the pre-campaign wave, so the coefficients on our measures of the social environment capture the extent to which voters gravitate toward the biases of their regions over the course of the campaign.

Vote Choice in Brazil

For vote choice in Brazil, we estimate three multinomial logit models. Vote for Dilma is the omitted baseline category in all three. Model 1 is a simplified estimation of regional "effects" only. Model 2 introduces measures of individual-level factors, including wealth-related variables, issue positions, and partisanship. These are factors that scholars often posit as underlying Brazil's regional divide. Model 3 then adds measures of political preferences within the respondent's social network. Because BEPS 2014 contains few measures of vertical intermediaries, we estimate just three models for this exercise. Table 6.2 reports the most relevant coefficients.

Model 1 shows the main regional "effect," shaded in gray, on shifts in vote choice during the campaign. Individuals in states that voted heavily for the PSDB in 2010 tended to move toward Aécio over the course of the campaign in 2014, while those in states that voted heavily for Dilma in 2010 switched toward Dilma. By introducing individual-level factors, Model 2 begins the effort of specifying the mechanisms behind this partial correlation between region and vote choice. The coefficient on the PSDB's previous vote share falls by about 15 percent. This reduction suggests that the campaign partially activated these factors, nudging some voters toward the candidate who most closely represented their individual values and interests. Still, the coefficient remains statistically distinguishable from zero. Introducing the measures of discussant preferences in model 3 attenuates this coefficient much more dramatically. It falls by 44 percent (or 37 percent of the original coefficient) and drops to statistical insignificance. In short, the regionalization of preferences between the PT's Dilma and the PSDB's Aécio in Brazil's 2014 election consisted of more than just the sum of individual interests, attitudes, and identities. Political discussions magnified this geographical clustering by exposing individuals to the political biases of their social environments.

On the right-hand half of the table, the pattern is repeated: the inclusion of discussant preferences attenuates the coefficient on state Marina support by 38 percent. It is important to note, additionally, that there is no statistically significant regional coefficient for change toward a Marina vote in any of the models—surely because Marina support was a weak aspect of politics in the states in which she had nonetheless performed well in the past.

Vote Choice in Mexico

Table 6.3 shows the results for the multinomial logit models of voting behavior in the Mexico 2006 election. With vote for Calderón as the omitted baseline category, we focus on the extent to which political leanings at the state level differentiate the AMLO versus Calderón vote (left-hand side) and the Madrazo versus Calderón vote (right-hand side). The key coefficients are shaded in gray. The Mexico 2006 Panel does contain measures of exposure to other political intermediaries—namely, party contact and television news viewership—so four models appear instead of three.

Focusing first on the PRD (AMLO) versus PAN (Calderón) divide, model 1 shows the regional "effect" to be large even when we control for lagged vote intention. By election day, the campaign had brought individuals more into line with the preferences of their states. Model 2 shows that the campaign's activation of individual-level predispositions explains part of this trend. The introduction of 13 traits that capture the standard explanations for Mexico's North/South political divide—issue positions, wealth, urbanization, partisanship—shrinks the regional coefficient by about 14 percent, but it remains highly statistically significant. Model 3 introduces measures of exposure to party contacting and television news, but their inclusion is *counterproductive* in accounting for the mechanisms behind the regional effect. Upon adding measures of discussants' preferences in model 4, we find that the lingering regional effect falls by 21 percent, more than it did when the individual-level factors were introduced. In other words, measures of social influence go further toward accounting for regional clustering than the commonly considered measures of individual-level interests and identities.

TABLE 6.2.
Ego's Vote Choice by State's Political Leaning and Possible Mediators in Brazil 2014: Results from Three Multinomial Logit Models

Dependent variable categories:	Aécio vote / Dilma vote			Marina vote / Dilma vote		
	Model 1	Model 2	Model 3	Model 1	Model 2	Model 3
Mediators:	None	Individual traits	Individual traits & discussants	None	Individual traits	Individual traits & discussants
Regional "Effects": State's Political Leaning						
State PSDB support	3.976* (1.745)	3.436* (1.608)	1.972 (1.599)	1.377 (1.453)	1.026 (1.438)	1.087 (1.227)
State Marina support	6.664* (3.303)	6.060* (2.798)	3.367 (2.764)	4.978 (3.845)	4.738 (3.417)	3.391 (3.373)
State PT support	Omitted baseline	Omitted baseline	Omitted baseline	Omitted baseline	Omitted baseline	Omitted baseline
Discussants' Vote Intentions (c wave)						
Pro-Aécio share among alters			3.716* (0.447)			0.185 (0.607)

Pro-Marina share among alters				2.802* (0.337)	3.028* (0.543)
Singleton				1.381* (0.280)	1.049* (0.354)
Pro-Dilma share among alters				Omitted baseline	Omitted baseline
Other Variables					
Ego vote intention (*pc* wave) (3 vars.)	Included	Included	Included	Included	Included
Individual-level traits (*pc* wave) (9 vars.)	Not included	Included	Not included	Included	Included

Notes: Entries are multinomial logit coefficients and robust standard errors (corrected for clustering within states) in parentheses. Dependent variable for each model is *Ego vote choice. pc* = pre-campaign wave, *c* = campaign wave. Table A.17 reports the complete set of coefficient estimates in numerical form.

$N = 913$. $* = p < 0.05$.

Source: BEPS 2014.

TABLE 6.3.
Ego's Vote Choice by State's Political Leaning and Possible Mediators in Mexico 2006: Results from Four Multinomial Logit Models

Dependent variable categories:	AMLO vote Calderón vote				Madrazo vote Calderón vote			
Mediators:	Model 1	Model 2	Model 3	Model 4	Model 1	Model 2	Model 3	Model 4
	None	Individual traits	Individual traits & other intermediaries	Individual traits & other intermediaries & discussants	None	Individual traits	Individual traits & other intermediaries	Individual traits & other intermediaries & discussants
Regional "Effects": State's Political Leaning								
State PRD support	5.507* (1.292)	4.717* (1.268)	5.330* (1.315)	4.221* (1.385)	3.217* (1.060)	3.770* (1.302)	3.624* (1.349)	3.124* (1.320)
State PRI support	3.321 (2.553)	3.556 (2.556)	3.505 (2.688)	2.600 (2.740)	3.595 (1.904)	5.464* (1.685)	5.497* (1.723)	4.155* (1.675)
State PAN support	Omitted baseline	Omitted baseline	Omitted baseline	Omitted baseline	Omitted baseline	Omitted baseline	Omitted baseline	Omitted baseline
Discussants' Vote Intentions (c wave)								
Pro-AMLO share among alters				3.346* (0.499)				0.720 (0.520)
Pro-Madrazo share among alters				1.924* (0.588)				2.581* (0.455)

	(1)	(2)	(3)	(4)	(5)	(6)
Singleton			1.781* (0.428)			1.669* (0.429)
Pro-Calderón share among alters			Omitted baseline			Omitted baseline
Other Variables						
Ego vote intention (pc wave) (4 vars.)	Included	Included	Included	Included	Included	Included
Individual-level traits (pc wave) (13 vars.)	Not included	Included	Included	Not included	Included	Included
Other political intermediaries (e wave) (6 vars.)	Not included	Not included	Included	Not included	Not included	Included

Notes: Entries are logit coefficients and robust standard errors (corrected for clustering within states) in parentheses. Dependent variable for each model is *Ego vote choice*. pc = pre-campaign wave, c = campaign wave, e = election wave. Table A.18 reports the complete set of coefficient estimates in numerical form. $N = 1{,}325$. $* = p < 0.05$.
Source: Mexico 2006 Panel.

Repeating the progression through the four models on the right-hand half of the table leads to a similar conclusion. In differentiating a Madrazo vote from a Calderón vote, the activation of individual-level factors plays no role in accounting for the regional "effect" on changes in vote choice during the campaign. In fact, their inclusion in the model is counterproductive. The coefficient on regional leanings, by contrast, falls by 25 percent when we introduce network measures in model 4.

Our fullest specifications have not completely eliminated regional "effects" from these regression models. For example, given a northerner and a southerner with identical (observed) individual-level traits, vertical intermediation sources, and discussant networks, the northerner is still more likely to vote for Calderón. Without exception, however, the inclusion of network characteristics moves the coefficients on regional leanings in the right direction—toward zero. Unmeasured factors at the individual level, regionally based media biases,[37] endorsements by subnational political leaders,[38] and discussion with individuals beyond the three whom respondents could name—all these factors might contribute to the continued statistical significance of the state-level coefficients in Mexico.

CONCLUSION

In Brazil and Mexico regional differences in vote choice are greater than the differences that individual factors alone dictate. Stated differently, citizens with similar personal and political traits who live in different regions cast different ballots. Social influence is one factor that makes regional differences more than the mere aggregation of micro-level traits. Spatial clustering is sharper than the sum of its individual parts because citizens are embedded in social networks that vary dramatically with their place of residence. Over the course of a campaign, voters are exposed to political suggestions and arguments from persuasive peers, and the political biases of these messages vary with the supply of candidate preferences in voters' social environments.

With these findings, we urge scholars to treat the presence of significant regional effects as a *starting point* for further inquiry into the mechanisms of geographical variation in voting behavior, not as a substantive conclusion about the causes of voting behavior. In Brazil and Mexico previous scholarship has accomplished much on this explanatory front, so we build on these efforts. Individual-level factors, such as wealth and attitudes about issues, are *partially* responsible for Mexico's yellow-state/blue-state divide, and they are *partially* responsible for Brazil's North/South divide. We move a step further to demonstrate that social influence deepens these divides. Many voters do not fit the dominant demographic and attitudinal profiles of their regions, but they still vote with the prevailing partisan leanings of their geographical surroundings after gravitating toward those leanings via influential conversations during the campaign. Plenty of southern Brazilians are poor, and lots of northern Brazilians dislike Bolsa Família, but many individuals like these absorb their regions' political biases after listening to persuasive peers. In this sense, social communication *magnifies* the political consequences of individual-level interests and values within a region. In the next chapter we consider the implications of these magnifying effects for the behavior of strategic political elites.

PART III

Implications of a Horizontally Networked World

7

Clientelism as the Purchase of Social Influence

Coauthored with Joby Schaffer

When a [medical] treatment exists but there is not enough money to offer it to everybody who needs it, we should primarily give it to the hubs.

—*Albert László Barabási*[1]

Parts I and II of this book demonstrated that election results in Latin America are more than the sum of private decisions reached in isolation. Rather, run-ups to election days involve a swirl of horizontal social interactions among voters, many of whom are open to the inputs of their peers as they decide on candidates. For strategic elites, the political tactics they should use on an electorate of interconnected voters are different from the tactics they should use on an electorate of social isolates. Despite this simple fact, scholarship on vertical intermediation and party linkages to voters typically assumes that citizens have no important horizontal ties.

Consider the rapidly expanding research agenda on clientelism, a common form of vertical intermediation in Latin America. If, hypothetically, the electorate consisted only of socially isolated citizens, party machines should target clientelistic payoffs to voters strictly on the basis of their individual traits. Though decidedly unrealistic, this scenario is assumed by the balance of scholarship on clientelistic targeting. Scholars have variously asserted that machine operatives should purchase the support of *swing voters*, buy the turnout of *unmobilized supporters*, reward the loyalty of *past supporters*, or encourage the activism of *loyal partisans*.[2] To the extent that scholarship on clientelism has considered citizens' networks, it has focused only on vertical ties between party and citizen.[3]

In the real world voters *are* embedded in politically influential horizontal networks, so the strategic calculus of parties is very different. Party machines should direct payoffs to citizens who are hubs—that is, citizens who are opinion-leading epicenters in their informal conversation networks. (Recall the epigraph.) Hubs give parties indirect access to voters who are not directly paid off themselves. In essence, party machines should buy the persuasive services of their clients, a strategy we call the purchase of social influence. This strategy has greater yield than the buying of, say, swing voters or turnout because it can create a social-magnification effect: the effect of the clientelistic gift is magnified via the conversion of multiple voters within a payoff recipient's existing conversational networks.

This chapter analyzes public opinion surveys from 22 Latin American countries to show that parties target individuals who engage in persuasive political talk. An important finding central to competing theories of clientelistic targeting—the finding that loyal partisans are the most likely targets—loses empirical support when we hold constant citizens' propensities to persuade. We then use the Mexico 2006 Panel to test the exogeneity of our (and other scholars') primary causal variables. The analysis confirms that party machines target individuals who, in the past, have been embedded in large discussion networks. It also shows how endogeneity bias drives the claim that loyal partisans are the most likely targets. Loyalty to the machine emerges only *after* payoffs have been made. Our argument suggests that clientelism can produce a higher yield for parties than previously thought, since the effects of payoffs can be magnified through discussion networks. This helps explain why an otherwise expensive and risky strategy is so common in the developing world. Finally, this chapter provides suggestive cross-national evidence to explain why clientelism declines as a society grows wealthier and more media-rich. Clientelism thrives in media-poor environments because persuasion via social communication is virtually the *only* way for parties to reach the many potential voters they cannot directly contact.

WHO IS BOUGHT?

Clientelism is the vertical form of intermediation by which politicians—mostly through party machine operatives—offer goods, services, or jobs to citizens in the expectation that these citizens will return the favor with some form of political support. We use "target" as shorthand for someone who has been offered a clientelistic enticement from a machine operative. The "operative" distributes favors on behalf of an election-seeking politician (the "patron"). Because not all targets accept the enticements, we refer to those who do accept as "clients." We exclude from this definition the practice of targeting a relatively large group of people with club goods, a practice better labeled as "pork barreling." Clientelism, in short, is the delivery of private goods in search of votes.

The central question in the scholarly literature on clientelism asks what kinds of voters are most likely to be offered enticements in exchange for their vote. Cross-national estimates show that, in most developing countries, between 5 percent and 35 percent of citizens receive payoffs.[4] Which 5 to 35 percent do operatives target? Susan Stokes puts the question in illustrative terms:

> About 40 voters live in [a machine operative's] neighborhood, and her responsibility is to get them to the polls and get them to vote for her party. But the party gives her only 10 bags of food to distribute. . . . How does she, and machine operatives like her in systems around the world, decide who among her neighbors shall and who shall not receive handouts?[5]

Initially it seemed almost self-evident that a party machine would target swing voters—those most likely to be favorably swayed by the enticement—or even the subset of swing voters weakly opposed to the party.[6] Under this so-called vote-buying strategy, machines view payoffs as a means of converting clients. The machine targets those non-supporters most easily moved, rather than those already firmly in their camp or firmly opposed. This view, however, has been challenged by a stubborn empirical fact: when choosing clients, the typical machine seems to favor supporters of its own party.[7] Our own findings provide a further challenge: in chapter 4 we found that clientelism did little to induce vote switching.[8]

Does clientelism make sense when the machine already has the beneficiaries of its payoffs in the bag? Three alternative logics have been proposed as solutions to this loyal-voter anomaly.[9] One sees targeted favors to already-strong supporters as the buying of maintenance, also called a rewarding-loyalists strategy.[10] When a machine fears that strong supporters will drift to opposing parties if they are taken for granted, the machine will channel benefits to these strong supporters, maintaining relationships that will keep these supporters within the party's core constituency. A second alternative consistent with targeting strong supporters is the turnout-buying strategy. Here a machine operative delivers favors to demobilized or passive supporters—that is, citizens who favor the party already but are unlikely to vote without a clientelistic prod.[11]

These answers to the loyal-voter anomaly are innovative, but they present their own problems. It is hard to see how a rewarding-loyalists approach is an equilibrium strategy for any party. Why would machines squander benefits on strong supporters in the current election, thus putting victory at risk just to maintain these voters as core constituents in a future election?[12] Parties focusing on the future risk losing in the present. The turnout-buying strategy, in contrast, is on more solid theoretical grounds. Its shortcomings are largely empirical. Scholars have mustered little evidence for the claim that targets were more likely to abstain (before receipt of a benefit) than non-targets. If anything, evidence shows the contrary: targets are *more* likely than non-targets to be participatory citizens.[13] Indeed, if targets are already supporters of a party, they are more likely to vote, according to empirical and theoretical findings, than the average citizen.[14]

In response to these failings, Stokes et al. offer a third solution to the loyal-voter anomaly.[15] Machine operatives, they claim, are brokers who may not have their patrons' best interests at heart. Brokers devote excessive payoffs to strong supporters, thus performing suboptimally for both patron and party, because of agency slack—that is, the inability of principals (patrons) to control their agents (brokers). In particular, brokers subordinate the goal of maximizing votes for their patrons to the goal of maintaining their own positions as brokers. Brokers hold desirable positions because they can withhold some of the clientelistic goods meant for distribution, thus benefiting themselves. Maintaining their positions requires brokers to demonstrate effectiveness to their patrons, which they do by recruiting as many clients as possible into their vertical partisan networks. A broker's preferred target is someone who is easy to recruit, meaning a citizen who already supports the patron's party and who is willing to do visible things such as attending rallies and performing campaign work.[16] Brokers, in other words, target loyalists of their own party to maximize the number of voters in their vertical partisan networks. This subordinates their patrons' primary goals of vote buying and turnout buying because these voters are already strong supporters. Payoffs yield few extra votes for the patron. We call this the engagement-buying strategy.

The engagement-buying solution to the loyal-voter anomaly is a major theoretical breakthrough, but its empirical grounding is thin. Scholars have yet to demonstrate that clientelistic payoffs go to those who can be swayed into becoming engaged, visible members of a broker's partisan network. In addition, the jury is still out on whether the loyal-voter anomaly results from endogeneity bias. Virtually all findings in support of this claim are post-receipt measures. The findings are typically based on survey questions in which respondents report their current partisanship and whether they *previously* received clientelistic benefits. While some scholars have been attentive to the specter of "endogenous loyalty"—gift recipients becoming loyal partisans only after receiving the benefit—they have yet to address the issue convincingly by comparing partisanship before and after the receipt of gifts.[17]

SOCIAL INFLUENCE BUYING AND THE MAGNIFICATION EFFECT

Whom do party machines buy? We offer a different answer to this question, an answer that recognizes citizens' embeddedness not just in *vertical* partisan networks but, more importantly, in *horizontal* social networks. Let us reconsider Stokes' illustration. A party operative with payoffs for just 10 of 40 persons would be wise to give them not to 10 swing voters, not to 10 potential nonvoters, not to 10 potential rally attenders, but rather to the 10 voters who are most likely to reach the other 30 with the machine's partisan message. In other words, machine operatives should target hubs—the opinion leaders in small informal discussion networks. They should seek to purchase social influence.

Figure 7.1 illustrates, with two sociograms, the logic behind this strategy of buying social influence within horizontal networks, contrasting these horizontal networks with the strictly vertical partisan networks[18] that predominate in the standard vote-, turnout-, and engagement-buying models.[19] Frame A depicts these standard models. They imply a vertical relationship between two nodes, a machine operative and a client.[20] Ties between the nodes are directional in the following ways: the operative grants a clientelistic favor with the expectation of garnering a vote for the patron (vote buying), mobilizing an otherwise abstaining client to vote for the patron (turnout buying), or rallying the client to become politically active for the patron (engagement buying). Note that the operative makes the payoff simply to influence the behavior of the client. In other words, operatives see clients as terminal nodes (in the language of network theory), so clientelistic influence arrives at a dead end upon reaching the client. This illustrates why standard models of clientelism see the practice as strictly hierarchical and socially atomizing, a phenomenon of one-to-one exchange between machine and voter.[21] Finally, frame A depicts, with the node colors, the partisan nature of the relationship implied by the loyal-voter anomaly: the client is already a supporter of the operative's (Black) party.

Frame B depicts the logic behind the strategy of buying social influence. The machine operative observes voters' embeddedness in their horizontal networks and selects one with the expectation that this recipient will engage in subsequent social persuasion. In the language of network theory, the operative targets a hub, meaning someone who is a high-degree node (i.e., has a large egocentric network) *and* has high outdegree (i.e., influence). The operative intends for the favor to energize the client to proselytize the machine's partisan message to non-client peers, essentially seeding a preexisting discussion network by paying off the individual who wields the most influence within it. In targeting the voter with a long-standing propensity to talk and persuade, the operative need not incur extra costs to create conversations or persuasive opportunities that would not otherwise exist. Conversely, the operative does not target the four nodes who have no outdegree and only one tie each. The central essence of our social-influence-buying framework is the choice by the operative to target the hub rather than the hub's less connected peers.[22]

This sociogram also builds in our finding that opinion leaders tend to be politically knowledgeable (designated by the client's large vertically hatched ring). In fact, this sociogram is a redrawing of the one in figure 1.4, but with the simple addition of the vertical tie to the operative. The knowledgeable uncle

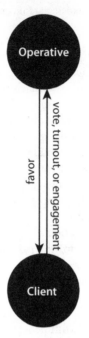

Frame A: The Vote-, Turnout- and Engagement-Buying Models

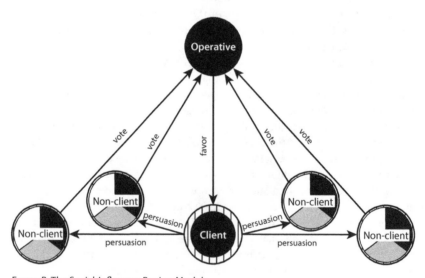

Frame B: The Social-Influence-Buying Model

FIGURE 7.1 Sociograms for Two Different Conceptualizations of Clientelism
Notes: Node color indicates support for Black party, White party, or Gray party. A tricolored node means the actor is undecided. Thickness of the rings with vertically hatched lines in frame B indicates amount of actor's political knowledge. Arrowheads indicate direction of resource flows (vote or favor) or of persuasion.

from figure 1.4 is now recast as the client, while Eva, her father, and the other undecided and less knowledgeable nodes are now nameless non-clients. The operative pays off the knowledgeable and well-connected node because so many individuals turn to that node for voting advice.

With respect to the partisan preferences of clients and non-clients, frame B depicts just one among many possible scenarios that are compatible with the framework. In this scenario the client is a co-partisan of the operative, consistent with the findings on the loyal-voter anomaly. Moreover, this client is particularly valuable to the operative because the client's peers are all undecided and thus highly amenable to persuasion. Other scenarios are also compatible with a strategy of buying social influence. A hub is still valuable if tied to co-partisans, since the hub can provide social reinforcement or encourage the non-client ties to provide turnout or engagement for the machine. Indeed, if the loyal-voter anomaly does not hold and the operative instead chooses among swing or even out-partisan voters, the operative would still be wise to target those who are well connected.

By targeting hubs, party machines seek to create a social-magnification effect,[23] increasing their returns from a single payoff. The impact of the payoff disseminates, via persuasive discussion within horizontal social networks, to non-clients like ripples in a pond.[24] Preference change, documented in chapter 4, occurs among those who were never direct beneficiaries of a clientelist enticement, and parties can forge indirect linkages with voters through direct targeting of relatively few individuals. For parties, therefore, the purchase of social influence potentially yields higher returns than the mere purchase of individual votes or turnout, making it more profitable than strategies that treat clients as terminal nodes. In fact, as Huckfeldt and Sprague point out, the existence of clientelism may *depend* on informal persuasion:

> Even at the height of the so-called machine era in [US] party politics, jobs and favors and assistance were not distributed on a tit-for-tat basis—one job for one vote. Such an enterprise would have bankrupted even the wealthiest party organization. Rather, party efforts at electoral mobilization inevitably depend upon a process of social diffusion and informal persuasion. If a party worker can succeed in convincing Sally to vote Democratic, then Sally might be able to convince Bill, and so on. The investment of party resources becomes more potent to the extent that the votes of individuals are interdependent because the initial contact has cascading consequences in the collective deliberations of democracy.[25]

The social-influence-buying argument implies a reinterpretation of the loyal-voter anomaly. Targets, to reiterate our claim, are chosen not for their partisanship but for their persuasive propensities and their access to relatively large pools of downstream voters. For instance, it could be worthwhile for a party operative to target an even minimally swayable out-partisan if that target provides the machine with indirect access to numerous voters. In this case the average vote yield to the machine may be higher than the yield from tar-geting a socially isolated swing voter or co-partisan.[26] Previous work does show that partisans of the machine are more likely than nonpartisans to receive gifts, but we believe that this result—depicted by the hub's loyalty to the operative's party in frame B—is due to omitted-variable and endogeneity bias. Recall from chapters 2 and 4 that opinion leaders are more likely to be politically knowl-edgeable. As a result, failure to control for the respondent's propensity to per-suade, for network size, or for political knowledge creates omitted-variable bias in any estimation of the effects of partisanship. The loyal-voter anomaly, more-over, may be partially due to endogeneity bias, whereby the payoff boosts the probability of strong partisanship, not vice versa.

Finally, our argument also reinterprets the machine's instrumental vision of horizontal ties. To reiterate, almost all previous studies of clientelism ignore horizontal social networks. The few studies that are exceptions to this rule see horizontal networks as a means for operatives to monitor whether clients vote in accordance with the wishes of the machine. An operative, the argument holds, can rely on a client's contacts to convey whether the client reciprocated the payoff, thereby resolving the compliance puzzle—that is, the puzzle of why clients vote for the party that paid them off when they could use the secret bal-lot to vote their conscience.[27] On its face, however, it is not clear why a client's social contacts would betray the client's lack of reciprocity. Moreover, the com-pliance puzzle contradicts the finding that clients are already machine loyal-ists. Finally, the compliance puzzle is a true puzzle only in a world where voters are strictly selfish. Research shows that nonrational norms of reci-procity in clientelistic relationships are widespread.[28] In the end, clients' horizontal networks are far more useful to machines as magnifiers than as enforcers.

HYPOTHESES

Party operatives seek targets, we argue, who have the capacity and proclivity to create indirect returns for the machine through informal social influence. To set the stage for the analysis, this section presents our primary hypotheses and compares them to those offered by the vote-, turnout-, and engagement-buying alternatives.

We expect to find that citizens who frequently attempt to influence the po-litical choices of others and who are embedded in large political-discussion net-works are more likely to be targeted by machines than are those less prone or less well-positioned to engage in social influence. Because a central premise of this book is that opinion leaders are politically knowledgeable, we also expect to find a correlation between knowledge and the propensity to be a target.

Furthermore, machines should prefer targets who are embedded in conversational networks with a low degree of insularity, meaning networks with ties to the community and not just immediate family. Individuals with a large number of ties to nonfamily contacts wield greater influence than those with few nonfamily ties, so the potential exists for larger social-magnification effects.[29] Among highly insular individuals—those whose political discussants are all family members—persuasive efforts are subject to a dead end, staying within their isolated familial bonds. Also, although local operatives are deeply knowledgeable about their bailiwicks, it is surely easier for them to identify those who talk politics outside the home than those who talk politics only inside the home.

In selecting their targets, party machines should be more focused on potential clients' persuasive capacities than on their partisan leanings. This contrasts with the turnout- and engagement-buying alternatives, which identify partisans of the operative's party as the most likely targets. We hypothesize that this loyal-partisan finding is partly spurious and partly endogenous. In other words, it will weaken when we control for a respondent's tendency to persuade others and when we control for declared partisanship measured *prior* to the receipt of a clientelistic benefit.

DATA AND RESULTS

To test these hypotheses, we use the 2010 Americas Barometer (conducted by the Latin American Public Opinion Project, LAPOP) and the Mexico 2006 Panel.[30] The LAPOP 2010 project asked respondents whether they were offered election-year clientelistic enticements and how frequently they tried to persuade others to vote a certain way.

Because the LAPOP data are cross-sectional, a positive correlation between the propensity to persuade and the likelihood of being a target fails to distinguish between two different causal scenarios. Do machines seek out preexisting opinion leaders, nudging them toward persuading on behalf of the machine? Or do they create opinion leaders through the payoff, enticing otherwise politically reticent citizens to become persuaders? We suspect that the former is at work. Research on the propensity to discuss politics and to be communally involved shows a high degree of temporal persistence within individuals.[31] In the Mexico 2006 Panel, for example, *Egocentric network size* is correlated at +0.79 between the campaign and election waves. This means that a campaign gift is unlikely to turn a politically mute person into a talkative one. Moreover, efficiency-minded machines should seek out individuals with proven records as frequent persuaders and as high-degree nodes, not try to create new social relationships via a nominal payoff.

To provide an empirical basis for this claim, we follow up our cross-sectional analysis of LAPOP responses with an analysis of the Mexico 2006 Panel. Its longitudinal structure allows us to distinguish between these two logics and to explore whether the loyal-voter anomaly is simply due to endogenous partisanship. In addition, the Mexico 2006 Panel is the rare survey dataset that contains both egocentric network data and a self-report of clientelistic targeting.

For both datasets, the dependent variable is a dichotomous measure of whether the respondent reported an experience with clientelism. The exact wording of the LAPOP variable, *Target of clientelism*, is as follows: "In recent years and thinking about election campaigns, has a candidate or someone from a political party offered you something like a favor, food, or any other benefit or object in return for your vote or support?" For the Mexico 2006 Panel, which asked respondents just after a campaign, the wording of the variable *Paid off by a party* is "Over the last few weeks, has a representative of a political party or candidate given you a gift, money, meals, groceries, or any other type of help?"[32]

Clientelistic Targets as Frequent Persuaders

We begin with an analysis of the full 22-country LAPOP sample. To test our main hypothesis, we use *Persuasion frequency*, a four-point scale ranging from "never" to "frequently." This question measures the frequency with which respondents tried "to convince others to vote for a party or candidate" during election times. Latin American party machines should target those who report a high frequency of persuasive attempts. Figure 7.2 shows clearly that this kind of targeting occurs. Benefit recipients are more than twice as likely as non-recipients to be frequent persuaders, and non-recipients are 27 percentage points more likely never to engage in persuasion.

To provide more rigorous statistical tests, we estimate statistical models that determine whether this strong relationship holds when one controls for alternative theories of clientelistic targeting. The models include a dummy variable measuring whether the respondent is a *Partisan identifier*. Unfortunately, LAPOP did not measure which party paid off the self-identified targets, so it is impossible for us to know whether parties are buying their own or someone else's partisans. Nonetheless, we can state what patterns in the available data would be consistent with each alternative theory. First, if the vote-buying (swing-voter) hypothesis is correct, the coefficient on partisan identifier will be *negatively* signed. This would mean that nonpartisans are receiving benefits at a higher rate than partisans. Second, if engagement buying is taking place, then the coefficient on partisan identifier will have a *positive* sign. Third, if social-influence buying drives client selection, then the coefficient on partisan identifier will be a statistical *zero* when we control for persuasion frequency. Fourth, if the turnout-buying model is correct, then partisan identifier will be

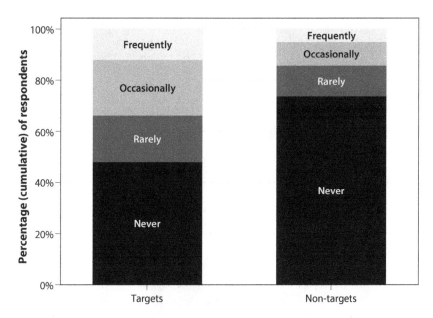

FIGURE 7.2 Persuasion Frequency among Targets and Non-targets in 22 Latin American Countries
Notes: The two categories on the horizontal axis are defined by *Target of clientelism.* Difference of means between the two is statistically significant at $p < .001$. $N = 36,622$.
Source: LAPOP 2010.

positively correlated with targeting *and* the coefficient on *Political participation index* will be *negatively* signed. The turnout model argues that parties are attempting to get unmobilized supporters to the polls, so those who are disinclined to participate should be targets of clientelism.[33] It is also important to control for these forms of participation because our measure of persuasion frequency could just be a proxy for participatory tendencies. Those who participate may be more likely to be rewarded with benefits, so a positive correlation between persuasion frequency and receipt of payoffs could be, in lieu of this control, spurious.[34]

Figure 7.3 plots the coefficient estimates from two models. Model 1 tests the vote-buying and turnout-buying arguments by estimating the effect of partisan identification and political participation. Both theoretical arguments, given these results, are inaccurate. Partisans and the highly participatory are more likely than nonpartisans and the unparticipatory, respectively, to report receipt of a campaign gift. In other words, neither swing voters nor unmobilized supporters are targeted. Instead, model 1 suggests that machine operatives target loyal and participatory voters, a pattern most consistent with the engagement-buying argument.

Dependent variable: target of clientelism

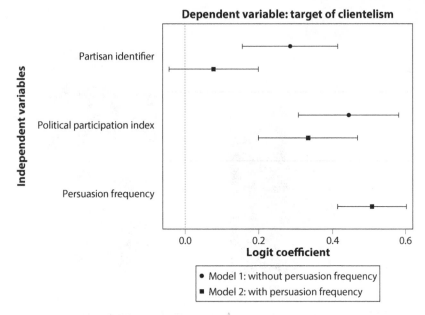

FIGURE 7.3 Clientelistic Targeting by Persuasion Frequency in 22 Latin American Countries in 2010: Results from Two Binary Logit Models
Notes: Each marker is a logit coefficient with 95 percent confidence interval. Table A.19 reports the complete sets of coefficient estimates in numerical form. $N = 35{,}854$.
Source: LAPOP 2010.

The introduction of persuasion frequency in model 2, however, dispels the notion that engagement buying underlies this pattern of findings. The coefficient on persuasion frequency is positive and highly statistically significant: moving from "never" to "frequently" yields a 0.20 increase in the probability of receiving a campaign gift. For an otherwise average respondent, the probability than triples, from 0.08 to 0.28. Just as important is the fact that the addition of persuasion frequency obliterates the coefficient on partisan identifier, as it declines in size by nearly 75 percent. In other words, partisanship appears relevant in the trim model (model 1) only because of its correlation with persuasion frequency. This is a strong indication that Latin American party machines are seeking *persuaders* when distributing clientelistic benefits. Operatives do not focus on potential recipients' partisan loyalties.

Another observable implication of our argument is that targets should be more knowledgeable about politics than non-targets. (Recall figure 7.1.) This is not because operatives are seeking out well-informed voters per se. Nor is it (as we established in figure 2.5) for endogenous reasons, whereby targets glean more knowledge about politics from the payoff itself. Rather, in targeting hubs,

TABLE 7.1.

Clientelistic Targeting by Persuasion Frequency in Brazil, Mexico, and Argentina in 2010: Coefficients from Six Binary Logit Models

	Brazil		Mexico		Argentina	
	Model 1	Model 2	Model 3	Model 4	Model 5	Model 6
Persuasion frequency		0.496*		0.418*		0.562*
		(0.056)		(0.082)		(0.075)
Partisan identifier	0.203	0.060	0.082	−0.025	0.611*	0.266
	(0.121)	(0.125)	(0.153)	(0.157)	(0.175)	(0.189)
Political partici-pation index	−0.014	−0.167	0.427*	0.367*	0.428	0.319
	(0.141)	(0.142)	(0.150)	(0.153)	(0.248)	(0.250)
Constant	−1.703*	−2.088*	−1.652*	−1.788*	−1.680*	−2.089*
	(0.070)	(0.087)	(0.083)	(0.089)	(0.086)	(0.109)
N	2,309		1,521		1,299	

Notes: Entries are logit coefficients with standard errors in parentheses. Dependent variable for each model is *Target of clientelism*.

$^* = p < .05.$

Source: LAPOP 2010.

operatives buy off the individuals to whom many poorly informed voters defer, and these individuals hold these opinion-leading roles precisely because they tend to be—as we have stressed throughout this book—politically knowledge-able. We evaluate this argument with two more models of clientelistic target-ing, reported as models 3 and 4 in table A.19 of appendix A. Using an index constructed from LAPOP's *Political knowledge* battery, we do find a statisti-cally significant relationship between knowledge and targeting in model 3. According to model-predicted probabilities, highly informed citizens are more than twice as likely to receive a payoff as poorly informed ones (0.15 versus 0.06). The statistically significant coefficient on political knowledge disappears, however, when we control for persuasion frequency (model 4). The apparent relevance of political knowledge to targeting is incidental to the more important attraction for operatives, a propensity to persuade peers.

Table 7.1 shows the statistical results for our two main cases, Brazil and Mex-ico, plus Argentina, a case that has weighed heavily in previous studies of cli-entelism. The table moves through the two model specifications (as in figure 7.3) for each of the three countries. The most important result from figure 7.3 is rep-licated across the three cases: *Persuasion frequency* is statistically significant, and its inclusion dramatically lowers the coefficients on *Partisan identifier*. Party machines, then, are not seeking co-partisans, swing voters, or unmo-bilized supporters. Rather, they seek hubs. Targets who frequently engage in influential political talk have real drawing power for party machines. The attraction of machines to these persuasive peers lies in the ability to harness networks of social communication.

Mexican Clients as High-Degree Nodes

In this subsection we tease out remaining questions about the direction of causality and assess the impact of a completely different measure of respondents' propensities to engage in horizontal political discussion. The Mexico 2006 Panel is valuable on both counts. Our primary expectation is that Mexican machine operatives seek to make clients out of high-degree, low-insularity nodes—that is, individuals with a relatively large number of nonfamilial political discussants. We also expect that clients were high-degree, low-insularity nodes *before* they became clients, but they were not necessarily strong partisans of the machine before becoming clients.

Our dependent variable is *Paid off by a party*, the election-wave measure of whether respondents reported receiving a gift in the preceding few weeks.[35] The primary independent variables are campaign-wave measures of network size. In contrast to the analysis of the LAPOP cross-sectional data above—not to mention most previous analyses of clientelistic targeting in the developing world—use of these variables puts the hypothesis test in the proper temporal order: operatives learn who wields social influence and then target those people. Two variables gauge respondents' relevant network traits: *Number of nonfamilial alters* and *Number of familial alters*. As a primary test of the theory of social-influence buying, we hypothesize that those with a large number of nonfamilial political discussants in the campaign wave drew the attention of political machines in the weeks prior to the July election. To capture the main alternative theories, *Strength of partisanship* is included as an ordinal trichotomy (0 for independents, 1 for weak partisans, 2 for strong partisans). We estimate three models that vary only in the timing of the strength of partisanship measure. These differences in timing allow us to distinguish between the loyal-voter hypothesis and the endogenous-loyalty hypothesis.

The model estimates, reported in figure 7.4, conform closely to the expectations generated by the social-influence-buying model. Most important, the number of nonfamilial discussants, as measured *before* the delivery of clientelistic benefits, is a statistically significant predictor of which Mexicans are targeted. Among respondents without nonfamilial discussants, the average predicted probability of being a client is 0.034. Among those with three nonfamilial discussants, the probability is 0.073, more than doubling the propensity to receive a clientelistic favor.[36] As expected, the impact of family network size is smaller and not statistically significant. Mexican machines seek to create clients of individuals who have many nonfamilial ties.

The results also cast serious doubt on the claim that machines seek already-loyal partisans. Instead, in line with the social-influence-buying approach,

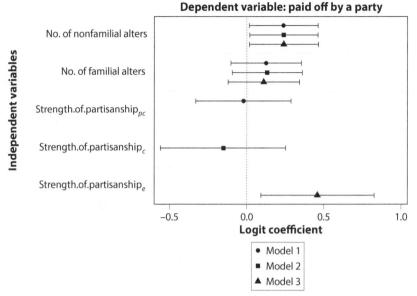

FIGURE 7.4 Clientelistic Targeting by Egocentric Network Size in Mexico 2006: Results from Three Binary Logit Models
Notes: Each marker is a logit coefficient with 95 percent confidence interval. *Number of nonfamilial alters* and *Number of familial alters* are both measured at the campaign wave. pc = pre-campaign, c = campaign wave, e = election wave. Table A.20 reports the complete sets of coefficient estimates in numerical form. $N = 1,358$.
Source: Mexico 2006 Panel.

targets are more likely to express partisanship *after* receiving the payoff. Before and during the campaign, those who later became clients were *not* more likely to express a partisan leaning than those who remained non-clients (models 1 and 2). Yet *Strength of partisanship* has a positive and statistically significant effect when measured in the election wave, *after the payoffs were made* (model 3). Stated differently, the observed correlation upon which turnout-buying and engagement-buying claims are based requires that we measure partisan loyalty after targeting has occurred. The standard gap in partisan loyalties between clients and non-clients emerged only *after* the delivery of campaign benefits. Collectively, these results are more supportive of the phenomenon of endogenous loyalty—whereby clientelistic targeting creates machine partisans—than of the loyal-voter anomaly fundamental to these alternative perspectives.

We address this issue more directly by depicting trends in partisanship and network size through time. During the campaign, did partisanship and network size increase more among those who received payoffs than among those who did not receive payoffs? Either finding would cast doubt on the variable as an exogenous driver of clientelistic targeting.

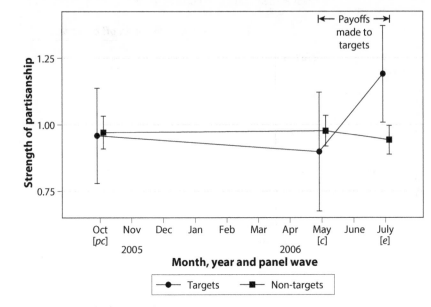

Frame A: Strength of Partisanship

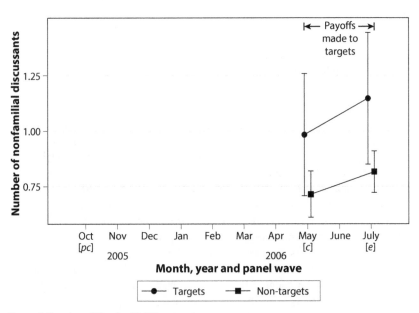

Frame B: Number of Nonfamilial Discussants

FIGURE 7.5 Trends in Strength of Partisanship and the Number of Nonfamilial Discussants among Clientelistic Targets and Non-targets: Mexico 2006
Notes: Each marker is an observed mean with 95 percent confidence interval. *Paid off by a party* is used to determine who was a target.
Source: Mexico 2006 Panel.

Figure 7.5 confirms the suspicions raised in figure 7.4 by plotting some observed means. Partisanship is largely endogenous to receipt of a payoff, while network size is not. Frame A of the figure depicts means (with 95 percent confidence intervals) of *Strength of partisanship* across the three panel waves for two groups: those who received a clientelistic payoff between the campaign and election waves ("targets," denoted with circles) and those who did not ("non-targets" with squares). To clarify, respondents tallied as targets did not become so until after the campaign wave; the set of respondents defined as targets and non-targets is fixed across all three waves. In the first two waves (pre-campaign and campaign), the two groups were statistically indistinguishable in their degree of partisanship, and those who were eventually paid off were actually a bit *less* partisan than those who were never targeted. In other words, those who received a payoff after the campaign wave were *not* more partisan before that wave than those who received no payoff. It is only after the payoff is made that a gap emerges, since recipients became more partisan while non-recipients remained stable. The simplest and most plausible explanation is that partisan loyalty is endogenous to clientelistic targeting. Merely looking at post-targeting, cross-sectional measures yields misleading estimates of the impact of partisanship on payoff receipt.

Network size, in contrast, seems unaffected by clientelistic targeting. Frame B of Figure 7.5 reports the means and confidence intervals of nonfamilial discussants for targets and non-targets in the campaign and election waves. In the campaign wave, those who later received a payoff (circle markers) already had more discussants than those who did not later receive a payoff (square markers). This gap remained nearly constant in size across the campaign and election waves, meaning clients did not increase their egocentric network sizes in response to a payoff.[37] Rather, both sets of individuals increased their network sizes at nearly equivalent rates. To reiterate, Mexicans' expressed loyalties to parties increase after they are paid off, whereas their egocentric network sizes do not increase.*

IMPLICATIONS

Our theory and empirical findings resolve an important puzzle in the literature on politics in developing countries: Why do so many politicians around the world consider clientelism to be a cost-effective way of winning votes? As currently understood by political scientists, clientelism is expensive and inefficient. The granting of particularistic benefits to individuals in exchange for

*Although opinion leaders tend to be, as we have stressed throughout, more stable voters, these results suggest that Mexican parties are targeting high-degree individuals who are not necessarily more partisan and stable.

their political support carries more costs than just the price of the payoffs themselves. Patrons must maintain an army of machine operatives. In turn, these operatives must devote time and effort to choosing which citizens to pay off, to delivering the benefits, and then to monitoring the subsequent voting behavior of their beneficiaries.[38] All the while, both patrons and operatives risk legal sanction, noncompliance by ungrateful targets, waste via the targeting of voters who are already supporters, and resentment from non-recipients.[39] All this occurs, moreover, in search of votes that are merely "picked up one at a time," putting clientelism "among the least-efficient strategies of manipulation."[40] Would it not be cheaper for patrons to reach voters with pork-barrel projects or programmatic stances benefiting entire communities or socioeconomic strata?[41] Would it not be cheaper to utilize media-based appeals that can reach broad segments of the population? Auyero summarizes this puzzle most effectively:

> The brokers' . . . capacity to deliver . . . is *limited* because the broker can get jobs, deliver medicine, do an essential (or founding) favor, and assist someone as if he or she were part of her family, for a restricted number of people. . . . The size of the brokers' inner circle can hardly account for the "conquest of the vote" and "building of electoral consensus" that is usually attributed to clientelism.[42]

Our answer to this puzzle is clear: scholars have misinterpreted the logic of clientelism by overlooking the persuasive potential of clients. Clients can magnify the effect of a payoff by convincing their peers of the merits of casting a vote for the patron. The paradigm of methodological individualism, it seems, has exerted a lasting pull on clientelism scholarship, leading a literature otherwise quite attentive to networks to treat clients, once they have been paid off, as socially isolated. Clientelism is not a narrow strategy of targeting a relatively small number of presumably high-yield voters. Rather, it is encompassing, pollinating the electorate by "treating the hubs" and enticing a minority directly while attempting to reach the non-client majority indirectly.[43]

The social-influence-buying argument also carries important macro-level implications for understanding the strong negative correlation between GDP per capita and the prevalence of clientelism.[44] The long-standing claim has been that clientelistic gifts, because of the diminishing marginal utility of income, produce a greater yield for the machine when given to the poor than when given to the rich.[45] The problem with this logic—when scaled up to the country level—is that virtually every country has relatively poor and precarious citizens whom party machines could afford to buy off. Politicians in developed countries can afford to pay off the relatively poor, even if the absolute cost of such payoffs is higher than for politicians in developing countries, because the politicians themselves have greater financial resources upon which to draw.

Our argument emphasizes the availability of mass media as a possible reason for the disappearance of clientelism as a country grows wealthier.[46] By this

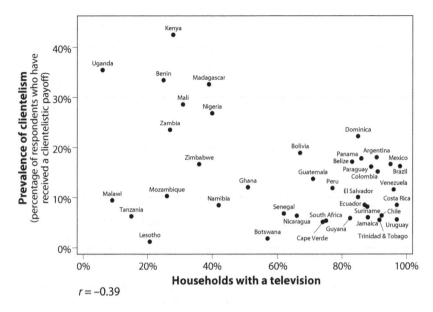

FIGURE 7.6 The Prevalence of Clientelism by TV Ownership in 31 African and Latin American Countries
Source: Afrobarometer, LAPOP, World Telecommunications Indicators database.

logic, clientelism thrives in media-poor environments because horizontal persuasion via informal discussion is virtually the *only* way for parties to reach the many potential voters they cannot directly contact. Where informal discussion among horizontal social relations is the primary source of political information—as is necessarily the case in media-poor countries—the benefits of engaging in clientelism are large. Once citizens are able to access mass-mediated sources of political information, clientelistic targeting of hubs is no longer the only way for politicians to reach non-targets. Politicians can reach them directly and, as we discussed in previous chapters, use media to shape the conversations that continue to take place within their electorates.

Consider, as merely suggestive evidence, the scattergram in figure 7.6, which plots 40 countries by two indicators. The *y*-axis variable, labeled *Prevalence of clientelism*, is the percentage of respondents in each country who report that in recent years they were offered a campaign gift by a politician. The *x*-axis variable is *Households with a television* (as a percentage of all households).[47] To boost the number of observations and expand variance on *x* and *y*, the figure includes the LAPOP sample plus some countries from the Afrobarometer survey, which in 2005 asked a similarly worded question on clientelistic targeting.[48] The cross-national correlation between the two variables is −0.39, and it is stronger than the correlation between GDP per capita and the *Prevalence of clientelism*. The partial correlation between television ownership and the *Prevalence of clientelism*, when GDP per capita is held constant, is −0.21, whereas the partial correlation between GDP per capita and *Prevalence of clientelism* is just −0.06 when television ownership is held constant. Thus a modest negative correlation exists across countries between exposure to modern mass media technologies and the extent of clientelism, and this correlation is stronger than the correlation between the extent of clientelism and average income.

CONCLUSION

For strategically minded political elites, an electorate of isolated voters, each of whom thinks and decides alone, is very different from an electorate of socially connected voters who discuss political choices with their peers. This chapter has shown that in Latin America, the party operatives in charge of delivering clientelistic payoffs seek targets based more on their social traits than on their individual political characteristics. Operatives pursue persuasive peers—that is, voters who are politically verbose and well-networked. This strategy of buying social influence carries the highest potential yield for the party because the payoff's effect can be magnified via the conversion of multiple voters within a recipient's informal social networks. Our empirical demonstration of this argument also showed that the propensity to persuade is the lurking variable behind the commonly observed correlation between partisan loyalty and clientelistic targeting. In fact, when not spurious, the alleged impact of partisan loyalty to the machine on payoff receipts is endogenous.

This chapter considered one implication of a horizontally networked world for elite behavior. What are the broader implications of horizontal intermediation and social influence for mass behavior? Thus far, we have demonstrated how everyday talk influences the decisions of voters, but we have been silent on its broader implications for mass politics—implications for issues such as the quality and fairness of democratic citizenship as well as the accountability mechanism of elections. The next chapter, which contains the book's final empirical exercises, addresses these topics.

8

Discussion, Societal Exclusion, and Political Voice

Carla: "When I speak with people right here in the street who pass
by and sit to drink a soda, the conversation begins. [They say,]
'Gosh, so who are you going to vote for?' 'I'm going to vote for
so-and-so.' And then I begin with 'Ah, so let's give Marina a
chance. Let's give a chance to, maybe . . .' aww, I forget the guy's
name. . . .
"My neighbor said she was going to vote for . . . I forgot the name, it
was on the tip of my tongue. . . .
"We speak about politics a lot [in my family], but I always forget the
guys' names."[TA8.1] (Brazil 2018)

Tiago: "[Who would I vote for] if I could vote? It's actually something
that I can't do, because now there's that Clean Record [*Ficha
Limpa*] bureaucracy. So as an ex-convict, we cannot vote. We are
banned from voting. To them, our opinion is worth nothing. But if
I could vote, I would vote for [Fernando] Haddad."[TA8.2] (Brazil 2018)

Carla and Tiago are a poor, Afro-Brazilian, married couple. They are
40-somethings who sell drinks and sandwiches as street vendors in one of
downtown Rio de Janeiro's primary thoroughfares. Both are opinionated about
politics and discuss it with friends, family, and even strangers, but, as illustrated by these quotations, their political voices are distorted or even muted.
Carla's voice is distorted by the fact that, as a poorly educated and extremely
busy woman, she is not very knowledgeable about politics. She repeatedly forgets politicians' names. Indeed, at the point of trying to influence someone else
to vote for her favorite candidate, Carla cannot remember that candidate's
name. For his part, Tiago's political voice is muted by misinformation. He did

not vote in 2018 because he thought he was ineligible, but this is false. Under Brazilian law, ex-convicts may (and indeed must) vote.

Effective political voice is the ability of citizens to influence, indirectly or directly, political elites and policy. Effective voice is unevenly distributed in all political systems, often weaker among groups who confront marginalization from society and the economy. Because the monetary costs of discussion are virtually nil, the realm of everyday talk could be a haven for under-resourced citizens, an easy way for them to acquire political knowledge and exert at least some political influence. Yet as Carla's experience shows, social and economic marginalization can complicate political self-expression, even in informal networks. Political discussion requires some minimal levels of articulateness, knowledge, and self-confidence, so those who live on the socioeconomic fringe may be excluded from the realm of social communication about politics. This exclusion, in turn, may yield negative consequences for the quality and effectiveness of their political voices.

This final empirical chapter explores implications of the book's argument for the quality of political voice and democratic citizenship in Latin America. We first ask whether individuals who face societal marginalization and exclusion—the poor, the darker-skinned, and women—participate in horizontal intermediation as frequently as individuals that are less marginalized. We find that, nearly without exception across Latin American countries, individuals of lower socioeconomic status (SES) are less likely to discuss politics than those of high SES. Lower-SES individuals also tend to have smaller egocentric networks of political discussion. The effects of SES on engagement in, and exposure to, informal political discussion are huge. They are also consequential, as they lead the poor and less educated to have far less political knowledge. Race and gender, however, have a much weaker effect on engagement in political discussion. The CNEP and our own panel studies illuminate these patterns across 12 elections in six Latin American countries.

The second half of the chapter directly considers whether these stratification patterns affect the political voices of the marginalized. Our criterion of political voice is correct voting: individuals cast correct votes when they select the candidate who best represents their issue positions and values. On average, politically talkative individuals are more likely to vote correctly than politically mute individuals, and political discussion is the only form of intermediation that yields this effect. These patterns do not, it turns out, create consistent differences across social classes in the propensity to vote correctly. In some elections the poor are less likely to vote correctly, but in others they are not. We also find that socially informed preferences—those reached at the end of the campaign—are not necessarily more correct than those held during the campaign.

SOCIETAL EXCLUSION, HORIZONTAL INTERMEDIATION, AND POLITICAL INFORMATION

The information exchanged through political discussion and through other forms of political intermediation is crucial for navigating the world of power and authority.[1] Research outside Latin America has shown that political knowledge facilitates political voice and, thus, elite responsiveness and accountability.[2] As we saw with Tiago above, political participation requires accurate information about engagement opportunities and about the specifics of getting involved. In addition, knowledge is necessary for citizens when they must navigate local bureaucracies in order to fulfill a legal requirement or resolve a problem. Moreover, groups that possess high levels of political information are better able than groups that possess low levels of information to hold politicians accountable for their actions.[3] Finally, political knowledge advances an individual's community standing. An important implication of our central argument—voters defer to more knowledgeable peers—is that the opinions of knowledgeable citizens are more likely to be magnified through political discussion than the opinions of unknowledgeable ones.

When the degree of exposure to political information within an electorate is not distributed equitably, its benefits are also not distributed equitably. Furthermore, if those who are otherwise marginalized by society possess this resource in smaller quantities than those who are not marginalized, then political intermediation reinforces existing inequalities.[4] For this reason, we wish to understand how political discussion and the use of other political intermediaries are distributed across groups in Latin America. Do groups with different class, gender, and racial affiliations engage equally in horizontal political intermediation?

Theoretical Expectations

Among the major forms of political intermediation, discussion carries the greatest potential for democratizing and equalizing access to information. It is partly for this reason, in fact, that some scholars advocate more deliberative forms of democracy.[5] Discussion requires little technology or money. Instead, it emerges naturally from the most human of activities—conversation. Recall from figure 2.2, for instance, that Kenya and Mozambique, the poorest countries in the CNEP study, have the highest rates of political discussion of any national samples. Moreover, because political discussion emerges organically from a commonly practiced activity, its marginal cost in time is also relatively minimal. Finally, conversation is a bottom-up activity, one almost always initiated by citizen choice, not elite choice.

Vertical intermediation, in contrast, seemingly carries less potential to equalize access to political information. Mass media consumption is, like discussion, initiated by citizen choice, but it requires costly technologies and a specific devotion of time. The Mozambique example is again telling, as the country has the lowest rate of political news consumption in the CNEP.[6] Party contacting and clientelism are elite-initiated, top-down activities that are highly episodic and have minimal potential to deepen political knowledge. (Recall the evidence in figure 2.5.)

Still, the notion of political discussion as the great equalizer—or at least more equalizing than other intermediary forms—has its own detractors. Although discussion seems less costly, it is naive to assume that the self-motivation to discuss politics is equitably distributed. Because discussion requires civic skills, a certain degree of eloquence, and self-esteem, its frequency may correlate with educational attainment and social capital, qualities more abundant among individuals with higher SES.[7] Furthermore, informal conversations can *reinforce* resource inequalities and power imbalances: "status and hierarchy shape patterns of talking and listening."[8] Women, for instance, are less likely to be listened to and more likely to be interrupted.[9]

Vertical intermediation, moreover, may not be as inequitable as imagined. Radios and televisions are now nearly universal in Latin America, thus minimizing the marginal financial cost of consuming these common forms of media. Also, research on clientelism has shown that parties often seek to pay off poor and rural residents.[10] When payoffs are made disproportionately to the lower class, expectations about a bias to elite-initiated intermediation are turned on their heads.

Results

With these ambivalent theoretical expectations in mind, we turn to our Brazil and Mexico panel studies. We first estimate the relationship between societal exclusion—SES, gender, and race—and exposure to different intermediaries. Then we estimate the relationship between societal exclusion and levels of political knowledge. Our dependent variables, each a measure of exposure to a particular intermediary form, are five different indicators. *Frequency of political discussion* and *Egocentric network size* capture the prevalence of horizontal political intermediation. For vertical intermediation, we use three indicators. *Media exposure*[11] measures consumption of traditional news, while *Contacted by a party* and *Paid off by a party* measure direct party-to-citizen intermediation. Not all five variables are available in every survey, and the measurement of each one varies slightly across the surveys. (See appendix B.) To ease comparisons, we standardize each variable, and we scored each one so that higher values correspond to greater exposure (greater frequency, larger size, more contact).

The independent variables gauge four concepts related to societal exclusion: wealth, education, gender, and race. *Wealth* is an index compiled from "yes" or "no" responses to an asset indicator battery (e.g., "Do you own a refrigerator?

A cellular phone?").[12] *Education* is the respondent's (logged) educational attainment. *Gender* is 1 for male respondents and 0 for female ones. *Race* is based on an ordinal trichotomy that is, in Brazil, (1) black or indigenous, (2) mixed race (*pardo*) or Asian (*amarelo*), and (3) white. In Mexico it is (1) *moreno oscuro*, (2) *moreno claro*, and (3) white.[13] For all four measures, lower numbers correspond to groups experiencing greater societal marginalization.

Figure 8.1 reports substantive effects and 95 percent confidence intervals from sixteen different OLS regressions, each with four independent variables. For race and gender, the substantive effects are the differences in predicted values between the maximum and minimum on each independent variable (e.g., from female to male for gender and black/indigenous/*moreno oscuro* to white for race). The variables *Wealth* and *Education*, collectively referred to as SES, enter separately in our regression models because they can produce different effects.[14] The figure, however, reports just one substantive effect per model for both of them—the effect that results from moving both variables from the 5th to the 95th percentile. For all independent variables, a positive effect means that the societally excluded group has less exposure to the intermediary form than the more included group. A negative effect means the converse.

The figure reveals numerous statistically significant relationships. The propensity to discuss politics is highly stratified by socioeconomic status. In the Brazil samples, the differences between low-SES and high-SES individuals in discussion frequency and network size range from 0.7 to 1.1 standard deviations. In Mexico the differences are even larger at 1.5 (discussion frequency) and 1.9 (network size) standard deviations. The consumption of political news is also highly stratified by SES. In the two-city sample the effect of SES on news consumption (about 1.5 standard deviations) is even stronger than the effect of SES on discussion frequency, and in Brazil 2014 and Mexico 2006 SES yields equally sized effects on both discussion and media exposure. Both *Wealth* and *Education* are responsible for these large SES effects; the coefficients on both variables are statistically significant in all instances. (See regression coefficients in table A.21.) We have demonstrated, in sum, that engagement in the two most commonly practiced intermediation activities—discussion and media consumption—is highly stratified by wealth and education in Brazil and Mexico.

The propensity to be contacted or paid off by a party, in comparison, is much less stratified by SES. In the two Brazilian cities and in Mexico 2006, parties are indeed more likely to contact individuals of high SES, but the effect sizes of SES range only from 0.3 to 0.5 of a standard deviation. As for clientelism, in Mexico 2006 wealth had virtually no effect on whether a party paid off a respondent. Previous arguments notwithstanding, the poor were *not* more likely than the rich to be approached for clientelistic reasons.

Gender also has significant effects on exposure to intermediaries. Women discuss politics less often than men in all four instances, and the difference approaches a quarter of a standard deviation in Brazil 2006 and Mexico 2006. Despite this, women do not have smaller networks than men, except for a

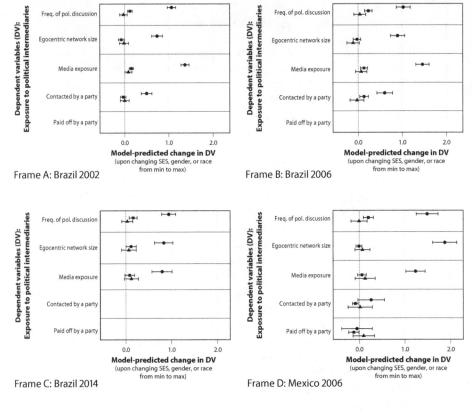

FIGURE 8.1 The Stratification of Intermediation Exposure by SES, Gender, and Race in Brazil and Mexico: Predicted Changes from 16 OLS Regression Models
Notes: Each marker is a model-predicted change in standard deviations (with 95 percent confidence intervals). Change in SES is from 5th percentile to 95th percentile (not from minimum to maximum) on wealth and education. Table A.21 reports the sample sizes and the complete sets of coefficient estimates in numerical form.
Sources: Two-City Panel, BEPS 2014, Mexico 2006 Panel.

FIGURE 8.2 The Stratification of Intermediation Exposure by SES and Gender in 10 Latin American Election Campaigns: Predicted Changes from 27 OLS Regression Models
Notes: Each marker is a model-predicted change in standard deviations (with 95 percent confidence interval). Change in SES is from 5th percentile to 95th percentile (not from minimum to maximum) on wealth and education. Table A.22 reports the sample sizes and the complete sets of coefficient estimates in numerical form.
Source: CNEP.

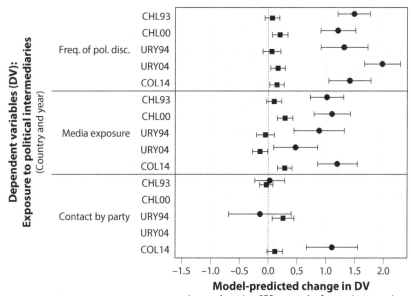

Frame A: Chile, Colombia, and Uruguay

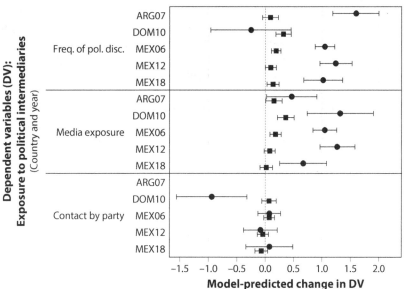

Frame B: Argentina, Dominican Republic, and Mexico

Independent
variable
● SES
■ Gender (male)

statistically significant but modestly sized difference in Brazil 2002. In Mexico 2006 women were more likely to be contacted and paid off by parties, but in Brazil 2006 men were more likely to be contacted. Finally, there are no differences in discussion frequency or network size by race and only a small effect of race on news consumption in Brazil 2014 and Mexico 2006.

We also conduct the same exercise with the CNEP data, using one measure each of three major intermediary types. The *Frequency of political discussion* and *Media exposure* are both indexes calculated from multiple items. *Contacted by a party* is based on self-reports of party canvassing efforts.[15] Figure 8.2 provides these results for the ten available Latin American elections. The figure reports estimated effects of SES (measured with *Income* and *Education* measures) and *Gender*. (The CNEP contains no indicator of race.)

Figure 8.2 yields the same broad conclusion as figure 8.1: engagement in political discussion and engagement in media news consumption are stratified by SES but the propensity to be contacted by a party is not.[16] Across 20 different statistical tests, discussion and news consumption are stratified by SES in all but one instance (Dominican Republic 2010). The results also show that men are more likely than women to discuss politics and consume political news. The typical effect sizes of gender are moderate (usually between 0.2 and 0.3 standard deviations), although they are statistically significant only about half the time. In one exceptional case (Uruguay 2000), women are more likely than men to consume political news. Finally, gender is linked to differences in party contacting in only one of seven cases: men were more likely than women to be contacted by a party in Uruguay 1994.

From one perspective, this collection of findings is counterintuitive. Elite-initiated forms of intermediation (canvassing and payoffs by parties) are less stratified by SES than citizen-initiated forms (discussion and media consumption). Stated differently, party contacting and clientelism are more leveling as intermediaries than political discussion and news consumption. Men also engage in citizen-initiated intermediation more than women, although this gender gap is far from ubiquitous. (The findings regarding race are a bit more sanguine, as there is little stratification by skin color.) Overall, concerns that discussion and deliberation in Latin America are somewhat exclusionary are well-founded. Discussions about politics, not to mention exposure to mass media, tend to be the domain of the richer and better educated. Party contacts and payoffs are less biased toward the upper crust, but (recall from figure 2.5) these practices yield little by way of political knowledge.

Figure 8.3 confirms that the disparities by SES in the frequency of discussion and news consumption translate into concrete differences in *Political knowledge*. The figure reports the effects of SES and gender on political knowledge in all the country-year cases referenced in figures 8.1 and 8.2. High-SES individuals have political knowledge levels exceeding those of low-SES individuals by anywhere from 0.5 to 2.5 standard deviations.[17] Gender effects are

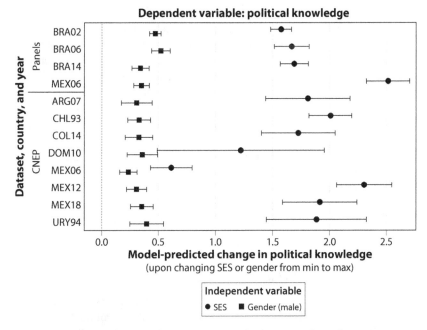

FIGURE 8.3 The Stratification of Political Knowledge by SES and Gender in 11 Latin American Election Campaigns: Predicted Changes from 12 OLS Regression Models
Notes: Each marker is a model-predicted change in standard deviations (with 95 percent confidence interval). Change in SES is from 5th percentile to 95th percentile (not from minimum to maximum) on wealth and education. Table A.23 reports the sample sizes and the complete sets of coefficient estimates in numerical form.
Source: Two-City Panel, BEPS 2014, Mexico 2006 Panel, CNEP.

also sizable and always statistically significant, ranging from a quarter to more than a half standard deviation.[18] In other words, even though political discussion is free, lower-SES Latin Americans are less motivated to engage in it than their higher-SES compatriots. Because discussion is a crucial form of information acquisition, poorer citizens are less politically knowledgeable. These two findings are nearly ubiquitous across the cases.

SOCIETAL EXCLUSION, HORIZONTAL INTERMEDIATION, AND CORRECT VOTING

Poorer citizens have less exposure to political intermediaries. Does this compromise their political voices? Typically, scholars address this question by looking at the relationship between SES and political participation, treating the latter as the primary form of political voice. Empirical results for Latin America have been mixed. Sometimes the poor participate at rates similar to those of the rich,[19] while sometimes patterns of stratification are strong.[20]

In this section we employ a different indicator of effective political voice, correct voting. Scholarship on correct voting asks how many and which voters choose the candidate who best represents their expressed values and issue attitudes. While it may be tempting to assert that every voter casts a ballot for her or his correct candidate, recall that voters' information is incomplete. For example, it might be hard for Carla, given her struggles to remember candidates' names, to link her beliefs about the economy and redistribution to actual candidates. In this section we address these questions by estimating the cross-sectional relationships among societal exclusion, exposure to political intermediaries, and correct voting in our four main election cases. We also use our panel data to consider a lingering question about horizontal intermediation in general: Are socially informed preferences more correct than pre-campaign preferences?

Definitions and Expectations

A voter casts a correct vote when she selects the candidate for whom she would have voted if she had complete information about all the candidates.[21] Incorrect voting occurs when a voter selects the candidate for whom she would *not* have voted under complete information. Voting "correctness" is thus defined according to the *expressed* interests, attitudes, and values of each voter. Consider, for instance, a hypothetical Brazilian voter who had socialist and redistributionist issue positions, a left-leaning ideological stance, and a positive evaluation of recent macroeconomic trends. That Brazilian voted correctly in 2014 if he voted for left-of-center incumbent Dilma Rousseff. He voted incorrectly if he voted for Dilma's right-of-center opponent Aécio Neves.

To clarify, correct voting does *not* consider whether citizens vote in line with some *imputed*—and in practice economic—interest. Conclusions and (often) criticisms about voters along these lines are legion in political commentary. One of the better-known conclusions is the "What's the matter with Kansas?" argument, which derides white rural US citizens for seemingly voting against their income-maximizing interests because of their conservative religious and racial values.[22] In Brazil the line "the people don't know how to vote" (*o povo não sabe votar*), a saying sometimes attributed to soccer legend Pelé, captures a similar sentiment. During the pre-2002 era, when the PT suffered repeated electoral losses, many frustrated leftists invoked the line to explain why so many poor voters preferred right-of-center, clientelistic elites who protected the status quo. Other examples of observers faulting a group of voters for failing to vote their interests abound: Marxian and Gramscian notions of false consciousness and hegemony, Barack Obama's "cling to guns and religion" gaffe, and commentary on the phenomenon of working-class Tories in the UK. All of these arguments notwithstanding, our analysis of correct voting takes a voter's own set of expressed beliefs, whether they are in line with that voter's objective interests or not, as the proper criterion for assigning the voter's correct candidate.

The correct-voting framework also departs from the opposite extreme: a relativist notion that all votes are *by definition* correct ones. Because voters have cognitive limitations and flawed information environments, they make their decisions with incomplete knowledge about candidates. Experiments have shown that voters change their votes under conditions of fuller information.[23] Thus we accept the notion that, for each voter, one candidate represents and would (in office) promote that voter's expressed values and issue positions better than the other candidates.

Research on whether informal political discussion boosts correct voting has been of two minds. On the one hand, the information provided through social networks can be an important resource in helping voters identify their correct candidates. Political knowledge is an important, positive correlate of the propensity to vote correctly.[24] Given the homophily instinct, moreover, discussion can provide individuals with important cues about how others with similar traits and values are voting.[25] For this reason, information gathered from peers may be more valuable than information gleaned from mass media in nudging voters toward their correct choices.

On the other hand, there is no guarantee that political discussion moves a voter toward the candidate who shares his issue positions. Recall our finding that many egos seek help with their vote decisions from knowledgeable alters. Rare is the benevolent alter whose sole interest lies in guiding ego toward ego's correct candidate. Instead, the typical alter seeks to nudge ego toward alter's own preferred candidate, regardless of whether alter's candidate represents ego's expressed beliefs. As we have shown, discussion induces many a voter to choose the candidate who is most popular in the voter's social context, and this candidate may not always be the best to promote the voter's values and beliefs. Some empirical research shows that discussion can increase ideological inconsistency and lower the propensity to vote correctly.[26]

Design of the Correct-Voting Analysis

As in previous studies of the topic, our process for evaluating the correlates of correct voting entails two broad steps. The first step identifies the correct candidate for each respondent by summing distances between the respondent and each candidate over five to eight issue spaces.[27] We limit the issue spaces to divisive values and positional issues plus performance-oriented valence issues.[28] By doing so, we stay true to our definition of correct voting as the selection of the candidate with the nearest *values and positions* on policies and policy outcomes. We do not include partisan identities or evaluations of candidate personalities, as these criteria can divert voters from choosing candidates who best represent them on genuine policy issues.[29]

For positional issues, we include pre-campaign measures of attitudes on issues such as social policy, land reform, free trade, and privatization. We also include left-to-right ideological placement and religious identification.[30] We place candidates in these positional spaces by using either average placements of the candidates by politically knowledgeable respondents (when such placements are available) or expert placements of the candidates/parties.[31] For valence issues, our models include respondents' pre-campaign self-placements on measures of sociotropic economic evaluations and presidential approval. We locate candidates in these spaces with the following simple rules: incumbents receive the score on one extreme of the dimension, and challengers receive the score at the opposite extreme.[32] For each respondent and each candidate, we sum the respondent's distances from the candidate in all the issue spaces, and then we repeat this for all major-party candidates. In other words, each respondent gets J scores, where J is the number of major candidates. A respondent's correct candidate is that candidate from whom the respondent has the *smallest* summed distances.

Using these procedures, we find that between 47 and 56 percent of respondents voted correctly in our Brazilian and Mexican cases. These percentages may seem small, but recall that the models include an intentionally narrow set of criteria in the first step—a set oriented around issues. We could easily boost these percentages by including such variables as partisanship and evaluations of the personal traits of candidates.[33] Our interest, however, lies less in the absolute size of correct-voting percentages and more in the ways in which the propensities for citizens to vote in line with their issue preferences vary across individuals and through time.

The second step estimates cross-sectional models of correct voting. A binary dependent variable, *Voted correctly*, measures whether a respondent's actual election-day vote, as reported in the election panel wave, matches our estimate of her or his correct candidate. If so, the variable equals one. Otherwise it is zero. A logit model then regresses these binary measures on the variables of interest—namely, political knowledge, exposure to political intermediaries, and indicators of societal exclusion. This second step thus reveals which factors are correlated with the correct-voting form of expressing political voice. More details on the execution of these steps, along with the full results, are presented in appendix C. The text here reports only the most important results from the second step.

Cross-sectional Results

For the second step, we estimate three logit models per election. Each model contains an independent variable or set of independent variables that was employed in the previous section of this chapter. In order to discern whether

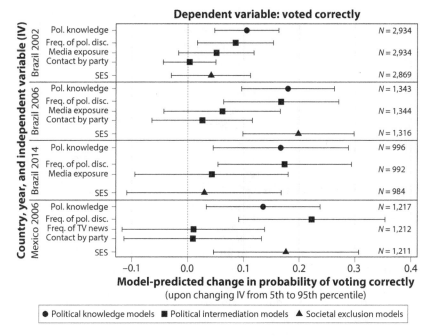

FIGURE 8.4 Voted Correctly by Political Knowledge, Exposure to Political Intermedi-aries, and Societal Exclusion: Predicted Changes in Probability from 12 Binary Logit Models
Notes: Each marker is a model-predicted change in the probability of voting correctly (with 95 percent confidence interval). Three models are estimated for each country year. Table C.1 reports the complete sets of coefficient estimates in numerical form.
Source: Two-City Panel, BEPS 2014, Mexico 2006 Panel.

politically knowledgeable citizens are more likely to vote correctly, the first model contains only *Political knowledge* as an independent variable ("Politi-cal knowledge models"). The second model contains measures of exposure to different political intermediaries ("Political intermediation models"). The third includes the four measures of societal exclusion ("Societal exclusion models").[34]

Figure 8.4 reports the most important results from the 12 logit models. The figure plots the predicted change in the probability of voting correctly by each independent variable. For each election, estimates with the same marker are from the same model, and estimates with different markers are from different models.

Consider first the circular point plotted for each election. Politically knowl-edgeable individuals are more likely to vote correctly than less knowledgeable individuals, as the effect of political knowledge is always statistically significant and double digits in size. Political sophistication is clearly an important re-source in Brazil and Mexico, since it increases the likelihood that individuals match their candidate choices to their own positional and valence issue standings. Indeed, political knowledge has a much larger effect in these two countries than it does elsewhere; previous scholarship on more than 30 other countries has found political knowledge to yield, on average, just a four-point increase in the probability of voting correctly.[35] In Brazil and Mexico the po-litically informed clearly enjoy an advantage in political voice over the unin-formed: they are more likely to vote correctly.

The next set of estimates reveals which type of political intermediary has the strongest correlation with this advantage. The square markers are derived from logit models that regress the *Voted correctly* variable on exposure to three different intermediaries. The markers clearly show that engagement in hori-zontal intermediation is more strongly correlated with correct voting than are other intermediaries. *Frequency of political discussion* has a positive and sta-tistically significant correlation in all four cases, whereas both *Media expo-sure* and *Contact by a party* have no correlation with correct voting in any of the four cases. In summary, the politically talkative are more likely to vote cor-rectly than the politically mute, but exposure to traditional news media is un-correlated with the propensity to vote correctly.[36]

Does correct voting correlate with societal exclusion? Here the results paint a slightly less pessimistic scenario than does the previous section on interme-diation, information, and factors of exclusion. The bottom set of results for each election (plotted with triangles) depicts the relationship between SES and cor-rect voting. In Brazil 2006 and Mexico 2006, correct voting is stratified by SES—and strongly so. In the other two instances, high-SES individuals are *not* more likely to vote correctly than low-SES ones.[37] Sometimes the political voices of the poor are more distorted by incorrect voting than those of the rich, but this is not always the case.

Socially Informed Preferences and Correct Voting

These results demonstrate that politically knowledgeable and politically talk-ative citizens are more likely than the politically uninformed and mute to se-lect presidential candidates who match their issue positions, but the finding does not speak to timing and dynamics. Politically informed and talkative citi-zens may already have their correct vote in place before the campaign begins. In other words, this cross-sectional finding says little about whether the so-cially informed preferences that voters develop over the course of a campaign are more likely to be correct than their mid-campaign preferences. A social process unfolds over the campaign, but do persuasive peers lead the aver-age voter toward a "better" candidate choice? Previous analyses of correct voting—all cross-sectional in nature—have ignored the relationship between

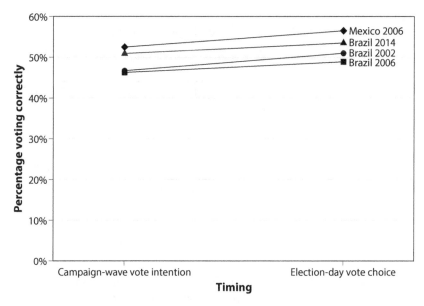

FIGURE 8.5 Rates of Correct Voting by Panel Wave in Brazil and Mexico
Notes: Each marker is the observed percentage of respondents who *Voted correctly*.
The designation of each respondent's correct candidate is based on the respondent's
pre-campaign issue positions. Sample sizes are reported in table 8.1.
Source: Two-City Panel, BEPS 2014, Mexico 2006 Panel.

campaign dynamics and the quality of candidate choice, but we now exploit
our panel data to address it.

Figure 8.5 suggests that rates of correct voting increase minimally during
campaigns. The figure plots (on the left) the percentage of twice-opinionated
voters holding a correct vote intention at the campaign wave and (on the right)
the percentage casting a correct vote on election day (as reported in the election wave). Recall that we assign each respondent's correct candidate based on
the respondent's pre-campaign-wave issue positions, so each respondent's
correct candidate does not change through time. As a result, the figure reveals
whether, on balance, voters gravitate toward their correct candidates between
these two waves.[38] The lines connecting the rates of correct voting from each
pair of waves are upward sloping, meaning correct voting increases from the
campaign wave to election day. The sizes of these increases, however, are
small, ranging from 2 to 4 percentage points, and only the increase for Brazil
2002 is statistically significant.

Moving to the individual level of analysis, table 8.1 yields a similar conclusion. We estimate four logit regressions to discern whether those who change
their vote during the campaign move toward a correct vote. The main test of

TABLE 8.1.
Correct Voting by Vote Switching in Brazil and Mexico: Coefficients from Four
Binary Logit Models

	Brazil 2002	Brazil 2006	Brazil 2014	Mexico 2006
Changed vote preference	0.101	0.247	−0.156	0.365
	(.114)	(.190)	(.530)	(.517)
Lagged DV (correct vote intention at c wave)	2.527*	3.154*	3.647*	4.053*
	(.107)	(.170)	(.307)	(.315)
N	2,287	1,068	686	878

Notes: Entries are logit coefficients with standard errors in parentheses. Dependent variable for each model is *Voted correctly.* Intercepts and candidate fixed effects for vote choice are included but not shown. $* = p < .05$.

Source: Two-City Panel, BEPS 2014, Mexico 2006 Panel.

this hypothesis is the coefficient on *Changed vote preference* (a variable previously used in chapters 3 and 4), which measures whether twice-opinionated voters switched preferences across party lines between the campaign and election waves (1 if they did, 0 if they did not). To isolate whether this change moves more voters toward their correct votes, the models also include a lagged dependent variable, meaning a measure of whether the respondent's campaign-wave vote intention was correct. Although three of the four coefficients on vote switching are positively signed, none are statistically significant. In the end, campaigns and the social processes they unleash in Brazil and Mexico do *not* draw citizens toward their correct votes.

CONCLUSION

The world of horizontal intermediation and social influence that this book has explored carries important implications for the equality and effectiveness of democratic citizenship. In Latin America the poor and less educated do not engage in informal conversations about politics as frequently as the wealthy and well-educated. This contributes to a large gap in political knowledge between rich and poor. To be sure, in Brazil and Mexico people of color do discuss politics at the same frequency as whites, and women do so at the same rate as men in some Latin American countries, though not in others. But the effect of financial and educational resources on participation in, and exposure to, horizontal intermediation is huge. To paraphrase E. E. Schattschneider, the informal airwaves of mass political discussion in Latin America have a "strong upper-class accent."[39]

Partly as a result, the upper crust sometimes has a less distorted political voice. Frequent political talkers are more likely to select a presidential candidate in line with their values and beliefs—that is, to vote correctly. The relationship between discussion frequency and correct voting is much larger and more consistent than the relationship between media consumption and correct voting. In turn, poor voters, in some settings, are less likely to select candidates representing their values and issue attitudes. Moreover, the socially informed preferences toward which Brazilian and Mexican voters move by the end of a campaign are *not* significantly better fits with their values and beliefs than the preferences they held during the campaign.

Overall, these two broad sets of findings seemingly cast informal political discussion in a negative light, at least with respect to normative questions around citizenship and equality. Nonetheless, let us postpone our final judgments on this front for the next, and final, chapter. There we reach a more measured conclusion.

9

Conclusion

We should not lament social influences or wish them away. Much of the time, people do better when they take close account of what others do. . . . But social influences . . . threaten, much of the time, to lead individuals and institutions in the wrong directions.

—*Cass Sunstein*[1]

The Doctor: "Do you know what thinking is? It's just a fancy word for changing your mind."
Zygella: "I will not change my mind."
The Doctor: "Then you will die stupid."

—*"The Zygon Inversion,"* Doctor Who[2]

Consider four of our Brazilian interviewees, each exemplifying a different side of political discussion:

> Janira: "At my work, [political] opinions are totally mixed. . . . We don't fight, but there's a lot of exchange of ideas."[TA9.1]

> Jairo: "[My brother-in-law] is more knowledgeable, you know? He's more knowledgeable, more intelligent about Lula, so he might have a more thought-out opinion. Yes, [I trust his opinion]. He's also more opinionated." [TA9.2]

> Valdenor: "I don't talk about politics much with people, because you know that in politics, soccer, and religion each person has their own [opinion]." [TA9.3]

> Rosa: "In the last election, my family influenced me, but now I've decided for myself that no one will ever influence me again. I think my opinion is the one that counts." [TA9.4]

These four reactions to conversations about politics carry a range of implications for the relationship between horizontal intermediation and the quality of democratic citizenship. They move, roughly, from the most positive implications to the most negative ones. Janira fits, in many ways, a deliberative ideal, since she is willing to discuss politics peacefully across lines of partisan difference.[3] Jairo fits a Downsian ideal, because he uses a more knowledgeable relative as an information shortcut. His relative's expertise gets multiplied in the electorate.[4] But does Jairo's reliance on someone else constitute genuinely active and engaged thought about candidate options, or is he just mindlessly conforming? Is Jairo's socially informed preference the best for his interests? Valdenor fits no ideal. Out of distaste and perhaps even fear of disagreement, he rarely discusses politics, so he excludes himself from the potential benefits of discussion and deliberation.[5] Finally, Rosa's reflection carries the most dystopian take on social influence: it has betrayed her. She regrets that peers pushed her away from her personal best choice, and she vows to eschew social influence forever.[6]

Which implication best fits our findings? What does the widespread prevalence of social influences on voting behavior say about the nature of citizenship and democracy in Brazil, Mexico, and the rest of Latin America? The answer to this question is complex, and in many ways it is beyond the scope of our argument and data. Still, some speculation is certainly in order, so in this conclusion we speculate. Our purpose is to show the necessary ambivalence, as in the epigraph by Cass Sunstein, of any answer. On the one hand, our argument illuminates a form of citizenship and engagement that is beyond the purview of elite control, and we add this form to a literature focused on elite-initiated intermediation. In addition, despite this radically decentralized, citizen-centered form of political communication, voters still prefer more information to less, as many defer to their more knowledgeable peers. On the other hand, the process of social communication about politics is stratified. Upper-class Latin Americans discuss politics more frequently than their lower-class counterparts, and upper-class voters have greater political knowledge because of this disparity. Lower-class individuals, moreover, are sometimes more likely to have distorted political voices, at least in part because of this disparity. When it comes to the quality of democratic citizenship, the world of social influence cuts multiple ways.

This concluding chapter first summarizes our main argument and findings. It then comments on avenues for future scholarship, especially the burgeoning wave of research on online political discussion. We close by considering the implications of the argument and results of our research for the depth and quality of citizenship in new democracies.

SUMMARY OF FINDINGS

In the study of mass politics in the US, the central empirical models portray the voter as a "socially disembodied individual whose decisions, judgments, and voting choices are based on individually held preferences, opinions, beliefs, attitudes, and identification."[7] As we pointed out in chapter 1, this characterization applies in even greater measure to research on mass politics in Latin America. Economistic and psychological models dominate research on voting in the region's nascent democracies, largely ignoring the relational aspects of attitude and preference formation. Final vote tallies, however, are not merely aggregations of socially isolated decisions. Our book seeks to correct this "individualistic fallacy" by demonstrating the *truly social* side of voting in Latin America—that is, the impact of peers and horizontal communication networks on the decisions of voters.[8] In doing so, we hope to raise Latin Americanists' awareness of the extent of social influence on the region's voters. We also wish to inform the scholarship on political networks about the ways that social influence plays out in new democracies.

Chapter 2 closed part I by demonstrating that a large majority of Latin Americans, unlike Valdenor above, discuss politics with peers. Politically mute individuals like Valdenor exist, but they are rare. In fact, Latin Americans discuss politics at rates close to international norms. Like Jairo, they tend to discuss politics with individuals who are more politically knowledgeable than themselves. Latin Americans also prefer discussion partners with whom they agree politically. Individuals like Janira, in other words, are a minority. Nonetheless, the rate at which they encounter political disagreement in their conversations is greater than the rate prevailing in the US, largely because Latin America's multiparty systems create more opportunities for disagreement. We illustrated these descriptive patterns with survey data from dozens of countries, including ten Latin American countries.

Part II of the book presented our core findings on the ways in which social communication within peer networks in Brazil and Mexico influences the evolution of voters' choices during a campaign, producing socially informed preferences by election day. We began in chapter 3 by documenting the number of voters in these two countries who change their minds during presidential election campaigns. The number of voters changing their vote intentions, unlike the number in the US, is relatively high—ranging between 20 and 50 percent. Collectively, these individual-level changes produce some exciting momentum changes in the polls, shifting the fortunes of candidates dramatically. Still, election-day vote tallies in each of our four main election cases (Brazil 2002, 2006, 2014, and Mexico 2006) did not diverge significantly from the distribution of vote intentions prevailing at the campaign's onset. In other words, momentum runs by outsider candidates were short-lived.

Voters like Janira, who discuss politics during the campaign across partisan lines, have a relatively high probability of changing candidate preferences before election day (chapter 4). They often gravitate toward the preference of a disagreeing discussant, but individuals who discuss politics only with agreeing discussants have a relatively low probability of switching because discussion reinforces their early campaign preference. The mechanism of social influence is largely informational: individuals seek to feel more certain in their own vote choices by consulting with more informed—and therefore more attitudinally stable—peers. Recall the example of Jairo and his more knowledgeable and more opinionated brother-in-law. This process of peer influence draws many voters toward candidates who polled strongly in the pre-campaign period. For this reason, outsider candidates who made surges during Brazilian campaigns, such as Ciro, Heloísa Helena, and Marina, could not sustain their runs. We demonstrated these empirical patterns by analyzing panel data from our four main election cases.

Peer effects can create and explain important geographical patterns in voting behavior. Where neighborhoods have strong political leanings, political discussion during campaigns exerts a gravitational pull on their residents, assimilating many voters, by election day, to their neighborhoods' partisan tendencies (chapter 5). This occurs because neighborhoods shape social networks, particularly the balance of partisan opinions that individuals encounter in their networks. Voters who live in left-leaning neighborhoods, for instance, are more likely than voters living in right-leaning neighborhoods to have discussants supporting left-leaning candidates. This occurs not just because of homophily, but also because there are more left-leaning individuals in the social environments from which voters in left-leaning neighborhoods select discussants. As a result, influential political conversations during the campaign bring the preferences of many voters into line with those of their neighborhood social environments. We showed how this process unfolded in 2002 in Caxias do Sul, a Brazilian city with a history of polarized and politicized neighborhoods. In contrast, no similar process unfolded in Juiz de Fora, a city where neighborhoods lacked stable partisan leanings.

This logic also works over larger geographical territories. States and even subnational regions have political leanings that shape the supply of certain political opinions among the potential discussants from which individuals select their alters (chapter 6). A voter in a right-leaning state or region is more likely, just by chance, to encounter and discuss politics with right-leaning discussants than a voter in a left-leaning state or region. The regionalization of voters' political preferences influences, by the sheer force of chance, the balance of political opinions in their discussion networks. As in politicized neighborhoods, the geographical clustering of preferences moves many voters toward the region's political tendency over the course of a campaign via influential social communication. Political discussion, in other words, is a means by which the partisan orientations of the community and even region are implanted in the minds of individual voters. We demonstrated this with nationwide data from the Brazil 2014 and the Mexico 2006 elections.

Part III explored broader implications of a horizontally networked world. When it comes to patterns of clientelistic redistribution, party machines seeking to buy votes with private payoffs should target citizens who hold the greatest potential for magnifying the electoral effect of the payoff (chapter 7).

This means buying off hubs, citizens who are likely to spread the machine's partisan message to their peers and likely to have many peers with whom they discuss politics. We showed that machine operatives did in fact favor voters with these traits during the Mexico 2006 election campaign and in more than 20 other Latin American countries.

What are the normative implications of horizontal social influence on vote choice? Despite the potential of social influence to create a channel of communication that is beyond elite control, the middle and upper classes dominate political discussion in Latin American electorates (chapter 8). Surveys from ten countries show this pattern to be virtually ubiquitous in the region. Partly for this reason, lower-class individuals are sometimes less likely to vote in line with their expressed values and issue positions. Overall, the social process that occurs during a campaign does not necessarily make the decisions of voters more correct. Socially informed preferences, in other words, are not better preferences, but nor are they worse.

FUTURE RESEARCH

To arrive at this collection of findings on social influence in Latin American election campaigns, we employed three powerful methodologies: population-representative survey research, measurement of egocentric networks, and (in Brazil and Mexico) repeated interviews. Not surprisingly, we argue that panel surveys measuring potential sources of social influence should be routine rather than rare in scholarship on Latin American politics. At the same time, we also welcome other methodological approaches to measuring social influence. In particular, studies of online political discussion in the region are set to proliferate, but it is important to recognize that the logic and processes underlying this new realm of social interaction are largely similar to what we have documented in this book. We consider, in turn, these two broad points about future research.

Panel Studies of Egonets

Why have so few studies of Latin American political behavior used our primary research design: panel surveys with repeated measures of egonets? It is beyond the scope of this conclusion to trace the intellectual history of the Michigan and Columbia schools of voting behavior. In scholarship on US and Latin American voting, Michigan won the theoretical rivalry, but cost largely drove that victory. Cross-sectional surveys of atomized individuals are cheaper to field.[9] For scientific goals, of course, this rationale should be unpersuasive. The vote decision in Latin America is clearly a dynamic process, since citizens arrive at a decision as the campaign unfolds.[10] To understand the true roots of voting choices, scholars must observe and analyze these changes in preferences with panel data. In addition, while vote choice is partly a function of (Michigan-style) individual-level psychological factors, such as identities and issue positions, much of mass politics is relational and requires observations of social ties.[11]

Fortunately, efforts to incorporate dynamics and social networks into political surveys need not be cost prohibitive. Name generators and name interpreters take up questionnaire space, but this is clearly well-spent space. Expenses do rise even further with interviews of discussants, but these can be implemented inexpensively with brief telephone or internet questionnaires. Indeed, our findings in chapter 2 on the accuracy of perceived preferences suggest that direct interviews with discussants are not always necessary.

Cost considerations partly motivated our decision to limit the first panel study to two Brazilian cities. Like this panel study, the classic panel studies of social influence in politics examine single cities: Elmira, Erie, and South Bend.[12] Despite this initial coupling between geographically narrow samples and measures of egocentric networks, egocentric measures are easily obtainable in nationally representative surveys, as we and others have shown.[13] The value of focusing on two cities lies not in the measures of egonets per se, but in merging egonets with aspects of the neighborhood and municipal contexts. Population-representative surveys still carry tremendous value for the study of mass political behavior in Latin America, and their value can be increased through the inclusion of dynamic measures of preferences and of social network ties.

Online Political Discussion

Future investigations of horizontal intermediation in Latin America, not to mention political communication elsewhere, will surely reflect the dramatic rise of online political discussion via social media such as Facebook and Twitter and via texting apps like WhatsApp.[14] We welcome this trend in research and look forward to its findings. Social media and texting apps may have swung voters and even entire elections by enabling candidates to communicate directly and inexpensively with voters, by aiding the rapid dissemination of unsubstantiated conspiracy theories and fake news, and by mobilizing new movements and new groups of voters.[15] Scholars should test these hypotheses with respect to specific elections when they arise.

We wish to emphasize, however, that the behavioral instincts and processes underlying the use and influence of these online technologies are not novel, so our arguments about the social roots of Latin American voting behavior can inform this coming wave of research.[16] The allure to researchers of online discussion lies in the fact that its content is written and recorded, making it easier to observe and analyze than the informal offline discussion with which we have wrestled. Online political discussion, moreover, may produce effects that are of different magnitudes than the effects of offline discussion.[17] Still, scholarship on Latin American politics and elections must resist the conclusion that these technologies have somehow created horizontal social communication where none previously existed. Nor are social media outlets necessarily destined to overtake traditional face-to-face discussion as the primary form of peer-to-peer intermediation. Despite numerous headlines about WhatsApp in Brazil's 2018 election campaign, for example, just 24 percent of voters said they discussed politics during the campaign via the texting app. This is a sizable minority, but it is still far fewer than the percentage that discussed politics face-to-face.[18] As they have always done, Latin Americans will continue to discuss politics face-to-face. Scholars of the region should avoid the assumption that social media present an entirely new way for citizens to learn and communicate about politics.

A brief discussion of Brazil's 2018 presidential election campaign illustrates these points. One of the leading stories from the campaign was the seemingly newfound role for WhatsApp in shaping the flow of political information. Campaigns, parties, business leaders, and avid partisans created fake images, false news stories, and other forms of electronic misinformation, including memes designed to spread confusion about a candidate's policy proposals or voting-machine number (i.e., the identifying number a voter enters in the electronic voting machine). One study found that 56 percent of shared political images were misleading.[19] These spread horizontally through the electorate, mostly via sharing in WhatsApp.[20] The messages were so widespread that electoral authorities sought to crack down on their authors, and during the campaign WhatsApp responded to widespread calls for intervention by shutting down the accounts of hundreds of thousands of users.

WhatsApp, however, did not initiate the practice of spreading misinformation through peer networks. False rumors have often been spread about Brazilian candidates, with their targets denouncing these rumors as "electoral crimes." During the 1989 presidential campaign, Lula's opponents propagated multiple falsehoods, including a claim that Lula's party was behind a recent high-profile kidnapping, and that Lula as president would allow homeless people to occupy vacant rooms in large homes.[21] Some evangelicals were convinced that Lula intended to implement an atheist, Communist dictatorship that would close churches.[22] The realities of political competition and human nature, with its intergroup biases and need for social exchange, will obstruct efforts to prevent the spread of misinformation through social media and through conversation.[23]

WhatsApp and social media, moreover, did not invent news sharing, which is a merger of vertical and horizontal intermediation. WhatsApp users can easily forward and simultaneously comment on news content. This blurs the line between vertically and horizontally generated political information and exposes individuals to immediate peer feedback on professional news. This book, however, has offered multiple qualitative examples of citizens orally discussing the nightly television news with their social contacts, often in real time as the news was airing. Horizontal commentary on vertically mediated information has always existed.

Experts have also noted the more direct role that WhatsApp played in shaping vote choice in 2018. Voters used WhatsApp to send *colas eleitorais*—crib sheets with the numbers they need to enter a vote for their preferred candidates—and to seek peer advice on how to vote. Eleven percent of respondents received a *cola eleitoral* via WhatsApp, and the majority of these respondents reported that a friend or relative had sent it.[24] Similarly, many individuals used WhatApp to get advice from the more politically knowledgeable nodes in their social networks. Consider the following WhatsApp exchange, which our qualitative respondent Juliana showed us in 2018:

Fábio: • I am having a hard time choosing a candidate for deputy.
          • Do you have any recommendations to give me?
Juliana: • Vote for black women, Fábio.
Fábio: • Yes, but that's why I'm asking you.
Juliana   • I'm going to vote for Talíria 5077 for federal deputy. For state deputy Rose Cipriano 50800, but there's also Thais Ferreira 50010 and Mónica Francisco 50888.
Fábio: • I'm going to research it.
          • Thank you very much![TA9.5]

Now consider the following exchange, documented during Rio's 1992 municipal election, long before the advent of WhatsApp and social media:

FELIPE, 39, MECHANIC: We had to vote for [Luiz Otávio Campos for city council]. I voted for him, my wife voted for him, and I got more votes for him, you know.
RESEARCHER: How was it you got the votes?
FELIPE: Talking to friends . . . I asked if they had a candidate. [If] they said, "Look, I don't have a candidate," I said, "If you want, you know, you could help us out. I have a candidate." I gave the candidate's number and name . . . I got some 10 [votes] for him.[25]

To summarize, relying on knowledgeable ties for voting advice is hardly new in Brazil. Online political discussion will help researchers better observe and document social influence, but *online political discussion did not create social influence*. Social influence is a basic fact of human existence.

NORMATIVE IMPLICATIONS FOR
DEMOCRATIC CITIZENSHIP

What does the existence of this social world—a world of informal political discussion and persuasive peers—imply for the nature and quality of democratic citizenship in Latin America's new democracies? In adapting previous ideas on the matter to the Latin American context, we see two opposing views.

A Positive View

Our picture of the Latin American voter fits a certain democratic ideal—the deliberative citizen—far better than that ideal fits most voters in the US and other established democracies. During election campaigns, as this book has shown, many Brazilians and Mexicans *think*, at least in the sense of changing one's mind (from the fictional Doctor's definition of "think" in the epigraph). They listen to and absorb new information about their candidate options, and they update their preferences when this information is compelling. This behavior contrasts sharply with the highly partisan and stable US voter.[26] Furthermore, many Brazilians and Mexicans reflect on their choices in response to discussion and consultation with peers—peers who are typically more politically knowledgeable and who sometimes disagree with them. In other words, many Latin American voters seek out expert opinions, a practice that can multiply expertise through the electorate, and many are also willing to engage in an exchange of ideas across lines of political difference.[27]

To advocates of deliberative democracy, discussion of this consequential sort provides numerous advantages for citizenship and even for institutions.[28] It is an indicator, a cause, and a consequence of social capital.[29] Discussion and deliberation also give voters more and better reasons to support their political attitudes.[30] Discussion also provides a realm of informational exchange and decision making that is largely beyond elite control. This is particularly important in a region of the world with deep power inequalities and where, according to many scholarly portrayals, voters are available to the highest vote-buying bidder. After all, campaigns "lose much of their importance as democratic instruments if partisan elites alone are in the driver's seat."[31] As we showed, moreover, discussion and deliberation boost political knowledge, and politically talkative individuals are more likely to cast a "better" (more correct) vote than the politically mute.[32] Finally, political discussion, when it crosses lines of disagreement, can increase tolerance of the other side.[33] Perhaps Latin Americans have revived the public sphere that, to the lament of Jürgen Habermas, has declined with modernity.[34]

Our findings are even consistent with crucial notions of democratic accountability. Even though campaign fundamentals are not our focus, our argument is wholly compatible with findings on their importance in shaping Latin American election outcomes. Campaign fundamentals are the economic trends, corruption scandals, issue positions, demographic patterns, and other slow-moving factors that tend to be (1) in place before a campaign's onset, (2) highly influential on election outcomes, and (3) meaningful for holding ruling elites accountable to masses.[35] To reiterate, we do not claim that voters are switching preferences haphazardly at the whim of each contact and each persuasive conversation. In deferring to knowledgeable peers, they are instead deferring to those who have relatively stable campaign preferences. This deference draws many voters toward preferences that reflect these pre-campaign factors. Our portrait of the Latin American voter also leaves plenty of space for individual and regional interests and, as a result, positional issue voting.

Overall, our claim that voters arrive at their socially informed preferences over the course of the campaign paints them in a flattering light. Their vote choices are an amalgamation of Habermasian deliberation and communitarianism along with Downsian rationality and accountability. Yet this rosy interpretation, not surprisingly, is too one-sided.

A Negative View

The changing of a voter's mind, although seemingly a manifestation of deliberative thought, has a bad reputation in some scholarship on comparative politics and especially on party systems. According to this strand of research, parties should be institutionalized, meaning they should be stable, predictable, and rooted in their electorates.[36] Voter volatility both undermines and symbolizes weak party systems. Even worse, volatility may indicate that voters are unsophisticated and easily manipulated—susceptible to clientelism or charismatic appeals that are irrelevant to how and for whom a candidate will govern.

Furthermore, the process by which many voters arrive at their socially informed preferences smacks of Christopher Achen and Larry Bartels's famous phrase, "it feels like we're thinking."[37] Rather than multiplying expertise, deference to more expert contacts can be a strategy for voters with little self-motivation to get informed about candidate options. These voters sometimes let associates think for them, free riding on others' information and engagement. Calling this process deep, engaged, and knowledgeable citizenship is a stretch.

It would also be an exaggeration to claim that we have uncovered massive amounts of deliberation—discussion, yes, but genuine deliberation, not necessarily. Deliberation implies hearing and thoughtfully engaging the other side while being open to changing one's mind. Admittedly, there are higher numbers of disagreeing dyads in Latin America than in the US, and exposure to a disagreeing discussant is a leading indicator during a campaign of opinion change. Despite these facts, exposure to disagreement—Janira's experience—is not the norm. In all four of our main election cases, only a minority of voters named at least one disagreeing discussant. In this respect, Latin America is again typical of other multiparty systems in its rates of dyadic disagreement, but disagreeing dyads still remain minorities. Moreover, our finding that exposure to agreement reinforces and strengthens preferences is just as important. There is no guarantee that discussion leads to open minds and reevaluations of preferences. It can further entrench and polarize points of view.[38]

Furthermore, socially informed preferences are not necessarily "better" preferences. Recall from chapters 5 and 6 that regional and neighborhood political leanings, conveyed through social networks, can sometimes pull voters away from voting in line with their individual-level traits and issue positions. Similarly, chapter 8 showed that voters' socially informed preferences were only slightly more likely to be correct than their pre-campaign preferences. For these reasons, social contacts can sometimes provide suboptimal guidance and can even, as Rosa experienced, create regret.

Finally, political discussion in Latin America has exclusionary tendencies, a trait that is the basis of a recurring critique of deliberative democracy.[39] The wealthy and the well-educated are more likely to engage in political discussion, and they have larger political-discussion networks than the poor and less educated. This relationship is paradoxical: horizontal intermediation creates political communications outside the realm of elite control, but in practice it is dominated by the middle and upper classes. Partly for this reason, the poor are sometimes less likely to vote correctly.

A Balanced Normative Conclusion

Do our findings lean to the positive perspective or to the negative perspective? In the end, the most reasonable conclusion draws from both and strikes a measured stance, while also inviting future research on the matter. On the positive side, Latin American voters are receptive during campaigns to new persuasive information. As a result, they are willing to change their preferences. This result reflects an open-mindedness absent in current US politics. Campaigns in Latin America provide truly valuable and meaningful information, making them more than mere epiphenomena. Not all Latin American voters simply disregard new facts that are inconvenient to their partisan predispositions and then return to a predictable home. In this sense, some campaign and electoral volatility is acceptable, even healthy, in new democracies.

Our findings, moreover, paint elections and voters in Latin America in a more flattering light than common scholarly depictions, most of which put political elites in control. According to many depictions, voters are highly susceptible to the short-term allure of a clientelistic payoff, too confused to vote on positional issues, easily swayed by shallow charismatic appeals transmitted through traditional media, and vulnerable to misinformation and false news.[40] Our argument highlights a way that voters supplement or even substitute elite-driven vertical intermediation with information that is more bottom-up in character. Voters seek commentary, insight, advice, reassurance, and even counterargumentation from peers—individuals who are not themselves political elites. Furthermore, voters seek these horizontal inputs from non-elites who are nonetheless well-qualified—or at least more qualified than they are themselves—to provide such inputs. In relying so heavily on available peers, voters are not actively resisting elites and elite-generated information, but horizontal intermediation does give them access to interpretations that can circumvent elite sources and frames. This practice is especially useful because elites are not always trusted and because peers can put a more colloquial spin on political information.

Still, the implications of our findings are not all positive. Many Latin American voters do change their minds during campaigns, but the votes they ultimately cast—their socially informed preferences—are not more in line with their issue positions than are their pre-campaign vote intentions. As a result, we cannot conclude that the social influences occurring during presidential campaigns improve accountability and representation of the beliefs and values of voters. Furthermore, we remain struck by the finding, seemingly ubiquitous across the region, that lower-class Latin Americans are less likely to participate in the social communication processes we highlight. This limits their ability to acquire political knowledge and to influence others—all in a region with deep socioeconomic inequalities. In some instances, the more limited engagement of lower-class Latin Americans in horizontal intermediation even means that their political voices are more distorted by incorrect voting than the voices of higher-status citizens.

Overall, political discussion is a double-edged sword. It informs, but it does not inform everyone equally. Discussion invokes a reexamination of preferences, but it also reinforces blindly held preferences. It influences, but not always for the better. In the end, socially informed voters are neither ideal nor deeply flawed citizens, but they are an empirical reality that scholars of Latin American politics must recognize.

APPENDIX A

Statistical Results

TABLE A.1 (*MODEL RESULTS DEPICTED IN FIGURE 2.5*).
Campaign Knowledge by Exposure to Political Intermediaries in Mexico 2006:
Coefficients from Three OLS Models

	Model 1	Model 2	Model 3
Dependent Variable:	Campaign knowledge (*pc* wave)	Campaign knowledge (*c* wave)	Campaign knowledge (*c* wave)
Frequency of political discussion	0.025* (0.004)	0.021* (0.004)	
Egocentric network size			0.169* (0.024)
Frequency of TV news consumption	0.008* (0.003)	0.013* (0.003)	0.012* (0.003)
Contacted by a party		0.007 (0.007)	0.008 (0.007)
Paid off by a party		−0.009 (0.012)	−0.009 (0.014)
Constant	−0.328* (0.055)	−0.376* (0.058)	−0.456* (0.054)
N	2,231	1,632	1,653

Notes: Entries are OLS coefficients with standard errors in parentheses. The original
Contacted by party and *Paid off by a party* variables are multiplied by 10 to improve readability
in figure 2.5.
* $= p < 0.05$
Source: Mexico 2006 Panel Study.

TABLE A.2 (*MODELS USED FOR FIGURE 2.7*).
Selection of a Social Alter to Be a Political Alter by the Perceived Political Knowledge
of That Alter in Four Latin American Countries: Results from Three Binary Logit
Models

	Dependent Variable		
	Spouse selected as a political alter	Alter 2 selected as a political alter	Alter 3 selected as a political alter
Perceived political knowledge of spouse	1.232* (0.220)		
Perceived political knowledge of alter 2		1.125* (0.088)	
Perceived political knowledge of alter 3			1.221* (0.122)
Campaign interest (of main respondent)	0.155* (0.056)	0.182* (0.048)	0.139* (0.053)
Political knowledge (of main respondent)	0.119 (0.091)	0.147* (0.052)	0.242* (0.072)
Frequency of political discussion (by main respondent)	0.514 (0.301)	1.152* (0.092)	0.906* (0.101)
Constant	1.359 (1.054)	3.015* (0.298)	2.568* (0.325)
N	3,251	4,669	2,312

Notes: Entries are logit coefficients with robust standard errors (corrected for clustering
within country years) in parentheses. Coefficients for country-year fixed effects are not shown.
All variables except *Perceived political knowledge of spouse/alter 2/alter 3* are held at their
means to generate predicted probabilities in figure 2.7.
  $* = p < 0.05$
Source: CNEP.

TABLE A.3 (*MODELS USED FOR FIGURE 4.3*).
The Likelihood of Changing Vote Preference between Campaign and Election Waves by Campaign-Wave Network Traits: Results from Four Binary Logit Models

	Brazil 2002	Brazil 2006	Brazil 2014	Mexico 2006
Network disagreement	1.207*	1.276*	1.709*	2.033*
	(0.166)	(0.235)	(0.408)	(0.326)
Disagreeing alters' diversity	−0.139	−0.051		−1.074
	(0.356)	(0.520)		(0.825)
Singleton	0.745*	0.935*	0.667*	1.027*
	(0.105)	(0.146)	(0.230)	(0.258)
Juiz de Fora resident	−0.516*	0.066		
	(0.106)	(0.145)		
Constant	−0.481*	−1.530*	−1.749*	−2.300*
	(0.181)	(0.265)	(0.235)	(0.199)
N	2,278	1,184	710	1,043

Notes: Entries are logit coefficients with standard errors in parentheses. Dependent variable for each model is *Changed vote preference*. *Juiz de Fora resident* is held at its mean to generate predicted probabilities in figure 4.3.

* = *p* < 0.05

Source: Two-City Panel, BEPS 2014, Mexico 2006 Panel Study.

TABLE A.4 (*MODEL RESULTS DEPICTED IN FIGURE 4.4*).
Changed Vote Preference by Network Traits in Brazil and Mexico: Results from Four
Binary Logit Models (Restrictive Definition of Disagreement)

	Brazil 2002	Brazil 2006	Brazil 2014	Mexico 2006
Horizontal Intermediation				
Network.disagreement$_e$	2.700*	2.335*	3.037*	3.360*
	(0.223)	(0.268)	(0.386)	(0.418)
Network.disagreement$_c$	−0.060	−0.555*	0.832*	0.852*
	(0.207)	(0.261)	(0.403)	(0.320)
Disagreeing.alters'. diversity$_e$	−1.089*	0.586		−3.637*
	(0.432)	(0.498)		(0.976)
Disagreeing.alters'. diversity$_c$	0.061	−1.224		−1.536
	(0.460)	(0.649)		(1.159)
Singleton$_e$	2.120*	1.022*	1.559*	2.067*
	(0.272)	(0.287)	(0.461)	(0.343)
Singleton$_c$	−0.171	0.291	0.476	0.128
	(0.215)	(0.225)	(0.248)	(0.283)
Vertical Intermediation				
Contacted by a disagreeing party	0.035	0.194		
	(0.272)	(0.440)		
Not contacted by a party	0.244	0.263		
	(0.244)	(0.418)		
Paid off by a disagreeing party				−0.520
				(1.222)
Not paid off by a party				−0.296
				(1.135)
Ciro intention × HEG exposure	−0.220			
	(0.291)			
Exposure to disagreeing media	−0.140			
	(0.129)			
Unexposed to media	0.544			
	(0.299)			
Exposed only to uncoded media	0.139			
	(0.232)			

Table A.4 (continued)

	Brazil 2002	Brazil 2006	Brazil 2014	Mexico 2006
Exposure to disagreeing TV news				−0.059 (0.175)
Unexposed to TV news				0.037 (0.290)
Exposure to uncoded media				−0.749 (0.386)
Media exposure		−0.324* (0.160)	0.220 (0.237)	
Alckmin intention × Media exposure		0.178 (0.229)		
HH intention × Media exposure		−0.084 (0.181)		
Other intention × Media exposure		0.110 (0.395)	1.299* (0.371)	
Aécio intention × Media exposure			−0.225 (0.370)	
Marina intention × Media exposure			−0.456 (0.281)	
Juiz de Fora resident	−0.246 (0.131)	0.150 (0.167)		
Constant	−0.777* (0.327)	−3.018* (0.449)	−4.641* (0.881)	−3.715* (1.191)
N	2,278	1,184	710	1,043

Notes: Entries are logit coefficients with standard errors in parentheses. Dependent variable for each model is *Changed vote preference*. Measures of vote intention are from campaign waves, and measures of vertical intermediation are from election waves. Coefficients (one per candidate) for fixed effects for campaign-wave vote intention are not shown.

* = $p < 0.05$

Source: Two-City Panel, BEPS 2014, Mexico 2006 Panel Study.

TABLE A.5 (*MODELS REFERENCED ONLY IN CHAPTER 4 TEXT*).
Changed Vote Preference by Network Traits in Brazil and Mexico: Results from Four
Binary Logit Models (Inclusive Definition of Disagreement)

	Brazil 2002	Brazil 2006	Brazil 2014	Mexico 2006
Horizontal Intermediation				
Network.disagreement$_e$	3.144*	1.905*	2.991*	2.885*
	(0.254)	(0.282)	(0.500)	(0.393)
Network.disagreement$_c$	0.030	−0.045	0.844*	0.377
	(0.198)	(0.241)	(0.341)	(0.299)
Disagreeing.alters'. diversity$_e$	−0.610*	0.895*	−0.427	−0.371
	(0.296)	(0.396)	(0.918)	(0.647)
Disagreeing.alters'. diversity$_c$	−0.461	−1.722*	−2.418	−1.050
	(0.349)	(0.510)	(1.378)	(0.867)
Singleton$_e$			1.660*	2.222*
			(0.467)	(0.371)
Singleton$_c$	2.281*	1.469*	0.515	−0.011
	(0.244)	(0.274)	(0.337)	(0.309)
Vertical Intermediation				
Contacted by a disagreeing party	0.048	0.264		
	(0.286)	(0.441)		
Not contacted by a party	0.186	0.299		
	(0.239)	(0.401)		
Paid off by a disagreeing party				−0.421
				(0.889)
Not paid off by a party				−0.331
				(0.799)
Ciro intention × HEG exposure	−0.220			
	(0.289)			
Exposure to disagreeing media	−0.143			
	(0.126)			
Unexposed to media	0.508			
	(0.303)			
Exposed only to uncoded media	0.136			
	(0.251)			
Exposure to disagreeing TV news				−0.067
				(0.168)

TABLE A.5 (continued)

	Brazil 2002	Brazil 2006	Brazil 2014	Mexico 2006
Unexposed to TV news				0.002
				(0.294)
Exposure to uncoded media				−0.665
				(0.364)
Media exposure		−0.299*	0.222	
		(0.144)	(0.195)	
Alckmin intention × Media exposure		0.131		
		(0.202)		
HH intention × Media exposure		−0.074		
		(0.206)		
Other intention × Media exposure		0.104	1.034	
		(0.333)	(0.631)	
Aécio intention × Media exposure			−0.141	
			(0.317)	
Marina intention × Media exposure			−0.540*	
			(0.257)	
Juiz de Fora resident	−0.255*	0.106		
	(0.124)	(0.156)		
Constant	−1.170*	−3.095*	−4.845*	−3.565*
	(0.392)	(0.488)	(0.710)	(0.836)
N	2,278	1,184	710	1,042

Notes: Entries are logit coefficients with standard errors in parentheses. Dependent variable for each model is *Changed vote preference*. Measures of vote intention are from campaign waves, and measures of vertical intermediation are from election waves. Coefficients (one per candidate) for fixed effects for campaign-wave vote intention are not shown.

* = $p < 0.05$

Source: Two-City Panel, BEPS 2014, Mexico 2006 Panel Study.

TABLE A.6 (*MODEL RESULTS PARTIALLY DEPICTED IN FIGURE 4.5, FRAME A, AND FIGURE 4.6, FRAME A*).
Ego's Vote Choice (Y_e) by Alter's Vote Choice at the Dyadic Level in Brazil 2002: Results from Two Multinomial Logit Models

Dependent variable categories:	Full Sample			Stable-Alters Sample		
	Lula vote *Serra vote*	*Garo. vote* *Serra vote*	*Ciro vote* *Serra vote*	*Lula vote* *Serra vote*	*Garo. vote* *Serra vote*	*Ciro vote* *Serra vote*
Horizontal Intermediation						
Alter vote choice (e wave)						
Lula	2.010* (0.157)	1.106* (0.217)	1.035* (0.194)			
Garotinho	0.955* (0.345)	3.074* (0.330)	0.928* (0.387)			
Ciro	1.187* (0.231)	1.256* (0.309)	1.771* (0.242)			
No one	1.362* (0.172)	1.030* (0.244)	0.737* (0.222)			
Serra	Omitted baseline	Omitted baseline	Omitted baseline			
Alter vote intention (c wave)						
Lula	−0.290 (0.207)	−0.048 (0.266)	−0.211 (0.285)	1.535* (0.239)	1.012* (0.339)	0.587 (0.322)
Garotinho	−0.039 (0.368)	−0.285 (0.401)	0.466 (0.488)	1.737* (0.771)	3.325* (0.766)	1.286 (0.864)

Ciro	−0.334 (0.202)	−0.219 (0.263)	0.097 (0.257)	0.651 (0.337)	1.162* (0.447)	1.690* (0.345)
No one	−0.377 (0.217)	−0.099 (0.277)	−0.197 (0.295)	0.869* (0.309)	0.861* (0.422)	0.295 (0.422)
Serra	Omitted baseline	Omitted baseline	Omitted baseline	Omitted baseline	Omitted baseline	Omitted baseline
Political Predispositions (pc wave)						
Macroeconomic evaluations	−0.142 (0.075)	−0.048 (0.094)	−0.160 (0.095)	−0.051 (0.099)	−0.007 (0.122)	−0.130 (0.125)
PT partisanship	2.337* (0.412)	0.626 (0.490)	0.573 (0.531)	2.497* (0.529)	0.851 (0.635)	0.857 (0.624)
Partisanship toward another party or no partisanship	0.748* (0.287)	0.088 (0.330)	0.573 (0.343)	1.114* (0.364)	0.453 (0.427)	0.721 (0.423)
PSDB partisanship	Omitted baseline	Omitted baseline	Omitted baseline	Omitted baseline	Omitted baseline	Omitted baseline
Position in issue space	0.133 (0.087)	0.106 (0.117)	−0.041 (0.104)	0.306* (0.121)	0.153 (0.144)	0.024 (0.140)
Ego.vote.intention$_c$						
Lula	3.930* (0.318)	2.377* (0.432)	3.487* (0.777)	3.997* (0.399)	1.628* (0.551)	16.427* (0.469)

(continued)

TABLE A.6 (continued)

Dependent variable categories:	Full Sample			Stable-Alters Sample		
	$\dfrac{Lula\ vote}{Serra\ vote}$	$\dfrac{Garo.\ vote}{Serra\ vote}$	$\dfrac{Ciro\ vote}{Serra\ vote}$	$\dfrac{Lula\ vote}{Serra\ vote}$	$\dfrac{Garo.\ vote}{Serra\ vote}$	$\dfrac{Ciro\ vote}{Serra\ vote}$
Garotinho	1.404*	3.405*	2.048*	1.817*	3.389*	−2.413*
	(0.411)	(0.455)	(0.967)	(0.496)	(0.558)	(0.402)
Ciro	1.547*	1.401*	4.588*	1.881*	1.309*	17.935*
	(0.242)	(0.351)	(0.696)	(0.332)	(0.453)	(0.200)
No one	1.913*	1.578*	3.225*	1.881*	1.464*	16.505*
	(0.293)	(0.438)	(0.756)	(0.369)	(0.553)	(0.380)
Serra	Omitted baseline	Omitted baseline	Omitted baseline	Omitted baseline	Omitted baseline	Omitted baseline
Ego.vote.intention$_{pc}$						
Lula	2.227*	1.336*	1.536*	2.260*	1.678*	1.676*
	(0.389)	(0.510)	(0.528)	(0.537)	(0.667)	(0.716)
Garotinho	0.807*	1.614*	0.533	0.846*	1.981*	0.988
	(0.342)	(0.401)	(0.453)	(0.420)	(0.520)	(0.572)
Ciro	0.568	0.262	1.019*	0.317	−0.050	0.575
	(0.359)	(0.461)	(0.373)	(0.472)	(0.590)	(0.468)
Other	0.701*	0.195	0.066	0.541	−0.030	0.137
	(0.251)	(0.375)	(0.330)	(0.307)	(0.477)	(0.430)

	(1)	(2)	(3)	(4)	(5)	(6)
No one	0.638*	0.489	0.566	0.647	0.507	0.758
	(0.277)	(0.408)	(0.370)	(0.341)	(0.537)	(0.461)
Serra	Omitted baseline	Omitted baseline	Omitted baseline	Omitted baseline	Omitted baseline	Omitted baseline
Juiz de Fora resident	1.552*	0.694*	1.828*	1.780*	0.995*	1.982*
	(0.188)	(0.264)	(0.244)	(0.227)	(0.315)	(0.303)
Constant	−5.639*	−4.733*	−8.261*	−6.420*	−5.407*	−21.737*
	(0.470)	(0.674)	(0.955)	(0.614)	(0.800)	(0.682)
N		5,169			2,698	

Notes: Entries are multinomial logit coefficients with robust standard errors (corrected for clustering within main respondents) in parentheses. Dependent variable for each model is *Ego vote choice*. Shaded coefficients correspond to those labeled in boldface in the figures. pc = pre-campaign wave, c = campaign wave, e = election wave.

$* = p < 0.05$

Source: Two-City Panel.

TABLE A.7 (*MODEL RESULTS PARTIALLY DEPICTED IN FIGURE 4.5, FRAME B, AND FIGURE 4.6, FRAME B*).
Ego's Vote Choice (Y_e) by Alter's Vote Choice at the Dyadic Level in Brazil 2006: Results from Two Multinomial Logit Models

Dependent variable categories:	Full Sample		Stable-Alters Sample	
	Alckmin vote / Lula vote	HH vote / Lula vote	Alckmin vote / Lula vote	HH vote / Lula vote
Horizontal Intermediation				
Alter vote choice (*e* wave)				
Alckmin	2.437* (0.224)	1.074* (0.288)		
Heloísa Helena	1.558* (0.422)	2.902* (0.409)		
Other	1.148* (0.282)	0.563 (0.405)		
No one	0.811* (0.232)	0.890* (0.301)		
Lula	Omitted baseline	Omitted baseline		
Alter vote intention (*c* wave)				
Alckmin	−0.224 (0.265)	−0.116 (0.305)	2.034* (0.288)	1.038* (0.430)
Heloísa Helena	0.167 (0.394)	−0.490 (0.408)	2.079* (0.712)	2.629* (0.761)
Other	−0.552 (0.471)	−0.783 (0.589)	1.081 (0.584)	−14.445* (0.819)
No one	−0.356 (0.248)	−0.466 (0.270)	0.114 (0.347)	0.406 (0.362)
Lula	Omitted baseline	Omitted baseline	Omitted baseline	Omitted baseline
Political Predispositions (c wave)				
Macroeconomic evaluations	−0.163 (0.118)	0.164 (0.171)	−0.233 (0.165)	0.100 (0.210)

TABLE A.7 (continued)

Dependent variable categories:	Full Sample		Stable-Alters Sample	
	Alckmin vote / Lula vote	HH vote / Lula vote	Alckmin vote / Lula vote	HH vote / Lula vote
Presidential approval	−0.708*	−0.665*	−0.645*	−0.482*
	(0.136)	(0.175)	(0.176)	(0.233)
PSDB partisanship	4.741*	3.416*	4.430*	2.021
	(1.180)	(1.384)	(1.348)	(1.657)
Partisanship toward another party or no partisanship	0.723*	0.222	0.764*	0.248
	(0.282)	(0.363)	(0.357)	(0.442)
PT partisanship	Omitted baseline	Omitted baseline	Omitted baseline	Omitted baseline
Position in issue space	−0.116	0.234	−0.160	0.399
	(0.116)	(0.156)	(0.153)	(0.209)
Ego.vote.intention$_c$				
Alckmin	3.222*	1.906*	3.717*	2.061*
	(0.330)	(0.585)	(0.408)	(0.687)
Heloísa Helena	1.779*	3.625*	1.758*	3.554*
	(0.350)	(0.484)	(0.429)	(0.544)
Other	1.828*	2.510*	2.183*	2.489*
	(0.676)	(0.891)	(0.897)	(1.181)
No one	2.169*	2.508*	2.683*	2.687*
	(0.349)	(0.499)	(0.468)	(0.570)
Lula	Omitted baseline	Omitted baseline	Omitted baseline	Omitted baseline
Juiz de Fora resident	−0.996*	0.213	−0.829*	0.526
	(0.225)	(0.290)	(0.301)	(0.369)
Constant	0.962	−2.761*	0.747	−3.668*
	(0.723)	(0.971)	(0.877)	(1.237)
N	2,577		1,336	

Notes: Entries are multinomial logit coefficients with robust standard errors (corrected for clustering within main respondents) in parentheses. Dependent variable for each model is *Ego vote choice*. Shaded coefficients correspond to those labeled in boldface in the figures. pc = pre-campaign wave, c = campaign wave, e = election wave.

* = $p < 0.05$

Source: Two-City Panel.

TABLE A.8 (*MODEL RESULTS PARTIALLY DEPICTED IN FIGURE 4.5, FRAME C, AND FIGURE 4.6, FRAME C*).

Ego's Vote Choice (Y_e) by Alter's Vote Choice at the Dyadic Level in Brazil 2014: Results from Two Multinomial Logit Models

Dependent variable categories:	Full Sample		Stable-Alters Sample	
	Aécio vote / Dilma vote	*Marina vote* / Dilma vote	*Aécio vote* / Dilma vote	*Marina vote* / Dilma vote
Horizontal Intermediation				
Alter vote choice (*e* wave)				
Aécio	4.260* (0.525)	1.620* (0.657)		
Marina	0.805 (0.675)	3.003* (0.540)		
Other	−10.331* (1.389)	−10.378* (1.301)		
No one	1.386 (0.956)	0.435 (0.822)		
Dilma	Omitted baseline	Omitted baseline		
Alter vote intention (*c* wave)				
Aécio	−1.833* (0.627)	−0.544 (0.690)	2.762* (0.774)	0.283 (0.929)
Marina	1.045* (0.526)	−0.268 (0.621)	2.179* (0.765)	2.984* (0.961)
Other	−2.890 (1.710)	2.117* (0.833)		
No one	−0.331 (0.934)	1.536* (0.697)	1.204 (0.954)	2.759* (1.099)
Dilma	Omitted baseline	Omitted baseline	Omitted baseline	Omitted baseline
Pol. Predispositions (pc wave)				
Macroeconomic evaluations	0.585 (0.309)	−0.055 (0.270)	1.030* (0.438)	−0.763* (0.302)
Presidential approval	−0.093 (0.271)	−0.449 (0.260)	−0.592 (0.466)	−1.354* (0.389)

TABLE A.8 (continued)

Dependent variable categories:	Full Sample		Stable-Alters Sample	
	Aécio vote / *Dilma vote*	*Marina vote* / *Dilma vote*	*Aécio vote* / *Dilma vote*	*Marina vote* / *Dilma vote*
PSDB partisanship	2.418 (1.270)	4.109* (1.576)	0.383 (1.390)	5.903* (1.831)
PSB partisanship	0.867 (1.533)	2.188 (1.266)	−3.663 (2.293)	4.414* (1.670)
PT partisanship	Omitted baseline	Omitted baseline	Omitted baseline	Omitted baseline
Partisanship toward another party or no partisanship	0.151 (0.623)	2.562* (0.887)	−1.377 (1.069)	3.471* (1.090)
Position in issue space	0.672* (0.249)	−0.126 (0.269)	0.527 (0.326)	−0.547 (0.487)
Ego.vote.intention$_c$				
Aécio	4.317* (0.896)	2.408* (0.978)	3.921* (1.266)	3.052* (1.506)
Marina	1.927* (0.650)	4.189* (0.701)	0.976 (0.824)	6.407* (1.052)
Other	1.115 (0.970)	2.358 (1.223)	−16.268* (1.103)	6.212* (1.355)
No one	1.266 (0.848)	2.883* (0.730)	0.474 (1.396)	3.065* (1.395)
Dilma	Omitted baseline	Omitted baseline	Omitted baseline	Omitted baseline
Ego.vote.intention$_{pc}$				
Aécio	−0.935 (0.931)	−0.320 (0.762)	−0.983 (1.373)	−3.186* (1.177)
Marina	0.817 (0.957)	1.227 (0.897)	1.483 (1.446)	−1.079 (1.166)
Other	1.023 (0.928)	0.318 (0.813)	1.756 (1.231)	−1.953 (1.072)
No one	−0.993 (0.784)	−0.907 (0.732)	−0.053 (0.980)	−1.946 (1.084)

(continued)

TABLE A.8 (continued)

Dependent variable categories:	Full Sample		Stable-Alters Sample	
	Aécio vote / *Dilma vote*	*Marina vote* / *Dilma vote*	*Aécio vote* / *Dilma vote*	*Marina vote* / *Dilma vote*
Dilma	Omitted baseline	Omitted baseline	Omitted baseline	Omitted baseline
Constant	−0.010	−5.605*	2.968	−7.083*
	(1.804)	(1.647)	(2.158)	(2.008)
N	566		356	

Notes: Entries are multinomial logit coefficients with robust standard errors (corrected for clustering within main respondents) in parentheses. Dependent variable for each model is *Ego vote choice*. Shaded coefficients correspond to those labeled in boldface in the figures. pc = pre-campaign wave, c = campaign wave, e = election wave. c wave corresponds to waves $c4$ and $c5$, and e wave corresponds to $e6$.

$^{*} = p < 0.05$

Source: BEPS 2014.

TABLE A.9 (*MODEL RESULTS PARTIALLY DEPICTED IN FIGURE 4.5, FRAME D, AND FIGURE 4.6, FRAME D*).

Ego's Vote Choice by Alter's Vote Choice at the Dyadic Level in Mexico 2006: Results from Two Multinomial Logit Models

Dependent variable categories:	Full Sample		Stable-Alters Sample	
	AMLO vote Calderón vote	*Madrazo vote* Calderón vote	*AMLO vote* Calderón vote	*Madrazo vote* Calderón vote
Horizontal Intermediation				
Alter vote choice (*e* wave)				
AMLO	2.390* (0.502)	0.077 (0.603)		
Madrazo	0.549 (0.717)	2.547* (0.615)		
Other	1.287 (0.862)	0.443 (1.201)		
No one	0.988 (0.625)	0.222 (0.636)		
Calderón	Omitted baseline	Omitted baseline		
Alter vote intention (*c* wave)				
AMLO	0.773 (0.539)	0.400 (0.603)	2.408* (0.630)	0.645 (0.745)
Madrazo	1.452* (0.675)	−0.094 (0.663)	1.247 (0.847)	2.607* (0.601)
Other	0.845 (0.918)	1.908 (1.208)	−7.644* (1.406)	−6.553* (1.531)
No one	−0.264 (0.660)	0.724 (0.566)	0.114 (0.912)	1.226 (0.949)
Calderón	Omitted baseline	Omitted baseline	Omitted baseline	Omitted baseline
Political Predispositions (pc wave)				
Macroeconomic evaluations	−0.209 (0.265)	−0.665* (0.333)	−0.287 (0.317)	−0.676 (0.358)
Presidential approval	−0.585* (0.226)	−0.618* (0.246)	−0.149 (0.233)	−0.322 (0.270)

(*continued*)

TABLE A.9 (continued)

Dependent variable categories:	Full Sample		Stable-Alters Sample	
	AMLO vote / *Calderón vote*	*Madrazo vote* / *Calderón vote*	*AMLO vote* / *Calderón vote*	*Madrazo vote* / *Calderón vote*
PRI partisanship	0.389	0.254	1.210	0.457
	(1.196)	(1.124)	(1.313)	(1.278)
PRD partisanship	2.332	2.013	4.825*	3.733
	(1.424)	(1.971)	(2.118)	(4.530)
Partisanship toward another party or no partisanship	0.522	0.828	0.889	0.612
	(0.653)	(0.717)	(0.695)	(0.917)
PAN partisanship	Omitted baseline	Omitted baseline	Omitted baseline	Omitted baseline
Position on trade with US	0.229	0.182	0.018	0.149
	(0.172)	(0.207)	(0.196)	(0.242)
Position on privatization	−0.268*	−0.250	−0.211	−0.324
	(0.128)	(0.160)	(0.167)	(0.199)
Position on abortion	0.041	0.407*	0.090	0.312*
	(0.156)	(0.135)	(0.208)	(0.155)
Position on capital punishment	−0.060	0.082	−0.158	−0.016
	(0.129)	(0.130)	(0.197)	(0.156)
Ego.vote.intention$_c$				
AMLO	3.751*	1.650	4.553*	2.365*
	(0.679)	(0.933)	(0.869)	(1.127)
Madrazo	0.352	5.284*	1.066	5.057*
	(0.842)	(0.782)	(1.105)	(1.078)
Other	1.245	0.679	3.321*	2.011
	(1.013)	(1.443)	(1.214)	(1.583)
No one	2.848*	0.033	2.646*	−0.075
	(1.087)	(1.079)	(0.902)	(1.327)
Calderón	Omitted baseline	Omitted baseline	Omitted baseline	Omitted baseline
Ego.vote.intention$_{pc}$				
AMLO	0.646	−1.342	0.804	−1.452
	(0.799)	(1.077)	(0.909)	(1.356)

TABLE A.9 (continued)

Dependent variable categories:	Full Sample		Stable-Alters Sample	
	AMLO vote Calderón vote	*Madrazo vote* Calderón vote	*AMLO vote* Calderón vote	*Madrazo vote* Calderón vote
Madrazo	−0.452 (1.029)	−0.356 (1.054)	−0.071 (1.091)	−0.268 (1.419)
Other	−0.952 (0.892)	−2.639 (1.426)	−0.039 (0.995)	−2.174 (1.952)
No one	−2.488* (1.063)	−0.046 (0.830)	−0.955 (0.864)	0.801 (1.193)
Calderón	Omitted baseline	Omitted baseline	Omitted baseline	Omitted baseline
Constant	−1.244 (1.469)	−1.525 (1.413)	−2.657 (1.691)	−2.321 (1.499)
N	928		644	

Notes: Entries are multinomial logit coefficients with robust standard errors (corrected for clustering within main respondents) in parentheses. Dependent variable for each model is *Ego vote choice*. Shaded coefficients correspond to those labeled in boldface in the figures. pc = pre-campaign wave, c = campaign wave, e = election wave.

$*$ = $p < 0.05$

Source: Mexico 2006 Panel.

Table A.10 (*MODELS USED FOR FIGURE 4.7*).
Ego's Runoff Vote Choice by Alter's First-Round Vote Choice in Brazil: Results from Three Models

Dependent variable categories:	2002 *Lula vote* / *Serra vote*	2006 *Alckmin vote* / *Lula vote*	2014 *Aécio vote* / *Dilma vote*
Horizontal Intermediation			
Alter vote choice (*e* wave)			
Lula('02)/Dilma('14)	0.381 (0.286)	Omitted baseline	Omitted baseline
Garotinho('02)/HH('06)/ Marina('14)	−0.077 (0.340)	0.760 (0.540)	0.385* (0.148)
Ciro	0.087 (0.340)		
Other		0.313 (0.526)	0.218 (0.413)
No one	0.281 (0.313)	0.680 (0.477)	0.626* (0.174)
Serra('02)/Alckmin('06)/Aécio('14)	Omitted baseline	0.888* (0.437)	0.526* (0.148)
Alter vote intention (*c* wave)			
Lula	0.781* (0.348)	Omitted baseline	Omitted baseline
Garotinho('02)/HH('06)/ Marina('14)	0.497 (0.442)	−0.149 (0.584)	−0.059 (0.167)
Ciro	0.614 (0.343)		
Other		1.397* (0.704)	−0.144 (0.170)
No one	0.056 (0.380)	0.464 (0.356)	−0.052 (0.217)
Serra('02)/Alckmin('06)/Aécio('14)	Omitted baseline	0.895* (0.416)	−0.135 (0.188)

Table A.10 (continued)

Dependent variable categories:	2002 Lula vote Serra vote	2006 Alckmin vote Lula vote	2014 Aécio vote Dilma vote
Political Predispositions (pc wave)			
Macroeconomic evaluations	−0.170 (0.124)	0.282 (0.268)	−0.003 (0.065)
Presidential approval		−0.881* (0.302)	−0.129 (0.071)
PT partisanship	0.635 (0.667)	Omitted baseline	Omitted baseline
Partisanship toward another party or no partisanship	−0.491 (0.481)	1.035* (0.512)	−0.178 (0.120)
PSDB partisanship	Omitted baseline	2.849* (1.004)	−0.285 (0.281)
Position in issue space	0.010 (0.128)	−0.397 (0.241)	0.036 (0.080)
Ego.vote.intention$_c$			
Lula('02)/Dilma('14)	1.742* (0.788)	Omitted baseline	Omitted baseline
Garotinho('02)/HH('06)/ Marina('14)	0.027 (0.741)	2.919* (1.132)	−0.195 (0.286)
Ciro	0.800 (0.675)		
Other		2.141 (1.303)	−0.278 (0.339)
No one	0.988 (0.777)	2.045 (1.159)	−0.245 (0.288)
Serra('02)/Alckmin('06)/Aécio('14)	Omitted baseline	3.034* (1.283)	−0.835* (0.375)
Ego.vote.intention$_{pc}$			
Lula('02)/Dilma('14)	1.319 (0.743)		Omitted baseline
Garotinho('02)/HH('06)/ Marina('14)	0.379 (0.608)		0.242 (0.239)

(continued)

TABLE A.10 (continued)

Dependent variable categories:	2002 Lula vote / Serra vote	2006 Alckmin vote / Lula vote	2014 Aécio vote / Dilma vote
Ciro	0.644 (0.587)		
Other	−0.117 (0.566)		−0.042 (0.316)
No one	0.288 (0.601)		0.055 (0.235)
Serra('02)/Alckmin('06)/Aécio('14)	Omitted baseline		0.356 (0.238)
Juiz de Fora resident	2.034* (0.328)	−0.920* (0.464)	
Constant	−4.051* (1.027)	−0.785 (2.260)	1.078 (0.552)
N	841	392	120

Notes: Entries are logit coefficients with robust standard errors (corrected for clustering within main respondents) in parentheses, although the 2014 model is estimated as a linear probability model (OLS regression) because the small sample size makes logit estimates unstable. Dependent variable for each model is *Ego runoff vote choice.* Samples are limited to main respondents who voted for candidates not contesting the runoff election. Shaded coefficients correspond to variables we manipulate to generate predicted probabilities in figure 4.7. All other variables are held at their means. For 2006, political predispositions are estimated using c wave measures. pc = pre-campaign wave, c = campaign wave, e = election wave.

* $= p < 0.05$

Source: Two-City Panel, BEPS 2014.

TABLE A.11 (*MODELS USED FOR FIGURE 4.9*).
Preference Stability by Degree of Political Knowledge in Brazil and Mexico

Frame A: Timing of Vote Decision: Results from Four Ordered Logit Models

	Brazil 2002	Brazil 2006	Brazil 2014	Mexico 2006
Political knowledge	−0.193*	−0.406*	−0.165*	−0.211*
	(.046)	(.045)	(.077)	(.075)
Juiz de Fora resident	−0.640	−0.181		
	(.105)	(.110)		
Responded in $c2$			0.345	
			(.228)	
Responded in $c3$			Omitted baseline	
Cut point 1	−1.322	−0.112	−0.659	0.238
	(.168)	(.160)	(.158)	(.086)
Cut point 2	−0.439		0.119	1.167
	(.160)		(.156)	(.101)
N	1,761	1,513	697	1,053

(continued)

Frame B: Changed vote preference: Results from Eight Binary Logit Models

	Brazil 2002		Brazil 2006		Brazil 2014		Mexico 2006	
	Always opinionated sample	≥ once opinionated sample	Always opinionated sample	≥ once opinionated sample	Always opinionated sample	≥ once opinionated sample	Always opinionated sample	≥ once opinionated sample
Political knowledge	−0.455* (0.087)	−0.213* (0.054)	−0.490* (0.084)	−0.406* (0.045)	−0.199 (0.108)	−0.275* (0.110)	−0.267* (0.094)	−0.218* (0.078)
Responded in c2					0.067 (0.357)	0.074 (0.234)		
Responded in c3					Omitted baseline	Omitted baseline		
Juiz de Fora resident	−0.286* (0.128)	−0.562* (0.111)	0.145 (0.163)	−0.181 (0.110)				
Constant	2.369* (0.362)	1.206* (0.177)	−1.824* (0.317)	0.112 (0.160)	−1.070* (0.200)	0.816* (0.173)	−1.327* (0.265)	−0.244* (0.086)
N	1,268	1,761	1,172	1,513	359	697	914	1,053

Notes: Entries are ordered logit (frame A) or binary logit (frame B) coefficients with standard errors in parentheses. Dependent variable for each model in frame A is *Timing of vote decision.* Dependent variable for each model in frame B is *Changed vote preference.* Coefficients (one per candidate) for fixed effects for pre-campaign and campaign-wave vote intention (one per candidate) are not shown. c2 and c3 denote different campaign waves in BEPS 2014.

* = p < 0.05

Source: Two-City Panel, BEPS 2014, Mexico 2006 Panel.

TABLE A.12 (*MODELS USED FOR FIGURE 5.6*).
The Distribution of Vote Intentions among Alters by Neighborhood Type and City in Brazil 2002: Results from Two Fractional Multinomial Logit Models

	Caxias do Sul			Juiz de Fora		
Dependent variable categories:	Pro-Lula share / Pro-Serra share	Pro-Garo. share / Pro-Serra share	Pro-Ciro share / Pro-Serra share	Pro-Lula share / Pro-Serra share	Pro-Garo. share / Pro-Serra share	Pro-Ciro share / Pro-Serra share
Neighborhood's Political Leaning						
Neighborhood PT support	0.348* (0.063)	0.378* (0.139)	0.199* (0.087)	-0.133 (0.100)	-0.239 (0.134)	-0.130 (0.078)
Ego's Political Predispositions (pc wave)						
PT partisanship	0.998* (0.182)	-0.412 (0.580)	0.220 (0.295)	0.396 (0.427)	-0.324 (0.633)	-0.691 (0.424)
PMDB partisanship	0.290 (0.217)	0.056 (0.539)	0.370 (0.245)	0.026 (0.255)	-0.082 (0.689)	-0.333 (0.265)
Partisans of other parties and nonpartisans	0.414* (0.167)	0.192 (0.462)	0.226 (0.238)	-0.202 (0.254)	-0.197 (0.564)	-0.404 (0.270)
PSDB partisanship	Omitted baseline	Omitted baseline	Omitted baseline	Omitted baseline	Omitted baseline	Omitted baseline
Ego vote intention						
Lula	1.777* (0.149)	1.645* (0.532)	0.837* (0.204)	1.783* (0.347)	2.345* (0.645)	1.430* (0.382)

(*continued*)

TABLE A.12 (continued)

Dependent variable categories:	Caxias do Sul			Juiz de Fora		
	Pro-Lula share / Pro-Serra share	Pro-Garo. share / Pro-Serra share	Pro-Ciro share / Pro-Serra share	Pro-Lula share / Pro-Serra share	Pro-Garo. share / Pro-Serra share	Pro-Ciro share / Pro-Serra share
Garotinho	0.629* (0.222)	1.909* (0.393)	0.308 (0.223)	0.620* (0.218)	2.870* (0.484)	0.485 (0.322)
Ciro	0.379 (0.221)	0.894 (0.482)	0.691* (0.203)	0.738* (0.374)	1.273 (0.802)	1.071* (0.428)
Other or none	0.524* (0.162)	1.000 (0.557)	0.455* (0.093)	0.987* (0.303)	1.905* (0.535)	1.043* (0.268)
Serra	Omitted baseline	Omitted baseline	Omitted baseline	Omitted baseline	Omitted baseline	Omitted baseline
Individual-level Demographics (pc wave)						
Socioeconomic status	-0.062 (0.079)	-0.419* (0.112)	0.173 (0.097)	0.022 (0.095)	-0.325* (0.112)	0.255* (0.105)
Woman	-0.212* (0.081)	-0.147 (0.261)	-0.191 (0.102)	-0.154 (0.144)	0.309 (0.211)	-0.039 (0.166)
Evangelical church attendance	-0.078 (0.088)	0.624* (0.088)	0.040 (0.075)	0.049 (0.101)	0.569* (0.107)	0.080 (0.105)
Constant	-0.243 (0.169)	-2.668* (0.582)	0.173 (0.097)	0.968* (0.447)	-3.014* (0.842)	0.460 (0.331)
N	1,183			1,307		

Notes: Entries are fractional multinomial logit coefficients with robust standard errors (corrected for clustering within neighborhoods) in parentheses. Dependent variables for each model, estimated jointly, are *Pro-Lula share among alters, Pro-Serra share among alters, Pro-Garotinho share among alters,* and *Pro-Ciro share among alters.* Dependent variables are measured in the campaign wave.

$\star = p < 0.05$

Source: Two-City Panel.

TABLE A.13 (*MODEL RESULTS PARTIALLY REPORTED IN TABLE 5.5*).
Ego's Vote Choice by Neighborhood's Political Leaning and Possible Mediators in Caxias do Sul 2002: Results from Four Multinomial Logit Models

Dependent variable categories:	Lula vote / Serra vote				Garotinho vote / Serra vote			
	Model 1	Model 2	Model 3	Model 4	Model 1	Model 2	Model 3	Model 4
Mediators:	None	Individual traits	Individual traits & other intermediaries	Individual traits & other intermediaries & discussants	None	Individual traits	Individual traits & other intermediaries	Individual traits & other intermediaries & discussants
Neighborhood "Effects": Neighborhood's Political Leaning								
Neighborhood PT support	0.279* (0.089)	0.203* (0.089)	0.238* (0.094)	0.176 (0.099)	0.230* (0.108)	0.125 (0.107)	−0.042 (0.143)	−0.089 (0.143)
Discussants' Vote Intentions (c wave)								
Pro-Lula share among alters				1.875* (0.331)				1.417* (0.479)
Pro-Garotinho share among alters				−0.162 (0.677)				1.282 (0.679)
Pro-Ciro share among alters				−0.154 (0.357)				0.332 (0.483)
Singleton				0.672* (0.293)				0.563 (0.423)
Pro-Serra share among alters				Omitted baseline				Omitted baseline

(continued)

TABLE A.13 (continued)

Dependent variable categories:	Lula vote				Garotinho vote			
	Serra vote				Serra vote			
Mediators:	Model 1	Model 2	Model 3	Model 4	Model 1	Model 2	Model 3	Model 4
	None	Individual traits	Individual traits & other intermediaries	Individual traits & other intermediaries & discussants	None	Individual traits	Individual traits & other intermediaries	Individual traits & other intermediaries & discussants
Ego's Vote Intention (pc wave)								
Lula	3.832*	3.041*	3.091*	2.887*	1.784*	1.574*	1.459*	1.225*
	(0.350)	(0.350)	(0.326)	(0.338)	(0.443)	(0.433)	(0.499)	(0.512)
Garotinho	1.258*	1.232*	1.224*	1.213*	2.202*	2.122*	1.784*	1.652*
	(0.297)	(0.299)	(0.322)	(0.336)	(0.249)	(0.252)	(0.381)	(0.391)
Ciro	0.390	0.437	0.398	0.444	0.033	0.028	−0.190	−0.257
	(0.264)	(0.325)	(0.364)	(0.379)	(0.482)	(0.483)	(0.587)	(0.605)
Other or none	1.154*	1.163*	1.174*	1.131*	0.633	0.574	0.527	0.449
	(0.234)	(0.251)	(0.231)	(0.244)	(0.341)	(0.351)	(0.339)	(0.343)
Serra	Omitted baseline	Omitted baseline	Omitted baseline	Omitted baseline	Omitted baseline	Omitted baseline	Omitted baseline	Omitted baseline
Individual Traits (pc wave)								
PT partisanship		2.655*	2.667*	2.396*		0.336	−0.027	−0.157
		(0.475)	(0.448)	(0.463)		(0.530)	(0.692)	(0.700)

	(1)	(2)	(3)	(4)	(5)	(6)
PMDB partisanship	−0.175 (0.401)	−0.228 (0.430)	−0.424 (0.449)	0.040 (0.390)	0.188 (0.572)	0.085 (0.576)
Partisans of other parties and nonpartisans	0.695 (0.378)	0.666 (0.380)	0.492 (0.395)	0.041 (0.401)	0.021 (0.537)	−0.086 (0.542)
PSDB partisanship	Omitted baseline	Omitted baseline	Omitted baseline	Omitted baseline	Omitted baseline	Omitted baseline
SES	−0.171 (0.098)	−0.151 (0.098)	−0.134 (0.105)	−0.414* (0.108)	−0.421* (0.147)	−0.410* (0.153)
Position in issue space	−0.377* (0.079)	−0.386* (0.091)	−0.327* (0.094)	−0.234 (0.124)	−0.342* (0.137)	−0.309* (0.139)
Woman	−0.676* (0.157)	−0.684* (0.180)	−0.694* (0.187)	−0.289 (0.207)	−0.360 (0.264)	−0.344 (0.267)
Other Political Intermediaries (c wave)						
Evangelical church attendance		−0.284 (0.157)	−0.257 (0.166)		1.080* (0.118)	1.077* (0.122)
Contacted by pro-Lula party		−0.753 (0.389)	−0.642 (0.405)		−0.515 (0.559)	−0.452 (0.569)
Contacted by pro-Garo. Party		−2.407 (2.178)	−2.540 (2.705)		−13.142 (879.034)	−12.326 (639.937)
Contacted by pro-Ciro party		−0.592 (0.415)	−0.475 (0.435)		−0.001 (0.536)	0.043 (0.544)

(continued)

TABLE A.13 (continued)

Dependent variable categories:	Lula vote / Serra vote				Garotinho vote / Serra vote			
	Model 1	Model 2	Model 3	Model 4	Model 1	Model 2	Model 3	Model 4
Mediators:	None	Individual traits	Individual traits & other intermediaries	Individual traits & other intermediaries & discussants	None	Individual traits	Individual traits & other intermediaries	Individual traits & other intermediaries & discussants
Contacted by other party or not contacted			−0.742* (0.371)	−0.553 (0.387)			−0.677 (0.508)	−0.566 (0.512)
Contacted by pro-Serra party			Omitted baseline	Omitted baseline			Omitted baseline	Omitted baseline
Constant	−1.243* (0.193)	−0.824 (0.521)	−0.031 (0.590)	−0.701 (0.655)	−2.039* (0.238)	−1.554* (0.397)	−1.340 (0.820)	−1.922* (0.888)

Notes: Entries are multinomial logit coefficients with robust standard errors (corrected for clustering within neighborhoods) in parentheses. Dependent variable for each model is *Ego vote choice*. *pc* = pre-campaign, *c* = campaign. Coefficients for *Ciro vote / Serra vote* were estimated but are not shown.

$N = 1,143$. * = $p < .05$.
Source: Two-City Panel.

TABLE A.14 (*MODELS REFERENCED ONLY IN CHAPTER 5 TEXT*).
Ego's Vote Choice by Neighborhood's Political Leaning and Possible Mediators in Juiz de Fora 2002: Results from Four Multinomial Logit Models

Dependent variable categories:	Lula vote *Serra vote*				Garotinho vote *Serra vote*			
	Model 1	Model 2	Model 3	Model 4	Model 1	Model 2	Model 3	Model 4
Mediators:	None	Individual traits	Individual traits & other intermediaries	Individual traits & other intermediaries & discussants	None	Individual traits	Individual traits & other intermediaries	Individual traits & other intermediaries & discussants
Neighborhood "Effects": Neighborhood's Political Leaning								
Neighborhood PT support	−0.159* (0.074)	−0.176* (0.076)	−0.190 (0.121)	−0.193 (0.127)	−0.337* (0.153)	−0.327* (0.111)	−0.310 (0.167)	−0.286 (0.173)
Discussants' Vote Intentions (c wave)								
Pro-Lula share among alters				2.898* (0.413)				2.125* (0.772)
Pro-Garotinho share among alters				1.866* (0.719)				3.228* (0.963)
Pro-Ciro share among alters				2.042* (0.447)				2.431* (0.798)
Singleton				2.389* (0.389)				2.886* (0.798)
Pro-Serra share among alters				Omitted baseline				Omitted baseline

(*continued*)

Table A.14 (continued)

Dependent variable categories:	Lula vote Serra vote				Garotinho vote Serra vote			
Mediators:	Model 1 None	Model 2 Individual traits	Model 3 Individual traits & other intermediaries	Model 4 Individual traits & other intermediaries & discussants	Model 1 None	Model 2 Individual traits	Model 3 Individual traits & other intermediaries	Model 4 Individual traits & other intermediaries & discussants
Ego's Vote Intention (pc wave)								
Lula	17.779* (0.428)	17.260* (0.372)	18.768 (1159.504)	17.491 (647.526)	16.390* (0.465)	16.514* (0.482)	18.144 (1159.504)	16.900 (647.526)
Garotinho	1.647* (0.494)	1.357* (0.535)	1.364* (0.466)	1.372* (0.503)	4.281* (0.468)	4.101* (0.499)	4.070* (0.728)	3.858* (0.771)
Ciro	1.802* (0.381)	1.754* (0.430)	1.743* (0.514)	1.775* (0.560)	1.863* (0.713)	1.995* (0.726)	2.500* (0.901)	2.599* (0.931)
Other or none	1.870* (0.303)	1.682* (0.303)	1.676* (0.278)	1.551* (0.300)	1.926* (0.390)	1.784* (0.414)	2.030* (0.621)	1.785* (0.646)
Serra	Omitted baseline	Omitted baseline	Omitted baseline	Omitted baseline	Omitted baseline	Omitted baseline	Omitted baseline	Omitted baseline
Individual Traits (pc wave)								
PT partisanship		2.154* (0.483)	2.229* (0.526)	2.377* (0.556)		0.500 (0.623)	0.537 (0.713)	0.720 (0.745)

PMDB partisanship	0.670 (0.407)	0.785* (0.387)	0.841* (0.403)	0.123 (0.545)	0.451 (0.571)	0.515 (0.587)
Partisans of other parties and nonpartisans	0.769* (0.286)	0.852* (0.330)	0.917* (0.344)	0.091 (0.425)	0.167 (0.492)	0.149 (0.508)
PSDB partisanship	Omitted baseline	Omitted baseline	Omitted baseline	Omitted baseline	Omitted baseline	Omitted baseline
SES	-0.209* (0.104)	-0.189 (0.107)	-0.175 (0.114)	-0.563* (0.148)	-0.502* (0.157)	-0.438* (0.166)
Position in issue space	-0.468* (0.135)	-0.481* (0.106)	-0.413* (0.113)	-0.376* (0.140)	-0.455* (0.161)	-0.467* (0.170)
Woman	-0.293 (0.214)	-0.212 (0.215)	-0.123 (0.225)	-0.363 (0.286)	-0.299 (0.305)	-0.318 (0.316)
Other political intermediaries (c wave)						
Evangelical church attendance		0.265 (0.212)	0.242 (0.213)		1.431* (0.215)	1.375* (0.217)
Contacted by pro-Lula party		0.699 (0.535)	0.782 (0.562)		0.888 (0.764)	0.801 (0.786)
Contacted by pro-Garo. party		17.766 (5428.003)	16.911 (2895.655)		15.983 (5428.003)	14.739 (2895.656)

(continued)

TABLE A.14 (continued)

Dependent variable categories:	Lula vote / Serra vote				Garotinho vote / Serra vote			
	Model 1	Model 2	Model 3	Model 4	Model 1	Model 2	Model 3	Model 4
Mediators:	None	Individual traits	Individual traits & other intermediaries	Individual traits & other intermediaries & discussants	None	Individual traits	Individual traits & other intermediaries	Individual traits & other intermediaries & discussants
Contacted by pro-Ciro party			−0.071 (0.275)	0.005 (0.294)			−0.410 (0.410)	−0.348 (0.428)
Contacted by other party or not contacted			0.323 (0.353)	0.391 (0.376)			0.308 (0.510)	0.162 (0.528)
Contacted by pro-Serra party			Omitted baseline	Omitted baseline			Omitted baseline	Omitted baseline
Constant	−1.243* (0.193)	−0.824 (0.521)	−0.031 (0.590)	−0.701 (0.655)	−2.007* (0.304)	−1.510* (0.656)	−3.010* (0.913)	−4.977* (1.166)

Notes: Entries are multinomial logit coefficients with robust standard errors (corrected for clustering within neighborhoods) in parentheses. Dependent variable for each model is *Ego vote choice*. *pc* = pre–campaign, *c* = campaign. Coefficients for $\frac{Ciro\ vote}{Serra\ vote}$ were estimated but are not shown.

$N = 1,463$. * = $p < .05$.
Source: Two-City Panel.

TABLE A.15 (*MODELS USED FOR FIGURE 6.6*).
The Distribution of Vote Intentions among Alters by State's Political Leaning in Brazil 2014: Results from a Fractional Multinomial Logit Model

Dependent variable categories:	Pro-Aécio share among alters / Pro-Dilma share among alters	Pro-Marina share among alters / Pro-Dilma share among alters
State's Political Leaning		
State PSDB support	6.101*	1.591
	(0.972)	(1.013)
State Marina support	9.831*	7.301*
	(2.295)	(1.992)
State other candidate support	−75.322*	−46.149
	(28.232)	(28.509)
State PT support	Omitted baseline	Omitted baseline
Ego's Political Predispositions (pc wave)		
PSDB partisan	1.844*	1.112
	(0.397)	(0.607)
PSB partisan	3.124*	0.570
	(0.942)	(0.668)
Partisans of other parties and nonpartisans	0.975*	1.059*
	(0.177)	(0.267)
PT partisan	Omitted baseline	Omitted baseline
Ego vote intention		
Aécio	1.710*	1.257*
	(0.446)	(0.297)
Campos	0.437	1.980*
	(0.294)	(0.253)
Other or none	0.513	0.826*
	(0.266)	(0.261)
Dilma	Omitted baseline	Omitted baseline
Individual-level Demographics (pc wave)		
Urban resident	0.519	0.443*
	(0.513)	(0.215)
Education	0.255	−0.201
	(0.334)	(0.199)

(*continued*)

TABLE A.15 (continued)

Dependent variable categories:	*Pro-Aécio share among alters* / *Pro-Dilma share among alters*	*Pro-Marina share among alters* / *Pro-Dilma share among alters*
Wealth	0.398*	0.222
	(0.161)	(0.121)
Woman	−0.162	−0.549*
	(0.217)	(0.214)
Constant	−6.366*	−3.248*
	(0.768)	(0.703)

Notes: Entries are fractional multinomial logit coefficients with robust standard errors (corrected for clustering within states) in parentheses. Dependent variables for each model, estimated jointly, are *Pro-Dilma share among alters*, *Pro-Aécio share among alters*, *Pro-Marina share among alters*, and *Pro-other share among alters*. Dependent variables are measured in $c4$ and $c5$. Vector of coefficients for *Pro-other share among alters* is not shown to reduce clutter. Shaded coefficients correspond to variables we manipulate to generate predicted probabilities in figure 6.6.

$N = 749$. $* = p < 0.05$

Source: BEPS 2014.

TABLE A.16 (*MODELS USED FOR FIGURE 6.7*).
The Distribution of Vote Intentions among Alters by State's Political Leaning in Mexico 2006: Results from a Fractional Multinomial Logit Model

Dependent variable categories:	Pro-AMLO share among alters Pro-Calderón share among alters	Pro-Madrazo share among alters Pro-Calderón share among alters
State's Political Leaning		
State PRD support	4.909* (1.015)	2.281 (1.166)
State PRI support	2.802 (2.250)	4.805* (1.636)
State other candidate support	19.834 (13.388)	−4.811 (12.725)
State PAN support	Omitted baseline	Omitted baseline
Ego's Political Predispositions (pc wave)		
PRD partisanship	1.944* (0.443)	0.720 (0.574)
PRI partisanship	0.724 (0.400)	1.590* (0.354)
Partisans of other party and nonpartisans	0.719* (0.282)	0.533* (0.252)
PAN partisanship	Omitted baseline	Omitted baseline
Ego vote intention		
AMLO	1.819* (0.311)	0.848* (0.242)
Madrazo	0.825* (0.362)	1.335* (0.275)
Other or none	1.174* (0.328)	0.771* (0.275)
Calderón	Omitted baseline	Omitted baseline
Individual-level Demographics (pc wave)		
Urban resident	0.025 (0.116)	0.024 (0.121)
Education	−0.060 (0.037)	−0.049 (0.044)

(*continued*)

TABLE A.16 (continued)

Dependent variable categories:	Pro-AMLO share among alters Pro-Calderón share among alters	Pro-Madrazo share among alters Pro-Calderón share among alters
Wealth	−0.045	−0.299*
	(0.126)	(0.121)
Woman	−0.325	−0.200
	(0.178)	(0.154)
Skin color	0.183	0.071
	(0.147)	(0.128)
Constant	−4.213*	−3.425*
	(1.310)	(0.993)

Notes: Entries are fractional multinomial logit coefficients with robust standard errors (corrected for clustering within states) in parentheses. Dependent variables for each model, estimated jointly, are *Pro-Calderón share among alters, Pro-AMLO share among alters, Pro-Madrazo share among alters*, and *Pro-other share among alters*. Dependent variables are measured in the campaign wave. Vector of coefficients for *Pro-other share among alters* is not shown to reduce clutter. Shaded coefficients correspond to variables we manipulate to generate predicted probabilities in figure 6.7.

$N = 948$. * $= p < 0.05$

Source: Mexico 2006 Panel

TABLE A.17 (*MODEL RESULTS PARTIALLY REPORTED IN TABLE 6.2*).
Ego's Vote Choice by State's Political Leaning and Possible Mediators in Brazil 2014: Results from Three Multinomial Logit Models

Dependent variable categories:	*Aécio vote / Dilma vote*			*Marina vote / Dilma vote*		
	Model 1	Model 2	Model 3	Model 1	Model 2	Model 3
Mediators:	None	Individual traits	Individual traits & discussants	None	Individual traits	Individual traits & discussants
Regional "Effects": State's Political Leaning						
State PSDB support	3.976*	3.436*	1.972	1.377	1.026	1.087
	(1.745)	(1.608)	(1.599)	(1.453)	(1.438)	(1.227)
State Marina support	6.664*	6.060*	3.367	4.978	4.738	3.391
	(3.303)	(2.798)	(2.764)	(3.845)	(3.417)	(3.373)
State other candidate support	-44.194	-43.285	-21.393	-80.127	-89.554	-77.352
	(35.623)	(34.743)	(37.996)	(56.267)	(50.084)	(46.803)
State PT support	Omitted baseline	Omitted baseline	Omitted baseline	Omitted baseline	Omitted baseline	Omitted baseline
Discussants' Vote Intentions (c wave)						
Pro-Aécio share among alters			3.716*			0.185
			(0.447)			(0.607)
Pro-Marina share among alters			2.802*			3.028*
			(0.337)			(0.543)
Pro-other share among alters			-0.060			0.056
			(2.259)			(2.002)

(continued)

TABLE A.17 (continued)

Dependent variable categories:	Aécio vote / Dilma vote			Marina vote / Dilma vote		
Mediators:	Model 1	Model 2	Model 3	Model 1	Model 2	Model 3
	None	Individual traits	Individual traits & discussants	None	Individual traits	Individual traits & discussants
Singleton			1.381* (0.280)			1.049* (0.354)
Pro-Dilma share among alters			Omitted baseline			Omitted baseline
Ego's Vote Intention (pc wave)						
Aécio	2.017* (0.342)	1.404* (0.371)	1.026* (0.417)	1.450* (0.423)	1.147* (0.457)	0.975* (0.458)
Campos	1.477* (0.343)	0.827* (0.375)	0.441 (0.434)	2.817* (0.395)	2.510* (0.370)	1.960* (0.349)
Other or none	0.931* (0.316)	0.257 (0.344)	0.135 (0.371)	1.579* (0.314)	1.134* (0.351)	0.922* (0.411)
Dilma	Omitted baseline	Omitted baseline	Omitted baseline	Omitted baseline	Omitted baseline	Omitted baseline
Individual-level Traits (pc wave)						
PSDB partisan		2.046* (0.716)	1.520 (1.276)		1.592* (0.672)	1.353 (0.898)

PSB partisan	0.779 (0.988)	1.111 (1.125)		0.363 (1.101)	1.893 (1.139)
Partisans of other parties and nonpartisans	1.575* (0.296)	1.346* (0.384)		1.037 (0.537)	1.260* (0.451)
PT partisan	Omitted baseline	Omitted baseline		Omitted baseline	Omitted baseline
Wealth	0.124 (0.160)	0.124 (0.160)		0.140 (0.139)	0.151 (0.135)
Education	0.280 (0.213)	0.375 (0.229)		0.547* (0.240)	0.540* (0.201)
Bolsa família recipient	−0.319 (0.316)	−0.251 (0.308)		−0.127 (0.503)	−0.105 (0.508)
Position in issue space	−0.085 (0.153)	−0.222 (0.151)		0.189 (0.128)	0.348 (0.193)
Urban resident	0.271 (0.364)	0.282 (0.415)		0.366 (0.490)	0.466 (0.500)
Woman	−0.215 (0.323)	0.006 (0.332)		0.288 (0.238)	0.196 (0.201)
Constant	−4.341* (1.191)	−5.557* (1.173)	−2.803* (0.831)	−5.455* (1.346)	−4.750* (1.389)

Constant (additional column): −3.464* (0.771)

Notes: Entries are multinomial logit coefficients and robust standard errors (corrected for clustering within states) in parentheses. Dependent variable for each model is *Ego vote choice*. *pc* = pre-campaign wave, *c* = campaign wave, *e* = election wave.
$N = 913$. * = $p < 0.05$.
Source: BEPS 2014.

TABLE A.18 (MODEL RESULTS PARTIALLY REPORTED IN TABLE 6.3).
Ego's Vote Choice by State's Political Leaning and Possible Mediators in Mexico 2006: Results from Four Multinomial Logit Models

Dependent variable categories:	AMLO vote / Calderón vote				Madrazo vote / Calderón vote			
	Model 1	Model 2	Model 3	Model 4	Model 1	Model 2	Model 3	Model 4
Mediators:	None	Individual traits	Individual traits & other intermediaries	Individual traits & other intermediaries & discussants	None	Individual traits	Individual traits & other intermediaries	Individual traits & other intermediaries & discussants
Regional "Effects": State's Political Leaning								
State PRD support	5.507* (1.218)	4.717* (1.268)	5.330* (1.315)	4.221* (1.385)	3.217* (1.059)	3.770* (1.302)	3.624* (1.349)	3.124* (1.320)
State PRI support	3.321 (2.668)	3.556 (2.556)	3.505 (2.688)	2.600 (2.740)	3.595 (2.020)	5.464* (1.685)	5.497* (1.723)	4.155* (1.675)
State other candidate support	32.736* (14.937)	38.424* (15.250)	39.585* (15.899)	33.451* (16.223)	-11.007 (13.602)	2.116 (14.395)	1.698 (14.509)	2.401 (14.986)
State PAN support	Omitted baseline	Omitted baseline	Omitted baseline	Omitted baseline	Omitted baseline	Omitted baseline	Omitted baseline	Omitted baseline
Discussants' Vote Intentions (c wave)								
Pro-AMLO share among alters				3.346* (0.499)				0.720 (0.520)
Pro-Madrazo share among alters				1.924* (0.588)				2.581* (0.455)

Pro-other share among alters					1.420 (1.334)			0.220 (1.950)
Singleton					1.781* (0.428)			1.669* (0.429)
Pro-Calderón share among alters					Omitted baseline			Omitted baseline
Ego's Vote Intention (pc wave)								
AMLO	3.296* (0.343)	2.657* (0.417)	2.649* (0.430)	2.251* (0.420)	1.765* (0.434)	1.414* (0.483)	1.401* (0.479)	1.263* (0.502)
Madrazo	1.695* (0.369)	1.517* (0.464)	1.472* (0.474)	1.205* (0.463)	3.670* (0.405)	2.652* (0.473)	2.631* (0.475)	2.367* (0.486)
Other or none	1.309* (0.400)	1.035* (0.476)	1.031* (0.484)	0.665 (0.472)	2.352* (0.449)	1.958* (0.466)	1.967* (0.471)	1.767* (0.480)
Calderón	Omitted baseline	Omitted baseline	Omitted baseline	Omitted baseline	Omitted baseline	Omitted baseline	Omitted baseline	Omitted baseline
Individual-level Traits (pc wave)								
PRD partisan	2.720* (0.578)	2.711* (0.577)			2.335* (0.620)	1.012 (0.727)	1.038 (0.731)	0.799 (0.819)

(continued)

Table A.18 (continued)

Dependent variable categories:	AMLO vote / Calderón vote				Madrazo vote / Calderón vote			
	Model 1	Model 2	Model 3	Model 4	Model 1	Model 2	Model 3	Model 4
Mediators:	None	Individual traits	Individual traits & other intermediaries	Individual traits & other intermediaries & discussants	None	Individual traits	Individual traits & other intermediaries	Individual traits & other intermediaries & discussants
PRI partisan		0.509 (0.537)	0.489 (0.529)	0.331 (0.509)		1.979* (0.377)	2.006* (0.393)	1.814* (0.414)
Partisans of other party and nonpartisans		0.686* (0.311)	0.685* (0.318)	0.613* (0.300)		0.427 (0.309)	0.437 (0.316)	0.389 (0.339)
PAN partisan		Omitted baseline	Omitted baseline	Omitted baseline		Omitted baseline	Omitted baseline	Omitted baseline
Wealth		0.181 (0.136)	0.180 (0.135)	0.167 (0.156)		0.160 (0.171)	0.150 (0.182)	0.217 (0.196)
Education		−0.052 (0.051)	−0.060 (0.050)	−0.033 (0.055)		−0.005 (0.063)	−0.002 (0.062)	0.011 (0.066)
Skin color		−0.056 (0.192)	−0.079 (0.195)	−0.116 (0.191)		−0.012 (0.184)	−0.002 (0.184)	0.036 (0.171)
USA trade		0.071 (0.080)	0.066 (0.079)	0.060 (0.079)		0.096 (0.087)	0.096 (0.084)	0.101 (0.079)
Private investment electricity		−0.124 (0.071)	−0.135 (0.070)	−0.108 (0.080)		−0.039 (0.089)	−0.049 (0.090)	−0.034 (0.095)
Frequency of church attendance		−0.003 (0.085)	−0.021 (0.085)	0.003 (0.091)		0.099 (0.095)	0.096 (0.096)	0.104 (0.102)

	(1)	(2)	(3)	(4)	(5)	(6)	(7)
Abortion attitude	0.089	0.094	0.081	0.122	0.118	0.102	
	(0.058)	(0.059)	(0.062)	(0.063)	(0.064)	(0.069)	
Capital punishment attitude	0.003	-0.005	0.022	-0.052	-0.059	-0.040	
	(0.059)	(0.060)	(0.061)	(0.061)	(0.062)	(0.063)	
Urban resident	-0.137	-0.149	-0.128	-0.195	-0.204	-0.156	
	(0.148)	(0.153)	(0.151)	(0.136)	(0.136)	(0.138)	
Woman	-0.512*	-0.495*	-0.433*	-0.461	-0.476*	-0.514*	
	(0.215)	(0.208)	(0.208)	(0.238)	(0.238)	(0.249)	
Other Political Intermediaries (e wave)							
Contacted by PAN		0.162	0.272		-0.450	-0.598	
		(0.324)	(0.344)		(0.323)	(0.348)	
Contacted by PRD		-0.177	-0.318		0.341	0.504	
		(0.278)	(0.335)		(0.318)	(0.311)	
Contacted by PRI		0.699*	0.593		0.146	0.180	
		(0.319)	(0.335)		(0.357)	(0.385)	
Televisa news exposure		-0.003	-0.023		-0.024	-0.020	
		(0.044)	(0.047)		(0.053)	(0.054)	
TV Azteca news exposure		0.043	0.027		-0.017	-0.027	
		(0.061)	(0.064)		(0.067)	(0.070)	
Other network news exposure		-0.049	-0.074		0.098	0.066	
		(0.085)	(0.097)		(0.084)	(0.096)	
Constant	-5.313*	-4.986*	-5.837*	-4.644*	-5.825*	-5.750*	-6.652*
	(1.437)	(1.589)	(1.707)	(1.119)	(1.133)	(1.155)	(1.124)

Notes: Entries are multinomial logit coefficients and robust standard errors (corrected for clustering within states) in parentheses. Dependent variable for each model is *Ego vote choice*. *pc* = pre-campaign wave, *c* = campaign wave, *e* = election wave.

N=1,325. * = p<0.05.

Source: Mexico 2006 Panel.

TABLE A.19 (*MODEL RESULTS PARTIALLY DEPICTED IN FIGURE 7.3 OR MENTIONED IN TEXT*):

Clientelistic Targeting by Persuasion Frequency in 22 Latin American Countries in 2010: Results from Four Binary Logit Models

	Model 1	Model 2	Model 3	Model 4
Persuasion frequency		0.508*		0.534*
		(0.048)		(0.046)
Partisan identifier	0.285*	0.078		
	(0.066)	(0.062)		
Political participation index	0.444*	0.334*		
	(0.070)	(0.069)		
Political knowledge			0.218*	0.064
			(0.055)	(0.050)
Constant	−1.719*	−1.863*	−1.623*	−1.843*
	(0.022)	(0.035)	(0.003)	(0.024)

Notes: Entries are logit coefficients with robust standard errors (corrected for clustering within countries) in parentheses. Dependent variable for each model is *Target of clientelism.* Coefficients for country-fixed effects are not shown.

$N = 35,584.$ * $= p < .05.$

Source: LAPOP 2010.

TABLE A.20 (*MODELS DEPICTED IN FIGURE 7.4*).
Clientelistic Targeting by Egocentric Network Size in Mexico 2006: Results from Three Binary Logit Models

	Model 1	Model 2	Model 3
Number of nonfamilial discussants	0.239*	0.240*	0.241*
	(.113)	(.112)	(.113)
Number of familial discussants	0.126	0.133	0.111
	(.116)	(.115)	(.117)
Strength.of.partisanship$_{pc}$	−0.021		
	(.156)		
Strength.of.partisanship$_c$		−0.151	
		(.204)	
Strength.of.partisanship$_e$			0.458*
			(.184)
Constant	−3.232	−3.117	−3.731
	(0.272)	(0.360)	(0.325)

Notes: Entries are logit coefficients with standard errors in parentheses. Dependent variable for each model is *Paid off by a party*, measured at the election wave. *Number of nonfamilial alters* and *Number of familial alters* are both measured at the campaign wave. pc = pre-campaign, c = campaign wave, e = election wave.
    N = 1,358. * = $p < .05$.
Source: Mexico 2006 Panel Study.

TABLE A.21 (*MODELS USED FOR FIGURE 8.1*):
The Stratification of Intermediation Exposure by SES, Gender, and Race in Brazil and
Mexico: Results from 16 OLS Regression Models

Frame A: Brazil 2002

	Dependent Variable			
	Frequency of political discussion	Egocentric network size	Media exposure	Contacted by a party
Wealth	0.175*	0.142*	0.297*	0.109*
	(0.020)	(0.024)	(0.019)	(0.024)
Education	0.397*	0.224*	0.388*	0.138*
	(0.027)	(0.033)	(0.026)	(0.033)
Male	0.124*	−0.080*	0.156*	−0.035
	(0.027)	(0.033)	(0.025)	(0.032)
Race	−0.015	−0.008	0.042*	−0.001
	(0.023)	(0.028)	(0.021)	(0.027)
Juiz de Fora resident	0.145*	−0.065*	−0.112*	0.442*
	(0.028)	(0.034)	(0.026)	(0.033)
Constant	−2.240*	−1.236*	−2.853*	−1.637*
	(0.135)	(0.163)	(0.127)	(0.162)
N	4,711	3,476	4,709	3,897

Frame B: Brazil 2006

	Dependent Variable			
	Frequency of political discussion	Egocentric network size	Media exposure	Contacted by a party
Wealth	0.160*	0.181*	0.289*	0.116*
	(0.033)	(0.034)	(0.031)	(0.038)
Education	0.361*	0.256*	0.423*	0.182*
	(0.042)	(0.044)	(0.040)	(0.048)
Male	0.232*	−0.026	0.132*	0.132*
	(0.043)	(0.045)	(0.041)	(0.050)
Race	0.019	−0.058	0.034	−0.014
	(0.035)	(0.036)	(0.033)	(0.041)
Juiz de Fora resident	0.182*	−0.201*	0.144*	0.300*
	(0.044)	(0.046)	(0.042)	(0.051)
Constant	−2.233*	−1.275*	−3.190*	−1.603*
	(0.219)	(0.226)	(0.208)	(0.255)
N	1,986	1,980	1,985	1,695

TABLE A.21 (continued)

Frame C: Brazil 2014

	Dependent Variable		
	Frequency of political discussion	Egocentric network size	Frequency of TV news consumption
Wealth	0.183*	0.126*	0.235*
	(0.028)	(0.037)	(0.036)
Education	0.372*	0.398*	0.160*
	(0.050)	(0.064)	(0.076)
Male	0.162*	0.116*	0.085
	(0.045)	(0.058)	(0.055)
Race	0.015	0.033	0.061
	(0.032)	(0.042)	(0.040)
Constant	−0.793*	−0.884*	−0.468*
	(0.123)	(0.161)	(0.171)
N	3,065	1,585	1,705

Frame D: Mexico 2006

	Dependent Variable				
	Frequency of political discussion	Egocentric network size	Frequency of TV news consumption	Contacted by a party	Paid off by a party
Wealth	0.207*	0.192*	0.280*	0.069*	−0.013
	(0.029)	(0.041)	(0.043)	(0.035)	(0.041)
Education	0.407*	0.602*	0.196*	0.028	−0.006
	(0.041)	(0.051)	(0.043)	(0.058)	(0.076)
Male	0.202*	−0.006	0.058	−0.088*	−0.122*
	(0.056)	(0.032)	(0.049)	(0.031)	(0.057)
Race	−0.001	0.035	0.064	0.009	0.048
	(0.045)	(0.042)	(0.056)	(0.068)	(0.060)
Constant	−0.718*	−0.935*	−0.429*	−0.072	−0.007
	(0.099)	(0.102)	(0.145)	(0.128)	(0.209)
N	1,973	1,987	1,936	1,976	1,979

Notes: Entries are OLS coefficients with standard errors in parentheses. *Juiz de Fora resident* is held at its mean to generate predicted values in figure 8.1.

$* = p < 0.05$

Source: Two-City Panel, BEPS 2014, Mexico 2006 Panel Study.

TABLE A.22 (*MODELS USED FOR FIGURE 8.2*):
The Stratification of Intermediation Exposure by SES and Gender in 10 Latin American Election Campaigns: Results from 27 OLS Regression Models

	Chile 1993	Chile 1993	Chile 1993	Chile 2000	Chile 2000
	Dependent Variable				
	Frequency of political discussion	Media exposure	Contacted by a party	Frequency of political discussion	Media exposure
Wealth	0.126*	0.113*	−0.031	0.015	0.094*
	(0.043)	(0.044)	(0.038)	(0.046)	(0.044)
Education	0.556*	0.336*	0.066	0.561*	0.385*
	(0.083)	(0.087)	(0.082)	(0.092)	(0.088)
Male	0.071	0.104	−0.031	0.206*	0.295*
	(0.066)	(0.068)	(0.059)	(0.069)	(0.068)
Constant	−1.873*	−1.482*	0.198	−1.038*	−1.546*
	(0.325)	(0.331)	(0.279)	(0.354)	(0.342)
N	833	834	1,193	794	794
	Uruguay 1994	Uruguay 1994	Uruguay 1994	Uruguay 2004	Uruguay 2004
	Dependent Variable				
	Frequency of political discussion	Media exposure	Contacted by a party	Frequency of political discussion	Media exposure
Wealth	0.156*	0.086	0.097	0.235*	0.193*
	(0.062)	(0.061)	(0.074)	(0.045)	(0.047)
Education	0.421*	0.313*	−0.235	0.615*	−0.049
	(0.097)	(0.105)	(0.125)	(0.086)	(0.097)
Male	0.063	−0.048	0.261*	0.170*	−0.141*
	(0.079)	(0.080)	(0.097)	(0.064)	(0.068)
Constant	−1.956*	−1.136*	−0.452	−3.041*	−1.594*
	(0.494)	(0.497)	(0.603)	(0.353)	(0.389)
N	657	661	662	923	929

Table A.22 (continued)

	Colombia 2014	Colombia 2014	Colombia 2014	Argentina 2007	Argentina 2007
	Dependent Variable				
	Frequency of political discussion	Media exposure	Contacted by a party	Frequency of political discussion	Media exposure
Wealth	0.151*	0.250*	0.346*	0.091	0.030
	(0.053)	(0.050)	(0.072)	(0.063)	(0.067)
Education	0.460*	0.210*	0.026	0.681*	0.194
	(0.091)	(0.087)	(0.064)	(0.111)	(0.122)
Male	0.151*	0.290*	0.118	0.090	0.153*
	(0.065)	(0.064)	(0.069)	(0.071)	(0.075)
Constant	−2.098*	−2.672*	−3.109*	−1.891*	−0.580
	(0.423)	(0.397)	(0.604)	(0.523)	(0.553)
N	1,080	1,077	1,080	798	798

	Dom. Rep. 2010	Dom. Rep. 2010	Dom. Rep. 2010	Mexico 2006	Mexico 2006	Mexico 2006
	Dependent Variable					
	Frequency of political discussion	Media exposure	Contacted by a party	Frequency of political discussion	Media exposure	Contacted by a party
Wealth	−0.065*	0.044	−0.074*	0.211*	0.151*	0.042
	(0.033)	(0.026)	(0.030)	(0.030)	(0.035)	(0.033)
Education	0.235*	0.398*	−0.049	0.232*	0.310*	−0.020
	(0.063)	(0.061)	(0.060)	(0.044)	(0.050)	(0.051)
Male	0.321*	0.363*	0.068	0.192*	0.181*	0.071
	(0.069)	(0.075)	(0.065)	(0.043)	(0.051)	(0.048)
Constant	0.204	−0.923*	0.662*	−2.333*	−1.865*	−0.302
	(0.271)	(0.215)	(0.239)	(0.248)	(0.292)	(0.276)
N	1,211	1,211	1,465	2,078	1,498	2,098

(continued)

TABLE A.22 (continued)

	Mexico 2012	Mexico 2012	Mexico 2012	Mexico 2018	Mexico 2018	Mexico 2018
	Dependent Variable					
	Frequency of political discussion	Media exposure	Contacted by a party	Frequency of political discussion	Media exposure	Contacted by a party
Wealth	0.196*	0.181*	−0.029	0.139*	0.092	0.087
	(0.046)	(0.050)	(0.046)	(0.056)	(0.066)	(0.067)
Education	0.295*	0.332*	0.005	0.273*	0.177*	−0.100
	(0.058)	(0.054)	(0.056)	(0.060)	(0.061)	(0.062)
Male	0.096	0.079	−0.040	0.137*	0.018	−0.069
	(0.049)	(0.049)	(0.050)	(0.054)	(0.056)	(0.057)
Constant	−2.273*	−2.173*	0.285	−1.779*	−1.123	−0.625
	(0.394)	(0.440)	(0.406)	(0.493)	(0.596)	(0.598)
N	1,591	1,593	1,594	1,422	1,426	1,426

Notes: Entries are OLS coefficients with standard errors in parentheses.
* $p < 0.05$
Source: CNEP.

TABLE A.23 (*MODELS USED FOR FIGURE 8.3*):
The Stratification of Political Knowledge by SES and Gender in 11 Latin American Election Campaigns:
Results from 12 OLS Regression Models

			Panel Studies		
	Brazil 2002	Brazil 2006	Brazil 2014	Mexico 2006
Wealth	0.314*	0.299*	0.336*	0.220*
	(0.018)	(0.028)	(0.024)	(0.027)
Education	0.467*	0.460*	0.659*	0.859*
	(0.026)	(0.039)	(0.041)	(0.035)
Male	0.473*	0.523*	0.343*	0.352*
	(0.026)	(0.042)	(0.039)	(0.035)
Constant	−3.550*	−3.042*	−1.413*	−1.198*
	(0.118)	(0.186)	(0.084)	(0.057)
N	4,641	1,722	3,090	2,393

(*continued*)

TABLE A.23 (continued)

| | | | | | CNEP | | | | |
	Argentina 2007	Chile 1993	Colombia 2014	Dom. Rep. 2010	Mexico 2006	Mexico 2012	Mexico 2018	Uruguay 1994
Wealth	0.112	0.294*	0.374*	0.035	0.125*	0.291*	0.247*	0.307*
	(0.059)	(0.032)	(0.051)	(0.034)	(0.027)	(0.042)	(0.050)	(0.067)
Education	0.758*	0.539*	0.280*	0.396*	0.133*	0.657*	0.534*	0.460*
	(0.102)	(0.062)	(0.080)	(0.066)	(0.036)	(0.049)	(0.054)	(0.093)
Male	0.309*	0.332*	0.330*	0.360*	0.236*	0.309*	0.355*	0.398*
	(0.069)	(0.051)	(0.062)	(0.069)	(0.040)	(0.045)	(0.051)	(0.076)
Constant	−2.354*	−3.457*	−3.889*	−0.848*	−1.439*	−3.765*	−3.282*	−3.522*
	(0.484)	(0.234)	(0.399)	(0.276)	(0.238)	(0.365)	(0.448)	(0.540)
N	798	1,193	1,080	1,211	2,098	1,594	1,426	653

Notes: Entries are OLS coefficients with standard errors in parentheses. Dependent variable for each model is *Political knowledge.*
  * $p < 0.05$
Source: Two-City Panel, BEPS 2014, Mexico 2006 Panel Study, CNEP.

Measurement of Variables

This section contains only the variables mentioned in the main text. Numerous variables are mentioned in appendix A but not in the main text. The wordings and measurement decisions for these are not listed here in appendix B; they are available from the authors upon request.

Alter 2/Alter 3 selected as a political alter (CNEP) (figure 2.7). "How often did you talk to this person about the recent election? (0) Never. (1) Rarely. (1) Sometimes. (1) Often."

Alter vote choice (CNEP) (figure 2.9). "Which party, if any, did [discussant's name] support in the last election?"

Alter vote intention/choice (BEPS 2014) (figures 2.8, 4.5, 4.6, 4.7). "For which of these candidates do you think [discussant's name] voted? Dilma Rousseff, Aécio Neves, Marina Silva, Pastor Everaldo Pereira, Eduardo Jorge, Luciana Genro, some other candidate, spoiled their ballot or voted blank, did not vote."

Alter vote intention/choice (Mexico 2006 Panel) (figures 2.8, 4.5, 4.6). ▪Campaign wave: "Who do you think [discussant's name] will vote for in the presidential elections?" ▪Election wave: "Who do you think [discussant's name] voted for in the presidential elections?"

Alter vote intention/choice (Two-City Panel) (figures 2.8, 4.5, 4.6, 4.7). ▪Campaign wave, 2002: [Asked of main respondent] "If the election for president were held today, for which of these candidates *do you think* [named discussant] would vote? Ciro Gomes, Lula, José Serra, Anthony Garotinho, or some other candidate?" ▪Election wave, 2002: [Asked of discussant] "For whom did you vote for president in the first round of the election on October 6? Ciro Gomes, Lula, José Serra, Anthony Garotinho, some other candidate, or did you not vote for anyone?" ▪Election wave, 2002: [Asked of main respondent and used only when direct interview with discussant did not occur] "For whom did that person vote for president of the republic in the first-round election on October 6? Ciro, Lula, Serra, Garotinho, some other candidate, or did they not vote?" ▪Campaign wave, 2006: [Asked of main respondent] "If the election for president were held today, for which of these candidates *do you think* [named discussant] would vote?

Cristovam Buarque, Geraldo Alckmin, Heloísa Helena, José Maria Eymael, Luciano Bivar, Lula, Rui Pimenta, or some other candidate?" ▪Election wave, 2006: [Asked of main respondent] "For whom did [named discussant] vote for president of the republic in the first-round election on October 1? Cristovam Buarque, Geraldo Alckmin, Heloísa Helena, José Maria Eymael, Luciano Bivar, Lula, Rui Pimenta, Ana Maria Rangel, or some other candidate?"

Campaign interest (CNEP) (chapter 2 text). "To what extent were you interested in following the election campaign? (3) Very interested. (2) Somewhat interested. (1) Not very interested. (0) Not at all interested."

Campaign knowledge (Mexico 2006 Panel) (figure 2.5). For each wave, we convert each response to the items listed below to (1) correct or (0) incorrect, estimate a two-parameter item-response theory model on the set of binary items, and use the recovered latent trait (standardized). ▪Pre-campaign wave: "I am going to read you some campaign slogans. For each one please tell me which politician says it. A. 'Together we'll get Mexico moving' (Montiel). B. 'Happiness is just around the corner' (AMLO). C. 'Passion for Mexico' (Calderón). D. 'Get Mexico moving' (Madrazo)." ▪Campaign wave: "I am going to read you some campaign slogans. For each one please tell me which politician says it. A. 'Let's get things done' (Madrazo). B. 'I deliver' (AMLO). C. 'So we live better' (Calderón)."

Changed vote preference (Two-City Panel, BEPS 2014, Mexico 2006 Panel) (figures 3.1, 4.3, 4.4, 4.9). Using *Ego vote intention/choice*, this variable is (1) for voters who crossed party lines between panel waves and (0) for voters who did not cross party lines. Limited to twice-opinionated voters only, except in figure 4.9, where the "≥ once opinionated" entries use a version that is the reverse coding $(1=0)$ $(0=1)$ of *Maintained vote preference*.

Contacted by a disagreeing party (Two-City Panel) (figure 4.4). If respondents answered "yes" to *Not contacted by a party*, they were then asked, "Which parties or candidates asked for your vote?" This variable is the percentage of parties / candidates listed that were not in a coalition supporting the respondent's vote intention (*Ego vote intention*). If none listed, this variable is zero.

Contacted by a party (CNEP) (figure 8.2). "Did a representative of any of the following parties contact you in person during the campaign?" (1) Yes to at least one. (0) No to all.

Contacted by a party (Mexico 2006 Panel) (figures 2.5, 8.1, 8.4). "Over the last few weeks, has a representative of any political party or candidate knocked on your door? (1) Yes. (0) No."

Contacted by a party (Two-City Panel) (figure 8.1, 8.4). "During this campaign, did some candidate or party militant ask for your vote, either personally or by telephone or by telephone message? (0) No. (1) Yes."

Disagreeing alters' diversity (Two-City Panel, BEPS 2014, Mexico 2006) (figures 4.3, 4.4). This variable equals zero for egos who do *not* have at least two alters who disagree with ego *and* with one another. For egos for whom this condition holds, this variable is the probability that two of the disagreeing alters chosen at random (with replacement) hold opposing preferences. We use *Ego vote intention* and *Alter vote intention/choice* to define agreement and disagreement.

Education (BEPS 2014) (figures 8.1, 8.3, 8.4). "What was the last year of school that you completed? [Original Portuguese] (1) Creche, pré-escolar (maternal e jardim de infância), classe de alfabetização—CA. (2) Alfabetização de jovens e adultos. (3) Antigo primário (elementar). (4) Antigo ginásio (médio 1º ciclo). (5) Ensino fundamental ou 1º grau (da 1ª a 3ª série / do 1º ao 4º ano). (6) Ensino fundamental ou 1º grau (4ª série / 5º ano). (7) Ensino fundamental ou 1º grau (da 5ª a 8ª série / 6º ao 9º ano). (8) Supletivo do ensino fundamental ou do 1º grau. (9) Antigo científico, clássico, etc. . . . (médio 2º ciclo). (10) Regular ou supletivo do ensino médio ou do 2º grau. (11) Superior de graduação. (12) Especialização de nível superior (mínimo de 360 horas). (13) Mestrado. (14) Doutorado"

Education (CNEP) (figures 8.2, 8.3). "What is the highest level of education that you have completed? (0) No formal schooling. (1) Some primary education. (2) Completed primary education. (3) Some secondary education. (4) Completed secondary education. (5) Some university education. (6) University education completed. (7) Some or completed postgraduate education."

Education (Mexico 2006 Panel) (figures 8.1, 8.3, 8.4). "How many years of schooling have you had? (1) No schooling. (2) Incomplete elementary school. (3) Complete elementary school. (4) Incomplete middle school/Technical school. (5) Complete middle school / Technical school. (6) Incomplete high school. (7) Complete high school. (8) Incomplete college. (9) Complete college or more."

Education (Two-City Panel) (figures 8.1, 8.3, 8.4). "Up to what grade did you study or are you studying? (0) No instruction. (1) First year primary. (2) Second year primary (3) Third year primary. (4) Fourth year primary / primary complete. (5) Fifth year / first year middle school. (6) Sixth year / second year middle school. (7) Seventh year / third year middle school. (8) Eighth year / fourth year middle school / middle school complete. (9) First year secondary (10) Second year secondary. (11) Third year secondary, secondary complete. (12) Tertiary incomplete. (13) Tertiary complete. (14) Postgraduate incomplete. (15) Graduate complete."

Ego federal deputy vote choice (Two-City Panel, 2002) (chapter 5 text). "In the elections for federal deputy on October 6, did you vote for a party (*legenda*), a candidate, or did you not vote? [If "party"] Which party did you vote for? [If "candidate"] Which candidate did you vote for? If you can't remember their name, do you remember their number?"

Ego gubernatorial vote choice (Two-City Panel, 2002) (chapter 5 text). "For whom did you vote for governor in the first round of the October 6 election? [Caxias] Antônio

Britto, Caleb de Oliveira, Celso Bernardi, Germano Rigotto, Tarso Genro, some other candidate, or did you not vote for anyone? [Juiz de Fora] Aécio Neves, Nilmário Miranda, Newton Cardoso, some other candidate, or did you not vote for anyone?"

Ego runoff vote choice (Two-City Panel, 2002) (figure 4.7). "If the second round were today and the candidates were Lula and Serra, for whom would you vote? (0) Serra. (1) Lula."

Ego runoff vote choice (Two-City Panel, 2006) (figure 4.7). "If the second round were today and the candidates were Lula and Geraldo Alckmin, for whom would you vote? (0) Lula. (1) Alckmin."

Ego runoff vote choice (BEPS 2014) (figure 4.7). "On the 26th of October, the second round of the presidential elections will occur. If the election were today, for whom would you vote for president of the republic? (0) Dilma. (1) Aécio."

Ego vote choice (CNEP) (figure 2.9). "For which party [or candidate] did you vote [in the most recent election]?"

Ego vote intention/choice (BEPS 2014) (figures 2.8, 4.5, 4.6; table 6.2). ▪Pre-campaign wave: "In October there will be elections for president. If the election were today, and these were the candidates, for whom would you vote? Dilma Rousseff, Aécio Neves, Eduardo Campos, Pastor Everaldo Pereira, Levy Fidelix, Randolfe Rodrigues, spoil my ballot / vote blank, would not vote." ▪c2 wave: "Let's talk a little about the election in October of this year. If the election for president were today, for whom would you vote? [Order of candidates randomized] Dilma Rousseff, Aécio Neves, Eduardo Campos, Pastor Everaldo Pereira, Eduardo Jorge, Luciana Genro, some other candidate, spoil my ballot / vote blank, would not vote." ▪ c3, c4, c5 waves: "Let's talk a little about the election in October of this year. If the election for president were today, for whom would you vote? [Order of candidates randomized] Dilma Rousseff, Aécio Neves, Marina Silva, Pastor Everaldo Pereira, Eduardo Jorge, Luciana Genro, some other candidate, spoil my ballot / vote blank, would not vote." ▪ e6 wave: "For whom did you vote for president of the republic? [Order of candidates randomized] Dilma Rousseff, Aécio Neves, Marina Silva, Pastor Everaldo Pereira, Eduardo Jorge, Luciana Genro, some other candidate, spoiled your ballot, voted blank."

Ego vote intention/choice (Mexico 2006 Panel) (figures 2.8, 4.5, 4.6; table 6.3). ▪Pre-campaign and campaign waves: "For the purposes of this survey, we will assume that today is election day and that you will vote for president of the republic. I will give you a ballot that you can mark without my seeing you, after which you can deposit it in this bag. If elections were today, for whom would you vote?" ▪Election wave: "For the purposes of this survey, I will give you a ballot that you can mark without my seeing you, after which you can deposit it in this bag. For whom did you vote for president?"

Ego vote intention/choice (Two-City Panel) (figures 2.8, 4.5, 4.6; table 5.5). ▪Pre-campaign wave, 2002: "If the election for president were held today, for whom would you vote?

Ciro Gomes, Lula, Roseana Sarney, José Serra, Anthony Garotinho, Itamar Franco, or some other candidate?" ▪Campaign wave, 2002: "If the election for president were held today, for whom would you vote? Ciro Gomes, Lula, José Serra, Anthony Garotinho, or some other candidate?" ▪Election wave, 2002: "For whom did you vote for president in the first round of the election on October 6? Ciro Gomes, Lula, José Serra, Anthony Garotinho, some other candidate, or did you not vote for anyone?" ▪Campaign wave, 2006: "If the election for president were held today, for whom would you vote? Cristovam Buarque, Geraldo Alckmin, Heloísa Helena, José Maria Eymael, Luciano Bivar, Lula, Rui Pimenta, or some other candidate?" ▪Election wave, 2006: "In the election of October 1, 2006, for which presidential candidate did you vote? Cristovam Buarque, Geraldo Alckmin, Heloísa Helena, José Maria Eymael, Luciano Bivar, Lula, Rui Pimenta, Ana Maria Rangel, or some other candidate?"

Egocentric network size (BEPS 2014) (figure 8.1). "To finish, I'm going to ask you about two people with whom you discuss politics and the election. First, thinking about your family members, with whom do you most discuss politics: your spouse, your father or mother, your son or daughter, or with some other family member?" "Now, thinking about someone outside your family, with whom do you most discuss politics: a work colleague, a friend, a neighbor, or someone else?" This variable is the sum across both queries of discussants named.

Egocentric network size (Mexico 2006 Panel) (figures 2.3, 2.5, 8.1). "Could you name the three persons with whom you most frequently talk about politics? Would you mind telling me first and last name, or just the first name and the last name's initial?" This variable is a count of the discussants named.

Egocentric network size (Spencer) (figure 2.3). "From time to time, people discuss government, elections, and politics with other people. We'd like to know the first names or just the initials of people you talk with about these matters. These people might be from your family, from work, from the neighborhood, from some other organization you belong to, or they might be from somewhere else. Who is the person you've talked with most about politics?" ▪"Aside from this person, who is the person you've talked with most about politics?" ▪"Aside from anyone you've already mentioned, is there anyone else you've talked with about politics?" This variable is a count of the discussants named.

Egocentric network size (Two-City Panel) (figures 2.3, 8.1). "To finish, can you, please, tell me the first names of the three people with whom you most discuss politics?" This variable is a count of the discussants named.

Evangelical church attendance (Two-City Panel, 2002) (tables A.12, A.13, and A 14). "Would you say that you go to church (3) every week, (2) once or twice a month, (1) a few times per year, or (0) never?" Coded as nonzero only if respondents answered "evangelical" to the following question: "What is your religion?"

Exposure to disagreeing media (Two-City Panel, 2002) (figure 4.4). The political leanings of six major media sources are coded using the scores reported by Andy Baker, Barry Ames, and Lúcio R. Rennó.[1] These scores are based on content coders' answers to the following question: "Would the candidate(s) mentioned in this story like the fact that this story was aired / published? (1) Would dislike a lot. (2) Would dislike a little. (3) Balanced coverage. (4) Would like a little. (5) Would like a lot."[2] The degree of respondents' exposure to each of these six sources is determined with the seven *Media exposure* items. We create a single score for each respondent using the following procedure: we weight the media sources the respondent uses by each source's political bias toward the candidate of *Ego vote intention.*

Exposure to disagreeing TV news (Mexico 2006 Panel) (figure 4.4). The political leanings of the two major television news networks are coded using scores shared with us by Chappell Lawson. The degree of respondents' exposure to each of these two sources is determined with the following survey questions: "Do you normally watch any news program on TV? Which?" We create a single score for each respondent using the following procedure: we weight the media sources the respondent uses by each source's political bias toward the candidate of *Ego vote intention.*

Family income (Two-City Panel) (figures 8.1, 8.3, 8.4). "More or less, what is the total monthly income of your family, summing income from everyone who works or has some income source?"

Feeling thermometer scores (Two-City Panel, 2002) (figure 5.2). "I'm going to mention some groups / parties and I'd like you to give them a grade from 0 to 10 indicating how much you like them. A grade of zero means you don't like the group at all. A grade of 10 means you like the group a lot. You can give grades using values between 0 and 10. When I say the name of a group that you do not know, just say you don't know it." ▪PT. ▪PMDB. ▪CUT—Central Única dos Trabalhadores ▪MST—Movimento dos Sem Terra

Frequency of political discussion (BEPS 2014) (figures 8.1, 8.4). Mean of *Frequency of political discussion with family* and *Frequency of political discussion with friends.*

Frequency of political discussion (CNEP) (figure 8.2). This is the first factor score recovered from a polychoric principal components analysis conducted on *Frequency of political discussion with family* (CNEP), *Frequency of political discussion with friends* (CNEP), and *Frequency of political discussion with neighbors* (CNEP).

Frequency of political discussion (Mexico 2006 Panel) (figures 2.4, 2.5, 8.1, 8.4). "How often do you talk about politics with other people? (30) Daily. (15) A few days a week. (4) A few days a month. (1) Rarely. (0) Never."

Frequency of political discussion (Two-City Panel) (figures 8.1, 8.4). This is the first factor score recovered from a polychoric principal components analysis conducted on *Frequency of political discussion with family, Frequency of political discussion with friends,* and *Frequency of political discussion with neighbors.*

Frequency of political discussion on social network websites (BEPS 2014) (chapter 2 text). "And on social networks (Facebook, Twitter, Orkut, etc. . . .). Do you talk about politics (3) frequently, (2) sometimes, (1) rarely, (0) never?"

Frequency of political discussion with family (BEPS 2014) (figure 2.2). "How frequently do you talk about politics with people from your family? (3) Frequently. (2) Sometimes. (1) Rarely. (0) Never."

Frequency of political discussion with family (CNEP) (figure 2.2). "How frequently did you talk about the most recent election campaign with your family? (3) Often. (2) Sometimes. (1) Rarely. (0) Never."

Frequency of political discussion with family (Two-City Panel) (figure 2.2). "How frequently do you talk about politics with family members? (0) Never. (1) Rarely. (2) Sometimes. (3) Frequently."

Frequency of political discussion with friends (BEPS 2014) (figure 2.2). "And at work, school, or with friends. Do you talk about politics in these places (3) frequently. (2) sometimes. (1) rarely. (0) never?"

Frequency of political discussion with friends (CNEP) (figure 2.2). "How frequently did you talk about the most recent election campaign with your friends? (3) Often. (2) Sometimes. (1) Rarely. (0) Never."

Frequency of political discussion with friends (Two-City Panel) (figure 2.2). "How frequently do you talk about politics with friends? (0) Never. (1) Rarely. (2) Sometimes. (3) Frequently."

Frequency of political discussion with friends (WVS) (figure 2.1). "How often do you discuss political matters with friends? (2) Frequently. (1) Occasionally. (0) Never."

Frequency of political discussion with neighbors (CNEP) (figure 2.2). "And what about your neighbors? How frequently did you talk with them about the most recent election campaign? (3) Often. (2) Sometimes. (1) Rarely. (0) Never."

Frequency of political discussion with neighbors (Two-City Panel) (figure 2.2). "How frequently do you talk about politics with people from your neighborhood who are not members of the neighborhood association? (0) Never. (1) Rarely. (2) Sometimes. (3) Frequently."

Frequency of TV news consumption (Mexico 2006 Panel) (figures 2.4, 2.5, 8.1, 8.4). "Do you normally watch a news program on TV? [If "yes"] Which ones? How often do you watch it? (30) Daily. (15) A few times per week. (4) Once a week. (1) Sometimes. (0) [If "no"] Never."

HEG exposure (Two-City Panel, 2002) (figures 4.4, 4.10). "Since August 20, the free electoral hour has been on television and radio. Between the beginning of the free electoral hour in August and the October 6 election, more or less how much time per week did you watch on television and listen on radio to programs about presidential candidates? (0) Never. (15) Less than 30 minutes per week. (45) Between 30 and 60 minutes per week. (90) Between 1 and 2 hours per week. (180) Between 2 and 4 hours. (300) More than 4 hours."

Households with a television (figure 7.6). We use figures available in the World Telecommunications Indicators Database. For nine countries with missing values in this dataset, we imputed values based on responses to queries about TV ownership from Afrobarometer and LAPOP.

Income (CNEP) (figures 8.2, 8.3). Logged income, which CNEP converts into US$ at purchasing power parity.

Lost supporters (Two-City Panel, BEPS 2014, Mexico 2006) (figure 4.8). Using *Ego vote intention/choice*, this is the proportion of each candidate's campaign-wave supporters who did not vote for that candidate on election day. Limited to twice-opinionated respondents.

Maintained vote preference (Two-City Panel, BEPS 2014, Mexico 2006 Panel) (figure 3.2). Using *Ego vote intention/choice*, this variable is (0) for voters who crossed party lines between panel waves or were undecided in at least one panel wave and (1) for voters who did not cross party lines. Includes both once- and twice-opinionated voters.

Mean disagreement in the networks of supporters (Two-City Panel, BEPS 2014, Mexico 2006) (figure 4.8). The average of *Network disagreement* among each candidate's campaign-wave supporters.

Media exposure (BEPS 2014) (figures 4.4, 8.1, 8.4). "How often do you read or watch news about the candidates and elections? (5) More than once per day. (4) Once per day. (3) A few times per week. (2) Once a week. (1) Rarely or never." This question was asked in waves $c2$ through $e7$, so we take each respondent's average over all available answers.

Media exposure (CNEP) (figures 8.2, 8.4). This is the first factor score recovered from a polychoric principal components analysis conducted on the following three variables: "During the electoral campaign, how frequently did you follow political news through ▪Newspapers, including online editions. ▪Radio, including online and satellite broadcasts. ▪Television, including online broadcasts. (0) Never. (0.5) Less frequently. (1.5) One to two days per week. (3.5) Three to four days per week. (6) Daily or almost daily."

Media exposure (Two-City Panel) (figures 4.4, 4.10, 8.1, 8.4). This is the first factor score recovered from a polychoric principal components analysis conducted on seven variables. Respondents were asked in turn whether they watched TV news, read news magazines, read newspapers, and listened to political radio shows. If they responded "yes," they named up to two sources (one for radio) per category and their frequency of use of each. From these reports we created seven variables—used for the principal components analysis—that recorded the frequency of exposure to each of their seven sources.

Meet with friends (Two-City Panel, 2002) (chapter 5 text). "How often do you get together with friends to talk? Never, a few times per year, once or twice per month, or almost every week?"

Neighborhood income level (Two-City Panel, 2002) (figure 5.5). Each neighborhood's median answer to *Family income.*

Neighborhood PT support (figure 5.6; table 5.5). Neighborhood-level average across the 1998 presidential, 1998 gubernatorial, and 2000 mayoral elections in *PT's two-party vote share.*

Network disagreement (Two-City Panel, BEPS 2014, Mexico 2006) (figures 4.3, 4.4). The proportion of all opinionated alters who disagree with ego. For the inclusive definition of disagreement used in table A.5, it is the proportion of all named discussants who disagree with ego. We use *Ego vote intention* and *Alter vote intention/choice* to define agreement and disagreement.

Not contacted by a party (Two-City Panel) (figure 4.4). Reversed coding (0 = 1) (1 = 0) of *Contacted by a party.*

Not paid off by a party (Mexico 2006 Panel) (figure 4.4). Reversed coding (0 = 1) (1 = 0) of *Paid off by a party.*

Number of familial alters (Mexico 2006 Panel) (figures 7.4, 7.5). The number of named discussants (from *Egocentric network size*) who are relatives, as designated by *Relationship with discussant.*

Number of nonfamilial alters (Mexico 2006 Panel) (figures 7.4, 7.5). The number of named discussants (from *Egocentric network size*) who are friends, as designated by *Relationship with discussant.*

Paid off by a disagreeing party (Mexico 2006 Panel) (figure 4.4). If respondents answered "yes" to *Paid off by a party,* they were then asked, "Which party or candidate was it?" We compare this to *Ego vote intention* to measure disagreement.

Paid off by a party (Mexico 2006 Panel) (figures 2.5, 7.4, 7.5, 8.1). "Over the last few weeks, has a representative of a political party or candidate given you a gift, money, food, subsidy, or any other type of help? (1) Yes. (0) No."

Partisan identifier (LAPOP) (figure 7.3, table 7.1). "Do you currently identify with a political party? (0) No. (1) Yes."

Partisanship (BEPS 2014) (table 6.2). "Do you sympathize with a political party? [If "yes"] With which party do you sympathize? [If "no"] Is there a party for which you have a little more sympathy than the others?" We use this to create the following variables: *PSB partisanship*: (1) Strong PSB partisan, (0.5) Weak PSB partisan, (0) Everyone else; *PSDB partisanship*: (1) Strong PSDB partisan, (0.5) Weak PSDB partisan, (0) Everyone else; *Partisans of other parties and nonpartisans*: (1) Strong partisans of a non-PSDB /

PSB / PT party or nonpartisans, (.5) Weak partisans of a non-PSDB / PSB / PT party, (0) Everyone else. This makes *PT partisanship* the omitted baseline category.

Partisanship (Mexico 2006 Panel) (table 6.3). "In general, would you say you identify with the PAN, the PRI or the PRD? [If respondent names one] Would you say you identify strongly with that party or only somewhat with that party?" We use this to create the following variables: *PRD partisanship*: (1) Strong PRD partisan, (0.5) Weak PRD partisan, (0) Everyone else; *PRI partisanship*: (1) Strong PRI partisan, (0.5) Weak PRI partisan, (0) Everyone else; *Partisans of other parties and nonpartisans*: (1) Strong partisans of a non-PRD / PAN / PRI party or nonpartisans, (0.5) Weak partisans of a non-PRD / PAN / PRI party, (0) Everyone else. This makes *PAN partisanship* the omitted baseline category in the regressions.

Partisanship (Two-City Panel, 2002) (tables 5.3, 5.4, 5.5). "Do you sympathize with a political party? [If "yes"] Which? [If "no"] Is there a party for which you have a little more sympathy than the others?" We use this to create the following variables: *PT partisanship*: (1) Strong PT partisan, (0.5) Weak PT partisan, (0) Everyone else; *PMDB partisanship*: (1) Strong PMDB partisan, (0.5) Weak PMDB partisan, (0) Everyone else; *Partisans of other parties and nonpartisans*: (1) Strong partisans of a non-PMDB / PT / PSDB party or nonpartisans, (0.5) Weak partisans of a non-PMDB / PT / PSDB party, (0) Everyone else. This makes *PSDB partisanship* the omitted baseline category in the regressions.

Perceived political knowledge of spouse/alter 2/alter 3 (CNEP) (figure 2.7). "Generally speaking, how well informed would you say this person is when it comes to politics? (0) Not at all informed. (1) Not well informed. (2) Somewhat informed. (3) Very well informed."

Persuasion frequency (LAPOP) (figures 7.2, 7.3; table 7.1). "During election times, some people try to convince others to vote for a party or a candidate. How often have you tried to persuade others to vote for a party or candidate? (0) Never. (1) Rarely. (2) Occasionally. (3) Frequently."

Political knowledge (BEPS 2014) (figures 4.9, 8.3, 8.4). We convert each response to the items listed below to (1) correct or (0) incorrect (except for ordinal item G), estimate a two-parameter item-response theory model on the items, and use the recovered latent trait (standardized). ▪A. "Who is the president of the Chamber of Deputies?" (Henrique Eduardo Alves) ▪B. "Is Argentina a member of Mercosul?" (Yes) ▪C. "What is the name of the vice president of the republic?" (Michel Temer) ▪D. "Nicolás Maduro is president of what country?" (Venezuela) ▪E. "How many states does Brazil have?" (26 or 27)" ▪F. Whether the respondent placed self on 0 (left) to 10 (right) ideological scale. ▪G. A count of the number of feeling thermometer queries (of seven about politicians and parties) to which the respondent reported an opinion.

Political knowledge (CNEP) (figure 8.3). Respondents answered three to five quiz questions about objective political facts. These varied by country. For each country, we convert each response to (1) correct or (0) incorrect, estimate a two-parameter item-response theory model on the items, and use the recovered latent trait (standardized). For a few countries, only the total correct was reported, so we use this variable (standardized) as the measure of knowledge.

Political knowledge (LAPOP) (chapter 7 text). For each country, we convert each response to the items listed below to (1) correct or (0) incorrect (except the ordinal items D and E), estimate a two-parameter item-response theory model on the items, and use the recovered latent trait (standardized). ▪A. "How many provinces / departments / states are there in your country?" ▪B. "How long is the presidential term in your country?" ▪C. "What is the name of the current US president?" ▪D. A count of the number of political queries (i.e., presidential approval, congressional approval, Supreme Court approval, left/right self-placement) the respondent gave opinions for. ▪E. "How interested are you in politics? (4) A lot. (3) Somewhat. (2) A little. (1) Not at all."

Political knowledge (Mexico 2006 Panel) (figures 4.9, 8.3, 8.4). We convert each response to the items listed below to (1) correct or (0) incorrect (except the ordinal items H and L), estimate a two-parameter item-response theory model on the items, and use the recovered latent trait (standardized). ▪"I am going to read you some campaign slogans; for each one please tell me which politician says it. A. 'Together we'll get Mexico moving' (Montiel). B. 'Happiness is just around the corner' (AMLO). C. 'Passion for Mexico' (Calderón). D. 'Get Mexico moving' (Madrazo)." ▪"I am going to read you some campaign slogans; for each one please tell me which politician says it. D. 'Let's get things done' (Madrazo). E. 'I deliver' (AMLO). F. 'So we live better' (Calderón)." ▪G. "Together with Mexico and the United States, which of the following countries is a member of NAFTA: Canada (correct), Chile, or Cuba?" ▪H. "Could you tell me the names of the three branches of government, or you do not remember right now?" Count from 0 to 3. ▪"Could you tell me which former Mexican president . . . I. Nationalized oil (Cárdenas)? J. Created the National Solidarity Program (PRONASOL) (Salinas)? K. Created the PROGRESA program (Zedillo)?" ▪L. A count of the number of feeling thermometer queries (of seven about politicians and parties) the respondent gave opinions for.

Political knowledge (Two-City Panel, 2002) (figures 4.9, 8.3, 8.4). We convert each response to the items listed below to (1) correct or (0) incorrect, estimate a two-parameter item-response theory model on the items, and use the recovered latent trait (standardized) as the measure of political knowledge. ▪A. "Who is the vice president of Brazil? Inocêncio de Oliveira, Marco Maciel (correct), Íris Resende, or Marcello Alencar." ▪B. "What is the party of President Fernando Henrique Cardoso? PTB, PMDB, PSDB (correct), or PFL." ▪C. "Which of the following countries is a member of Mercosul? United States, Argentina (correct), Colombia, or Peru." ▪D. "Which of these politicians is a senator from your state? José Fogaça / José Alencar (correct), Saturnino Braga, Eduardo Suplicy, or Lindbergh Cury." ▪E. "Who is the president of the Chamber of Deputies? Roberto Jefferson, José Genoíno, Aécio Neves (correct), or Miro Teixeira?" ▪F. "What is the political office of Ana Corso / Paulo Delgado? Council (Corso), federal deputy (Delgado), state deputy, or senator." ▪G. "Who is currently the mayor of Caxias? Ana Corso, Germano Rigotto, José Sartori, or Pepe Vargas (correct)." "Who is currently the mayor of JF? Alberto Bejani, Newton Cardoso, Custódio Mattos, or Tarcísio Delgado (correct)."

Political knowledge (Two-City Panel, 2006) (figures 4.9, 8.3, 8.4). We convert each response to the items listed below to (1) correct or (0) incorrect, estimate a two-parameter item-response theory model on the items, and use the recovered latent trait (standardized). ▪A. "Who is the vice president of Brazil? Inocêncio de Oliveira, Marco Maciel, Íris Resende, or José Alencar (correct)." ▪B. "Which of the following countries is a member of Mercosul? United States, Argentina (correct), Colombia, or Peru." ▪C. "Which of these politicians is a senator from your state? Paulo Paím / Hélio Costa (correct), Saturnino Braga, Eduardo Suplicy, or Lindbergh Cury." ▪D. "Who is the president of the Chamber of Deputies? Roberto Jefferson, João Paulo Cunha, Patrus Ananias, or Aldo Rebelo (correct)." ▪E. "Who is currently the mayor of Caxias? Ana Corso, Germano Rigotto, José Sartori, or Pepe Vargas (correct)." ▪F. "What is the party of Pedro Simon [Caxias only]? PTB, PMDB (correct), PSDB, or PFL." "What is the party of Aécio Neves [JF only]? PTB, PMDB, PSDB (correct), or PFL." ▪G. "What is the political office of Rui Pauletti [Caxias only]? Council, federal deputy, state deputy (correct), or senator."

Political knowledge for ego ↔ alter comparison (Two-City Panel, 2002) (figure 2.6). We convert each response to the items listed below to (1) correct or (0) incorrect, estimate a two-parameter item-response theory model on the items, and use the recovered latent trait (standardized). ▪A. "Who is the vice president of Brazil? Inocêncio de Oliveira, Marco Maciel (correct), Íris Resende, or Marcello Alencar." ▪B. "What is the party of President Fernando Henrique Cardoso? PTB, PMDB, PSDB (correct), or PFL." ▪C. "Which of the following countries is a member of Mercosul? United States, Argentina (correct), Colombia, or Peru."

Political participation index (LAPOP) (figure 7.3, table 7.1). For each country, we estimate item-response theory models on the items listed below and use the recovered latent traits. ▪A. "In the last 12 months, have you participated in a demonstration or protest march? (0) No, (1) Yes." ▪B. "Have you attended a town meeting, city council meeting, or other meeting in the past 12 months? (0) No. (1) Yes." ▪C. "If the next presidential elections were being held this week, what would you do? (0) Wouldn't vote, (1) Would vote."

Prevalence of clientelism (Afrobarometer and LAPOP) (figure 7.6). For Latin America, we use the mean country response to *Target of clientelism*. For Africa, we use the mean country response to "And during the recent election, how often (if ever) did a candidate or someone from a political party offer you something, like food or a gift, in return for your vote? (0) Never. (1) Once or twice. (1) A few times. (1) Often. (0) No experience with this in the past year."

Pro-Aécio share among alters, *Pro-Marina share among alters*, and *Pro-Dilma share among alters* (BEPS 2014) (figure 6.6, table 6.2). These are based on *Alter vote intention* and sum to one for each ego.

Pro-AMLO share among alters, *Pro-Madrazo share among alters*, and *Pro-Calderón share among alters* (Mexico 2006 Panel) (figure 6.7, table 6.3). These are based on *Alter vote intention* and sum to one for each ego.

Pro-Lula share among alters, *Pro-Serra share among alters*, *Pro-Garotinho share among alters*, and *Pro-Ciro share among alters* (Two-City Panel) (figure 5.6, table 5.5). These are based on *Alter vote intention* and sum to one for each ego.

PT's two-party vote share (figure 5.6). ▪Presidential: $\dfrac{\#\,Lula\,votes}{\#\,Lula\,votes + \#\,Cardoso\,votes}$. ▪Guberna-torial in Caxias: $\dfrac{\#\,Dutra\,votes}{\#\,Dutra\,votes + \#\,Britto\,votes}$. ▪Gubernatorial in JF: $\dfrac{\#\,Ananias\,votes}{\#\,Ananias\,votes + \#\,Itamar\,votes}$. ▪Mayoral in Caxias: $\dfrac{\#\,Vargas\,votes}{\#\,Vargas\,votes + \#\,Sartori\,votes}$. ▪Mayoral in JF: $\dfrac{\#\,Valente\,votes}{\#\,Valente\,votes + \#\,Delgado\,votes}$.

Race (BEPS 2014) (figure 8.1). "Do you consider yourself a (3) white, (1) black, (2) brown (*parda*), (1) indigenous, or (2) yellow person?"

Race (Mexico 2006 Panel) (figure 8.1). Interviewer coded as (3) white, (2) light brown (*moreno claro*), (1) dark brown (*moreno oscuro*).

Race (Two-City) (figure 8.1). "I'm going to read some categories for skin color and I would like you to say which of these categories best describes your color: (3) White. (2) Brown (*pardo*) (1) Black. (2) Yellow. (1) Indigenous." We averaged this with the interviewer's score on the same scale: "Interviewer: Classify the respondent according to your opinion of their skin color."

Recall of 1998 gubernatorial vote (Two-City Panel, 2002) (chapter 5 text). "Did you vote in the 1998 elections for governor? [If "yes"] For whom did you vote? Antônio Britto, Olívio Dutra, or some other candidate (Caxias). Itamar Franco, Eduardo Azeredo, Patrus Ananias de Souza, or some other candidate (JF)."

Recall of 1998 presidential vote (Two-City Panel, 2002) (chapter 5 text). "Did you vote in the 1998 elections for president? [If "yes"] For whom did you vote? Fernando Henrique Cardoso, Lula, Ciro Gomes, or some other candidate?"

Recall of 2000 mayoral vote (Two-City Panel, 2002) (chapter 5 text). "Did you vote in the 1998 elections for mayor? [If "yes"] For whom did you vote? Pepe Vargas, José Ivo Sartori, or some other candidate (Caxias). Tarcisio Delgado, Carlos Alberto Bejani, or some other candidate (JF)."

Relationship with discussant (Mexico 2006 Panel) (figure 2.3). "What is your relationship with [named discussant]?" Spouse, son, daughter, parent (family). Relative (family).

Neighbor (friend). Very close friend (friend). Friend / acquaintance (friend). Church friend (friend). Coworker (friend). Other (unspecified). DK / NA (unspecified).

Relationship with discussant (Two-City Panel) (figures 2.3, 5.1). "What is your relationship with [named discussant]?" Partner / spouse (family). Relative (family). Child (family). Friend from the neighborhood (friend). Friend from work / school (friend). Other kind of friend (friend). Unspecified (unspecified). DK / NA (unspecified).

Respondent reports political bias of [intermediary] (CNEP) (figure 2.10). ▪Spouse, alter 2, and alter 3: In answer to *Alter vote choice*, main respondent (1) mentions a party or (0) does not mention a party. ▪TV News: "Do you think the television news broadcasts you watched most often favored a particular political party or candidate? Which political party or candidate?" (1) Mentions a party / candidate. (0) Does not mention a party / candidate. ▪Paper: "Do you think this newspaper you read most often favored a particular political party or candidate? Which political party or candidate?" (1) Mentions a party / candidate. (0) Does not mention a party / candidate. ▪Radio: "Do you think the radio program you listened to most often favored a particular political party or candidate? Which political party or candidate?" (1) Mentions a party / candidate. (0) Does not mention a party / candidate.

Secondary associations (Two-City Panel, 2002) (chapter 5 text). "Now I'd like to read to you a list of groups and associations. I'd like you to tell me how often you participate in meetings of each group? Never, a few times per year, once or twice per month, or almost every week." ▪Sports clubs. ▪Labor unions. ▪Self-help groups. ▪Political parties. ▪Cultural, music, reading, dance groups. ▪Social movements, such as Afro-Brazilian, feminist, environmentalist.

Singleton (Two-City Panel, BEPS 2014, Mexico 2006) (figures 4.3, 4.4; table 5.5, 6.2, 6.3). (1) *Egocentric network size* = 0. (0) *Egocentric network size* > 0.

Socioeconomic status (Two-City Panel, 2002) (table 5.5). We use the factor score extracted from a principal components analysis run on logged *Family income* and *Education*.

Source of friends (Two-City Panel, 2002) (chapter 5 text). "Where do most of your friends come from? Neighborhood, work, the groups in which you participate, or some other place?"

Spouse selected as a political alter (CNEP) (figure 2.7). "How often did you talk to your spouse / partner about the recent election? (0) Never. (1) Rarely. (1) Sometimes. (1) Often."

State Marina support (figure 6.6, table 6.2). Share of the vote in respondent's state won by Marina Silva in 2010 presidential election.

State PAN support (figure 6.7, table 6.3). Share of the vote in respondent's state won by Vicente Fox in 2000 presidential election.

State PRD Support (figure 6.7, table 6.3). Share of the vote in respondent's state won by Cuauhtémoc Cárdenas in 2000 presidential election.

State PRI support (figure 6.7, table 6.3). Share of the vote in respondent's state won by Francisco Labastida in 2000 presidential election.

State PSDB support (figure 6.6, table 6.2). Share of the vote in respondent's state won by José Serra in 2010 presidential election.

State PT support (figure 6.6, table 6.2). Share of the vote in respondent's state won by Dilma Rousseff in 2010 presidential election.

Strength of partisanship (Mexico 2006 Panel) (figures 7.4, 7.5). A recode of the *Partisanship* variable: (2) Strong partisans. (1) Weak partisans. (0) Nonpartisans.

Target of clientelism (LAPOP) (figures 7.2, 7.3; table 7.1). "In recent years and thinking about election campaigns, has a candidate or someone from a political party offered you something, like a favor, food, or any other benefit or object in return for your vote or support? (0) Never. (1) Sometimes or Often."

Timing of vote decision (Two-City Panel, 2002; Mexico 2006) (figure 4.9). (1) Before the campaign: Respondent expressed the same candidate intention and choice in the pre-campaign, campaign, and election waves. (2) Before mid-campaign: Respondent expressed the same candidate preference in the campaign and election waves but a different one in the pre-campaign wave. (3) Before election day: Respondent's campaign-wave intention is different from her or his election-wave vote choice.

Timing of vote decision (Two-City Panel, 2006) (figure 4.9). (2) Before mid-campaign: Respondent expressed the same candidate preference in both the campaign and election waves. (3) Before election day: Respondent's campaign-wave intention is different from her or his election-wave vote choice.

Timing of vote decision (BEPS 2014) (figure 4.9). (1) Before the campaign: Respondent expressed the same candidate intention and choice in the pre-campaign (*pc1*), campaign (*c2* or *c3*), and election waves (*e6*). (2) Before mid-campaign: Respondent expressed the same candidate preference in the campaign and election waves but a different one in the pre-campaign wave. (3) Before election day: Respondent's campaign-wave intention is different from her or his election-wave vote choice. We treat preferences for Marina and Campos as preferences for the same candidate.

TV news exposure (Two-City Panel, 2002) (figure 4.10). Averaged responses to the two frequency-of-TV-news items described under *Media exposure*.

Unexposed to media (Two-City Panel, 2002) (figure 4.4). Answer of "no" to all seven *Media exposure* items.

Unexposed to TV news (Mexico 2006 Panel) (figure 4.4). "Do you normally watch any news program on TV? (1) No. (0) Yes."

Voted correctly (Two-City Panel, BEPS 2014, Mexico 2006) (figure 8.4, 8.5). (1) Respondent voted correctly, (0) respondent did not vote correctly. Appendix C contains full details on how this is defined.

Wealth (BEPS 2014) (figures 8.1, 8.3, 8.4). We convert each response to the items listed below to (1) yes or (0) no (except for the ordinal bathrooms question), estimate a two-parameter item-response theory model on the items, and use the recovered latent trait (standardized). "Could you tell me whether, in your house, you have ▪TV ▪refrigerator ▪landline ▪cellular phone ▪car ▪computer?" ▪"Have you taken an international flight within the past year?" ▪"How many bathrooms do you have in your house, including any in the maid's quarters?"

Wealth (Mexico 2006) (figures 8.1, 8.3, 8.4). We convert each response to the items listed below to (1) yes or (0) no, estimate a two-parameter item-response theory model on the items, and use the recovered latent trait (standardized). "In this household, do you have ▪radio ▪TV ▪stove with oven ▪refrigerator ▪washing machine ▪automobile or truck of your own ▪computer ▪paid television (Sky, Direct TV, Cablevision)?" ▪[Asked of interviewer] "What material is the home mostly made of? (0) Discarded materials. (0) Cardboard. (0) Corrugated metal. (0) Thatch, bamboo, or palm. (0) Wood. (0) Adobe. (1) Plaster, brick, cement, concrete, stone."

Details of Correct-Voting Analyses

This appendix reports details on the four correct-voting analyses conducted in chapter 8. The analyses proceed in two broad steps. In step one, we sum up the respondent's distances from a candidate in a set of five to eight issue spaces. (All of the issue spaces and the questions that define them are listed below. All are from pre-campaign panel waves unless indicated otherwise.) This is repeated for all major-party candidates: each respondent gets J scores, where J is the number of major candidates. A respondent's correct candidate is that candidate for whom the respondent has the lowest score—that is, the candidate for whom the respondent has the smallest summed distances. Our approach makes two assumptions: (1) The relevant score is based on summing, rather than averaging, across the distances, and (2) respondents assign equal weight to each issue. The consequences of the first choice are mathematically trivial, as the difference boils down to how nonresponse is treated. The consequences of the second decision are greater, as the equal-weights assumption surely does not hold in all real-world voting decisions. In practice, however, relaxing even this assumption has little effect on results.[1]

For step two, we create a binary variable, *Voted correctly*, that measures whether a respondent's election-day vote, as reported in the election panel wave, matches our estimate of her correct candidate. If so, the variable equals one; it is zero otherwise. For each election, we regress this variable on *Political knowledge* in the "Political knowledge model"; *Frequency of political discussion*, *Media exposure/Frequency of TV news consumption*, and *Contacted by a party* in the "Political intermediation model"; and *Wealth, Education, Gender*, and *Race* in the "Societal exclusion model." These logit regression results are reported graphically in figure 8.4 (which refers to wealth and education jointly as SES) and numerically below in table C.1.

STEP ONE: ISSUE SPACES FOR DEFINING EACH
RESPONDENT'S CORRECT CANDIDATE

Brazil 2002

FEELING THERMOMETER SCORE OF CARDOSO

Respondent placements. "I'm going to mention some politicians, and I'd like you to give them a grade from 0 to 10 indicating how much you like them. A grade of zero means you don't like the politician at all. A grade of 10 means you like the politician a lot. You can give grades using values between 0 and 10. When I say the name of a politician that you do not know, just say you don't know." ▪Fernando Henrique Cardoso. (Recoded to the −1 to 1 interval.) Candidate placements. Lula = −1, Serra = 1, Garotinho = −1, Ciro = −1.

SOCIOTROPIC ECONOMIC EVALUATIONS

Respondent placements. "Speaking generally of the country over the past 12 months, do you think that the economic situation (1) improved a lot, (0.5) improved a little, (0) stayed the same, (−0.5) worsened a little, (−1) worsened a lot?" Candidate placements. Lula = −1, Serra = 1, Garotinho = −1, Ciro = −1.

IDEOLOGY

Respondent placements. "In relation to your political position, do you consider yourself (−1) left, (−0.5) center-left, (0) center, (0.5) center-right, or (1) right?" Candidate placements. "Do you think [Lula / Serra / Ciro / Garotinho] is a politician of the left, center-left, center, center-right, or right?" Lula = −0.77, Serra = 0.73, Ciro = −0.27, Garotinho = −0.40. These are the mean placements of each candidate by respondents with political knowledge in the top two quintiles.

PRIVATIZATION ATTITUDE

Respondent placements. "I'd now like to ask some questions about political issues. Over the last ten years, state-owned business, which were businesses directed by the government, were sold to private businesses in a process known as privatization. With which of the following statements about privatization do you agree the most? . . . Do you strongly agree or somewhat agree with this statement?" (1) Privatization is a good thing, strongly agree. (0.5) Privatization is a good thing, somewhat agree. (0) It depends. (−0.5) Privatization is a bad thing, somewhat agree. (−1) Privatization is a bad thing, strongly agree.
Candidate placements. "Based on what you know about him, according to [Lula / Serra / Ciro / Garotinho], is privatization a good thing or a bad thing? And does he think this strongly or only slightly?" Lula = −0.71, Serra = 0.68, Garotinho = −0.37, Ciro = −0.11. These are the mean placements of each candidate by respondents with political knowledge in the top two quintiles.

LAND REFORM ATTITUDE

Respondent placements. "Another important issue in Brazil is land reform. With which of the following statements do you agree the most? . . . Do you strongly agree or somewhat agree with this statement?" (1) The government should not give land from large farms to rural landless workers, strongly agree. (0.5) The government should not give land from large farms to rural landless workers, somewhat agree. (0) It depends. (−0.5) The government should give land from large farms to rural landless workers, somewhat agree. (−1) The government should give land from large farms to rural landless workers, strongly agree.

Candidate placements. "Based on what you know about him, according to [Lula / Serra / Ciro / Garotinho], should the government give land from large farms to rural landless workers, or should the government not give land from large farms to rural landless workers? And does he think this strongly or only slightly?" Lula = −0.70, Serra = 0.12. Garotinho = −0.36, Ciro = −0.18. These are the mean placements of each candidate by respondents with political knowledge in the top two quintiles.

EVANGELICAL CHRISTIAN

Respondent placements. "Would you say that you go to church (1) every week, (0.33) once or twice a month, (−0.33) a few times per year, or (0) never?" Coded as something other than −1 only if respondent answered "evangelical" to the following question: "What is your religion?"

Candidate placements. Lula = −1, Serra = −1. Garotinho = 1, Ciro = −1.

Brazil 2006

SOCIOTROPIC ECONOMIC EVALUATIONS

Respondent placements. "Speaking generally of the country over the past 12 months, do you think that the economic situation (1) improved a lot, (0.5) improved a little, (0) stayed the same, (−0.5) worsened a little, (−1) worsened a lot?" Candidate placements. Lula = 1, Alckmin = −1, Heloísa Helena = −1.

LULA PRESIDENTIAL APPROVAL

Respondent placements. "Do you think that President Lula is doing a (1) wonderful, (0.5) good, (0) fair, (−0.5) bad, or (−1) horrible job?" Candidate placements. Lula = 1, Alckmin = −1, Heloísa Helena = −1.

IDEOLOGY

Respondent placements. "In relation to your political position, do you consider yourself (−1) left, (−0.5) center-left, (0) center, (0.5) center-right, or (1) right?"

Candidate placements. "Do you think [Lula / Alckmin / Heloísa Helena] is a politician of the left, center-left, center, center-right, or right?" Lula = −0.25, Alckmin = 0.31, Heloísa Helena = −0.79. These are the mean placements of each candidate by respondents with political knowledge in the top two quintiles.

PRIVATIZATION ATTITUDE

Respondent placements. "I'd now like to ask some questions about political issues. Over the last ten years, state-owned business, which were businesses directed by the government, were sold to private businesses in a process known as privatization. With which of the following statements about privatization do you agree the most? . . . Do you strongly agree or somewhat agree with this statement?" (1) Privatization is a good thing, strongly agree. (0.5) Privatization is a good thing, somewhat agree. (0) It depends. (−0.5) Privatization is a bad thing, somewhat agree. (−1) Privatization is a bad thing, strongly agree.

Candidate placements. "Based on what you know about her/him, according to [Lula / Alckmin / Heloísa Helena], is privatization a good thing or a bad thing? And does s/he think this strongly or only slightly?" Lula = −0.32, Alckmin = 0.67, Heloísa Helena = −0.60. These are the mean placements of each candidate by respondents with political knowledge in the top two quintiles.

LAND REFORM ATTITUDE

Respondent placements. "Another important issue in Brazil is land reform. With which of the following statements do you agree the most? . . . Do you strongly agree or somewhat agree with this statement?" (1) The government should not give land from large farms to rural landless workers, strongly agree. (0.5) The government should not give land from large farms to rural landless workers, somewhat agree. (0) It depends. (−0.5) The government should give land from large farms to rural landless workers, somewhat agree. (−1) The government should give land from large farms to rural landless workers, strongly agree.

Candidate placements. "Based on what you know about her/him, according to [Lula / Alckmin / Heloísa Helena], should the government give land from large farms to rural landless workers, or should the government not give land from large farms to rural landless workers? And does s/he think this strongly or only slightly?" Lula = −0.35, Alckmin = 0.27, Heloísa Helena = −0.77. These are the mean placements of each candidate by respondents with political knowledge in the top two quintiles.

Brazil 2014

SOCIOTROPIC ECONOMIC EVALUATIONS

Respondent placements. "Now, talking about the economy. How do you evaluate the economic situation of the country?" (1) Wonderful, (0.5) good, (0) fair, (−0.5) bad, or (−1) horrible.

Candidate placements. Dilma = 1, Aécio = −1, Marina = −1.

DILMA PRESIDENTIAL APPROVAL

Respondent placements. "In your opinion, President Dilma is doing a (1) wonderful, (0.5) good, (0) fair, (−0.5) bad, or (−1) horrible job?"
Candidate placements. Dilma = 1, Aécio = −1, Marina = −1.

EVALUATION OF DILMA'S CORRUPTION

Respondent placements. "Currently, newspapers are writing about corruption in *Petrobras*. Do you think that President Dilma is responsible for the current problems documented by the newspapers?" (−1) Yes. (0) No. (1) They're just framing Dilma.
Candidate placements. Dilma = 1, Aécio = −1, Marina = −1.

ECONOMIC ISSUE SPACE

Respondent placements. This is the first factor score (rescaled to the −1 to 1 interval) recovered from a polychoric principal components analysis conducted on the following items:

- "Would you be inclined to pay more taxes than what you pay now so that the government can spend more on Family Grant (Bolsa Família)? Yes. No."
- "Would you be inclined to pay more taxes than what you pay now so that the government can spend more on public health services? Yes. No."
- "Do you approve or disapprove of income transfer programs like Family Grant (Bolsa Família) that make monthly payments to poor families? Approve. Disapprove."
- "Do you approve or disapprove of programs like More Doctors (Mais Médicos), which brings foreign doctors to work in Brazil? Approve. Disapprove."
- "Do you approve or disapprove of programs like My House My Life (Minha Casa Minha Vida) that finance the purchase of houses for families of low and medium income? Approve. Disapprove."
- "Do you approve or disapprove of programs like Social Subsidy for Electricity (Tarifa Social de Energia Elétrica), which gives discounts on lighting bills to families of low income? Approve. Disapprove."
- "Do you approve or disapprove of programs like Continuous Cash Benefit (Benefício de Prestação Continuado), which makes monthly payments to the elderly and incapacitated of low income? Approve. Disapprove."

Candidate placements. These are the means on the tax-and-spend issue dimension (rescaled to the −1 to 1 interval) from Nina Wiesehomeier and Kenneth Benoit.[2] Dilma = −0.48, Aécio = 0.26, Marina = −0.35.

EVANGELICAL CHRISTIAN

Respondent placements. "How often do you go to mass or religious services? (1) More than once per week (0.5) Weekly. (0) A few times per month. (−0.5) A few times per year. (−1) Almost never or never. Coded as something other than −1 only if respondent answered "evangelical" to the following question: "What is your religion, if you have one?"
Candidate placements. Dilma = −1, Aécio = −1, Marina = 1.

Mexico 2006

SOCIOTROPIC ECONOMIC EVALUATIONS UNDER FOX

Respondent placements. "Since Fox became president, would you say the national economy has gotten better, has gotten worse, or stayed the same? Would you say it has gotten a lot [better/worse] or a little [better/worse]?" (1) A lot better. (0.5) A little better. (0) Stayed the same. (−0.5) A little worse. (−1) A lot worse.
Candidate placements. Caldéron = 1, AMLO = −1, Madrazo = −1.

FOX PRESIDENTIAL APPROVAL

Respondent placements. "In general, do you approve or disapprove of the way in which Vicente Fox is doing his job as president? A lot or a little?" (1) Approve a lot. (0.5) Approve a little. (0) Neither. (−0.5) Disapprove a little. (−1) Disapprove a lot.
Candidate placements. Caldéron = 1, AMLO = −1, Madrazo = −1.

IDEOLOGY

Respondent placements. "In politics, would you consider yourself on the left, on the right, or in the center? [If "left" or "right"] Very or somewhat on the left/right? [If "center"] Center-left, center-right, or center-center?" (1) Very on the right. (0.66) Somewhat on the right. (0.33) Center-right. (0) Center-center. (−0.33) Center-left. (−0.66) Somewhat on the left. (−1) Very on the left.
Candidate placements. Caldéron = 0.62, AMLO = −0.63, Madrazo = 0.11. These are the means on the overall ideology scale (rescaled to the −1 to 1 interval) from Wiesehomeier and Benoit.

PRIVATIZATION ATTITUDE

Respondent placements. "Do you believe that more private investment should be allowed in the electricity sector or that the electricity sector should remain almost completely in the hands of the government? Are you sure about your opinion or do you think you could change your mind?" (1) More private investment should be allowed, sure. (0.5) More private investment should be allowed, could change. (0) DK / NA. (−0.5) Should remain in hands of government, could change. (−1) Should remain in hands of government, sure.

Candidate placements. "Do you believe that [Calderón / AMLO / Madrazo] is for or against allowing more private investment in the electricity sector?" Calderón = 0.63, AMLO = −0.42, Madrazo = 0.24. These are the mean election-wave placements of each candidate by respondents with political knowledge in the top two quintiles.

TRADE ATTITUDE

Respondent placements. Which would you prefer: that commercial relations between Mexico and the United States increase, decrease, or remain the same? Are you sure about your opinion or do you think you could change your mind? (1) Increase, sure. (0.5) Increase, could change. (0) remain the same. (−0.5) Decrease, could change. (−1) Decrease, sure.

Candidate placements. "Do you believe that [Calderón / AMLO / Madrazo] will try to (1) increase commercial relations between Mexico and the United States, (−1) decrease commercial relations between Mexico and the United States, or (0) keep commercial relations between Mexico and the United States the same?" Calderón = 0.74, AMLO = −0.17, Madrazo = 0.50. These are the mean election-wave placements of each candidate by respondents with political knowledge in the top two quintiles.

RELIGIOUS OBSERVANCE

Respondent placements. "How often do you attend religious services? (1) More than once a week. (0.5) Once a week. (0) Once a month. (−0.5) Only on special occasions. (−1) Never."

Candidate placements. Calderón = 0.19, AMLO = −0.83, Madrazo = −0.62. These are the means on the religion scale (rescaled to the −1 to 1 interval) from Wiesehomeier and Benoit.

MADRAZO WIN PROBABILITY

Respondent placements. "How likely is it that Roberto Madrazo will win the elections in 2006; would you say it is (1) totally certain that he will win, (0.33) likely that he will win, (−0.33) likely that he will lose, or (−1) totally certain that he will lose?" Measured in the campaign wave.

Candidate placements. Calderón = −1, AMLO = −1, Madrazo = 1.

STEP TWO: LOGIT REGRESSION RESULTS

TABLE C.1 (*MODELS USED FOR FIGURE 8.4*):
Voted Correctly by Political Knowledge, Exposure to Political Intermediaries, and Societal Exclusion: Results from 12 Binary Logit Models

	Brazil 2002			Brazil 2006		
	Political Knowledge Model	Political Intermediation Model	Societal Exclusion Model	Political Knowledge Model	Political Intermediation Model	Societal Exclusion Model
Political knowledge	0.133* (0.037)			0.236* (0.057)		
Freq. of pol. Discussion		0.109* (0.045)			0.204* (0.065)	
Media exposure		0.073 (0.050)			0.079 (0.069)	
Contact by party		0.006 (0.048)			0.034 (0.061)	
Wealth			0.089 (0.054)			0.220* (0.083)
Education			−0.056 (0.078)			0.155 (0.112)
Woman			−0.027 (0.077)			0.010 (0.115)
Race			0.005 (0.064)			0.173 (0.094)
Constant	−0.953* (0.184)	−0.881* (0.191)	−1.417* (0.413)	0.564* (0.211)	0.803* (0.227)	−1.709* (0.591)
N	2,934	2,934	2,869	1,343	1,344	1,316

Notes: Entries are logit coefficients with standard errors in parentheses. Dependent variable for each model is *Voted correctly. Frequency of political discussion* and *Media exposure* (*Frequency of TV news consumption* in Mexico) are average responses in the campaign and election waves, except in Brazil 2014 where we have only pre-campaign wave responses. Coefficients for fixed effects for *Ego vote choice* (one per candidate) are not shown.
* $= p < 0.05$
Source: Two-City Panel, BEPS 2014, Mexico 2006 Panel Study.

Brazil 2014			Mexico 2006		
Political Knowledge Model	Political Intermediation Model	Societal Exclusion Model	Political Knowledge Model	Political Intermediation Model	Societal Exclusion Model
0.212* (0.080)			0.170* (0.066)		
	0.235* (0.084)			0.264* (0.082)	
	0.048 (0.078)			0.015 (0.092)	
				0.038 (0.258)	
		0.040 (0.105)			0.188 (0.104)
		0.014 (0.186)			0.027 (0.034)
		−0.075 (0.159)			−0.262* (0.125)
		0.034 (0.118)			−0.120 (0.094)
0.061 (0.106)	−0.619* (0.257)	0.007 (0.478)	1.380* (0.169)	0.936* (0.223)	1.695* (0.301)
996	992	984	1,217	1,212	1,211

NOTES

PREFACE

1. "horror às distâncias . . . parece constituir . . . o traço mais específico do espirito brasileiro" (Buarque de Holanda 1995, 149). Note that the word *social* does not appear in the original Portuguese, but this can be safely added to clarify the original meaning. We are not the only scholars to have translated it in this way (Reid 2014, 20).

2. Passos 2018.

ACKNOWLEDGMENTS

1. Campbell et al. 1960.
2. Lazarsfeld, Berelson, and Gaudet 1944.
3. Huckfeldt and Sprague 1995.
4. Ames 2001a.

CHAPTER 1. SOCIAL COMMUNICATION AND VOTING BEHAVIOR

1. Aristotle 1895, 12.
2. Gelman and King 1993.
3. Finkel 1993.
4. Mainwaring 1999.
5. Samuels and Zucco 2018, chap. 2.
6. Duverger 1954.
7. Gay 1994, 110; Nichter 2018, 59.
8. According to the Two-City Panel discussed below, more than 85 percent of party-contacting efforts promote a candidate for a legislative post (i.e., federal or state deputy), while less than 5 percent promote a presidential candidate. Ames (1994) finds that upward endorsements mattered in the 1989 presidential election, but their effects were quite small in the aggregate.
9. Nichter 2008; Stokes et al. 2013.
10. Lins de Silva 2014.
11. Boas 2016; Greene 2011; Greene 2019.
12. Morgan 2011.
13. Hagopian 1996; Levitsky 2003.
14. Diniz 1982; Leal 1949; Weitz-Shapiro 2012. As one important example, the most encompassing tome to date on mass politics in Latin America, an authoritative edited volume entitled *The Latin American Voter*, contains a chapter on clientelism but nothing on other intermediary forms, such as mass media or discussion (Carlin, Singer, and Zechmeister 2015; Kitschelt and Altamirano 2015). Of course, one of us was more than honored to contribute to this volume (Baker and Greene 2015).

15. Calvo and Murillo 2019, 76–81; Gonzalez-Ocantos et al. 2012; Imai, Park, and Greene 2015.

16. Calvo and Murillo 2019, chap. 6; Greene 2020.

17. Diaz-Cayeros, Estévez, and Magaloni 2016; Stokes et al. 2013.

18. Cf. Szwarcberg 2014.

19. Beck and Gunther 2016, 51; Cleary and Stokes 2006, 130–38.

20. Hughes 2006; Lima 1988; Porto 2012.

21. Beck and Gunther 2016, 25.

22. Boas 2005; Geers and Bos 2017; Lawson and McCann 2005.

23. Siegel 2013, 786 (italics in the original).

24. Druckman and Nelson 2003.

25. Baker, Ames, and Rennó 2006; Flores-Macías 2009. The same is true about clientelism. Comparing the vote choices of payoff recipients to those of non-recipients is a poor way to assess the effectiveness and impact of the practice. If payoff recipients spread the favorable word about the payoff to social contacts, they may convert others to the machine's partisan message, which weakens the relationship between exposure and change in political attitudes. (This is one example of a violation of the stable unit treatment value assumption.) This model of clientelistic influence is the focus of chapter 7.

26. Cleary and Stokes 2006; Magalhães 2007; Zmerli and Castillo 2015.

27. Huckfeldt, Johnson, and Sprague 2004, 69.

28. Luna and Zechmeister 2005; Remmer 1991; Singer and Carlin 2013; Zechmeister 2008.

29. Collier and Collier 1991; Lipset and Rokkan 1967; Lupu and Stokes 2009; O'Donnell 1978.

30. Madsen and Snow 1991; Morgenstern and Zechmeister 2003.

31. Lupu 2016a; Samuels and Zucco 2015.

32. Bonner 1959, 4.

33. Kohler 2005.

34. Lazarsfeld, Berelson, and Gaudet 1944, 150.

35. Durkheim 1897, 320.

36. We can think of two sets of exceptions to this statement, but each constitutes only a small number of studies. First, a few studies, like this book, examine political-discussion effects (Ames, García-Sánchez, and Smith 2012; Crow and Pérez-Armendáriz 2018; Rojas 2008; Smith 2018; Torcal, Ruiz, and Maldonado 2017, chap. 7). Second, a smattering of studies considers social media and political behavior (Díaz-Domínguez and Moreno 2015; Gil de Zúñiga, Puig-I-Abril, and Rojas 2009; Iasulaitis 2013; Telles, Mundim, and Lopes 2013). There is also a research program on yard-sign displays, a form of social communication, but the literature treats this largely as a form of bottom-up communication to elites, not horizontal communication to peers (Nichter and Palmer-Rubin 2015).

37. Moreno and Mendizábal 2013; Straubhaar, Olsen, and Nunes 1993.

38. Karpowitz and Mendelberg 2014, 38.

39. Eveland and Thomson 2006; Mutz 2002b; Schmitt-Beck 2004.

40. Lawson 2002; Porto 2007.

41. Gentzkow and Shapiro 2011; Mutz and Martin 2001; Richardson and Beck 2007, 188–95.

42. Carlson and Settle 2016.

43. Auyero 2000; Stokes 2005.

44. Carlson 2019; Carlson 2017.

45. Abers 2000; Ahn, Huckfeldt, and Ryan 2014, 256.

46. Albuquerque 2002.

47. Bikhchandani, Hirshleifer, and Welch 1992; Mayer et al. 1990.

48. According to the network literature, a third possible mechanism of influence is social pressure. Social influence can occur when individuals feel pressured by socially communicated expectations that they internalize. Pressures to conform to a network norm can be strong and self-enforcing, as individuals wish to avoid embarrassment or the disappointment of others (Asch 1951; Milgram 1963; Noelle-Neumann 1984; Sinclair 2012). Despite this, our findings reveal minimal evidence of social pressure. The process of horizontal influence during Latin America's election campaigns involves genuine persuasion or reinforcement via open exchanges of political information.

49. Durlauf 2004.

50. Alt et al. 2020; Burnstein and Vinokur 1977.

51. Sunstein 2019, 6.

52. Downs 1957; Katz and Lazarsfeld 1955.

53. Ahn, Huckfeldt, and Ryan 2014, 145–46.

54. Dixit and Londregan 1996; Stokes 2005.

55. Cox and McCubbins 1986; Diaz-Cayeros, Estévez, and Magaloni 2016.

56. Schattschneider 1960, 35.

57. Ratliffe Sontoro and Beck 2017, 384.

58. Blais 2004.

59. Bartels 2006; Erikson and Wlezien 2012, 141–44.

60. Huckfeldt, Mendez, and Osborn 2004; Klofstad, Sokhey, and McClurg 2013; Nir and Druckman 2008. See Sinclair (2012) for a study that does consider vote choice in the US as a dependent variable, and see Bello and Rolfe (2014) for one on the UK. Scholars of political discussion in the US have also generated valuable insights using simulations to model volatility in vote intentions (Huckfeldt, Johnson, and Sprague 2004, chap. 7). Perhaps because of the lack of variance in individual-level voter dynamics, empirical studies of social influence and political participation—a separate dependent variable for which there is tremendous variation in the US—have mushroomed (Campbell 2010; Rolfe 2012; Rolfe and Chan 2017).

61. Berelson, Lazarsfeld, and McPhee 1954; Lazarsfeld, Berelson, and Gaudet 1944.

62. Converse 1969; Lupu 2014; Lupu, Oliveros, and Schiumerini 2019; Mainwaring and Scully 1995.

63. Huckfeldt, Johnson, and Sprague 2004, 176; Smith 2015b.

64. Fischer 1982; Wellman and Leighton 1979.

65. Canache 1996.

66. Bridges 1987; Stokes et al. 2013.

67. Frank 2004; Metzl 2019; Schkade, Sunstein, and Hastie 2007.

68. Gutmann and Thompson 2004.

69. The two egos are not connected, which reflects a plausible assumption that the probability any two randomly chosen respondents know one another is zero.

70. Marsden 1987; Sokhey and Djupe 2014.

71. The exception occurs when we use the Comparative National Elections Project in chapter 2 for descriptive purposes. Its name generator does query social ties, but the follow-up name interpreter items gather political information.

72. Ames 2001b.

73. Ames et al. 2016.

74. Lawson et al. 2007.

75. See Fitzgerald and Curtis (2012) for an exception.

76. Beck et al. 2002, 66; Carrington, Scott, and Wasserman 2005, 6; Fowler et al. 2011, 444.

77. Lazarsfeld, Merton, and Berger 1954; McPherson, Smith-Lovin, and Cook 2001.

78. Some recent research on the US and the UK suggests that concerns about homophily in dynamic political networks might be overblown (Bello and Rolfe 2014; Eveland, Appiah, and Beck 2018; Klofstad, McClurg, and Rolfe 2009; Lazer et al. 2010). During campaigns, individuals do not seem to drop political discussants simply because they disagree (Sokhey, Baker, and Djupe 2015).

79. See Zuckerman, Fitzgerald, and Dasović (2005) for an example.

80. Forgas and Williams 2001, xvii.

81. Klar 2014; Levitan and Visser 2009.

82. Brady, Johnston, and Sides 2006, 13–14; Ratliffe Sontoro and Beck 2017, 400; Sinclair 2012, 80.

83. Sociocentric (also whole-network) studies of social influence in politics have also proliferated in recent years (Pietryka et al. 2018; Szwarcberg 2012a). These map out and consider as potential sources of influence all ties among subjects, showing (in relation to figure 1.5) ego's second-degree ties (an alter's alter) and those beyond as well as all possible connections among these added nodes. For our research goals, sociocentric data are far less useful than egocentric data. Sociocentric data are valuable for studying actors in small, well-bounded entities (e.g., a college dormitory or military squadron) because one must observe the population, not a sample (Crossley et al. 2015, 21). This makes sociocentric data impractical for studies of even moderately sized populations: "The external validity issue is perhaps the most significant limitation of the sociocentric research design . . . [e]gonet designs are more conducive to making inferences from samples to population" (Perry, Pescosolido, and Borgatti 2018, 25, 27). The strongest social influences, moreover, emanate from direct contacts rather than from those separated by two or more degrees, so our egonets data observe the most important influences on our main respondents.

84. Price, Nir, and Cappella 2006; Walsh 2004; Walsh 2012.

CHAPTER 2. LATIN AMERICAN POLITICAL DISCUSSION IN COMPARATIVE PERSPECTIVE

1. Verba, Nie, and Kim 1978.

2. Handlin 2017; MacKuen et al. 2010.

3. Harrison 1985.

4. We first calculate the mean in each country year and then take the average of these country-year means (each weighted equally) by world region. Note that we apply survey weights, when made available by survey administrators, for all analyses in this book.

5. The Western Europe category includes Australia and New Zealand, and the Eastern Europe category includes Kyrgyzstan.

6. We use results from the first panel waves for Brazil 2002 and Brazil 2014. As the pre-attrition, population-representative waves, these have the best sampling properties. For Brazil 2006, we use results from wave 5.

7. Since BEPS 2014 did not contain a query about neighbors, we do not calculate this mean for Brazil 2014, but we place these 2014 results roughly in the order they would appear based on the averages for family and friends. Brazil 2014 is not plotted in frame B because of this missing question.

8. Surprisingly, previous studies suggest that queries about important matters do not yield a longer list of discussants, so we do consider some cross-national results from queries like these as shadow comparisons (Huckfeldt and Mendez 2008; Klofstad, McClurg, and Rolfe 2009).

9. Mutz 2002a.

10. In a previous publication (Ames, Baker, and Smith 2017), we erroneously reported the Brazil 2002 mean as 1.71. This underestimate was based on a coding error. About 900 respondents were newly added to the panel study in the campaign wave, but they were not asked the name-generator battery. Unfortunately, in Ames, Baker, and Smith (2017), we mistakenly treated all of them as singletons—meaning they were coded as having zero discussants—rather than dropping them from the calculation as we correctly do here.

11. Gibson 2001, 57.

12. These issues notwithstanding, our indicators of discussion frequency have good measurement validity. On the grounds of criterion-related validity, survey measures of discussion frequency and network size in the US correlate at the individual level with a variety of political behaviors that they should predict, such as political knowledge and political participation (Eveland and Thomson 2006; Leighley 1990). They also correlate with one another, and some evidence suggests that the propensity to discuss politics is related to stable personality traits (Eveland and Hively 2009; Hibbing, Ritchie, and Anderson 2011). These signs of measurement validity hold up in our data as well. In the Mexico 2006 Panel, for example, *Frequency of political discussion* and *Egocentric network size* have a polychoric correlation of +0.58 in the campaign wave and +0.72 in the election wave. Perhaps more important, each shows a high degree of test-retest reliability, evidence that they are capturing a stable behavioral propensity. The polychoric correlation between repeated measures of network size when administered two months apart is +0.79, and those between three repeated measures of discussion frequency average +0.66.

13. Fischer 2009; Krosnick 1999.

14. Eveland, Appiah, and Beck 2018. Research suggests that individuals in modern societies have roughly 70–130 people that they maintain as contacts (Eveland, Appiah, and Beck 2018; Eveland, Hutchens, and Morey 2013; Hill and Dunbar 2003; Roberts et al. 2009). At the same time, short name generators like ours remain useful because core networks (also "support cliques"), which are composed of contacts that provide egos with nearly daily conversation, emotional support, and advice, average just five alters in size (Dunbar and Spoors 1995). In short, network name generators undoubtedly underestimate network size, but they do capture the intimate and (thus) most influential ties.

15. Arias et al. 2019. Families are finite in size, yet relatives tend to be mentioned early in name generators. Thus capping egocentric network size at three (or four or five) underestimates the share of friends in the true network (Eveland and Hively 2009). Nonetheless, the shares that we report and that Gibson reports remain useful for understanding the ratio of relatives to nonrelatives in the core network.

16. Ames, Baker, and Smith 2017, 860.

17. Just one of these terms ("rarely") is unrooted in a concrete time interval, but its placement between "a few days a month" and "never" allowed respondents—and thereby allows us—to loosely translate it into a concrete rate.

18. Admittedly, asking respondents to estimate and report a more precise rate of political discussion ("once a month" or "once a week") can be fraught with respondents' recall biases, innumeracy, and differing understandings of what is political (Fitzgerald 2013; Lawrence and Sides 2014). Remember, however, that these items have good measurement validity.

19. Respondents could list two news shows, but we use the one they watched the most. The response options are not identical to those for discussion frequency, so we take some liberties in numerically equating "a few days a month" with "once a week" and in equating "sometimes" with "rarely." On its face, equating "sometimes" with "rarely" may seem the more problematic of the two decisions. This is defensible, however, given the relative placement in their respective lists of these options—in between once a week/few times a month and never.

20. Price and Zaller 1993.

21. Schmitt-Beck 2004.

22. DeMars 2010.

23. To ensure readability in the figure, we multiply the original *Contacted by party* and *Payoff by party* variables, which range from 0 to 1, by 10.

24. Dunbar et al. 2015, 39.

25. Bisbee and Larson 2017; Bond et al. 2012; Gil de Zúñiga, Puig-I-Abril, and Rojas 2009; Ho and McLeod 2008; Min 2007.

26. Beck and Gunther 2016, 37.

27. Moreno and Mendizábal 2013, 423.

28. Díaz-Domínguez and Moreno 2015, 247.

29. Calvo 2015.

30. Marshall 2018.

31. Downs 1957.

32. Huckfeldt 2001.

33. The pre-campaign wave's measure is the purest one because it is untainted by panel conditioning (i.e., main respondents learning the answers before the election wave precisely because they were asked the question). The only reason to prefer the election-wave measure of main respondents' knowledge is that it would carry the same period effect as the measure of discussants' knowledge. Perhaps information about these items was higher just after the election. The three items, however, had virtually nothing to do with the campaign. As it turns out, both the panel conditioning and period effect, if present at all, appear to be weak: reinterviewed main respondents improved their scores by only 1/17th of a standard deviation.

34. Bias in sampling coverage among our discussants could also increase the gap in knowledge between the full sample of egos and the full sample of alters. If discussants'

selection into our sample was positively correlated with political knowledge, then the gap would be artificially widened. One reassuring fact that refutes this is that our response rates for the discussant interviews, which were brief and occurred over the phone, were extremely high, greater than 80 percent.

35. Ahn, Huckfeldt, and Ryan 2014, 14.

36. For consistency, we maintain the "main respondent" label for CNEP respondents, although for the CNEP the qualifier "main" is superfluous since there is no sample of discussant respondents. Note that CNEP interviews are sometimes collected before and sometimes after the relevant election.

37. Huckfeldt, Johnson, and Sprague 2004.

38. Eveland and Hively 2009. Political disagreement holds a central causal position in the literature on a variety of other political behaviors, such as political demobilization (Mutz 2002a), political tolerance (Mutz 2002b), ambivalence about candidates (Huckfeldt, Mendez, and Osborn 2004), and delayed vote decisions (Nir and Druckman 2008).

39. Monnoyer-Smith and Talpin 2010, 252.

40. Bishop 2008; Finifter 1974; Mutz 2006, 43.

41. Mutz 2002b.

42. Keith et al. 1992; Klar and Krupnikov 2016.

43. Samuels and Zucco 2018.

44. Klofstad, Sokhey, and McClurg 2013.

45. Mutz 2006.

46. Huckfeldt, Johnson, and Sprague 2004.

47. Aside from this theoretical ambivalence, practical considerations also exist. An analysis based on the restrictive definition would drop this dyad because of its definitional ambiguity. An analysis based on the inclusive definition, however, poses apples-and-oranges problems in cross-national comparisons because of cross-national differences in rates of abstention and tendencies to express nonopinionation.

48. This is a quote from a newspaper article (Alves 2018, 3).

49. Because we use proxy reports, nonopinionated discussants are those who had preferences their main respondents did not know or who main respondents said were undecided/abstaining. Also, because we are working with the restrictive definition, we limit the sample to opinionated main respondents. We use campaign-wave data in all four instances.

50. Eveland, Appiah, and Beck 2018.

51. Mutz 2006, 39–41.

52. The CNEP battery is executed in a unique way that complicates cross-national comparability at the egocentric-network level (e.g., not all respondents have spouses). We thus discuss results at the dyadic level.

53. Huckfeldt, Ikeda, and Pappi 2005.

54. This is measured using official election returns.

55. Laakso and Taagepera 1979.

56. Independent candidate Ross Perot won 19 percent of the vote in 1992, and that election had 2.8 effective parties.

57. Rates of agreement are higher between spouses than they are in any other kind of dyad. Rates of agreement in the spousal dyads exceed 0.75 in most countries, but they range from 0.55 to 0.75 for most non-spousal dyads. Worldwide, individuals encounter more disagreement outside their marriages than they do within.

58. Bello and Rolfe 2014, 135.

59. Feldman 2011.

60. Mutz and Martin 2001.

61. Magalhães 2007.

62. Mutz and Martin 2001, 103.

63. Ross, Greene, and House 1977.

64. Beck et al. 2002, 65.

65. Huckfeldt and Sprague 1995, 153–55; Mutz 2006, 25; Sinclair 2012, 84.

66. Usually, there are fewer opportunities to be wrong in the US than in Latin America. In a typical two-party US election, a random guesser (who guessed the candidates at the rate of their national vote totals) would be accurate about her discussant roughly 50 percent of the time. This 1992 election in the US, however, was a three-candidate affair, so a random-guesser in 1992 would have been correct just 30 percent of the time, virtually the same baseline as in Brazil 2002. Furthermore, our figures for Brazil may slightly underestimate accuracy if alters misreported their own first-round vote choices. Because Lula won the second round just before the discussant interviews, there is risk of an overreport of Lula votes owing to a post-election bandwagon effect (Atkeson 1999).

CHAPTER 3. VOTER VOLATILITY AND STABILITY IN PRESIDENTIAL CAMPAIGNS

1. Zechmeister 2019, 239.

2. Cohen, Salles Kobilanski, and Zechmeister 2018; Roberts and Wibbels 1999.

3. Mainwaring, Gervasoni, and España-Najera 2017, 626–27; Roberts 2014, 35.

4. Huntington 1991.

5. Mainwaring, Gervasoni, and España-Najera 2017.

6. Converse 1969; Dalton and Weldon 2007; Norris 2004.

7. Mainwaring, Gervasoni, and España-Najera 2017, 632.

8. Mainwaring 2018a.

9. Lupu 2015, 235.

10. Cox 1997.

11. Huckfeldt, Johnson, and Sprague 2004, 176.

12. Mainwaring, Gervasoni, and España-Najera 2017.

13. Birnir 2007; Mainwaring, Gervasoni, and España-Najera 2017; Roberts and Wibbels 1999. For instance, virtually all the independent variables considered in the authoritative and sweeping *Latin American Voter* are factors—such as gender, ethnicity, religion, and incumbent performance—that change at most glacially during campaigns (Carlin, Singer, and Zechmeister 2015). The retrospective-voting school attributes voting outcomes to year-on-year changes in the macroeconomy (Gélineau and Singer 2015), while the structuralist tradition in Latin American politics sees voting behavior as the product of group material interests such as class or ethnicity (Mainwaring, Torcal, and Somma 2015).

14. Jennings and Wlezien 2018.

15. Mainwaring 2018a, 45.

16. Samuels 2006.

17. Baker and Dorr 2019; Carreirão and Kinzo 2004; Samuels and Zucco 2018. See Baker and Renno (2019) on the large effects that question wording can yield for these estimates. They make the case that the permissive metric is more valid.

18. Desposato and Scheiner 2008.

19. This result is from the four-city survey used in Baker (2009).

20. Ames, Baker, and Rennó 2008.

21. Almeida 2006.

22. Samuels and Zucco 2018.

23. Keck 1992; Samuels and Zucco 2015.

24. Lupu 2016b.

25. Baker et al. 2016.

26. This combination—two-party dominance in presidential elections with extreme fragmentation in the legislature—"is rare and perhaps unique in the history of presidential democracies" (Mainwaring, Power, and Bizzarro 2018, 174).

27. Braga and Pimentel 2011

28. Baker and Dorr 2019; Moreno 2018, 44.

29. Kitschelt et al. 2010, 320; Levitsky, Loxton, and Van Dyck 2016.

30. Bruhn 1997.

31. Greene and Sánchez-Talanquer 2018, 202.

32. Greene and Sánchez-Talanquer 2018, 201–2.

33. Green, Palmquist, and Schickler 2002; McCann and Lawson 2003.

34. Baker and Dorr 2019.

35. Moreno 2018, 44. This is according to the permissive definition.

36. Election panel studies have also been conducted in Costa Rica, El Salvador, and Uruguay, but the raw data for these are not yet publically available.

37. Erikson and Wlezien 2012, 9; Stimson 2004, 112.

38. Ames et al. 2010.

39. Rennó 2018.

40. Lawson et al. 2001.

41. Lawson et al. 2013.

42. Greene, Simpser, and Ponce 2018.

43. Lupu et al. 2015. For APES 2015, we drop campaign-wave respondents who reported a vote in the national primary for a candidate who lost the nomination in the primary and ultimately did not run in the general election. To be clear, the campaign-wave measure for Argentina is not a question about vote intentions in the general election, so users of this panel dataset treat self-reported vote in the national primary as the campaign-wave measure of general-election vote intention (Greene 2019; Lupu, Oliveros, and Schiumerini 2019; Weitz-Shapiro and Winters 2019).

44. For any given panel study, the number of possible dyads is $N(N-1)/2$, where N is the number of waves.

45. Clarke et al. 2004, 143; Erikson and Wlezien 2012, 144. In an exception that supports the rule, Bello and Rolfe (2014) find that 25 percent of British voters crossed party lines at least once before the 2010 election, a rate seemingly comparable to those in our two countries. This figure, however, is calculated over four panel waves and nine months. In BEPS 2014, roughly 40 percent of respondents switched at least once across four interviews conducted over just five months.

46. Blais 2004; Geers and Bos 2017.

47. For Brazil 2018, the figure may be slightly inflated by the fact that the PT's eventual candidate, Fernando Haddad, was not formally nominated until midway through the campaign, although the wording of the question we use does simulate an election that includes him as a candidate. Much of the change we observe occurred

via movement toward Bolsonaro during the campaign, something echoed in aggregate polling.

48. We use locally weighted scatterplot smoothing (LOWESS) to estimate the smoothed lines.

49. Party ideology scores are based on Wiesehomeier and Benoit (2009).

50. Erikson and Wlezien 2012, 44–46.

51. We cannot just attribute this to the balance of campaign advertising in the HEG, which favored the candidates from these two parties. By law, Serra did have twice as much advertising time as Ciro and Lula, but Ciro and Lula had roughly the same amount as each other.

52. Hunter 2010.

53. Apfeld and Branham 2016.

54. Cornejo 2018; Weitz-Shapiro and Winters 2019.

55. Moser and Scheiner 2012.

56. Duverger 1954, 240.

57. Cox 1997, 137.

58. Cox 1997, chap. 6.

59. Instituto Datafolha 2014.

60. Greene 2007, chap. 7; Magaloni and Poiré 2004.

61. Schussman and Earl 2004; Tsang and Larson 2016.

CHAPTER 4. DISCUSSION NETWORKS, CAMPAIGN EFFECTS, AND VOTE CHOICE

1. Our systematic coding of media content confirms that Ciro received the most negative coverage (Baker, Ames, and Rennó 2006, 397).

2. Eveland and Hively 2009.

3. This critique of conflation was made in Baker, Ames, and Rennó 2006, 385; see also Eveland and Hively 2009, 207; Nir 2005, 426.

4. Berelson, Lazarsfeld, and McPhee 1954, 126.

5. Lazarsfeld, Berelson, and Gaudet 1944, 53.

6. It is the standard $1 - D$ measure of heterogeneity, where D is Simpson's index of diversity.

7. Recall that, in the main text, we use the restrictive definition of agreement. This means that singletons are main respondents with no discussants or with no opinionated discussants. Similarly, nonopinionated discussants do not figure in the disagreement and diversity calculations; they are dropped. When we use the inclusive definition for results reported in appendix A, nonopinionated discussants are treated as if they hold a valenced choice that is different from all available candidates when calculating the three variables.

8. Visser and Mirabile 2004.

9. Centola 2018.

10. Huckfeldt, Johnson, and Sprague 2004.

11. For Brazil 2014, it is change between $c4$ or $c5$ and $e6$. We also estimated models using change between $c2$ or $c3$ and $e6$; they confirmed the main hypotheses.

12. There is one exception to this. In the election wave of BEPS 2014, respondents were asked to give the vote choices of the discussants they had named in the most re-

cent wave in which they participated *unless* this was wave *c5*—in which case they were asked about an earlier wave's discussants.

13. Perry, Pescosolido, and Borgatti 2018, 254; Rogowski and Sinclair 2017.

14. This addresses the homophily confound in a less satisfying way because homophily-minded main respondents can reshuffle their networks as a result of exogenous preference change, although evidence from four different countries suggests that this rarely occurs (Bello and Rolfe 2014). A big advantage of this measurement approach is that it provides valuable information about network stability, on which we have reported elsewhere (Sokhey, Baker, and Djupe 2015).

15. Beck and Heidemann 2014.

16. Moehler and Allen 2016. As an important accounting device, the models include *Unexposed to media* and *Unexposed to TV news* for Brazil 2002 and Mexico 2006, respectively. They each also include a measure of exposure to uncoded media sources. With the inclusion of these two extra variables per model, the implied baseline to which the coefficient on disagreeing media is compared is exposure to agreeing (and coded) media.

17. All measures of vertical intermediation are taken from election-wave reports.

18. The models of the Two-City Panel include a city fixed effect as well.

19. Many voters with agreement-only networks nonetheless switch (e.g., the minimum probability for Brazil 2002 is 0.23). Why? Disagreement is not the only game in town. Many main respondents changed in unison with their entire networks. In Brazil 2002, for example, 22 percent of all of Ciro's campaign-wave supporters adhered to the following trend: they had a completely agreeing, homogeneous pro-Ciro network in the campaign wave but switched to a new candidate in full unanimity with their network by election day.

20. The statistical power to test this hypothesis is too limited in the two-discussant, Brazil 2014 data.

21. Zaller 1992.

22. They also contain fixed effects for campaign-wave vote intentions.

23. Gay 1994, 110; Muñoz 2018; Nichter 2018.

24. The minor catch is that we need to make a simple correction for the statistical nonindependence introduced by the inclusion of the same ego multiple times. We cluster standard errors on main respondents.

25. Christakis and Fowler 2007.

26. A more aggregated means of accomplishing this at the ego level is employed in chapters 5 and 6. To avoid redundancy, we do not report such results in this chapter.

27. Election-day voters for minor-party candidates are dropped from all dyadic analyses. Sample sizes are too small to enable estimation of these coefficients.

28. "None" is defined inclusively, as alters who are nonopinionated because of abstention, indecision, or an ego's failure to perceive their opinions. In some years *Alter vote choice = other* is also included.

29. For Mexico 2006, a research assistant manually coded, based on the first-name reports by main respondents, which discussants were named in both waves (Sokhey, Baker, and Djupe 2015). Our dyadic analyses contain only these alters.

30. French 1956; Friedkin and Johnsen 2011, 46.

31. With the inclusion of these lags of the dependent variable and the lagged and contemporaneous measures of alter preferences, our dyadic models follow the logic of

an autoregressive distributed lag model, a flexible dynamic panel model that makes fewer assumptions than many standard specifications (De Boef and Keele 2008).

32. We also estimated models that include measures of vertical intermediation. Given our null results on these measures in the individual-level models, we were not surprised when they did not affect the main findings on social influence. We thus proceed with these more trim models.

33. When a confidence interval on one of these variables for an irrelevant option does include zero or the other point estimate, it does not necessarily undermine our claims about direction of social influence. According to the bottom half of the Mexico 2006 frame, for example, an AMLO discussant is not more important than a Calderón discussant in influencing the relative probability of a Madrazo versus a Calderón vote, even though a Madrazo discussant clearly is. Notice in the top half that an AMLO discussant *does* make a difference over a Calderón discussant in influencing the probability of a vote for the former relative to the latter.

34. Manski 1993.

35. Shalizi and Thomas 2011.

36. Lyons 2011.

37. VanderWeele 2011; VanderWeele and Arah 2011.

38. We use the *Relationship to discussant* variable introduced in chapter 2. Recall that we treat relative and friend as complements, meaning an alter is either a relative or a friend, unless the main respondent's answer to this question is missing or unclear.

39. Note the statistically significant coefficient on *Alter.vote.choice$_e$* in table A.10.

40. Instituto Datafolha 2002.

41. Ng 2001; Sinclair 2012, chap. 1.

42. Festinger 1954; Hardin and Higgins 1996; Stangor, Sechrist, and Jost 2001, 238.

43. Instituto Datafolha 2002.

44. These calculations are limited to twice-opinionated voters.

45. This is a familiar relationship in other countries (Dassonneville 2012). In the US scholars have found that "the well-informed are the most difficult to influence" (Ahn, Huckfeldt, and Ryan 2014, 108). The least politically aware have the smallest stores of background knowledge and, in practice, the weakest motivation to resist new persuasive information (Zaller 1992, chap. 7).

46. Centola 2018, 53–56; Galam and Jacobs 2007; Glaeser, Sacerdote, and Scheinkman 1996.

47. Price and Stone 2004.

48. Lazarsfeld, Berelson, and Gaudet 1944.

49. The one exception is Brazil 2006, for which we only have a campaign and an election wave. For Brazil 2014, we use the pre-campaign, the *c2* or *c3*, and the *e6* waves.

50. These are analogous to once- plus twice-opinionated voters in chapter 3.

51. Recall that nonvoters are dropped from both tallies. These probabilities are derived from binary logit models with political knowledge as an independent variable. The only other independent variables are candidate fixed effects for vote intention in the models on always-opinionated samples. This rids the estimates of the confound of demographic differences in candidates' vote bases.

52. In the first week of interviews for the campaign wave, Ciro polled between 25 and 30 percent in our sample, but in the final week he polled near 15 percent.

53. The "Serra02" outlier in figure 4.8 seemingly undermines this claim, but its extremity on the x-axis is actually driven by polling in Juiz de Fora, where pro-Serra discussants were needles in a haystack because of his deep unpopularity. (Chapter 5 discusses the two cities' political leanings.) In fact, a closer look at the Serra case supports our implication that pro-Serra discussants appeared more frequently than their sheer supply in the social environment would dictate. In Caxias do Sul, where Serra ultimately polled more closely to his national average, Ciro's mid-campaign supporters *did* face more disagreement (0.36) than Serra's mid-campaign supporters (0.33), even though Ciro supporters were more prevalent in the city (34 percent versus 24 percent, according to our campaign-wave polling). Similarly, mid-campaign Serra supporters in Juiz de Fora faced higher rates of disagreement (0.46) than did Ciro supporters (0.33), but this gap is smaller than the difference in discussant supply would dictate. Ciro supporters were nearly 2.5 times as prevalent (24 percent versus 10 percent according to our campaign-wave polling) as Serra supporters.

54. The partial correlation between the two variables in figure 4.8 falls by just 16 points (to +0.63) when we account for partisanship, which we measure as the proportion of the electorate that identifies with the candidate's party.

55. Huckfeldt and Sprague 1995, 123.

CHAPTER 5. NEIGHBORHOODS AND CITIES AS ARENAS OF SOCIAL INFLUENCE

1. Arias 2009; Gay 1994.

2. Just 20 percent of neighborhood-effects studies have an average neighborhood sample size of 100 or more (Arcaya et al. 2016, 21–22).

3. Sampson, Morenoff, and Gannon-Rowley 2002, 474.

4. Dietz 2002, 541; see also Sampson, Morenoff, and Gannon-Rowley 2002, 470; Sharkey and Faber 2014, 562–67.

5. Sinclair 2012, 36.

6. Canache 1996, 553; Córdova and Layton 2016.

7. Perlman 1976; Villarreal and Silva 2006.

8. Erbring and Young 1979, 401; Hauser 1974; Wilson 1987.

9. Brock and Durlauf 2002, 248; Cox 1969.

10. Books and Prysby 1991, 52.

11. Huckfeldt and Sprague 1995, 128.

12. King 1996, 160.

13. Eagles, Bélanger, and Calkins 2004.

14. Sinclair 2012, 133.

15. Fischer 1982; Wellman and Leighton 1979.

16. Johnston and Pattie 2006, 120–21.

17. Differences across the two cities (not reported) are negligible.

18. In a separate survey of JF residents conducted in 2008, Smith (2015a) found very similar numbers when asking respondents directly whether important-matters discussants lived in the same neighborhood. Seventy-eight percent of first-named discussants lived in the same neighborhood as the respondent, and the figures are 56 percent and 59 percent, respectively, for second- and third-named discussants.

19. Sharkey and Faber 2014, 569.

20. Gay 1994, 54–56.

21. Arias 2009; Vargas 2003.

22. Gay 1994, 111.

23. By contrast, the quest for club goods in Rio's *favelas*, documented by Gay, im-bued neighborhood leaders with "no allegiance to any politician, party, or ideology . . . beyond the dispute in question" (Gay 1994, 54–56).

24. Moreover, Caxias had enacted a participatory budgeting platform in the late 1990s, an idea that diffused from nearby state capital Porto Alegre and whose purpose was partly to combat the kind of clientelism that has been described in Rio de Janeiro (Baiocchi 2005). Participatory budgeting tends to marginalize municipal council mem-bers and state legislators, who can no longer focus on delivering petty pork barrel to targeted neighborhoods in exchange for votes.

25. Jencks and Mayer 1990.

26. Wittenberg 2006.

27. Feldmann 2002.

28. Gay 1994, 109.

29. Huckfeldt and Sprague 1995, chap. 12.

30. Alvarez 1990; Smith 2019.

31. See *Source of friends* in appendix B for question wording.

32. This is from the variable *Not contacted by party*. These contacts surely lack the intimacy and sustained nature of more informal social exchanges.

33. See *Meet with friends* in appendix B for question wording. Admittedly, atten-dance at religious services is relatively frequent (62 percent attend at least once per month), so this chapter does consider this vertical channel of political influence.

34. They are the Federal University of Juiz de Fora and the private University of Caxias do Sul.

35. Municipal statistics are from https://cidades.ibge.gov.br.

36. Ranincheski 1999; Trindade 1978.

37. Ames 2001a; Mainwaring 1999.

38. Feldmann 2002, 41–42.

39. The 1998 gubernatorial race also polarized between a *petista* (Olívio Dutra) and a *pemedebista* (Antônio Britto).

40. See *Partisanship* in appendix B for question wording. The next closest party (PDT) had just 2 percent.

41. These are based on respondent recall data from March/April 2002. See *Recall of 1998 presidential vote* and *Recall of 1998 gubernatorial vote* in appendix B for question wordings.

42. See *Recall of 2000 mayoral vote* in appendix B for question wordings.

43. This finding is from a crosstabulation of *Ego gubernatorial vote choice* and *Ego vote choice*.

44. This finding is from a crosstabulation of *Ego federal deputy vote choice* and *Ego vote choice*.

45. Ames, Baker, and Renno 2009.

46. Reis 1978.

47. Lupu 2014.

48. *Pemedebista* Tarcisio Delgado was the incumbent mayor as of 2002 and won 55 percent of the vote in the 2000 second round.

49. Ames, García-Sánchez, and Smith 2012.

50. We show in analyses elsewhere that only about 40 percent of these election-wave *petistas* reexpressed this partisanship 18 months later (Baker et al. 2016).

51. To clarify, these are *Feeling thermometer scores* adjusted for the response-set problem (and then standardized merely to aid interpretability). The presence of response set is manifest in the fact that respondents give average scores across the battery of feeling thermometers that vary by respondents, not just by party. Most telling, all five (pre-campaign wave) party feeling thermometer scores are, at the individual level, positively correlated with one another (Green 1988). To address this, we convert each party score to a deviation from the respondent's mean score across all five parties. We then take the merely cosmetic step of standardizing these deviations.

52. The mild asymmetry within Caxias—meaning the slightly lower rate of disdain that *petistas* have for the PMDB than the disdain that *pemedebistas* hold for the PT—is due to the fact that the PMDB does not unite and represent the anti-left to the same extent that the PT unites the left. The overall correlation between the PT and PMDB adjusted feeling thermometer scores is twice as strong in Caxias (–0.54) as it is in JF (–0.28).

53. In each city respondent selection followed a multistage cluster sampling approach. In the first stage we randomly selected 22 neighborhoods, weighting their probability of selection by population size. In the second stage we randomly chose between two and ten census tracts (*setores*) per neighborhood. Finally, within the selected census tracts, enumerators chose interviewees at every sixth residence using the most-recent-birthday technique. Our numerical target was roughly 100 pre-campaign-wave interviews per neighborhood, with a few more populous neighborhoods getting 200 or even 300 interviews.

54. Even these correlations surely overstate things, as it is a stretch to suggest that any neighborhoods in JF had PT leanings when the party was receiving less than 20 percent of the overall vote in nearly every neighborhood.

55. For use in regressions below, we standardize this variable by city.

56. We define these as the top tercile and bottom tercile, respectively, of neighborhoods on *Neighborhood PT support*.

57. In the end, the correlation in Caxias between 1998 and 2002 vote returns at the neighborhood level is +0.98.

58. We cannot conduct a formal mediation analysis because **M** includes multiple variables (Baron and Kenny 1986).

59. We introduce this new way of measuring network preferences—one that is different from those used in the preceding chapter—out of necessity. Here, we are working at the ego level, so the dyadic measures are not workable. At the same time, recall that the network measures in the ego-level analyses of the preceding chapter were apartisan, capturing only agreement or disagreement with the main respondent rather than partisan leanings. We thus use measures that, collectively, capture the distribution of candidate preferences within each main respondent's network (Lerman, Yan, and Wu 2016). The dependent variables sum to one under the restrictive definition of disagreement, which means nonopinionated discussants are dropped. In results not shown, the substantive findings are invariant to the inclusion of nonopinionated discussants and to the use of the inclusive definition of disagreement.

60. Huckfeldt and Sprague 1988.

61. Oakes 2004.

62. Mayer and Jencks 1989; Tiebout 1956.

63. In essence, we are suggesting that models 1 and 2 suffer from omitted-variable bias.

64. King 1996.

65. To reduce clutter, coefficients for Ciro vote are not shown. Ciro was a candidate in 1998, so we did run models that used Ciro vote in 1998 as a measure of neighborhood leanings toward him. He performed so poorly in Caxias in both years, however, that variation in neighborhood support was not meaningful and predictive of behavior.

66. We cannot entirely distinguish between the top-down effects of clergy leadership and the more bottom-up effects of evangelical identity itself. Garotinho did not campaign on any explicit evangelical platform, and in fact such a thing did not really exist at the national level in Brazil at the time.

CHAPTER 6. DISCUSSION AND THE REGIONALIZATION OF VOTER PREFERENCES

1. Huckfeldt and Sprague 1995, 160.

2. Axelrod 1997.

3. Jones and Mainwaring 2003; Morgenstern 2017.

4. Along with poverty, inequality is also distinctly worse in the North and Northeast. In 2004 the Gini coefficient was above 0.55 in all but one state in the Northeast, while in the rest of the country only the Federal District had a Gini above 0.55.

5. Lavareda 1991.

6. Ames 2001a, 21.

7. Singer 2012; Zucco 2008.

8. Hunter and Power 2007; Soares and Terron 2008; Zucco and Power 2013.

9. In contrast, just 8 percent of São Paulo residents earned the minimum (Foguel, Ramos, and Carneiro 2001).

10. Sperandio et al. 2017.

11. Góes and Karpowicz 2017.

12. Corrêa 2015.

13. Hunter 2010.

14. Alves and Hunter 2017; Montero 2012.

15. In 2014 Dilma's greatest challenge in the North was from Marina, who attracted votes more as a favorite daughter of the region than for her programmatic stances.

16. For example, the city legalized gay marriage in 2009.

17. Domínguez and McCann 1996; Klesner 1993; Magaloni 1999; Poiré 1999.

18. Lawson 2006, 2, 4; see also Klesner 2007.

19. Klesner 1995, 143.

20. At the state level the correlation between AMLO's 2006 and 2018 vote shares is +0.78, and that between his 2012 and 2018 vote shares is +0.76. The upward shift in his returns was slightly larger for AMLO in northern states than it was in southern ones and Mexico City, hence the increase in the nationalization of his returns. Likewise, the PAN performed similarly by state ($r = +0.73$) to its lackluster 2012 showing.

21. Magaloni 2006, 95–97.

22. Greene 2007.

23. Ames 1970.

24. Klesner 1995; Klesner 2004.

25. Domínguez and McCann 1996; Magaloni 1999.

26. Przeworski and Teune 1970.

27. Huckfeldt, Ikeda, and Pappi 2005.

28. Baker and Scheiner 2007.

29. Katz and King 1999; Philips, Rutherford, and Whitten 2016.

30. For Brasília and Mexico City, these are technically preferences at the level of the Federal District.

31. Recall that Marina switched parties between 2010 and 2014, but she contested both elections.

32. Both countries also include *State other candidate support*.

33. As in the preceding chapter, we run fractional multinomial logit models.

34. Unlike the prototypical northern state, Roraima is composed mostly of immigrants from other states, and it lacks the political traditions, especially the dominant families, that characterize other states in the region.

35. She had a nationalization score of 0.81 versus the PSDB's 0.79 and the PT's 0.86.

36. Guerrero was not only the strongest PRD state in 2000 but also one of the strongest PRI states.

37. Lawson 2002.

38. Ames 1994.

CHAPTER 7. CLIENTELISM AS THE PURCHASE OF SOCIAL INFLUENCE

1. Barabási 2014, 139.

2. Gans-Morse, Mazzuca, and Nichter 2014.

3. Calvo and Murillo 2013.

4. Gonzalez-Ocantos et al. 2012; Imai, Park, and Greene 2015.

5. Stokes 2005, 315.

6. Dixit and Londregan 1996; Stokes 2005.

7. Stokes et al. 2013, chap. 2.

8. See also Greene 2020.

9. Stokes et al. 2013, 66.

10. Cox and McCubbins 1986; Diaz-Cayeros, Estévez, and Magaloni 2016; Gans-Morse, Mazzuca, and Nichter 2014, 4.

11. Magaloni 2006; Nichter 2008.

12. If voters who were strong supporters in election $t-1$ find themselves on the fence in election t because the party has ignored them since $t-1$, then they are no longer strong supporters—they are now swing voters. A machine that gives them favors is thus pursuing a vote-buying, rather than a maintenance-buying, strategy.

13. Faughnan and Zechmeister 2011; Nichter 2018; Stokes et al. 2013, 66–72.

14. Verba, Nie, and Kim 1978.

15. Stokes et al, 2013, chap. 3.

16. Szwarcberg 2012b.

17. Stokes et al. 2013, 54–66.

18. Calvo and Murillo 2013, 855; Cruz, Labonne, and Querubín 2017.

19. Among other labels, partisan networks are variously referred to as "problem-solving networks" (Auyero 2000, 57; Levitsky 2003; Nichter and Peress 2017; Szwarcberg 2012a), "a loyal network of supporters" (Hicken 2011, 297), and in Japan *kōenkai* networks (Scheiner 2006, 71).

20. To simplify the presentation, frame A does not depict the operative's selection decision. This would entail adding more nodes. Some would be clients, like the one depicted, with the vertical directional ties drawn to the operative. Others would be non-clients, meaning they were not selected and thus have no ties to the operative.

21. Anderson 2010; Kitschelt 2000; Weyland 1996. In this formulation horizontal networking and persuasion, if it occurs at all, is considered "outsourcing," whereby operatives use their payoffs to create new mini-activists who will canvass and turn out non-client voters (Stokes et al. 2013, 72–73). Another argument that comes close to incorporating informal horizontal influence is that of Ronconi and Zarazaga (2019), who show that party machines give enticements to individuals residing in households with lots of adults so as to attract support from the largest possible voting-age population. Ronconi and Zarazaga do not specify, however, whether the influence occurs via conversational persuasion by the direct recipient of the payoff or because all family members benefit from the payoff.

22. Research on clientelism shows that machine operatives are deeply embedded in and knowledgeable about their local communities, so they typically can identify the hubs in the community's informal networks: "Brokers are engaged in sustained and frequent interactions with voters, observing their individual behavior and gaining knowledge of their inclinations and preferences" (Stokes et al. 2013, 75; see also Camp 2017, Holland and Palmer-Rubin 2015). Indeed, that is precisely why patrons and machines hire or draft particular brokers. They have effectively gathered information in their neighborhoods and know how to resolve the machine's own information problem about voters (Auyero 2000; Szwarcberg 2012a). Facts about potential clients are "basic craft knowledge," so operatives know who wields social influence, even in informal conversational networks (Stokes et al. 2013, 102).

23. A previous version of this chapter (Schaffer and Baker 2015) borrowed a term from economics and called this the "social multiplier" (Becker and Murphy 2000; Glaeser, Sacerdote, and Scheinkman 2003). In economics, however, the social multiplier refers to something slightly different: the fact that peers' possession of an attribute increases the utility one experiences from also adopting that attribute. In the 1980s, for example, the more one's contacts bought fax machines, the greater the value of getting a fax machine for oneself. Social multipliers can create cascades that are akin to social magnification, but the concepts are distinct. To avoid confusion, we now use social magnification effect.

24. Bikhchandani, Hirshleifer, and Welch 1992.

25. Huckfeldt and Sprague 1995, 230; see also Rosenstone and Hansen 1993, 29.

26. Some evidence from Mexico suggests that machines engage in a competitive bidding process whereby "parties channeled gifts to voters who were already targeted by other parties" (Díaz-Cayeros, Estevez, and Magaloni 2009, 241). Among the existing arguments, ours makes the most sense of this double-targeting phenomenon: parties are competing for the proselytizing services of high-degree individuals.

27. Cruz 2019.

28. Finan and Schechter 2012; Lawson and Greene 2014.

29. Granovetter 1973.

30. Latin American Public Opinion Project (2010). The two Brazil panel studies used throughout this book do not have questions on clientelism.

31. Hatemi and McDermott 2012; Mondak 2010.

32. Admittedly, both of these measures of clientelistic payoffs are obtrusive—that is, they require respondents to admit openly that they were offered or received a benefit. As a result, they are subject to underreporting from social desirability bias. Unfortunately, unobtrusive measures like list experiments that protect respondents from confessing to the interviewer are unavailable or implemented poorly in many countries. Still, the obtrusive measures are defensible. Neither wording asks citizens whether they *complied* with a payoff. The wording merely queries whether respondents were offered or given a payoff. This wording—especially LAPOP's use of "offered"—puts the illegality and shame of the matter strictly on the broker, mitigating social undesirability. In fact, in LAPOP the percentages of "yes" answers to these questions in Argentina (18 percent), Mexico (17 percent), and several other countries are close to the 24 percent that Gonzalez-Ocantos et al. (2012, 210) found in Nicaragua and the 20 percent that Imai et al. (2015) found in Mexico using *unobtrusive* measures.

33. We could have controlled for whether the respondent voted in the previous election, but this may have been the election in which the clientelist payment motivated the respondent to turn out. Given the available data, the better approach is to model each respondent's underlying propensity to participate.

34. Martin 2003. See Schaffer and Baker (2015) for models with a longer list of covariates and with multiple imputation of missing values. Our main substantive findings do not change with these decisions.

35. Perhaps because the question wording queried gifts received rather than merely offered, this query returned a lower rate of positive responses (5 percent) than the LAPOP wording.

36. This is the predicted probability when the number of familial discussants is zero and strength of partisanship is at its mean.

37. We also ran ordered logit and Poisson regression models with control variables to assess the conclusions drawn from figure 7.5. The statistical significance tests led to identical conclusions. These are available upon request.

38. Kitschelt and Wilkinson 2007.

39. Weitz-Shapiro 2012.

40. Schaffer 2007, 191.

41. Desposato 2007; Greene 2007.

42. Auyero 1999, 326.

43. Barabási 2014, 139.

44. Kitschelt 2011; Stokes et al. 2013, chap. 6.

45. Dixit and Londregan 1996.

46. Stokes et al. 2013, 186.

47. International Telecommunication Union 2013.

48. Afrobarometer 2006.

CHAPTER 8. DISCUSSION, SOCIETAL EXCLUSION, AND POLITICAL VOICE

1. Wolak and Juenke 2020.

2. Lau, Andersen, and Redlawsk 2008.

3. Lau et al. 2014; Lyons, Jaeger, and Wolak 2013.

4. Djupe and Sokhey 2014, 200; Karpowitz and Mendelberg 2014.

5. Fishkin 2011; Gutmann and Thompson 2004.

6. Beck and Gunther 2016.

7. Brady, Verba, and Schlozman 1995; Conover, Searing, and Crewe 2002.

8. Sanders 1997, 349; Young 2000.

9. Karpowitz, Mendelberg, and Shaker 2012.

10. Brusco, Nazareno, and Stokes 2004; Calvo and Murillo 2004; Gibson and Calvo 2000.

11. For Mexico 2006, we use *Frequency of TV news consumption*.

12. Such a battery is unavailable in the Two-City Panel, so instead we use logged *Family income*. (We still refer to it as "wealth" for ease of exposition.)

13. This variable is continuous, since we average over multiple self reports (if interviewed repeatedly) as well as interviewer reports of race. To reduce measurement error, we use means across multiple panel waves for dependent and independent variables when available.

14. Boulding and Holzner 2016.

15. This question is not available for three of the ten elections.

16. Also, it is reassuring that these CNEP Mexico 2006 results yield the same substantive conclusions as do those from the Mexico 2006 Panel reported in frame D of figure 8.1, although the effect sizes are larger in the panel study than the CNEP.

17. Oddly, the minimum (CNEP) and maximum (panel study) of this range are both from the Mexico 2006 election. We suspect the difference lies in the fact that the independent and dependent variables are better measured in the panel study than in the CNEP. The panel study uses an asset indicator of wealth and a more diverse array of knowledge items.

18. We cannot rule out the possibility that some or even all of these gender knowledge gaps are artifacts of measurement (Mondak and Anderson 2004).

19. Baker and Velasco-Guachalla 2018; Boulding 2014; Boulding and Holzner 2016.

20. Desposato and Norrander 2009.

21. Lau and Redlawsk 1997.

22. Frank 2004; Metzl 2019.

23. Calvo, Escolar, and Pomares 2009; Lupia 1994.

24. Lau et al. 2014; Lau, Andersen, and Redlawsk 2008.

25. Sokhey and McClurg 2012.

26. Jackman and Sniderman 2006; Ryan 2011.

27. Our choice of issue spaces is informed by some simple multinomial logit models (with a dependent variable of vote choice) that reveal which survey items divided voters of different candidates. The precise items used vary by country and survey, but all are recoded to vary between a minimum of –1 and a maximum of +1. All items are weighted equally.

28. Enelow and Hinich 1982; Stokes 1963.

29. Philpot 2017; Silveira 1994.

30. Baker and Greene 2015; Zechmeister 2006.

31. Wiesehomeier and Benoit 2009.

32. Because of the possibility of strategic voting in the Mexico 2006 election (table 3.5), we include a question gauging the respondent's perception of Madrazo's probability of winning the election.

33. Previous research on Brazil 2002, including some conducted with our dataset, has found rates close to 70 percent (Bello 2016; Lau et al. 2014).

34. In all of the models, we include candidate fixed effects to control for whom the respondent actually voted on election day. We see the inclusion of these candidate fixed effects to be crucial for isolating the effects of the independent variables on correct voting. Given inevitable limitations and errors in the first step of the procedure, the omission of fixed effects creates an undesirable correlation between correct voting and candidate choices.

35. Lau et al. 2014.

36. In Brazil this relationship is more about frequency than about network size. In models not shown, we replace frequency of political discussion with network size and find that it is statistically significant only in the Mexican election.

37. These logit models with SES also contain the gender and race measures used in the preceding section, but to reduce clutter we do not plot these. These variables have statistically significant coefficients in only two of eight instances (race in Brazil 2006 and gender in Mexico 2006).

38. We also maintain equivalent samples in both waves, limiting them to twice-opinionated voters who responded to both waves.

39. Schattschneider 1960, 35.

CHAPTER 9. CONCLUSION

1. Sunstein 2019, 7.

2. Harness and Moffat 2015.

3. Gutmann and Thompson 2004.

4. Ahn, Huckfeldt, and Ryan 2014.

5. Sanders 1997.

6. Asch 1951.

7. Ahn, Huckfeldt, and Ryan 2014, 6.

8. Huckfeldt and Sprague 1995, 29.

9. The private firms that dominate polling in Brazil and Mexico are primarily interested in predicting election outcomes, not in explaining why people vote the way they do.

10. Domínguez et al. 2015; Lupu, Oliveros, and Schiumerini 2019.

11. Even so, endogeneity contaminates these psychological orientations in a cross-sectional survey. Consider party identification. Any model of voting includes, beyond the usual socioeconomic and demographic measures, a variable for partisanship, but we know that Brazilian party identification is highly endogenous to vote choice. (Recall how identification with the PT nearly doubled in Juiz de Fora between March and August of 2002.) Only a panel design can separate the long-standing identifiers from the bandwagon identifiers.

12. Lazarsfeld, Berelson, and Gaudet 1944; Berelson, Lazarsfeld, and McPhee 1954; Huckfeldt and Sprague 1995, respectively.

13. Marsden 1987.

14. Calvo 2015; Carvalho and Mitozo 2016; Zago and Bastos 2013.

15. Guillén 2013.

16. Darnton 2010; Standage 2013.

17. Settle 2018.

18. Instituto Datafolha 2018.

19. Marés et al. 2018.

20. Facebook and other social media sites are monitored for political misinformation, but WhatsApp messages are encrypted and not viewable by third parties.

21. Krieger and Silva 1994.

22. Mariano and Pierucci 1992.

23. Manjoo 2018.

24. Instituto Datafolha 2018.

25. Guidry 1996, 252–53.

26. van der Meer et al. 2015.

27. Huckfeldt 2001.

28. Chambers 1996.

29. Putnam 1994.

30. Price, Cappella, and Nir 2002.

31. Box-Steffensmeier, Darmofal, and Farrell 2009, 310.

32. Luskin, Fishkin, and Jowell 2002.

33. Hochschild 1993; Mutz 2002b.

34. Habermas 1989.

35. Baker and Greene 2011; Zaller 1998.

36. Huntington 1968; Mainwaring and Scully 1995; Mainwaring 2018b; Roberts 2014.

37. Achen and Bartels 2016, 267.

38. Schkade, Sunstein, and Hastie 2007.

39. Karpowitz and Mendelberg 2014.

40. Larreguy, Marshall, and Querubín 2016; McCann and Lawson 2003; Straubhaar, Olsen, and Nunes 1993; Tardáguila, Benevenuto, and Ortellado 2018.

APPENDIX B. MEASUREMENT OF VARIABLES

1. Baker, Ames, and Rennó 2006, 397.

2. Dalton, Beck, and Huckfeldt 1998.

APPENDIX C. DETAILS OF CORRECT-VOTING ANALYSES

1. Lau, Andersen, and Redlawsk 2008, 400–401.

2. Wiesehomeier and Benoit 2009.

REFERENCES

Abers, Rebecca. 2000. *Inventing Local Democracy: Grassroots Politics in Brazil*. Boulder, CO: Lynne Rienner Publishers.

Achen, Christopher H., and Larry M. Bartels. 2016. *Democracy for Realists: Why Elections Do Not Produce Responsive Government*. Princeton, NJ: Princeton University Press.

Afrobarometer. 2006. "Afrobarometer Data Round 3: The Quality of Democracy and Governance in 18 African Countries, 2005–2006." At http://www.afrobarometer.org.

Ahn, T. K., Robert Huckfeldt, and John Barry Ryan. 2014. *Experts, Activists, and Democratic Politics: Are Electorates Self-Educating?* New York: Cambridge University Press.

Albuquerque, Liege. 2002. "Garotinho Invoca Deus Para Ir Ao 2° Turno." *Folha de São Paulo*, October 4. At https://www1.folha.uol.com.br/fsp/brasil/fc0410200230.htm.

Almeida, Alberto. 2006. "Amnésia Eleitoral: Em Quem Você Votou para Deputado em 2002? E em 1998?" In *Reforma Política: Lições da História Recente*, edited by Gláucio Ary Dillon Soares and Lúcio R. Rennó. Rio de Janeiro: FGV Editora.

Alt, James E., Amalie Jensen, Horacio Larreguy, David D. Lassen, and John Marshall. 2020. "Diffusing Political Concerns: How Unemployment Information Passed between Social Ties Influences Danish Voters." Working Paper, Harvard University.

Alvarez, Sonia E. 1990. *Engendering Democracy in Brazil: Women's Movements in Transition Politics*. Princeton, NJ: Princeton University Press.

Alves, Francisco Edson. 2018. "Política × Amizade: Em Tempos de Intolerância e Guerra Virtual de Ideais, Dicas de Como Manter as Amizades, Sobretudo nas Redes Sociais." *O Día*, September 30, sec. Eleições 2018: 3.

Alves, Jorge Antonio, and Wendy Hunter. 2017. "From Right to Left in Brazil's Northeast: Transformation, or 'Politics as Usual'?" *Comparative Politics* 49, no. 4: 437–55.

Ames, Barry. 1970. "Bases of Support for Mexico's Dominant Party." *American Political Science Review* 64, no. 1: 153–67.

Ames, Barry. 1994. "The Reverse Coattails Effect: Local Party Organization in the 1989 Brazilian Presidential Election." *American Political Science Review* 88, no. 1: 95–111.

Ames, Barry. 2001a. *The Deadlock of Democracy in Brazil*. Ann Arbor: University of Michigan Press.

Ames, Barry. 2001b. "The Dynamics of Political Attitude Formation in a Milieu of Multiple Weak Parties: A Context-Sensitive Analysis of Voting Behavior in Two Brazilian Cities." SES #0137088 National Science Foundation Proposal. Washington, DC: National Science Foundation.

Ames, Barry, Andy Baker, and Lúcio R. Rennó. 2008. "The Quality of Elections in Brazil: Policy, Performance, Pageantry, or Pork?" In *Democratic Brazil Revisited*, edited by Peter R. Kingstone and Timothy J. Power. Pittsburgh: University of Pittsburgh Press.

Ames, Barry, Andy Baker, and Lúcio R. Rennó. 2009. "Split-Ticket Voting as the Rule: Voters and Permanent Divided Government in Brazil." *Electoral Studies* 28, no. 1: 8–20.

Ames, Barry, Andy Baker, and Amy Erica Smith. 2017. "Social Networks in the Brazilian Electorate." In *The Oxford Handbook of Political Networks*, edited by Jennifer Nicoll Victor, Alexander H. Montgomery, and Mark Lubell. New York: Oxford University Press.

Ames, Barry, Miguel García-Sánchez, and Amy Erica Smith. 2012. "Keeping Up with the Souzas: Social Influence and Electoral Change in a Weak Party System, Brazil 2002–2006." *Latin American Politics and Society* 54, no. 2: 51–78.

Ames, Barry, Alyssa Huberts, Fabiana Machado, Lúcio R. Rennó, David Samuels, Amy Erica Smith, and Cesar Zucco. 2016. "Brazilian Electoral Panel Study: 2014 Results." Washington, DC: Inter-American Development Bank. At https://publications.iadb .org/bitstream/handle/11319/7445/Brazilian-Electoral-Panel-Study-2014-Results .pdf?sequence=1.

Ames, Barry, Fabiana Machado, Lúcio R. Rennó, David Samuels, Amy Erica Smith, and Cesar Zucco. 2010. "Brazilian Electoral Panel Studies (BEPS): Brazilian Public Opinion in the 2010 Presidential Elections." Washington, DC: Inter-American Development Bank.

Anderson, Leslie. 2010. *Social Capital in Developing Democracies: Nicaragua and Argentina Compared*. New York: Cambridge University Press.

Apfeld, Brendan, and J. Alexander Branham. 2016. "Campaign Shocks and Party Support: Evidence from Brazil's 2014 Presidential Election." *Journal of Elections, Public Opinion and Parties* 26, no. 3: 336–53.

Arcaya, Mariana C., Reginald D. Tucker-Seeley, Rockli Kim, Alina Schnake-Mahl, Marvin So, and S. V. Subramanian. 2016. "Research on Neighborhood Effects on Health in the United States: A Systematic Review of Study Characteristics." *Social Science & Medicine* 168: 16–29.

Arias, Enrique Desmond. 2009. *Drugs and Democracy in Rio de Janeiro: Trafficking, Social Networks, and Public Security*. Chapel Hill: University of North Carolina Press.

Arias, Eric, Pablo Balán, Horacio Larreguy, John Marshall, and Pablo Querubín. 2019. "Information Provision, Voter Coordination, and Electoral Accountability: Evidence from Mexican Social Networks." *American Political Science Review* 113, no. 2: 475–98.

Aristotle. 1895. *Aristotle's Politics: A Treatise on Government*. Translated by William Ellis. London: George Routledge and Sons.

Asch, Solomon E. 1951. "Effects of Group Pressure upon the Modification and Distortion of Judgement." In *Groups, Leadership and Men: Research in Human Relations*, edited by Harold Steere Guetzkow. Pittsburgh: Carnegie Press.

Atkeson, Lonna Rae. 1999. "'Sure, I Voted for the Winner!' Overreport of the Primary Vote for the Party Nominee in the National Election Studies." *Political Behavior* 21, no. 3: 197–215.

Auyero, Javier. 1999. "'From the Client's Point(s) of View': How Poor People Perceive and Evaluate Political Clientelism." *Theory and Society* 28, no. 2: 297–334.

Auyero, Javier. 2000. "The Logic of Clientelism in Argentina: An Ethnographic Account." *Latin American Research Review* 35, no. 3: 55–81.

Axelrod, Robert. 1997. "The Dissemination of Culture: A Model with Local Convergence and Global Polarization." *Journal of Conflict Resolution* 41, no. 2: 203–26.

Baiocchi, Gianpaolo. 2005. *Militants and Citizens: The Politics of Participatory Democracy in Porto Alegre*. Stanford, CA: Stanford University Press.

Baker, Andy. 2009. *The Market and the Masses in Latin America: Policy Reform and Consumption in Liberalizing Economies*. New York: Cambridge University Press.

Baker, Andy, Barry Ames, and Lúcio R. Rennó. 2006. "Social Context and Campaign Volatility in New Democracies: Networks and Neighborhoods in Brazil's 2002 Elections." *American Journal of Political Science* 50, no. 2: 382–99.

Baker, Andy, Barry Ames, Anand E. Sokhey, and Lúcio R. Rennó. 2016. "The Dynamics of Partisan Identification When Party Brands Change: The Case of the Workers Party in Brazil." *Journal of Politics* 78, no. 1: 197–213.

Baker, Andy, and Dalton Dorr. 2019. "Mass Partisanship in Three Latin American Democracies." In *Campaigns and Voters in Developing Democracies: Argentina in Comparative Perspective*, edited by Noam Lupu, Virginia Oliveros, and Luis Schiumerini. Ann Arbor: University of Michigan Press.

Baker, Andy, and Kenneth F. Greene. 2011. "The Latin American Left's Mandate: Free-Market Policies and Issue Voting in New Democracies." *World Politics* 63, no. 1: 43–77.

Baker, Andy, and Kenneth F. Greene. 2015. "Positional Issue Voting in Latin America." In *The Latin American Voter: Pursuing Representation and Accountability in Challenging Contexts*, edited by Ryan E. Carlin, Matthew M. Singer, and Elizabeth J. Zechmeister. Ann Arbor: University of Michigan Press.

Baker, Andy, and Lúcio Rennó. 2019. "Nonpartisans as False Negatives: The Mismeasurement of Party Identification in Public Opinion Surveys." *Journal of Politics* 81, no. 3: 906–22.

Baker, Andy, and Ethan Scheiner. 2007. "Electoral System Effects and Ruling Party Dominance in Japan: A Counterfactual Simulation Based on Adaptive Parties." *Electoral Studies* 26, no. 2: 477–91.

Baker, Andy, and Vania Ximena Velasco-Guachalla. 2018. "Is the Informal Sector Politically Different? (Null) Answers from Latin America." *World Development* 102: 170–82.

Barabási, Albert-László. 2014. *Linked: How Everything Is Connected to Everything Else and What It Means for Business, Science, and Everyday Life*. New York: Basic Books.

Baron, R. M., and D. A. Kenny. 1986. "The Moderator-Mediator Variable Distinction in Social Psychological Research: Conceptual, Strategic, and Statistical Considerations." *Journal of Personality and Social Psychology* 51, no. 6: 1173–82.

Bartels, Larry M. 2006. "Priming and Persuasion in Presidential Campaigns." In *Capturing Campaign Effects*, edited by Henry E. Brady and Richard Johnston. Ann Arbor: University of Michigan Press.

Beck, Paul A., Russell J. Dalton, Steven Greene, and Robert Huckfeldt. 2002. "The Social Calculus of Voting: Interpersonal, Media, and Organizational Influences on Presidential Choices." *American Political Science Review* 96, no. 1: 57–73.

Beck, Paul A., and Richard Gunther. 2016. "Global Patterns of Exposure to Political Intermediaries." In *Voting in Old and New Democracies*, edited by Richard Gunther, Paul A. Beck, Pedro Magalhães, and Alejandro Moreno. New York: Routledge.

Beck, Paul A., and Erik D. Heidemann. 2014. "Changing Strategies in Grassroots Canvassing: 1956–2012." *Party Politics* 20, no. 2: 261–74.

Becker, Gary S., and Kevin M. Murphy. 2000. *Social Economics: Market Behavior in a Social Environment.* Cambridge, MA: Belknap Press of Harvard University Press.

Bello, André. 2016. "A Lógica Social do Voto Correto no Brasil." *Opinião Pública* 22, no. 2: 466–91.

Bello, Jason, and Meredith Rolfe. 2014. "Is Influence Mightier than Selection? Forging Agreement in Political Discussion Networks during a Campaign." *Social Networks* 36: 134–46.

Berelson, Bernard, Paul F. Lazarsfeld, and William N. McPhee. 1954. *Voting: A Study of Opinion Formation in a Presidential Campaign.* Chicago: University of Chicago Press.

Bikhchandani, Sushil, David Hirshleifer, and Ivo Welch. 1992. "A Theory of Fads, Fashion, Custom, and Cultural Change as Informational Cascades." *Journal of Political Economy* 100, no. 5: 992–1026.

Birnir, Jóhanna Kristín. 2007. "Divergence in Diversity? The Dissimilar Effects of Cleavages on Electoral Politics in New Democracies." *American Journal of Political Science* 51, no. 3: 602–19.

Bisbee, James, and Jennifer M. Larson. 2017. "Testing Social Science Network Theories with Online Network Data: An Evaluation of External Validity." *American Political Science Review* 111, no. 3: 502–21.

Bishop, Bill. 2008. *The Big Sort: Why the Clustering of Like-Minded America Is Tearing Us Apart.* Boston: Houghton Mifflin Harcourt.

Blais, André. 2004. "How Many Voters Change Their Minds in the Month Preceding an Election?" *PS: Political Science & Politics* 37, no. 4: 801–3.

Boas, Taylor C. 2005. "Television and Neopopulism in Latin America: Media Effects in Brazil and Peru." *Latin American Research Review* 40, no. 2: 27–49.

Boas, Taylor C. 2016. *Presidential Campaigns in Latin America: Electoral Strategies and Success Contagion.* New York: Cambridge University Press.

Bond, Robert M., Christopher J. Fariss, Jason J. Jones, Adam D. I. Kramer, Cameron Marlow, Jaime E. Settle, and James H. Fowler. 2012. "A 61-Million-Person Experiment in Social Influence and Political Mobilization." *Nature* 489, no. 7415: 295–98.

Bonner, Hubert. 1959. *Group Dynamics: Principles and Applications.* New York: Ronald Press.

Books, John W., and Charles L. Prysby. 1991. *Political Behavior and the Local Context.* New York: Praeger Publishers.

Boulding, Carew. 2014. *NGOs, Political Protest, and Civil Society.* New York: Cambridge University Press.

Boulding, Carew, and Claudio Holzner. 2016. "Community Organizations and Strategic Mobilization: Explaining the Puzzle of Poor People's Participation in Latin America." Working Paper, University of Colorado.

Box-Steffensmeier, Janet M., David Darmofal, and Christian A. Farrell. 2009. "The Aggregate Dynamics of Campaigns." *Journal of Politics* 71, no. 1: 309–23.

Brady, Henry E., Richard Johnston, and John Sides. 2006. "The Study of Political Campaigns." In *Capturing Campaign Effects*, edited by Henry E. Brady and Richard Johnston. Ann Arbor: University of Michigan Press.

Brady, Henry E., Sidney Verba, and Kay Lehman Schlozman. 1995. "Beyond SES: A Resource Model of Political Participation." *American Political Science Review* 89, no. 2: 271–94.

Braga, Maria do Socorro Sousa, and Jairo Pimentel Jr. 2011. "Os Partidos Políticos Brasileiros Realmente Não Importam?" *Opinião Pública* 17, no. 2: 271–303.

Bridges, Amy. 1987. *A City in the Republic: Antebellum New York and the Origins of Machine Politics.* Ithaca, NY: Cornell University Press.

Brock, William A., and Steven N. Durlauf. 2002. "A Multinomial-Choice Model of Neighborhood Effects." *American Economic Review* 92, no. 2: 298–303.

Bruhn, Kathleen. 1997. *Taking on Goliath: The Emergence of a New Left Party and the Struggle for Democracy in Mexico.* University Park: Pennsylvania State University Press.

Brusco, Valeria, Marcelo Nazareno, and Susan C. Stokes. 2004. "Vote Buying in Argentina." *Latin American Research Review* 39, no. 2: 66–88.

Buarque de Holanda, Sérgio. 1995. *Raízes do Brasil.* São Paulo: Companhia das Letras.

Burnstein, Eugene, and Amiram Vinokur. 1977. "Persuasive Argumentation and Social Comparison as Determinants of Attitude Polarization." *Journal of Experimental Social Psychology* 13, no. 4: 315–32.

Calvo, Ernesto. 2015. *Anatomía Política de Twitter en Argentina: Tuiteando #Nisman.* Buenos Aires: Capital Intelectual.

Calvo, Ernesto, Marcelo Escolar, and Julia Pomares. 2009. "Ballot Design and Split Ticket Voting in Multiparty Systems: Experimental Evidence on Information Effects and Vote Choice." *Electoral Studies* 28, no. 2: 218–31.

Calvo, Ernesto, and Maria Victoria Murillo. 2004. "Who Delivers? Partisan Clients in the Argentine Electoral Market." *American Journal of Political Science* 48, no. 4: 742–57.

Calvo, Ernesto, and Maria Victoria Murillo. 2013. "When Parties Meet Voters: Assessing Political Linkages through Partisan Networks and Distributive Expectations in Argentina and Chile." *Comparative Political Studies* 46, no. 7: 851–82.

Calvo, Ernesto, and Maria Victoria Murillo. 2019. *Non-Policy Politics: Richer Voters, Poorer Voters, and the Diversification of Electoral Strategies.* New York: Cambridge University Press.

Camp, Edwin. 2017. "Cultivating Effective Brokers: A Party Leader's Dilemma." *British Journal of Political Science* 47, no. 3: 521–43.

Campbell, Angus, Philip E. Converse, Warren E. Miller, and Donald E. Stokes. 1960. *The American Voter.* New York: Wiley.

Campbell, David E. 2010. *Why We Vote: How Schools and Communities Shape Our Civic Life.* Princeton, NJ: Princeton University Press.

Canache, Damarys. 1996. "Looking Out My Back Door: The Neighborhood Context and Perceptions of Relative Deprivation." *Political Research Quarterly* 49, no. 3: 547–71.

Carlin, Ryan E., Matthew M. Singer, and Elizabeth J. Zechmeister, eds. 2015. *The Latin American Voter: Pursuing Representation and Accountability in Challenging Contexts.* Ann Arbor: University of Michigan Press.

Carlson, Taylor N. 2017. "Modeling Political Information Transmission as a Game of Telephone." *Journal of Politics* 80, no. 1: 348–52.

Carlson, Taylor N. 2019. "Through the Grapevine: Informational Consequences of Interpersonal Political Communication." *American Political Science Review* 113, no. 2: 325–39.

Carlson, Taylor N., and Jaime E. Settle. 2016. "Political Chameleons: An Exploration of Conformity in Political Discussions." *Political Behavior* 38, no. 4: 817–59.

Carreirão, Yan de Souza, and Maria D'Alva G. Kinzo. 2004. "Partidos Políticos, Preferência Partidária e Decisão Eleitoral No Brasil (1989/2002)." *Dados* 47, no. 1: 131–68.

Carrington, Peter J., John Scott, and Stanley Wasserman. 2005. Introduction to *Models and Methods in Social Network Analysis*, edited by Peter J. Carrington, John Scott, and Stanley Wasserman. New York: Cambridge University Press.

Carvalho, Fernanda Cavassana de, and Isabele Batista Mitozo. 2016. "Novos Ambientes, Mesmas Funções: O Jornalismo Profissional Fomentando o Debate sobre Eleições nas Redes Sociais Digitais." *Brazilian Journalism Research* 12, no. 3: 74.

Centola, Damon. 2018. *How Behavior Spreads: The Science of Complex Contagions*. Princeton, NJ: Princeton University Press.

Chambers, Simone. 1996. *Reasonable Democracy: Jürgen Habermas and the Politics of Discourse*. Ithaca, NY: Cornell University Press.

Christakis, Nicholas A., and James H. Fowler. 2007. "The Spread of Obesity in a Large Social Network over 32 Years." *New England Journal of Medicine* 357, no. 4: 370–79.

Clarke, Harold D., David Sanders, Stewart C. Marianne, and Paul Whiteley. 2004. *Political Choice in Britain*. New York: Oxford University Press.

Cleary, Matthew R., and Susan C. Stokes. 2006. *Democracy and the Culture of Skepticism: The Politics of Trust in Argentina and Mexico*. New York: Russell Sage Foundation.

Cohen, Mollie J., Facundo E. Salles Kobilanski, and Elizabeth J. Zechmeister. 2018. "Electoral Volatility in Latin America." *Journal of Politics* 80, no. 3: 1017–22.

Collier, Ruth Berins, and David Collier. 1991. *Shaping the Political Arena: Critical Junctures, the Labor Movement, and Regime Dynamics in Latin America*. Princeton, NJ: Princeton University Press.

Conover, Pamela Johnston, Donald D. Searing, and Ivor M. Crewe. 2002. "The Deliberative Potential of Political Discussion." *British Journal of Political Science* 32: 21–62.

Converse, Philip E. 1969. "Of Time and Partisan Stability." *Comparative Political Studies* 2, no. 2: 139–71.

Córdova, Abby, and Matthew L. Layton. 2016. "When Is 'Delivering the Goods' Not Good Enough? How Economic Disparities in Latin American Neighborhoods Shape Citizen Trust in Local Government." *World Politics* 68, no. 1: 74–110.

Cornejo, Rodrigo Castro. 2018. "Do Electoral Polls Affect Voters' Electoral Behavior? Strategic Behavior and Swing Voters in New Democracies." University of Virginia.

Corrêa, Diego Sanches. 2015. "Conditional Cash Transfer Programs, the Economy, and Presidential Elections in Latin America." *Latin American Research Review* 50, no. 2: 63–85.

Cox, Gary W. 1997. *Making Votes Count: Strategic Coordination in the World's Electoral Systems*. New York: Cambridge University Press.

Cox, Gary W., and Mathew D. McCubbins. 1986. "Electoral Politics as a Redistributive Game." *Journal of Politics* 48, no. 2: 370–89.

Cox, Kevin R. 1969. "The Spatial Structuring of Information Flows and Partisan Attitudes." In *Quantitative Ecological Analysis in the Social Sciences*, edited by Mattei Dogan and Stein Rokkan. Cambridge, MA: MIT Press.

Crossley, Nick, Elisa Bellotti, Gemma Edwards, Martin G. Everett, Johan Koskinen, and Mark Tranmer. 2015. *Social Network Analysis for Ego-Nets*. Thousand Oaks, CA: Sage Publications.

Crow, David, and Clarisa Pérez-Armendáriz. 2018. "Talk without Borders: Why Political Discussion Makes Latin Americans with Relatives Abroad More Critical of Their Democracies." *Comparative Political Studies* 51, no. 2: 238–76.

Cruz, Cesi. 2019. "Social Networks and the Targeting of Vote Buying." *Comparative Political Studies* 52, no. 3: 382–411.

Cruz, Cesi, Julien Labonne, and Pablo Querubín. 2017. "Politician Family Networks and Electoral Outcomes: Evidence from the Philippines." *American Economic Review* 107, no. 10: 3006–37.

Dalton, Russell J., Paul A. Beck, and Robert Huckfeldt. 1998. "Partisan Cues and the Media: Information Flows in the 1992 Presidential Election." *American Political Science Review* 92, no. 1: 111–26.

Dalton, Russell J., and Steven Weldon. 2007. "Partisanship and Party System Institutionalization." *Party Politics* 13, no. 2: 179–96.

Darnton, Robert. 2010. *Poetry and the Police: Communication Networks in Eighteenth-Century France*. Cambridge, MA: Harvard University Press.

Dassonneville, Ruth. 2012. "Electoral Volatility, Political Sophistication, Trust and Efficacy: A Study on Changes in Voter Preferences during the Belgian Regional Elections of 2009." *Acta Politica* 47, no. 1: 18–41.

De Boef, Suzanna, and Luke Keele. 2008. "Taking Time Seriously." *American Journal of Political Science* 52, no. 1: 184–200.

DeMars, Christine. 2010. *Item Response Theory*. New York: Oxford University Press.

Desposato, Scott. 2007. "How Does Vote Buying Shape the Legislative Arena?" In *Elections for Sale: The Causes and Consequences of Vote Buying*, edited by Frederic Charles Schaffer. Boulder, CO: Lynne Rienner Publishers.

Desposato, Scott, and Barbara Norrander. 2009. "The Gender Gap in Latin America: Contextual and Individual Influences on Gender and Political Participation." *British Journal of Political Science* 39, no. 1: 141–62.

Desposato, Scott, and Ethan Scheiner. 2008. "Governmental Centralization and Party Affiliation: Legislator Strategies in Brazil and Japan." *American Political Science Review* 102, no. 4: 509–24.

Díaz-Cayeros, Alberto, Federico Estévez, and Beatriz Magaloni. 2009. "Buying-off the Poor: Effects of Targeted Benefits in the 2006 Presidential Race." In *Consolidating Mexico's Democracy: The 2006 Presidential Campaign in Comparative Perspective*, edited by Jorge I. Domínguez, Chappell Lawson, and Alejandro Moreno. Baltimore: Johns Hopkins University Press.

Díaz-Cayeros, Alberto, Federico Estévez, and Beatriz Magaloni. 2016. *The Political Logic of Poverty Relief: Electoral Strategies and Social Policy in Mexico*. New York: Cambridge University Press.

Díaz-Domínguez, Alejandro, and Alejandro Moreno. 2015. "Effects of #YoSoy132 and Social Media in Mexico's 2012 Campaign." In *Mexico's Evolving Democracy: A Comparative Study of the 2012 Elections*, edited by Jorge Domínguez, Kenneth F. Greene,

Chappell Lawson, and Alejandro Moreno. Baltimore: Johns Hopkins University Press.

Dietz, Robert D. 2002. "The Estimation of Neighborhood Effects in the Social Sciences: An Interdisciplinary Approach." *Social Science Research* 31, no. 4: 539–75.

Diniz, Eli. 1982. *Voto e Máquina Política: Patronagem e Clientelismo no Rio de Janeiro.* Rio de Janeiro: Paz e Terra.

Dixit, Avinash, and John Londregan. 1996. "The Determinants of Success of Special Interests in Redistributive Politics." *Journal of Politics* 58, no. 4: 1132–55.

Djupe, Paul A., and Anand E. Sokhey. 2014. "The Distribution and Determinants of Socially Supplied Political Expertise." *American Politics Research* 42, no. 2: 199–225.

Domínguez, Jorge I., Kenneth F. Greene, Chappell H. Lawson, and Alejandro Moreno, eds. 2015. *Mexico's Evolving Democracy: A Comparative Study of the 2012 Elections.* Baltimore: Johns Hopkins University Press.

Domínguez, Jorge I., and James McCann. 1996. *Democratizing Mexico: Public Opinion and Electoral Choices.* Baltimore: Johns Hopkins University Press.

Downs, Anthony. 1957. *An Economic Theory of Democracy.* New York: Harper.

Druckman, James N., and Kjersten R. Nelson. 2003. "Framing and Deliberation: How Citizens' Conversations Limit Elite Influence." *American Journal of Political Science* 47, no. 4: 729–45.

Dunbar, R.I.M., Valerio Arnaboldi, Marco Conti, and Andrea Passarella. 2015. "The Structure of Online Social Networks Mirrors Those in the Offline World." *Social Networks* 43: 39–47.

Dunbar, R.I.M., and M. Spoors. 1995. "Social Networks, Support Cliques, and Kinship." *Human Nature* 6, no. 3: 273–90.

Durkheim, Emile. 1897. *Suicide: A Study in Sociology.* New York: Free Press.

Durlauf, Steven N. 2004. "Neighborhood Effects." In *Handbook of Regional and Urban Economics*, edited by J. Vernon Henderson and Jacques-François Thisse. Amsterdam: Elsevier B.V.

Duverger, Maurice. 1954. *Political Parties.* New York: Wiley.

Eagles, Munro, Paul Bélanger, and Hugh W. Calkins. 2004. "The Spatial Structure of Urban Political Discussion Networks." In *Spatially Integrated Social Science*, edited by Michael F. Goodchild and Donald G. Janelle. New York: Oxford University Press.

Enelow, James M., and Melvin J. Hinich. 1982. "Nonspatial Candidate Characteristics and Electoral Competition." *Journal of Politics* 44, no. 1: 115–30.

Erbring, Lutz, and Alice A. Young. 1979. "Individuals and Social Structure: Contextual Effects as Endogenous Feedback." *Sociological Methods & Research* 7, no. 4: 396–430.

Erikson, Robert S., and Christopher Wlezien. 2012. *The Timeline of Presidential Elections: How Campaigns Do (and Do Not) Matter.* Chicago: University of Chicago Press.

Eveland, William P., Jr., Osei Appiah, and Paul A. Beck. 2018. "Americans Are More Exposed to Difference Than We Think: Capturing Hidden Exposure to Political and Racial Difference." *Social Networks* 52: 192–200.

Eveland, William P., and Myiah Hutchens Hively. 2009. "Political Discussion Frequency, Network Size, and 'Heterogeneity' of Discussion as Predictors of Political Knowledge and Participation." *Journal of Communication* 59, no. 2: 205–24.

Eveland, William P., Myiah J. Hutchens, and Alyssa C. Morey. 2013. "Political Network Size and Its Antecedents and Consequences." *Political Communication* 30, no. 3: 371–94.

Eveland, William P., and Tiffany Thomson. 2006. "Is It Talking, Thinking, or Both? A Lagged Dependent Variable Model of Discussion Effects on Political Knowledge." *Journal of Communication* 56, no. 3: 523–42.

Faughnan, Brian M., and Elizabeth J. Zechmeister. 2011. "AmericasBarometer Insights." Latin American Public Opinion Project Insights Series, number 57. At http://www.vanderbilt.edu/lapop/insights/I0857en.pdf.

Feldman, Lauren. 2011. "Partisan Differences in Opinionated News Perceptions: A Test of the Hostile Media Effect." *Political Behavior* 33, no. 3: 407–32.

Feldmann, Antônio. 2002. *Eleições 2000: Uma Disputa Que Não Terminou*. Caxias do Sul, RS: Maneco Livraria & Editora.

Festinger, Leon. 1954. "A Theory of Social Comparison." *Human Relations* 7: 117–40.

Finan, Frederico, and Laura Schechter. 2012. "Vote-Buying and Reciprocity." *Econometrica* 80, no. 2: 863–81.

Finifter, Ada W. 1974. "The Friendship Group as a Protective Environment for Political Deviants." *American Political Science Review* 68, no. 2: 607–25.

Finkel, Steven E. 1993. "Reexamining the 'Minimal Effects' Model in Recent Presidential Campaigns." *Journal of Politics* 55, no. 1: 1–21.

Fischer, Claude S. 1982. *To Dwell among Friends: Personal Networks in Town and City*. Chicago: University of Chicago Press.

Fischer, Claude S. 2009. "The 2004 GSS Finding of Shrunken Social Networks: An Artifact?" *American Sociological Review* 74, no. 4: 657–69.

Fishkin, James S. 2011. *When the People Speak: Deliberative Democracy and Public Consultation*. New York: Oxford University Press.

Fitzgerald, Jennifer. 2013. "What Does 'Political' Mean to You?" *Political Behavior* 35, no. 3: 453–79.

Fitzgerald, Jennifer, and K. Amber Curtis. 2012. "Partisan Discord in the Family and Political Engagement: A Comparative Behavioral Analysis." *Journal of Politics* 74, no. 1: 129–41.

Flores-Macías, Francisco. 2009. "Electoral Volatility in 2006." In *Consolidating Mexico's Democracy: The 2006 Presidential Campaign in Comparative Perspective*, edited by Jorge I. Domínguez, Chappell H. Lawson, and Alejandro Moreno. Baltimore: Johns Hopkins University Press.

Foguel, Miguel Natan, Lauro Ramos, and Francisco Carneiro. 2001. "The Impact of the Minimum Wage on the Labor Market, Poverty and Fiscal Budget in Brazil." IPEA Discussion Paper 839, Institute of Applied Economic Research. At https://papers.ssrn.com/abstract=290623.

Forgas, Joseph P., and Kipling D. Williams. 2001. Preface to *Social Influence: Direct and Indirect Processes*, edited by Joseph P. Forgas and Kipling D. Williams. Philadelphia: Psychology Press.

Fowler, James H., Michael T. Heaney, David W. Nickerson, John F. Padgett, and Betsy Sinclair. 2011. "Causality in Political Networks." *American Politics Research* 39, no. 2: 437–80.

Frank, Thomas. 2004. *What's the Matter with Kansas? How Conservatives Won the Heart of America*. New York: Henry Holt and Company.

French, John R. P., Jr. 1956. "A Formal Theory of Social Power." *Psychological Review* 68, no. 3: 181–94.

Friedkin, Noah E., and Eugene C. Johnsen. 2011. *Social Influence Network Theory: A Sociological Examination of Small Group Dynamics*. New York: Cambridge University Press.

Galam, Serge, and Frans Jacobs. 2007. "The Role of Inflexible Minorities in the Breaking of Democratic Opinion Dynamics." *Physica A: Statistical Mechanics and Its Applications* 381: 366–76.

Gans-Morse, Jordan, Sebastián Mazzuca, and Simeon Nichter. 2014. "Varieties of Clientelism: Machine Politics during Elections." *American Journal of Political Science* 58, no. 2: 415–32.

Gay, Robert. 1994. *Popular Organization and Democracy in Rio De Janeiro: A Tale of Two Favelas*. Philadelphia: Temple University Press.

Geers, Sabine, and Linda Bos. 2017. "Priming Issues, Party Visibility, and Party Evaluations: The Impact on Vote Switching." *Political Communication* 34, no. 3: 344–66.

Gélineau, François, and Matthew M. Singer. 2015. "The Economy and Incumbent Support in Latin America." In *The Latin American Voter: Pursuing Representation and Accountability in Challenging Contexts*, edited by Ryan E. Carlin, Matthew M. Singer, and Elizabeth J. Zechmeister. Ann Arbor: University of Michigan Press.

Gelman, Andrew, and Gary King. 1993. "Why Are American Presidential Election Campaign Polls So Variable When Votes Are So Predictable?" *British Journal of Political Science* 23, no. 4: 409–51.

Gentzkow, Matthew, and Jesse M. Shapiro. 2011. "Ideological Segregation Online and Offline." *Quarterly Journal of Economics* 126, no. 4: 1799–839.

Gibson, Edward L., and Ernesto Calvo. 2000. "Federalism and Low-Maintenance Constituencies: Territorial Dimensions of Economic Reform in Argentina." *Studies in Comparative International Development* 35, no. 3: 32–55.

Gibson, James L. 2001. "Social Networks, Civil Society, and the Prospects for Consolidating Russia's Democratic Transition." *American Journal of Political Science* 45, no. 1: 51–68.

Gil de Zúñiga, Homero, Eulàlia Puig-I-Abril, and Hernando Rojas. 2009. "Weblogs, Traditional Sources Online and Political Participation: An Assessment of How the Internet Is Changing the Political Environment." *New Media & Society* 11, no. 4: 553–74.

Glaeser, Edward L., Bruce Sacerdote, and José A. Scheinkman. 1996. "Crime and Social Interactions." *Quarterly Journal of Economics* 111, no. 2: 507–48.

Glaeser, Edward L., Bruce I. Sacerdote, and Jose A. Scheinkman. 2003. "The Social Multiplier." *Journal of the European Economic Association* 1, nos. 2–3: 345–53.

Góes, Carlos, and Izabela Karpowicz. 2017. "Inequality in Brazil: A Regional Perspective." IMF Working Paper 17/225, International Monetary Fund.

Gonzalez-Ocantos, Ezequiel, Chad Kiewiet de Jonge, Carlos Meléndez, Javier Osorio, and David W. Nickerson. 2012. "Vote Buying and Social Desirability Bias: Experimental Evidence from Nicaragua." *American Journal of Political Science* 56, no. 1: 202–17.

Granovetter, Mark S. 1973. "The Strength of Weak Ties." *American Journal of Sociology* 78, no. 6: 1360–80.

Green, Donald P. 1988. "On the Dimensionality of Public Sentiment toward Partisan and Ideological Groups." *American Journal of Political Science* 32, no. 3: 758–80.

Green, Donald P., Bradley Palmquist, and Eric Schickler. 2002. *Partisan Hearts and Minds: Political Parties and the Social Identities of Voters.* New Haven, CT: Yale University Press.

Greene, Kenneth F. 2007. *Why Dominant Parties Lose: Mexico's Democratization in Comparative Perspective.* New York: Cambridge University Press.

Greene, Kenneth F. 2011. "Campaign Persuasion and Nascent Partisanship in Mexico's New Democracy." *American Journal of Political Science* 55, no. 2: 398–416.

Greene, Kenneth F. 2019. "Dealigning Campaign Effects in Argentina in Comparative Perspective." In *Campaigns and Voters in Developing Democracies: Argentina in Comparative Perspective*, edited by Noam Lupu, Virginia Oliveros, and Luis Schiumerini. Ann Arbor: University of Michigan Press.

Greene, Kenneth F. 2020. "Campaign Effects and the Elusive Swing Voter in Modern Machine Politics." *Comparative Political Studies.*

Greene, Kenneth F., and Mariano Sánchez-Talanquer. 2018. "Authoritarian Legacies and Party System Stability in Mexico." In *Party Systems in Latin America: Institutionalization, Decay, and Collapse*, edited by Scott Mainwaring. New York: Cambridge University Press.

Greene, Kenneth F., Alberto Simpser, and Alejandro Ponce. 2018. "The Mexico Elections and Quality of Democracy Panel Study." Datafile.

Guidry, John Alexis. 1996. "The Everyday Life of Politics: Class, Democracy and Popular Discourse in Urban Brazil." PhD diss., Ann Arbor: University of Michigan. At https://deepblue.lib.umich.edu/handle/2027.42/105097.

Guillén, Diana. 2013. "Mexican Spring? #YoSoy132, the Emergence of an Unexpected Collective Actor in the National Political Arena." *Social Movement Studies* 12, no. 4: 471–76.

Gutmann, Amy, and Dennis Thompson. 2004. *Why Deliberative Democracy?* Princeton, NJ: Princeton University Press.

Habermas, Jürgen. 1989. *The Structural Transformation of the Public Sphere: An Inquiry into a Category of Bourgeois Society.* Cambridge, MA: MIT Press.

Hagopian, Frances. 1996. *Traditional Politics and Regime Change in Brazil.* New York: Cambridge University Press.

Handlin, Samuel. 2017. *State Crisis in Fragile Democracies: Polarization and Political Regimes in South America.* New York: Cambridge University Press.

Hardin, Curtis D., and E. Tory Higgins. 1996. "Shared Reality: How Social Verification Makes the Subjective Objective." In *Handbook of Motivation and Cognition*, vol. 3, *The Interpersonal Context*, edited by Richard M. Sorrentino and E. Tory Higgins. New York: Guilford Press.

Harness, Peter, and Steven Moffat. 2015. "The Zygon Inversion." *Doctor Who.* BBC One.

Harrison, Lawrence E. 1985. *Underdevelopment Is a State of Mind: The Latin American Case.* New York: Madison Books.

Hatemi, Peter K., and Rose McDermott. 2012. "The Genetics of Politics: Discovery, Challenges, and Progress." *Trends in Genetics* 28, no. 10: 525–33.

Hauser, Robert M. 1974. "Contextual Analysis Revisited." *Sociological Methods & Research* 2, no. 3: 365–75.

Hibbing, Matthew V., Melinda Ritchie, and Mary R. Anderson. 2011. "Personality and Political Discussion." *Political Behavior* 33, no. 4: 601–24.

Hicken, Allen. 2011. "Clientelism." *Annual Review of Political Science* 14: 289–310.

Hill, R. A., and R.I.M. Dunbar. 2003. "Social Network Size in Humans." *Human Nature* 14, no. 1: 53–72.

Ho, Shirley S., and Douglas M. McLeod. 2008. "Social-Psychological Influences on Opinion Expression in Face-to-Face and Computer-Mediated Communication." *Communication Research* 35, no. 2: 190–207.

Hochschild, Jennifer L. 1993. "Disjunction and Ambivalence in Citizens' Political Outlooks." In *Reconsidering the Democratic Public*, edited by George E. Marcus and Russell L. Hanson. University Park: Pennsylvania State University Press.

Holland, Alisha C., and Brian Palmer-Rubin. 2015. "Beyond the Machine: Clientelist Brokers and Interest Organizations in Latin America." *Comparative Political Studies* 48, no. 9: 1186–223.

Huckfeldt, Robert. 2001. "The Social Communication of Political Expertise." *American Journal of Political Science* 45, no. 2: 425–38.

Huckfeldt, Robert, Ken'ichi Ikeda, and Franz Urban Pappi. 2005. "Patterns of Disagreement in Democratic Politics: Comparing Germany, Japan, and the United States." *American Journal of Political Science* 49, no. 3: 497–514.

Huckfeldt, Robert, Paul E. Johnson, and John D. Sprague. 2004. *Political Disagreement: The Survival of Diverse Opinions within Communication Networks*. New York: Cambridge University Press.

Huckfeldt, Robert, and Jeanette Morehouse Mendez. 2008. "Moths, Flames, and Political Engagement: Managing Disagreement within Communication Networks." *Journal of Politics* 70, no. 1: 83–96.

Huckfeldt, Robert, Jeanette Morehouse Mendez, and Tracy Osborn. 2004. "Disagreement, Ambivalence, and Engagement: The Political Consequences of Heterogeneous Networks." *Political Psychology* 25, no. 1: 65–95.

Huckfeldt, Robert, and John Sprague. 1988. "Choice, Social Structure, and Political Information: The Information Coercion of Minorities." *American Journal of Political Science* 32, no. 2: 467–82.

Huckfeldt, Robert, and John Sprague. 1995. *Citizens, Politics, and Social Communication: Information and Influence in an Election Campaign*. Cambridge: Cambridge University Press.

Hughes, Sallie. 2006. *Newsrooms in Conflict: Journalism and the Democratization of Mexico*. Pittsburgh: University of Pittsburgh Press.

Hunter, Wendy. 2010. *The Transformation of the Workers' Party in Brazil, 1989–2009*. New York: Cambridge University Press.

Hunter, Wendy, and Timothy J. Power. 2007. "Rewarding Lula: Executive Power, Social Policy, and the Brazilian Elections of 2006." *Latin American Politics and Society* 49, no. 1: 1–30.

Huntington, Samuel P. 1968. *Political Order in Changing Societies*. New Haven, CT: Yale University Press.

Huntington, Samuel P. 1991. *The Third Wave: Democratization in the Late Twentieth Century*. Norman: University of Oklahoma Press.

Iasulaitis, Sylvia. 2013. "Experiências Interativas em Websites de Campanhas Eleitorais: Os Fóruns de Discussão de Propostas de Governo na Argentina e no Chile." In

Comportamento Eleitoral e Comunicação Política na América Latina: O Eleitor Latino-Americana, edited by Helcimara Telles and Alejandro Moreno. Belo Horizonte: Editora UFMG.

Imai, Kosuke, Bethany Park, and Kenneth F. Greene. 2015. "Using the Predicted Responses from List Experiments as Explanatory Variables in Regression Models." *Political Analysis* 23, no. 2: 180–96.

Instituto Datafolha. 2002. "Intenção de Voto para Presidente—2° turno—02496." At https://www.cesop.unicamp.br/por/banco_de_dados/v/2373.

Instituto Datafolha. 2014. "Intenção de Voto Para Presidente da República: PO813760: 08 e 09/09/2014." At http://media.folha.uol.com.br/datafolha/2014/09/11/intencao_de _voto_e_avaliacao_presidente.pdf.

Instituto Datafolha. 2018. "Uso de Redes Sociais: Eleições 2018." São Paulo, Brazil: Instituto Datafolha. At http://datafolha.folha.uol.com.br/opiniaopublica/2018/10 /1983765-24-dos-eleitores-usam-whatsapp-para-compartilhar-conteudo-eleitoral .shtml.

Instituto Nacional Electoral. 2006. "Elecciones de Presidente de los EUM." Mexico City, Mexico: Instituto Nacional Electoral. At https://portalanterior.ine.mx/archivos3 /portal/historico/contenido/2006_PC/.

International Telecommunication Union. 2013. "World Telecommunication/ICT Indicators Database." At https://www.itu.int/en/ITU-D/Statistics/Pages/publications /wtid.aspx.

Jackman, Simon, and Paul M. Sniderman. 2006. "The Limits of Deliberative Discussion: A Model of Everyday Political Arguments." *Journal of Politics* 68, no. 2: 272–83.

Jencks, Christopher, and Susan E. Mayer. 1990. "The Social Consequences of Growing Up in a Poor Neighborhood." In *Inner-City Poverty in the United States*, edited by Laurence E. Lynn Jr. and Michael G. H. McGeary. Washington, DC: National Academy Press.

Jennings, Will, and Christopher Wlezien. 2018. "Election Polling Errors across Time and Space." *Nature Human Behaviour* 2, no. 4: 276–83.

Johnston, Ron, and Charles Pattie. 2006. *Putting Voters in Their Place: Geography and Elections in Great Britain*. New York: Oxford University Press.

Jones, Mark P., and Scott Mainwaring. 2003. "The Nationalization of Parties and Party Systems: An Empirical Measure and an Application to the Americas." *Party Politics* 9, no. 2: 139–66.

Karpowitz, Christopher F., and Tali Mendelberg. 2014. *The Silent Sex: Gender, Deliberation, and Institutions*. Princeton, NJ: Princeton University Press.

Karpowitz, Christopher F., Tali Mendelberg, and Lee Shaker. 2012. "Gender Inequality in Deliberative Participation." *American Political Science Review* 106, no. 3: 533–47.

Katz, Elihu, and Paul F. Lazarsfeld. 1955. *Personal Influence: The Part Played by People in the Flow of Mass Communications*. New York: Free Press.

Katz, Jonathan N., and Gary King. 1999. "A Statistical Model for Multiparty Electoral Data." *American Political Science Review* 93, no. 1: 15–32.

Keck, Margaret E. 1992. *The Workers' Party and Democratization in Brazil*. New Haven, CT: Yale University Press.

Keith, Bruce E., David B. Magleby, Candice J. Nelson, Elizabeth A. Orr, and Mark C. Westlye. 1992. *The Myth of the Independent Voter*. Berkeley: University of California Press.

King, Gary. 1996. "Why Context Should Not Count." *Political Geography* 15, no. 2: 159–64.

Kitschelt, Herbert. 2000. "Linkages between Citizens and Politicians in Democratic Politics." *Comparative Political Studies* 33, no. 6–7: 846–79.

Kitschelt, Herbert. 2011. "Clientelistic Linkage Strategies: A Descriptive Exploration." Paper prepared for the Workshop on Democratic Accountability Strategies, Duke University.

Kitschelt, Herbert, and Melina Altamirano. 2015. "Clientelism in Latin America: Effort and Effectiveness." In *The Latin American Voter: Pursuing Representation and Accountability in Challenging Contexts*, edited by Ryan E. Carlin, Matthew M. Singer, and Elizabeth J. Zechmeister. Ann Arbor: University of Michigan Press.

Kitschelt, Herbert, Kirk Andrew Hawkins, Juan Pablo Luna, Guillermo Rosas, and Elizabeth J. Zechmeister. 2010. *Latin American Party Systems*. New York: Cambridge University Press.

Kitschelt, Herbert, and Steven Wilkinson. 2007. "Citizen-Politician Linkages: An Introduction." In *Patrons, Clients, and Policies: Patterns of Democratic Accountability and Political Competition*, edited by Herbert Kitschelt and Steven Wilkinson. New York: Cambridge University Press.

Klar, Samara. 2014. "Partisanship in a Social Setting." *American Journal of Political Science* 58, no. 3: 687–704.

Klar, Samara, and Yanna Krupnikov. 2016. *Independent Politics: How American Disdain for Parties Leads to Political Inaction*. New York: Cambridge University Press.

Klesner, Joseph L. 1993. "Modernization, Economic Crisis, and Electoral Alignment in Mexico." *Mexican Studies/Estudios Mexicanos* 9, no. 2: 187–223.

Klesner, Joseph L. 1995. "The 1994 Mexican Elections: Manifestation of a Divided Society?" *Mexican Studies/Estudios Mexicanos* 11, no. 1: 137–49.

Klesner, Joseph L. 2004. "The Structure of the Mexican Electorate: Social, Attitudinal, and Partisan Bases of Vicente Fox's Victory." In *Mexico's Pivotal Democratic Election: Candidates, Voters, and the Presidential Campaign of 2000*, edited by Jorge I. Domínguez and Chappell Lawson. Stanford, CA: Stanford University Press.

Klesner, Joseph L. 2007. "The 2006 Mexican Elections: Manifestation of a Divided Society?" *PS: Political Science & Politics* 40, no. 1: 27–32.

Klofstad, Casey A., Scott D. McClurg, and Meredith Rolfe. 2009. "Measurement of Political Discussion Networks: A Comparison of Two 'Name Generator' Procedures." *Public Opinion Quarterly* 73, no. 3: 462–83.

Klofstad, Casey A., Anand E. Sokhey, and Scott D. McClurg. 2013. "Disagreeing about Disagreement: How Conflict in Social Networks Affects Political Behavior." *American Journal of Political Science* 57, no. 1: 120–34.

Kohler, Ulrich. 2005. "Changing Class Locations and Partisanship in Germany." In *The Social Logic of Politics: Personal Networks as Contexts for Political Behavior*, edited by Alan S. Zuckerman. Philadelphia: Temple University Press.

Krieger, Gustavo, and Eumano Silva. 1994. "Petistas Montam Central Contra Boatos." *Folha de São Paulo*, August 3. At https://www1.folha.uol.com.br/fsp/1994/8/03/caderno_especial/22.html.

Krosnick, Jon A. 1999. "Survey Research." *Annual Review of Psychology* 50, no. 1: 537–67.

Laakso, Markku, and Rein Taagepera. 1979. "'Effective' Number of Parties: A Measure with Application to West Europe." *Comparative Political Studies* 12, no. 1: 3–27.

Larreguy, Horacio, John Marshall, and Pablo Querubín. 2016. "Parties, Brokers, and Voter Mobilization: How Turnout Buying Depends upon the Party's Capacity to Monitor Brokers." *American Political Science Review* 110, no. 1: 160–79.

Latin American Public Opinion Project. 2010. "AmericasBarometer." At www.Lapop Surveys.org.

Lau, Richard R., David J. Andersen, and David P. Redlawsk. 2008. "An Exploration of Correct Voting in Recent U.S. Presidential Elections." *American Journal of Political Science* 52, no. 2: 395–411.

Lau, Richard R., Parina Patel, Dalia F. Fahmy, and Robert R. Kaufman. 2014. "Correct Voting across Thirty-Three Democracies: A Preliminary Analysis." *British Journal of Political Science* 44, no. 2: 239–59.

Lau, Richard R., and David P. Redlawsk. 1997. "Voting Correctly." *American Political Science Review* 91, no. 3: 585–98.

Lavareda, José Antônio. 1991. *A Democracia nas Urnas: O Processo Partidário-Eleitoral Brasileiro (1945–1964)*. Rio de Janeiro: IUPERJ.

Lawrence, Eric D., and John Sides. 2014. "The Consequences of Political Innumeracy." *Research & Politics* 1, no. 2: 1–8.

Lawson, Chappell. 2002. *Building the Fourth Estate: Democratization and the Rise of a Free Press in Mexico*. Berkeley: University of California Press.

Lawson, Chappell. 2006. "Preliminary Findings from the Mexico 2006 Panel Study Memo #1: Blue States and Yellow States." July 27. Available at http://web.mit.edu /polisci/research/mexico06/Region_and_demographics8.doc.

Lawson, Chappell, et al. 2007. "Mexico 2006 Panel Study." At http://mexicopanelstudy .mit.edu/.

Lawson, Chappell, et al. 2001. "Mexico 2000 Panel Study." At http://mexicopanelstudy .mit.edu/.

Lawson, Chappell, Jorge I. Domínguez, Alejandro Moreno, and Kenneth F. Greene. 2013. "Mexico 2012 Panel Study." At http://mexicopanelstudy.mit.edu/.

Lawson, Chappell, and Kenneth F. Greene. 2014. "Making Clientelism Work: How Norms of Reciprocity Increase Voter Compliance." *Comparative Politics* 47, no. 1: 61–85.

Lawson, Chappell, and James A. McCann. 2005. "Television News, Mexico's 2000 Elections and Media Effects in Emerging Democracies." *British Journal of Political Science* 35, no. 1: 1–30.

Lazarsfeld, Paul F., Bernard Berelson, and Hazel Gaudet. 1944. *The People's Choice: How the Voter Makes Up His Mind in a Presidential Campaign*. New York: Dell, Sloan, and Pearce.

Lazarsfeld, Paul F., and Robert K. Merton. 1954. "Friendship as a Social Process: A Substantive and Methodological Analysis." In *Freedom and Control in Modern Society*, edited by Monroe Berger, Theodore Abel, and Charles H. Page. New York: Van Nostrand.

Lazer, David, Brian Rubineau, Carol Chetkovich, Nancy Katz, and Michael Neblo. 2010. "The Coevolution of Networks and Political Attitudes." *Political Communication* 27, no. 3: 248–74.

Leal, Victor Nunes. 1949. *Coronelismo, Enxada e Voto: O Município e o Regime Representativo no Brasil*. São Paulo: Nova Fonteira.

Leighley, Jan E. 1990. "Social Interaction and Contextual Influences on Political Participation." *American Politics Quarterly* 18, no. 4: 459–75.

Lerman, Kristina, Xiaoran Yan, and Xin-Zeng Wu. 2016. "The 'Majority Illusion' in Social Networks." *PLOS ONE* 11, no. 2: e0147617.

Levitan, Lindsey Clark, and Penny S. Visser. 2009. "Social Network Composition and Attitude Strength: Exploring the Dynamics within Newly Formed Social Networks." *Journal of Experimental Social Psychology* 45, no. 5: 1057–67.

Levitsky, Steven. 2003. *Transforming Labor-Based Parties in Latin America: Argentine Peronism in Comparative Perspective*. New York: Cambridge University Press.

Levitsky, Steven, James Loxton, and Brandon Van Dyck. 2016. Introduction to *Challenges of Party-Building in Latin America*, edited by Steven Levitsky, James Loxton, Brandon Van Dyck, and Jorge I. Domínguez. New York: Cambridge University Press.

Lima, Venício A. de. 1988. "The State, Television, and Political Power in Brazil." *Critical Studies in Mass Communication* 5, no. 2: 108–28.

Lins de Silva, Carlos Eduardo. 2014. "Propaganda Não Decide Eleição." *Folha de São Paulo Online*, September 18. At https://www1.folha.uol.com.br/fsp/opiniao/186195-propaganda-nao-decide-eleicao.shtml.

Lipset, Seymour, and Stein Rokkan. 1967. "Cleavage Structures, Party Systems, and Voter Alignments: An Introduction." In *Party Systems and Voter Alignments: Cross-National Perspectives*, edited by Seymour Lipset and Stein Rokkan. New York: Free Press.

Luna, Juan P., and Elizabeth J. Zechmeister. 2005. "Political Representation in Latin America: A Study of Elite-Mass Congruence in Nine Countries." *Comparative Political Studies* 38, no. 4: 388–416.

Lupia, Arthur. 1994. "Shortcuts versus Encyclopedias: Information and Voting Behavior in California Insurance Reform Elections." *American Political Science Review* 88, no. 1: 63–76.

Lupu, Noam. 2014. "Brand Dilution and the Breakdown of Political Parties in Latin America." *World Politics* 66, no. 4: 561–602.

Lupu, Noam. 2015. "Partisanship in Latin America." In *The Latin American Voter: Pursuing Representation and Accountability in Challenging Contexts*, edited by Ryan E. Carlin, Matthew M. Singer, and Elizabeth J. Zechmeister. Ann Arbor: University of Michigan Press.

Lupu, Noam. 2016a. *Party Brands in Crisis: Partisanship, Brand Dilution, and the Breakdown of Political Parties in Latin America*. New York: Cambridge University Press.

Lupu, Noam. 2016b. "Building Party Brands in Argentina and Brazil." In *Challenges of Party-Building in Latin America*, edited by Steven Levitsky, James Loxton, Brandon Van Dyck, and Jorge I. Domínguez. New York: Cambridge University Press.

Lupu, Noam, Carlos Gervasoni, Virginia Oliveros, and Luis Schiumerini. 2015. "Argentine Panel Election Study." At http://www.noamlupu.com/data.html.

Lupu, Noam, Virginia Oliveros, and Luis Schiumerini. 2019. "Toward a Theory of Campaigns and Voters in Developing Democracies." In *Campaigns and Voters in Developing Democracies: Argentina in Comparative Perspective*, edited by Noam Lupu, Virginia Oliveros, and Luis Schiumerini. Ann Arbor: University of Michigan Press.

Lupu, Noam, and Susan C. Stokes. 2009. "The Social Bases of Political Parties in Argentina, 1912–2003." *Latin American Research Review* 44, no. 1: 58–87.

Luskin, Robert C., James S. Fishkin, and Roger Jowell. 2002. "Considered Opinions: Deliberative Polling in Britain." *British Journal of Political Science* 32, no. 3: 455–87.

Lyons, Jeffrey, William P. Jaeger, and Jennifer Wolak. 2013. "The Roots of Citizens' Knowledge of State Politics." *State Politics & Policy Quarterly* 13, no. 2: 183–202.

Lyons, Russell. 2011. "The Spread of Evidence-Poor Medicine via Flawed Social-Network Analysis." *Statistics, Politics, and Policy* 2, no. 1.

MacKuen, Michael, Jennifer Wolak, Luke Keele, and George E. Marcus. 2010. "Civic Engagements: Resolute Partisanship or Reflective Deliberation." *American Journal of Political Science* 54, no. 2: 440–58.

Madsen, Douglas, and Peter G. Snow. 1991. *The Charismatic Bond: Political Behavior in Time of Crisis*. Cambridge, MA: Harvard University Press.

Magalhães, Pedro. 2007. "Voting and Intermediation: Informational Biases and Electoral Choices in Comparative Perspective." In *Democracy, Intermediation, and Voting on Four Continents*, edited by Richard Gunther, José Ramón Montero, and Hans-Jürgen Puhle. New York: Oxford University Press.

Magaloni, Beatriz. 1999. "Is the PRI Fading? Economic Performance, Electoral Accountability, and Voting Behavior in the 1994 and 1997 Elections." In *Toward Mexico's Democratization: Parties, Campaigns, Elections, and Public Opinion*, edited by Jorge I. Domínguez and Alejandro Poiré. New York: Routledge.

Magaloni, Beatriz. 2006. *Voting for Autocracy: Hegemonic Party Survival and Its Demise in Mexico*. New York: Cambridge University Press.

Magaloni, Beatriz, and Alejandro Poiré. 2004. "Strategic Coordination in the 2000 Mexican Presidential Race." In *Mexico's Pivotal Democratic Election: Candidates, Voters, and the Presidential Campaign of 2000*, edited by Jorge I. Domínguez and Chappell Lawson. Stanford, CA: Stanford University Press.

Mainwaring, Scott. 1999. *Rethinking Party Systems in the Third Wave of Democratization: The Case of Brazil*. Stanford, CA: Stanford University Press.

Mainwaring, Scott. 2018a. "Party System Institutionalization in Contemporary Latin America." In *Party Systems in Latin America: Institutionalization, Decay, and Collapse*, edited by Scott Mainwaring. New York: Cambridge University Press.

Mainwaring, Scott. 2018b. "Party System Institutionalization, Predictability, and Democracy." In *Party Systems in Latin America: Institutionalization, Decay, and Collapse*, edited by Scott Mainwaring. New York: Cambridge University Press.

Mainwaring, Scott, Carlos Gervasoni, and Annabella España-Najera. 2017. "Extra- and Within-System Electoral Volatility." *Party Politics* 23, no. 6: 623–35.

Mainwaring, Scott, Timothy J. Power, and Fernando Bizzarro. 2018. "The Uneven Institutionalization of a Party System: Brazil." In *Party Systems in Latin America: Institutionalization, Decay, and Collapse*, edited by Scott Mainwaring. New York: Cambridge University Press.

Mainwaring, Scott, and Timothy Scully. 1995. "Introduction: Party Systems in Latin America." In *Building Democratic Institutions: Party Systems in Latin America*, edited by Scott Mainwaring and Timothy Scully. Stanford, CA: Stanford University Press.

Mainwaring, Scott, Mariano Torcal, and Nicolás M. Somma. 2015. "The Left and the Mobilization of Class Voting in Latin America." In *The Latin American Voter: Pursuing Representation and Accountability in Challenging Contexts*, edited by Ryan E. Carlin, Matthew M. Singer, and Elizabeth J. Zechmeister. Ann Arbor: University of Michigan Press.

Manjoo, Farhad. 2018. "The Problem with Fixing WhatsApp? Human Nature Might Get in the Way." *New York Times*, October 24. At https://www.nytimes.com/2018/10 /24/technology/fixing-whatsapp-disinformation-human-nature.html.

Manski, Charles F. 1993. "Identification of Endogenous Social Effects: The Reflection Problem." *Review of Economic Studies* 60, no. 3: 531–42.

Marés, Chico, Clara Becker, Cristina Tardáguila, Natália Leal, Pablo Ortellado, and Fabrício Benevenuto. 2018. "Só 4 das 50 Imagens Mais Compartilhadas por 347 Grupos de WhatsApp São Verdadeiras." São Paulo. At https://piaui.folha.uol.com.br /lupa/wp-content/uploads/2018/10/Relat%C3%B3rio-WhatsApp-1-turno-Lupa-2F -USP-2F-UFMG.pdf.

Mariano, Ricardo, and Antônio Flávio Pierucci. 1992. "O Envolvimento dos Pentecostais na Eleição de Collor." *Novos Estudos Cebrap* 3, no. 34: 92–106.

Marsden, Peter V. 1987. "Core Discussion Networks of Americans." *American Sociological Review* 52, no. 1: 122–31.

Marshall, John. 2018. "Signaling Sophistication: How Social Expectations Can Increase Political Information Acquisition." *Journal of Politics* 81, no. 1: 167–86.

Martin, Paul S. 2003. "Voting's Rewards: Voter Turnout, Attentive Publics, and Congressional Allocation of Federal Money." *American Journal of Political Science* 47, no. 1: 110–27.

Mayer, Michael E., William B. Gudykunst, Norman K. Perrill, and Bruce D. Merrill. 1990. "A Comparison of Competing Models of the News Diffusion Process." *Western Journal of Speech Communication* 54, no. 1: 113–23.

Mayer, Susan E., and Christopher Jencks. 1989. "Growing Up in Poor Neighborhoods: How Much Does It Matter?" *Science* 243, no. 4897: 1441–45.

McCann, James A., and Chappell Lawson. 2003. "An Electorate Adrift? Public Opinion and the Quality of Democracy in Mexico." *Latin American Research Review* 38, no. 3: 60–81.

McPherson, Miller, Lynn Smith-Lovin, and James M. Cook. 2001. "Birds of a Feather: Homophily in Social Networks." *Annual Review of Sociology* 27, no. 1: 415–44.

Metzl, Jonathan M. 2019. *Dying of Whiteness: How the Politics of Racial Resentment Is Killing America's Heartland*. New York: Basic Books.

Milgram, Stanley. 1963. "Behavioral Study of Obedience." *Journal of Abnormal and Social Psychology* 67: 371–78.

Min, Seong-Jae. 2007. "Online vs. Face-to-Face Deliberation: Effects on Civic Engagement." *Journal of Computer-Mediated Communication* 12, no. 4: 1369–87.

Moehler, Devra, and Douglas Michael Allen. 2016. "The Media Diet Imbalance Score: A Measure of Aggregate Media Diet." *Communication Methods and Measures* 10, no. 1: 4–12.

Mondak, Jeffery J. 2010. *Personality and the Foundations of Political Behavior*. New York: Cambridge University Press.

Mondak, Jeffery J., and Mary R. Anderson. 2004. "The Knowledge Gap: A Reexamination of Gender-Based Differences in Political Knowledge." *Journal of Politics* 66, no. 2: 492–512.

Monnoyer-Smith, Laurence, and Julien Talpin. 2010. "Participatory Frames in Deliberative Devices: The Ideal-EU Case Study." *Proceedings of the Fourth International Conference on Online Deliberation*. Leeds, UK: University of Leeds.

Montero, Alfred P. 2012. "A Reversal of Political Fortune: The Transitional Dynamics of Conservative Rule in the Brazilian Northeast." *Latin American Politics and Society* 54, no. 1: 1–36.

Moreno, Alejandro. 2018. *El Cambio Electoral: Votantes, Encuestas, y Democracia en México*. Mexico City: Fondo de Cultura Económica.

Moreno, Alejandro, and Karla Yuritzi Mendizábal. 2013. "O Uso das Redes Sociais e o Comportamento Político no México." In *Compartamento Eleitoral e Comunicação Política na América Latina: O Eleitor Latino-Americana*, edited by Helcimara Telles and Alejandro Moreno. Belo Horizonte: Editora UFMG.

Morgan, Jana. 2011. *Bankrupt Representation and Party System Collapse*. University Park: Pennsylvania State University Press.

Morgenstern, Scott. 2017. *Are Politics Local? The Two Dimensions of Party Nationalization around the World*. New York: Cambridge University Press.

Morgenstern, Scott, and Elizabeth Zechmeister. 2003. "Better the Devil You Know than the Saint You Don't? Risk Propensity and Vote Choice in Mexico." *Journal of Politics* 63, no. 1: 93–119.

Moser, Robert G., and Ethan Scheiner. 2012. *Electoral Systems and Political Context: How the Effects of Rules Vary across New and Established Democracies*. New York: Cambridge University Press.

Muñoz, Paula. 2018. *Buying Audiences: Clientelism and Electoral Campaigns When Parties Are Weak*. New York: Cambridge University Press.

Mutz, Diana C. 2002a. "The Consequences of Cross-Cutting Networks for Political Participation." *American Journal of Political Science* 46, no. 4: 838–55.

Mutz, Diana C. 2002b. "Cross-Cutting Social Networks: Testing Democratic Theory in Practice." *American Political Science Review* 96, no. 1: 111–26.

Mutz, Diana C. 2006. *Hearing the Other Side: Deliberative versus Participatory Democracy*. New York: Cambridge University Press.

Mutz, Diana C., and Paul S. Martin. 2001. "Facilitating Communication across Lines of Political Difference: The Role of Mass Media." *American Political Science Review* 95, no. 1: 97–114.

Ng, Sik Hung. 2001. "Influencing through the Power of Language." In *Social Influence: Direct and Indirect Processes*, edited by Joseph P. Forgas and Kipling D. Williams. Philadelphia: Psychology Press.

Nichter, Simeon. 2008. "Vote Buying or Turnout Buying? Machine Politics and the Secret Ballot." *American Political Science Review* 102, no. 1: 19–31.

Nichter, Simeon. 2018. *Votes for Survival: Relational Clientelism in Latin America*. New York: Cambridge University Press.

Nichter, Simeon, and Brian Palmer-Rubin. 2015. "Clientelism, Declared Support and Mexico's 2012 Campaign." In *Mexico's Evolving Democracy: A Comparative Study of the 2012 Elections*, edited by Jorge Domínguez, Kenneth F. Greene, Chappell Lawson, and Alejandro Moreno. Baltimore: Johns Hopkins University Press.

Nichter, Simeon, and Michael Peress. 2017. "Request Fulfilling: When Citizens Demand Clientelist Benefits." *Comparative Political Studies* 50, no. 8: 1086–117.

Nir, Lilach. 2005. "Ambivalent Social Networks and Their Consequences for Participation." *International Journal of Public Opinion Research* 17, no. 4: 422–42.

Nir, Lilach, and James N. Druckman. 2008. "Campaign Mixed-Message Flows and Timing of Vote Decision." *International Journal of Public Opinion Research* 20, no. 3: 326–46.

Noelle-Neumann, Elisabeth. 1984. *The Spiral of Silence: Public Opinion—Our Social Skin*. Chicago: University of Chicago Press.

Norris, Pippa. 2004. *Electoral Engineering: Voting Rules and Political Behavior*. Cambridge: Cambridge University Press.

Oakes, J. Michael. 2004. "The (Mis)Estimation of Neighborhood Effects: Causal Inference for a Practicable Social Epidemiology." *Social Science & Medicine* 58, no. 10: 1929–52.

O'Donnell, Guillermo. 1978. "State and Alliances in Argentina, 1956–1976." *Journal of Development Studies* 15, no. 1: 3–33.

Papke, Leslie E., and Jeffrey M. Wooldridge. 1996. "Econometric Methods for Fractional Response Variables with an Application to 401(k) Plan Participation Rates." *Journal of Applied Econometrics* 11, no. 6: 619–32.

Passos, Úrsula. 2018. "Para Maioria dos Eleitores, Pensar No Brasil Gera Tristeza e Desânimo." *Folha de São Paulo*, October 3, sec. Eleições 2018. At https://www1.folha .uol.com.br/poder/2018/10/para-maioria-dos-eleitores-pensar-no-brasil-gera -tristeza-e-desanimo.shtml.

Pedersen, Mogens N. 1979. "The Dynamics of European Party Systems: Changing Patterns of Electoral Volatility." *European Journal of Political Research* 7, no. 1: 1–26.

Perlman, Janice E. 1976. *The Myth of Marginality: Urban Poverty and Politics in Rio de Janeiro*. Berkeley: University of California Press.

Perry, Brea L., Bernice A. Pescosolido, and Stephen P. Borgatti. 2018. *Egocentric Network Analysis: Foundations, Methods, and Models*. New York: Cambridge University Press.

Philips, Andrew Q., Amanda Rutherford, and Guy D. Whitten. 2016. "Dynamic Pie: A Strategy for Modeling Trade-Offs in Compositional Variables over Time." *American Journal of Political Science* 60, no. 1: 268–83.

Philpot, Tasha S. 2017. *Conservative but Not Republican: The Paradox of Party Identification and Ideology among African Americans*. New York: Cambridge University Press.

Pietryka, Matthew T., Jack Lyons Reilly, Daniel M. Maliniak, Patrick R. Miller, Robert Huckfeldt, and Ronald B. Rapoport. 2018. "From Respondents to Networks: Bridging between Individuals, Discussants, and the Network in the Study of Political Discussion." *Political Behavior* 40: 711–35.

Poiré, Alejandro. 1999. "Retrospective Voting, Partisanship, and Loyalty in Presidential Elections in 1994." In *Toward Mexico's Democratization: Parties, Campaigns, Elections, and Public Opinion*, edited by Jorge I. Domínguez and Alejandro Poiré. New York: Routledge.

Porto, Mauro P. 2007. "Framing Controversies: Television and the 2002 Presidential Election in Brazil." *Political Communication* 24, no. 1: 19–36.

Porto, Mauro P. 2012. *Media Power and Democratization in Brazil: TV Globo and the Dilemmas of Political Accountability.* New York: Routledge.

Price, Paul C., and Eric R. Stone. 2004. "Intuitive Evaluation of Likelihood Judgment Producers: Evidence for a Confidence Heuristic." *Journal of Behavioral Decision Making* 17, no. 1: 39–57.

Price, Vincent, Joseph N. Cappella, and Lilach Nir. 2002. "Does Disagreement Contribute to More Deliberative Opinion?" *Political Communication* 19, no. 1: 95–112.

Price, Vincent, Lilach Nir, and Joseph N. Cappella. 2006. "Normative and Informational Influences in Online Political Discussions." *Communication Theory* 16, no. 1: 47–74.

Price, Vincent, and John Zaller. 1993. "Who Gets the News? Alternative Measures of News Reception and Their Implications for Research." *Public Opinion Quarterly* 57, no. 2: 133–64.

Programa de las Naciones Unidas para el Desarrollo. 2014. *Índice de Desarollo Humano Municipal en México: Nueva Metodología.* Mexico City: PNUD. At http://www.mx .undp.org/content/mexico/es/home/library/poverty/idh-municipal-en-mexico- -nueva-metodologia.html.

Przeworski, Adam, and Henry Teune. 1970. *The Logic of Comparative Social Inquiry.* New York: Wiley.

Putnam, Robert D. 1994. *Making Democracy Work: Civic Traditions in Modern Italy.* Princeton, NJ: Princeton University Press.

Ranincheski, Sonia. 1999. "A História Política do Rio Grande do Sul: Breve Comentário." *BIBLOS: Revista do Instituto de Ciências Humanas e da Informação* 11: 7–15.

Ratliffe Sontoro, Lauren, and Paul A. Beck. 2017. "Social Networks and Vote Choice." In *The Oxford Handbook of Political Networks*, edited by Jennifer Nicoll Victor, Alexander H. Montgomery, and Mark Lubell. New York: Oxford University Press.

Reid, Michael. 2014. *Brazil: The Troubled Rise of a Global Power.* New Haven, CT: Yale University Press.

Reis, Fábio Wanderley. 1978. "Classe Social e Opção Partidária: As Eleições de 1976 Em Juiz de Fora." In *Os Partidos e o Regime: A Lógica do Processo Eleitoral Brasileiro*, edited by Fábio Wanderley Reis. São Paulo: Editora Símbolo.

Remmer, Karen L. 1991. "The Political Impact of Economic Crisis in Latin America in the 1980s." *American Political Science Review* 85, no. 3: 777–800.

Rennó, Lúcio R. 2018. "Brazilian Electoral Panel Studies (BEPS) 2018."

Richardson, Bradley, and Paul A. Beck. 2007. "The Flow of Political Information: Personal Discussants, the Media, and Partisans." In *Democracy, Intermediation, and Voting on Four Continents*, edited by Richard Gunther, José Ramón Montero, and Hans-Jürgen Puhle. New York: Oxford University Press.

Roberts, Kenneth M. 2014. *Changing Course in Latin America.* New York: Cambridge University Press.

Roberts, Kenneth M., and Erik Wibbels. 1999. "Party Systems and Electoral Volatility in Latin America: A Test of Economic, Institutional, and Structural Explanations." *American Political Science Review* 93, no. 3: 575–90.

Roberts, Sam G. B., Robin I. M. Dunbar, Thomas V. Pollet, and Toon Kuppens. 2009. "Exploring Variation in Active Network Size: Constraints and Ego Characteristics." *Social Networks* 31, no. 2: 138–46.

Rogowski, Jon C., and Betsy Sinclair. 2017. "Causal Inference in Political Networks." In *The Oxford Handbook of Political Networks*, edited by Jennifer Nicoll Victor, Alexander H. Montgomery, and Mark Lubell. New York: Oxford University Press.

Rojas, Hernando. 2008. "Strategy versus Understanding: How Orientations toward Political Conversation Influence Political Engagement." *Communication Research* 35, no. 4: 452–80.

Rolfe, Meredith. 2012. *Voter Turnout: A Social Theory of Political Participation*. New York: Cambridge University Press.

Rolfe, Meredith, and Stephanie Chan. 2017. "Voting and Political Participation." In *The Oxford Handbook of Political Networks*, edited by Jennifer Nicoll Victor, Alexander H. Montgomery, and Mark Lubell. New York: Oxford University Press.

Ronconi, Lucas, and Rodrigo Zarazaga. 2019. "Household-Based Clientelism: Brokers' Allocation of Temporary Public Works Programs in Argentina." *Studies in Comparative International Development* 54, no. 3: 365–80.

Rosenstone, Steven J., and John Mark Hansen. 1993. *Mobilization, Participation, and Democracy in America*. New York: Macmillan Publishing Company.

Ross, Lee, David Greene, and Pamela House. 1977. "The 'False Consensus Effect': An Egocentric Bias in Social Perception and Attribution Processes." *Journal of Experimental Social Psychology* 13, no. 3: 279–301.

Ryan, John Barry. 2011. "Social Networks as a Shortcut to Correct Voting." *American Journal of Political Science* 55, no. 4: 753–66.

Sampson, Robert J., Jeffrey D. Morenoff, and Thomas Gannon-Rowley. 2002. "Assessing 'Neighborhood Effects': Social Processes and New Directions in Research." *Annual Review of Sociology* 28, no. 1: 443–78.

Samuels, David. 2006. "Sources of Mass Partisanship in Brazil." *Latin American Politics and Society* 48, no. 2: 1–27.

Samuels, David, and Cesar Zucco. 2015. "Crafting Mass Partisanship at the Grass Roots." *British Journal of Political Science* 45, no. 4: 755–75.

Samuels, David, and Cesar Zucco. 2018. *Partisans, Anti-Partisans, and Non-Partisans: Voting Behavior in Brazil*. New York: Cambridge University Press.

Sanders, Lynn M. 1997. "Against Deliberation." *Political Theory* 25, no. 3: 347–76.

Schaffer, Frederic Charles. 2007. "Lessons Learned." In *Elections for Sale: The Causes and Consequences of Vote Buying*, edited by Frederic Charles Schaffer. Boulder, CO: Lynne Rienner Publishers.

Schaffer, Joby, and Andy Baker. 2015. "Clientelism as Persuasion-Buying: Evidence from Latin America." *Comparative Political Studies* 48, no. 9: 1093–126.

Schattschneider, E. E. 1960. *The Semisovereign People: A Realist's View of Democracy in America*. New York: Holt, Rinehart and Winston.

Scheiner, Ethan. 2006. *Democracy without Competition in Japan: Opposition Failure in a One-Party Dominant State*. New York: Cambridge University Press.

Schkade, David, Cass R. Sunstein, and Reid Hastie. 2007. "What Happened on Deliberation Day?" *California Law Review* 95, no. 3: 915–40.

Schmitt-Beck, Rüdiger. 2004. "Political Communication Effects: The Impact of Mass Media and Personal Conversations on Voting." In *Comparing Political Communication: Theories, Cases, and Challenges*, edited by Frank Esser and Barbara Pfetsch. New York: Cambridge University Press.

Schussman, Alan, and Jennifer Earl. 2004. "From Barricades to Firewalls? Strategic Voting and Social Movement Leadership in the Internet Age." *Sociological Inquiry* 74, no. 4: 439–63.

Settle, Jaime E. 2018. *Frenemies: How Social Media Polarizes America*. New York: Cambridge University Press.

Shalizi, Cosma Rohilla, and Andrew C. Thomas. 2011. "Homophily and Contagion Are Generically Confounded in Observational Social Network Studies." *Sociological Methods & Research* 40, no. 2: 211–39.

Sharkey, Patrick, and Jacob W. Faber. 2014. "Where, When, Why, and for Whom Do Residential Contexts Matter? Moving Away from the Dichotomous Understanding of Neighborhood Effects." *Annual Review of Sociology* 40, no. 1: 559–79.

Siegel, David A. 2013. "Social Networks and the Mass Media." *American Political Science Review* 107, no. 4: 786–805.

Silva, Denisson, Fernando Meireles, and Beatriz Costa. 2017. "Package 'ElectionBR': Version 0.3.0." At https://cran.r-project.org/web/packages/electionsBR/electionsBR.pdf.

Silveira, Flávio Eduardo. 1994. "Escolha Intuitiva: Nova Modalidade de Decisão do Voto." *Opinião Pública* 2, no. 2: 95–116.

Sinclair, Betsy. 2012. *The Social Citizen: Peer Networks and Political Behavior*. Chicago: University of Chicago Press.

Singer, André. 2012. *Os Sentidos do Lulismo: Reforma Gradual e Pacto Conservador*. São Paulo: Companhia das Letras.

Singer, Matthew M., and Ryan E. Carlin. 2013. "Context Counts: The Election Cycle, Development, and the Nature of Economic Voting." *Journal of Politics* 75, no. 3: 730–42.

Smith, Amy Erica. 2015a. "Networks and Neighborhoods in Local Politics: The Case of Brazil." Harvard Dataverse. At https://doi.org/10.7910/DVN/JJ3F53.

Smith, Amy Erica. 2015b. "The Diverse Impacts of Politically Diverse Networks: Party Systems, Political Disagreement, and the Timing of Vote Decisions." *International Journal of Public Opinion Research* 27, no. 4: 481–96.

Smith, Amy Erica. 2018. "Talking It Out: Political Conversation and Knowledge Gaps in Unequal Urban Contexts." *British Journal of Political Science* 48, no. 2: 407–25.

Smith, Amy Erica. 2019. *Religion and Brazilian Democracy: Mobilizing the People of God*. New York: Cambridge University Press.

Soares, Gláucio Ary Dillon, and Sonia Luiza Terron. 2008. "Dois Lulas: A Geografia Eleitoral da Reeleição (Explorando Conceitos, Métodos e Técnicas de Análise Geoespacial)." *Opinião Pública* 14, no. 2: 269–301.

Sokhey, Anand E., Andy Baker, and Paul A. Djupe. 2015. "The Dynamics of Socially Supplied Information: Examining Discussion Network Stability over Time." *International Journal of Public Opinion Research* 27, no. 4: 565–87.

Sokhey, Anand E., and Paul A. Djupe. 2014. "Name Generation in Interpersonal Political Network Data: Results from a Series of Experiments." *Social Networks* 36: 147–61.

Sokhey, Anand E., and Scott D. McClurg. 2012. "Social Networks and Correct Voting." *Journal of Politics* 74, no. 3: 751–64.

Sperandio, Naiara, Cristiana Tristão Rodrigues, Sylvia do Carmo Castro Franceschini, Silvia Eloiza Priore, Naiara Sperandio, Cristiana Tristão Rodrigues, Sylvia do Carmo

Castro Franceschini, and Silvia Eloiza Priore. 2017. "The Impact of the Bolsa Família Program on Food Consumption: A Comparative Study of the Southeast and Northeast Regions of Brazil." *Ciência & Saúde Coletiva* 22, no. 6: 1771–80.

Standage, Tom. 2013. *Writing on the Wall: Social Media—The First 2,000 Years*. New York: Bloomsbury.

Stangor, Charles, Gretchen B. Sechrist, and John T. Jost. 2001. "Social Influence and Intergroup Beliefs: The Role of Perceived Social Consensus." In *Social Influence: Direct and Indirect Processes*, edited by Joseph P. Forgas and Kipling D. Williams. Philadelphia: Psychology Press.

Stimson, James A. 2004. *Tides of Consent: How Public Opinion Shapes American Politics*. New York: Cambridge University Press.

Stokes, Donald E. 1963. "Spatial Models of Party Competition." *American Political Science Review* 57, no. 2: 368–77.

Stokes, Susan C. 2005. "Perverse Accountability: A Formal Model of Machine Politics with Evidence from Argentina." *American Political Science Review* 99, no. 3: 315–25.

Stokes, Susan C., Thad Dunning, Marcelo Nazareno, and Valeria Brusco. 2013. *Brokers, Voters, and Clientelism: The Puzzle of Distributive Politics*. New York: Cambridge University Press.

Straubhaar, Joseph, Organ Olsen, and Maria C. Nunes. 1993. "The Brazilian Case: Influencing the Voter." In *Television, Politics, and the Transition to Democracy in Latin America*, edited by Thomas E. Skidmore. Baltimore: Johns Hopkins University Press.

Sunstein, Cass R. 2019. *Conformity: The Power of Social Influences*. New York: New York University Press.

Szwarcberg, Mariela. 2012a. "Revisiting Clientelism: A Network Analysis of Problem-Solving Networks in Argentina." *Social Networks* 34, no. 2: 230–40.

Szwarcberg, Mariela. 2012b. "Uncertainty, Political Clientelism, and Voter Turnout in Latin America: Why Parties Conduct Rallies in Argentina." *Comparative Politics* 45, no. 1: 88–106.

Szwarcberg, Mariela. 2014. "Political Parties and Rallies in Latin America." *Party Politics* 20, no. 3: 456–66.

Tardáguila, Cristina, Fabrício Benevenuto, and Pablo Ortellado. 2018. "Fake News Is Poisoning Brazilian Politics. WhatsApp Can Stop It." *New York Times*, October 19, sec. Opinion. At https://www.nytimes.com/2018/10/17/opinion/brazil-election-fake-news-whatsapp.html.

Telles, Helcimara, Pedro Mundim, and Nayla Lopes. 2013. "Internautas, Verdes e Pentecostais: Novos Padrões de Comportamento Político No Brasil?" In *Comportamento Eleitoral e Comunicação Política na América Latina: O Eleitor Latino-Americano*, edited by Helcimara Telles and Alejandro Moreno. Belo Horizonte: Editora UFMG.

Tiebout, Charles M. 1956. "A Pure Theory of Local Expenditures." *Journal of Political Economy* 64, no. 5: 416–24.

Torcal, Mariano, Leticia M. Ruiz, and Gerardo Maldonado. 2017. *El Votante Dominicano: Ciudadanos y Elecciones En La República Dominicana*. Santo Domingo, Dominican Republic: FUNGLODE.

Trindade, Hélgio. 1978. "Padrões e Tendências no Comportamento Eleitoral no Rio Grande do Sul." In *Os Partidos e as Eleições no Brasil*, edited by Bolívar Lamounier and Fernando Henrique Cardoso. Rio de Janeiro: Editora Paz e Terra.

Tsang, Alan, and Kate Larson. 2016. "The Echo Chamber: Strategic Voting and Homophily in Social Networks." *Proceedings of the 2016 International Conference on Autonomous Agents & Multiagent Systems.* AAMAS '16 Richland, SC: International Foundation for Autonomous Agents and Multiagent Systems. At http://dl.acm.org/citation.cfm?id=2936924.2936979.

van der Meer, Tom W. G., Erika van Elsas, Rozemarijn Lubbe, and Wouter van der Brug. 2015. "Are Volatile Voters Erratic, Whimsical or Seriously Picky? A Panel Study of 58 Waves into the Nature of Electoral Volatility (The Netherlands 2006–2010)." *Party Politics* 21, no. 1: 100–114.

VanderWeele, Tyler J. 2011. "Sensitivity Analysis for Contagion Effects in Social Networks." *Sociological Methods & Research* 40, no. 2: 240–55.

VanderWeele, Tyler J., and Onyebuchi A. Arah. 2011. "Unmeasured Confounding for General Outcomes, Treatments, and Confounders: Bias Formulas for Sensitivity Analysis." *Epidemiology* 22, no. 1: 42–52.

Vargas, João Costa. 2003. "The Inner City and the Favela: Transnational Black Politics." *Race & Class* 44, no. 4: 19–40.

Verba, Sidney, Norman H. Nie, and Jae-on Kim. 1978. *Participation and Political Equality: A Seven-Nation Comparison.* New York: Cambridge University Press.

Villarreal, Andrés, and Bráulio F. A. Silva. 2006. "Social Cohesion, Criminal Victimization and Perceived Risk of Crime in Brazilian Neighborhoods." *Social Forces* 84, no. 3: 1725–53.

Visser, Penny, and Robert R. Mirabile. 2004. "Attitudes in the Social Context: The Impact of Social Network Composition on Individual-Level Attitude Strength." *Journal of Personality and Social Psychology* 87, no. 6: 779–95.

Walsh, Katherine Cramer. 2004. *Talking about Politics: Informal Groups and Social Identity in American Life.* Chicago: University of Chicago Press.

Walsh, Katherine Cramer. 2012. "Putting Inequality in Its Place: Rural Consciousness and the Power of Perspective." *American Political Science Review* 106, no. 3: 517–32.

Weitz-Shapiro, Rebecca. 2012. "What Wins Votes: Why Some Politicians Opt Out of Clientelism." *American Journal of Political Science* 56, no. 3: 568–83.

Weitz-Shapiro, Rebecca, and Matthew S. Winters. 2019. "Strategic Voting in a Two-Round, Multi-Candidate Election." In *Campaigns and Voters in Developing Democracies: Argentina in Comparative Perspective*, edited by Noam Lupu, Virginia Oliveros, and Luis Schiumerini. Ann Arbor: University of Michigan Press.

Wellman, Barry, and Barry Leighton. 1979. "Networks, Neighborhoods, and Communities: Approaches to the Study of the Community Question." *Urban Affairs Quarterly* 14, no. 3: 363–90.

Weyland, Kurt. 1996. *Democracy without Equity: Failures of Reform in Brazil.* Pittsburgh: University of Pittsburgh Press.

Wiesehomeier, Nina, and Kenneth Benoit. 2009. "Presidents, Parties, and Policy Competition." *Journal of Politics* 71, no. 4: 1435–47.

Wilson, William Julius. 1987. *The Truly Disadvantaged: The Inner City, the Underclass, and Public Policy.* Chicago: University of Chicago Press.

Wittenberg, Jason. 2006. *Crucibles of Political Loyalty: Church Institutions and Electoral Continuity in Hungary.* New York: Cambridge University Press.

Wolak, Jennifer, and Eric Gonzalez Juenke. 2020. "Descriptive Representation and Political Knowledge." *Politics, Groups, and Identities.*

Young, Iris Marion. 2000. *Inclusion and Democracy*. New York: Oxford University Press.

Zago, Gabriela da Silva, and Marco Toledo Bastos. 2013. "Visibilidade de Notícias no Twitter e no Facebook: Análise Comparativa das Notícias mais Repercutidas na Europa e nas Américas." *Brazilian Journalism Research* 9, no. 1: 116–33.

Zaller, John R. 1992. *The Nature and Origins of Mass Opinion*. New York: Cambridge University Press.

Zaller, John R. 1998. "Monica Lewinsky's Contribution to Political Science." *PS: Political Science & Politics* 31, no. 2: 182–89.

Zechmeister, Elizabeth J. 2006. "What's Left and Who's Right? A Q-Method Study of Individual and Contextual Influences on the Meaning of Ideological Labels." *Political Behavior* 28, no. 2: 151–73.

Zechmeister, Elizabeth J. 2008. "Policy-Based Voting, Perceptions of Issue Space, and the 2000 Mexican Elections." *Electoral Studies* 27, no. 4: 649–60.

Zechmeister, Elizabeth J. 2019. "Conclusion: The Significance of Unmoored Voters." In *Campaigns and Voters in Developing Democracies: Argentina in Comparative Perspective*, edited by Noam Lupu, Virginia Oliveros, and Luis Schiumerini. Ann Arbor: University of Michigan Press.

Zmerli, Sonja, and Juan Carlos Castillo. 2015. "Income Inequality, Distributive Fairness and Political Trust in Latin America." *Social Science Research* 52: 179–92.

Zucco, Cesar. 2008. "The President's 'New' Constituency: Lula and the Pragmatic Vote in Brazil's 2006 Presidential Elections." *Journal of Latin American Studies* 40, no. 1: 29–49.

Zucco, Cesar, and Timothy J. Power. 2013. "Bolsa Família and the Shift in Lula's Electoral Base, 2002–2006: A Reply to Bohn." *Latin American Research Review* 48, no. 2: 3–24.

Zuckerman, Alan S., Jennifer Fitzgerald, and Josip Dasović. 2005. "Do Couples Support the Same Political Parties? Sometimes: Evidence from British and German Household Panel Surveys." In *The Social Logic of Politics: Personal Networks as Contexts for Political Behavior*, edited by Alan S. Zuckerman. Philadelphia: Temple University Press.

INDEX